Between the Guerrillas and the State

Between the Guerrillas and the State

The Cocalero Movement, Citizenship,
and Identity in the Colombian Amazon

María Clemencia Ramírez

Translated by Andy Klatt

Duke University Press   Durham & London   2011

© 2011 Duke University Press
All rights reserved
Printed in the United States of America on acid-free paper ⊗
Typeset in Arnhem by Tseng Information Systems, Inc.
Library of Congress Cataloging-in-Publication Data appear on the
last printed page of this book.

This book is dedicated to the campesinos of Putumayo

in the hope that its message will contribute

to their voices being heard and their

proposals being taken into account

to my daughter Ana Manuela

and to my new granddaughter Abril

Contents

Acknowledgments

This book is a concrete reflection of what I have learned about the long-term but always dynamic state of affairs of *campesinos* in the department of Putumayo between 1997 and 2008, the period that I have spent conducting fieldwork there. I owe my very sincere gratitude to the members and leaders of the peasant community in Putumayo who were ready to give me their perspective on the changing situation in Putumayo at different stages of my fieldwork. The ongoing theoretical discussion I maintained with the four professors who comprised my thesis committee at the Harvard University Department of Anthropology, David Maybury-Lewis, Sally Falk Moore, Begoña Aretxaga, and MIT professor Jean Jackson, helped me refine my analysis. I have not yet been able to accept the premature death of Begoña Aretxaga, and I can only say that she continues to be my inspiration. Jean Jackson has become a very close friend, the first person to whom I turn for academic and practical advice. She is always ready and willing to read and discuss my work, and her comments have been invaluable to me in writing the final version of this book.

I am especially grateful to Margot Nelson Gill, Administrative Dean of the Graduate School of Arts and Sciences at Harvard University, who helped me secure financial assistance, allowing me to extend my time at Harvard and complete my dissertation, which is the core of this book. My time spent as the 2004–5 Santo Domingo Visiting Scholar at Harvard's David Rockefeller Center for Latin American Studies gave me the opportunity to update the Spanish version of my book published in 2001 in Colombia by the Colombian Institute of Anthropology and Colciencias, and to write its last chapter, focused on Plan Colombia.

This work would not have been possible without funding from the following sources: in the United States, the Wenner-Gren Foundation for Anthropological Research, the United States Institute of Peace, the Mellon Foundation, The Cora Du Bois Charitable Trust, and The Edmund J. Curley Scholarship; in Colombia, the Colombian Institute for the Promotion of Science and Technology, known as *Colciencias*, and the Colombian Institute of Anthropology and History.

I thank all the people who welcomed me into their homes during my fieldwork, who answered my questions without hesitation, and who pointed me in right directions. To Gaby Lorena Reyes, my field assistant, without whom I could not have operated as I did in a conflict-ridden region. Her family network in Putumayo and Cauca always welcomed me warmly and made me feel at home. Thank you to all the public officials who shared their time with me to answer my questions and to discuss the events of July and August 1996; to Nancy Sánchez for providing me with audiotapes of the Orito negotiations and of meetings subsequent to the signing of the accords; to Teófilo Vásquez for providing draft copies of the Orito Agreement, materials that were key to the ethnography central to this book; and to Eduardo Díaz and Jaime Navarro for their trust in me and the frankness with which they shared their perspectives on events from a human point of view and as government officials.

Thanks go to Marta Herrera and Andrés Leonardo Pinzón, who designed and produced the maps; to María Lucía Sotomayor, with whom I first traveled to the Baja Bota of Cauca and later to the Sibundoy Valley. Her long friendship has been invaluable. I am also grateful to many other people who have helped in this project; to Luz Piedad Caicedo, for classifying the journalistic documentation; to Magadalena Arango, for her help in locating photographs and videos; to Mónica Ruán and Margarita Sandino for their help in classifying information; to Patricia Morales for her help with the transcription of interviews; to César Rozo, with whom I traveled to Puerto Asís and Mocoa at the beginning of my fieldwork and who helped me with my initial information gathering; and to Henry Salgado, Juliana Iglesias, and Elsy Castillo, researchers with the Colombian Institute of Anthropology and Colciencias. Henry and Elsy conducted research analogous to mine in Guaviare and Caquetá, respectively, so we were able to share and exchange information. Juliana has worked as my assistant since 2003 and has been invaluable in systemizing information related to Plan Colombia.

Thanks go to *Colcultura*, the Ministry of Culture, and the Colombian Institute of Anthropology and History, which granted me the leaves of absence necessary to further my graduate studies, write my dissertation, and spend a year as a Visiting Scholar at the David Rockefeller Center for Latin American Studies; and to my colleagues at the Colombian Institute of Anthropology and History who always believed in my work and accompanied me in their various capacities on this journey. To Fernando Coronil and Silvia Álvarez-Curbelo, who offered thoughtful feedback as fellows at Harvard's David Rockefeller Center for Latin American Studies, and to Winifred Tate, Colleta Youngers, and my colleagues at WOLA's Drugs, Democracy and Human Rights Project, for their insights on Plan Colombia.

Thanks go to Valerie Millholland, editor of Duke University Press, who has expressed her interest in the manuscript since the first time I talked to her about it at a Yale University Conference on Plan Colombia; to the two reviewers, whose detailed first and second round of comments helped me to rethink, revise, and convey my theoretical and ethnographic ideas in a straightforward fashion for the English-speaking audience; to Joanne Rappaport for her encouragement to publish the English version of the book and her suggestions for its improvement; to Katy Henrikson, who edited the final draft of the manuscript and helped me to clarify and synthesize the text; to Timothy Elfenbein, my managing editor at Duke University Press; and to Carol Roberts for preparing the index.

Thank yous also go to Bret Gustafson, Ben Penglase, and Kathleen Gallagher for their friendship during our years of graduate school, as well as to Lucia Volk, whose support at that time and over the ensuing years have been precious; to the members of the Colombian Colloquium at Harvard, June Erlick, Rodrigo Villar, Claudia Uribe, Franciso Ortega, Liliana Obregón, Claudia Pineda, Santiago Morales, Juan Federico Vélez, Claudia Mejía, Cesar Abadía, María LaRusso, Enrique Chaux and Angelika Rettberg, for their ongoing friendship, encouragement and interest in my work; and finally to Pia Maybury-Lewis, Richard and Pilar Brunnet, Linda Ordogh, Ann Conry, Monica Munson, and Patricia Villareal, who helped me in many ways during my time in Cambridge.

Finally, thanks go to my children, Santiago and Ana Manuela for their unconditional and selfless support. They have been consistently ready to help me, above all when my own efforts flagged. They did so with great affection, providing the love and solidarity necessary for the three of us to overcome whatever obstacle presented itself. To my mother and my brothers for their willingness to help us in any way they could during my doctoral work. And to Andy Klatt, my translator, soul mate, and husband, whose questions and our ensuing discussions helped me to clarify the text. His affection, his interest in Colombia, and his admiration for my work helped me to finish this book.

THE AUTHOR THANKS the Colombian Institute of Anthropology and History (ICANH) for permission to reprint parts of the earlier Spanish version of this book, *Entre el estado y la guerrilla: Identidad y ciudadanía en el movimiento de los campesinos cocaleros de Putumayo*, published by ICANH and Colciencias in 2001. An earlier version of Chapter 4 also appeared in *Journal of Drug Issues* Volume 35, no. 1, 2005.

Acronyms

ANAPO — Alianza Nacional Popular (National Popular Alliance)

ANNCOL — Agencia de Noticias Nueva Colombia (New Colombia News Agency)

ANUC — Asociación Nacional de Usuarios Campesinos (National Association of Campesinos)

ASOJUNTAS — Asociación de Juntas Comunales de Puerto Asís (Association of Communal Action Committees of Puerto Asís)

AUC — Autodefensas Unidas de Colombia (United Self Defense Forces of Colombia)

CAJ — Comisión Andina de Juristas (Andean Commission of Jurists)

CECOIN — Centro de Cooperación al Indígena (Center for Indigenous Cooperation)

CICAD — Interamerican Drug Abuse Control Commission

CINEP — Centro de Investigación y Educación Popular (Center for Research and Popular Education)

CMDR — Consejo Municipal de Desarrollo Rural (Municipal Rural Development Council)

CNE — Consejo Nacional de Estupefacientes (Colombian National Narcotics Council)

CODHES — Consultoría para los Derechos Humanos y el Desplazamiento (Consultancy for Human Rights and Forced Displacement)

COLCIENCIAS — Instituto Colombiano para el Desarrollo de la Ciencia y la Tecnología (Colombian Institute for the Promotion of Science and Technology)

CONPES — Consejo Nacional de Política Económica y Social (National Council for Economic and Social Policy)

CONVIVIR — Cooperativas de Vigilancia y Seguridad Privada (Private Security and Vigilance Cooperatives)

CORPES — Consejos Regionales de Planificación Económica y Social (Regional Councils for Economic and Social Planning)

CORPOAMAZONIA — Corporación para el Desarrollo Sostenible del Sur de la Amazonia (Corporation for Sustainable Development in the Southern Amazon)

CORPOICA — Corporación Colombiana de Investigación Agropecuaria (Colombian Agricultural Research Corporation)

CORPOS — Corporación Colombiana de Proyectos Sociales (Colombian Corporation for Social Projects)

DAINCO — Departamento Administrativo de Intendencias y Comisarías (Administrative Department for Intendencias and Comisarías)

DANE — Departamento Administrativo Nacional de Estadística (National Administrative Department of Statistics)

DAS — Departamento Administrativo de Seguridad (Department of Administrative Security)

DASALUD — Departamento Administrativo de Salud de Putumayo (Putumayo Health Department)

DDR — Desmovilización, Desarme y Reintegración (Demobilization, Disarmament, and Reintegration)

DNE — Departamento Nacional de Estupefacientes (National Narcotics Directorate)

DRI — Desarrollo Rural Integrado (Integrated Rural Development Fund)

ECOPETROL — Empresa Colombiana de Petróleos (Colombian Oil Company)

ELN — Ejército de Liberación Nacional (National Liberation Army)

EPL — Ejército Popular de Liberación (Popular Liberation Army)

FARC — Fuerzas Armadas Revolucionarias de Colombia (Revolutionary Armed Forces of Colombia)

FENSUAGRO — Federación Sindical Unitaria Agropecuaria (National Agricultural Union Federation)

ICA — Instituto Colombiano Agropecuario (Colombian Institute of Agriculture)

ICEL — Instituto Colombiano de Energía Eléctrica (Colombian Institute of Electrical Energy)

IDEA — Instituto de Estudios Ambientales (Institute of Environmental Studies)

IEPRI   Instituto de Estudios Políticos y Relaciones Internacionales (Institute of Political Studies and International Relations)

IICA   Instituto Interamericano de Cooperación para la Agricultura (Inter-American Institute of Agricultural Cooperation)

IGAC   Instituto Geográfico Agustín Codazzi (Agustín Codazzi Geographic Institute)

INCORA   Instituto Colombiano de Reforma Agraria (Colombian Institute of Agrarian Reform)

INDERENA   Instituto de Desarrollo de los Recursos Renovables (Institute for Renewable Natural Resources and the Environment)

INURBE   Instituto Nacional de Vivienda de Interés Social y Reforma Urbana (National Affordable Housing and Urban Reform Institute)

INVIAS   Instituto Nacional de Vías (National Highway Institute)

JAC   Junta de Acción Comunal (Community Action Committees)

OAS   Organization of American States

ONDCP   The US Office of National Drug Control Policy

OZIP   Organización Zonal Indígena del Putumayo (Putumayo Regional Indigenous Organization)

PILDAET   Programa de Iniciativas Locales para el Desarrollo Alternativo y la Erradicación Temprana (Local Initiatives for Alternative Development and Early Eradication)

PLANTE   Plan Nacional de Desarrollo Alternativo (National Alternative Development Plan)

PNR   Plan Nacional de Rehabilitación (National Rehabilitation Plan)

UMATA   Unidades Municipales de Asistencia Técnica Agropecuaria (Municipal Unit for Technical Assistance to Agriculture)

UNODC   United Nations Office on Drugs and Crime

UNRISD   United Nations Research Institute for Social Development

UP   Unión Patriótica (Patriotic Union)

URPA   Unidad Regional de Planificación Agropecuaria (Regional Agricultural Planning Unit)

USO   Unión Sindical Obrera (Oil Workers Union)

Introduction

In 1996 the United States "decertified" the Colombian government after then-President Ernesto Samper was accused of having received campaign donations from drug traffickers. In legal terms, the decertification was a consequence of Colombia's noncompliance with counter-narcotics efforts led by the United States. Nevertheless, the U.S. declared that its action was "a decertification not of Colombia but of President Samper . . . , a vote of no confidence for him, not the country" (Marc Thiessen; quoted in Crandall 2002, 119). Despite this alleged distinction, decertification "resulted in the cancellation or delay of US$35 million in counter-narcotics assistance to Colombia" (Crandall 2002, 138), a suspension of trade preferences for Colombian exports, an automatic veto by the United States of Colombian requests for funding from international financial institutions, and a hold on guarantees for U.S. investments in the country (De Rementería 1996).

In response to the action by the United States, President Samper hardened his stance against drug trafficking, increasing aerial fumigation of coca plantations in the Amazon region and tightening controls on the sale of cement and gasoline which are used for processing coca leaf into paste. This crackdown on illicit drug cultivation and processing sparked an uprising among *cocaleros* (coca producers and harvest workers) in the departments (equivalent to states or provinces) of Putumayo, Caquetá and Guaviare, and in the Baja Bota area of the department of Cauca in the western Amazon region (see map 1).[1] In the summer of 1996, more than 200,000 *campesinos*, including women, children and indigenous people, marched from their farms to the nearest towns and department capitals to protest the heightened threat to their livelihood.

It is important to clarify that when inhabitants of this region mention their activity as *cocaleros*, they refer to themselves in several different ways. At certain times they identify themselves as *colonos* (settlers who came from the Andean region of Colombia) and *cocaleros*, while at other times they call themselves *campesino colonos* or *campesino cocaleros*. It is clear throughout this work that they identify more as campesinos and/or colonos than as coca-

National Capital ★

International Boundary ———————

Department Boundary —·—·—·—·—·—

Map 1. Western Amazonia.

leros, given that coca is seen by them as a crop like any other. They distinguish themselves from the "drug trafficking mafia" by asserting their identity as small campesinos or colonos who grow coca leaf. Movement leaders will be quoted repeating this distinction throughout this book. The terms *campesino cocaleros* and *cocalero campesinos* will be used without distinction.

This book analyzes this cocalero uprising as a "diagnostic event" that "reveals ongoing contests and conflicts and competitions and the efforts to

Figure 1. Women and children at the cocalero marches. The poster says, "Yes to the strike, No to fumigation." (León Darío Pelaez, Casa Editorial, *El Tiempo*)

prevent, suppress, or repress them" (Moore 1987, 730). It was also a "critical event" as described by Das (1995, 5–6) in reference to consequences: "new models of action came into being, which redefined traditional categories . . . equally new forms were acquired by a variety of political actors."[2] The book also examines a paradox: it was precisely the illegality of coca that enabled the campesinos to put the region's social and economic crisis onto the national and international agenda, finally overcoming the government's apparent lack of interest in their plight.

During the cocalero uprising and mobilization of July–August 1996, Colombia came face to face with the previously unrecognized reality that its place in the Andean cocaine production chain had been transformed. Although Colombia had long been a processor and distributor of cocaine, by 1996 the country was the second largest producer of unprocessed coca leaf in the world. The following year, Colombia overtook Peru as the largest producer and remains so as of 2009. Coca had been grown by some indigenous groups in what is now Colombia since time immemorial, and its use was a significant part of their cultural heritage, but the 1996 cocalero marches drew the country's attention to a new social phenomenon: the cultivation of coca had increased dramatically to supply the international drug trade. Large quantities of coca were being grown by small campesinos in marginal and peripheral areas of the country.

The first of these regions was the western Amazon, comprising the departments of Putumayo, Caquetá, and Guaviare, where cultivation of coca as a commodity began in the 1970s. This was an area where the state had never successfully consolidated its control. In fact, the region was dominated by non-state armed actors at the very time of the 1996 marches. The state's presence was so weak that guerrillas and drug traffickers were free to carry out their illegal activities without interference, as became evident in my interview with Putumayan campesino Miguel Lucero. Miguel recalled how the United Nations arrived in his department in 1991 for the first voluntary coca eradication and alternative development program, and how the anti-narcotics police arrived at the same time. According to Miguel people began to believe that they would have to stop growing coca, but someone said, "Wait. Maybe there'll be a way to do business with the anti-narcotics police." "Of course," Miguel told me, "people who had more money got some resources together so they could make offers if it became necessary, and the anti-narcotics police made alliances with producers, so coca survived."[3] In fact, coca not only survived but spread, since in practice it was not being suppressed by the police who were ready to accept bribes.

While the 1996 cocalero movement constituted a coherent social phenomenon across the three departments in the Amazon, it unfolded and was resolved differently in each of them. The movement had different outcomes in Putumayo, Caquetá, and Guaviare as a result of the varied organizational histories and distinct politico-spatial identities of these departments, among other factors.[4] This book's analysis will focus primarily on the cocalero social movement in Putumayo but will reference certain moments of the social movement in the other two departments.

The Setting

Amazonia—and specifically the department of Putumayo—has always existed "at the margin," both geographically and conceptually, with respect to Colombia's central order. The characteristics of the tropical forest and the inaccessible location of the region made it marginal to the rest of the country. Putumayo was not even made a department until 1991. Up to that time it was territory that depended on the central government for all political and administrative matters, with no say in the choice of local authorities or policies.

Today, the department of Putumayo's thirteen municipalities depend on only two roads to move people and goods to and from the center of the country.[5] One road across the Sibundoy Valley in Upper Putumayo runs between the municipality of Mocoa and the city of Pasto in the department of Nariño. It is almost completely unpaved and takes seven to nine hours for a motor vehicle to travel. Another road from Mocoa goes to Pitalito in the department of Huila. This road was fully paved by the end of 2007 as a result of persistent popular demands that began in 1986. This trip takes six hours (these areas are depicted in maps 2 and 3).

The limited public transportation within Putumayo consists of service by bus or improvised bus (fashioned on a small truck frame) between town centers (*cascos urbanos*) on mostly unpaved roads.[6] Although the poor condition of these inter-municipal roads is a problem, campesinos complain more about the condition of the secondary and tertiary roads used to reach their own *veredas*, the rural precincts.[7] People commonly travel these minor roads by foot and frequently cross rivers and streams without the benefit of bridges. When roads are impassable for motor vehicles, campesinos must walk hours or days to reach the nearest town center. For example, to reach the center of Puerto Asís from the veredas near the Ecuadorean border one must walk two or three hours to reach a bus route, ride two hours on the bus, spend twenty minutes crossing the Putumayo River by ferry, and then travel ten minutes in another small vehicle. To get to Puerto Asís from a vereda on the Lower Putumayo River near the Piñuña River, one must walk up to three hours, wait for a boat that comes from Puerto Leguízamo, travel three to four hours on the river, and walk ten minutes from the river into town. The price of river transport, currently 50,000 pesos (US$26.90) per person, is an additional obstacle.[8] During the rainy seasons, transportation becomes more complicated, as the water rises and makes many rivers and streams impossible to cross without the use of small boats.

Not surprisingly, Putumayo is also marginal with respect to the market economy. This is a key factor with regard to why coca is so strongly preferred over crops such as corn and plantain that are grown in other regions. Unlike indigenous peoples with a coca tradition, campesinos in the western Amazon think of the crop exclusively as a means of economic survival in a context of inadequate public services.[9]

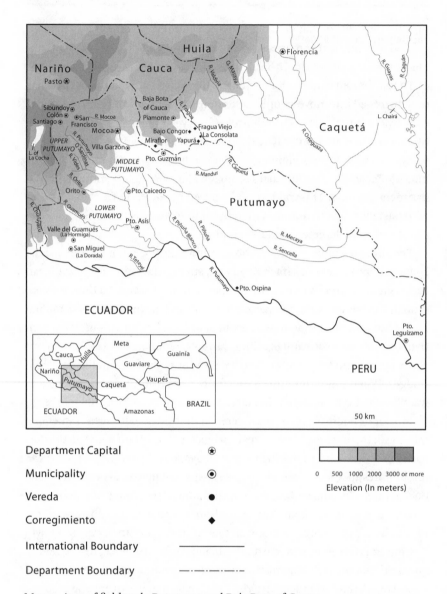

Department Capital   ⊛

Municipality   ◉

Vereda   ●

Corregimiento   ◆

International Boundary   ──────

Department Boundary   ──·──·──

0   500   1000   2000   3000 or more

Elevation (In meters)

Map 2. Area of fieldwork: Putumayo and Baja Bota of Cauca.

The Construction of a Marginal and Uncivilized Territory

This book takes its place within a body of scholarship (Aretxaga 2003; Das and Poole 2004; Tsing 1993, 1994; Borneman 1992; Ferguson 2001) that has called attention to the importance of borderlines and margins as peripheries where inhabitants find themselves between inclusion and exclusion, legality and illegality, order and disorder, ruled and unruled. These ambiguous spaces pose threats and demands and contest the relationship of their inhabitants to the central state, although they are legally intrinsic to the state and its constitution.

Tsing (1994, 279–80) defines margins as places where "contradictory discourses overlap, or where discrepant kinds of meaning-making converge," and she calls attention "to the tension between the constraining versus the empowering aspects of 'culture.'" The forms of dialogue established between the state and its margins are paramount in shaping communities. To explain the configuration of socio-economic and political processes in the region, we need first a historical analysis of the cultural and political construction of marginality by the state, and second an analysis of the marginalized people's perceptions and interpretations of the state and of their own situation. The case of Putumayo provides an opportunity to make sense of the role of the nation-state in social experience by examining the meanings and interpretations that people ascribe to the large-scale context in which they are immersed (Herzfeld 1985). My aim is to explore the dialectic between periphery and center within the nation-state from the perspectives of these different actors. I will examine the way in which this marginal space is imagined and constructed by both the central state and its inhabitants as well as how these actors resist, reinforce, and reconfigure its ascribed meanings.

Due to fierce resistance by the native population and its dense forest environment, Putumayo remained "uncivilized" for three hundred years after the Spanish conquest. Beginning in the early nineteenth century it was populated by people displaced from the central areas of Colombia identified as colonos. These colonos have been depicted ever since as migrants without roots—therefore without any regional identity—and, since the 1960s, as people in search of "easy money." This population has become the first and weakest link in the global chain of cocaine trafficking and has long been subject to the de facto "rule" of guerrilla armies dominating the region. As a result, the central state represents the region as uncivilized and disorderly, where inhabitants follow alternative codes of behavior and justice beyond its hegemonic control. In sum, the region poses a challenge to the status quo. Since guerrillas and drug traffickers have operated in Putumayo for over thirty years, outsiders associate its inhabitants with the barbarity and violence of these groups. The population is seen as contaminated by these traits and is accused of promoting violence by accepting and submitting to these forces. When paramilitaries entered Putumayo in 1997 to fight the guerrillas, the predicament caused by such perceptions was worsened. The paramilitaries accused many in the local population of being "guerrilla auxiliaries" and declared such collaborators "military targets." Well-documented ties between paramilitary and Colombian military forces have made this stigma even more dangerous for residents.[10]

The Colombian state has been driven by a longstanding crisis of sovereignty to exert control over the peripheral areas of its territory (Lefebrve 1991). Meta-narratives offered by the central government refer to the "reconquest" of the territory: the cleansing of the region of illegal crops and laboratories, the relocation of migrants and adventurers and the mending of a social fabric destroyed by violence and coca. A more recent example is a Colombian senator's description of anti-guerrilla marches held in 2008 in Colombia's big cities as "against barbarity" and "a symbol of civilization and tolerance."[11] Social benefits such as incorporation of the borderland into the nation-state and the imposition of the rule of law, as well as the state's attempt to acquire a monopoly over the use of arms, have legitimized military operations and aerial fumigation programs in the area.[12] The military is pictured as advancing from the center on a civilizing mission, conquistadors arriving to set the periphery in order. Many of the actions and debates before, during, and after the 1996 cocalero mobilization can be viewed as struggles over the meaning of civilization and the transformation of uncivil into civil behavior responsive to the nation-state (Keane 1998).

The coca growers contested their marginalization by demanding their rights as citizens under the law. They disputed the state's goal of bringing the rule of law to the region by enacting their citizenship on their own, as a way of being included in the legal and "civilized" nation-state. Consequently, it can be argued that the cocaleros were simultaneously inside and outside the law. As coca growers they were considered criminals, yet they rejected that status by exercising their right to participate as citizens.

State Exclusion vis-à-vis Citizen Participation

Dryzek (1996) has noted that the state itself engenders social movements by being "actively or passively exclusive."[13] In his discussion of Latin American social movements, Foweraker questions whether these movements in fact expand the public sphere—as has been assumed in social movement theory (for example, in Cohen and Arato 1994)—calling attention to the characteristics of Latin American public space, which "has been lacking, or is far more restricted [than in Europe or the United States], with the state a bulwark of social and economic exclusion" (Foweraker 1995, 32). This picture becomes more complex in Putumayo when to the historical exclusion of the Amazon region by the central state we add the presence of armed non-state actors and illicit ventures, which further both the state exclusion and the feeling of abandonment. The state intervened in the zone not to meet its responsibilities and compensate those who suffered by its absence but to represent them as criminals and punish them with violence reinforcing their exclusion and marginality. In response, politicized collective identities (Laclau 1994) emerged and gave birth to a social movement. Moreover, in Colombia a dirty war against grassroots leaders has been waged since the 1980s with the cooperation or acquiescence of the armed forces to thwart the opening of new political spaces. With this in mind, we can argue that the state has been both actively and passively exclusive in maintaining the long-term structural marginality of Amazonia.

Aretxaga (2003, 407) has pointed out that state "exclusion is always present as a potentiality, a *sine qua non* of the law and the state as an embodiment of its form" and she concludes that "those who are excluded are included through their exclusion." Though the cocalero social movement was born out of struggles against political and other types of exclusion, it sought to redress the campesino cocaleros' exclusion through their participation and influence in government, in particular *concertación* (a cooperative effort between the movement and government agencies to provide basic services).

Furthermore, the relation between the cocalero social movement and the state was strategic to the continuity of the movement itself. The fact that the movement depended on its engagement with the state for its existence meant that its social identity was not an autonomous phenomenon. The line between the internal and external realities of the movement was as diffuse as the distinction between the contingent and the essential. In the light of a social opening or at a moment of social change, hegemony as "a type of political relation" results from interactions between multiple factors. Thus, considering that "autonomy, far from being incompatible with hegemony, is a form of hegemonic construction" (Laclau and Mouffe 1985, 140), I argue that the cocalero movement sought to interact with and exert its influence on the hegemonic state discourse of democracy and citizen participation as a form of its own empowerment. Having experienced their exclusion as a negation of citizenship, the campesinos' demand for citizenship rights and inclusion of themselves and the region in the nation-state was a meaningful political act with cultural implications for their regional identity. In a country where campesino displacement is commonplace and despite the fact that many of them or their parents had already been displaced from other regions, the cocaleros insisted that Putumayo was the place where they legitimately belonged, from which they would resist further displacement.

In the context of exclusion, the state also became a nucleus of affection. The population desired and demanded its presence precisely because they felt abandoned by it. Finding a way to come to terms with the state so that it would take care of its citizens the way a responsible father meets the needs of his children became the motor of the movement. For the campesino colonos the return of a paternalistic state (*estado paternalista*) was a form of reparation after years of mistreatment.[14] I argue that the *politics of recognition* (Taylor 1995) was at the core of the emergence and constitution of collective identity in the cocalero social movement and its demands on the state.

The Cocalero Social Movement and the Recomposition of Collective Identities

The state's skewed representations of the western Amazon and the repressive policies applied and legitimized as a result of those characterizations helped trigger the 1996 social movement. Not only did this movement create a collective social identity for its members as cocaleros, but it also redefined this label, used previously only to stigmatize and criminalize them. In Putumayo, an imposed collective identity enabled a subaltern group to mobilize and articulate subjective positions in order to contest the regional political and ideological hegemony. Through collective action to protest fumigation of their coca crops, campesino cocaleros rejected the notions that they had no roots in the Amazon region and that they only wanted to enrich themselves as individuals and return "home" to their places of origin.

Cocaleros cast their social movement as a civic moment—*civic* in reference to citizenship, civility, and being "good citizens" (Moliner 1998, 646) as in the phrase "a civic act"—to encapsulate the message that the residents of Putumayo wanted to convey to the central government. The movement adopted various strategies to call attention to the needs of Putumayan citizens without using force or violence to get their way. In other words, they behaved as good citizens should. This was their response to their portrayal as barbarians or uncivilized people who use force over reason.

However, these negative identifying markers still led to the use of repressive measures in response to the civic mobilizations. Although the marches were not violent, similar demonstrations had been characterized since the 1980s as "guerrilla instigated." This blanket portrayal denied the region's inhabitants their agency and subsumed their demands, their needs, and the construction of their collective local and regional identities into the dynamics of the armed conflict and international war on drugs.

The cocalero movement can be categorized as a "new social movement," a newly structured base of collective action that transcended class struggle with struggles over meanings (Escobar 1992a, 1992b). A redefined cocalero identity emerged in the search for institutional reforms to increase members' opportunities to participate in decision making. Although it can be argued that small-scale campesino cocaleros have social demands as a subordinate social class, their condition as such was not what defined their social movement.[15]

The campesinos' self-identification as small coca growers and harvesters—in spite of the illegality of these activities—determined the configuration of the social movement. It was their open acknowledgment of this role that provided an opportunity to negotiate as valid interlocutors with state representatives and to propose their own alternatives for the region. Furthermore, the cocalero campesinos became empowered as a social group as they began to show they could defend their "right to have rights" (Arendt 1949) and right to be heard. This book describes how the cocalero movement fought not only for social and political rights but for civil rights, democratization, the protection of human dignity and life, and for overall recognition of campesinos as Putumayan citizens.

The movement's exercise of the rights of citizens enabled cocalero campesinos to establish a new role for themselves in relation to the state that affected the configuration of the state at the local level. In an area experiencing sharp conflict, this meant the state recognizing how Putumayan communities were affected by government social and economic policies and, above all, by political violence.

Local State Formation and Civil Society in a Conflict-Ridden Region

Various authors have challenged the conceptualization of the state as monolithic (Abrams 1988; Corrigan and Sayer 1985; Joseph and Nugent 1994; Mitchell 1991, 1999; Aretxaga 2003; Trouillot 2001; Hansen and Stepputat 2001). Their work enriches the discussion of local state formation in Putumayo, a region where the state's monopoly over violence is contested by the presence of two non-state armed actors (the guerrillas and the paramilitaries), and where internal state fissures are so deep that local mayors at times have become part of a *non-state within the state*. Putumayo is an example of how "margins break up the solidity often ascribed to the state" (Das and Poole 2004, 20).

I will analyze the ambiguities and ambivalence of relations between central and local state representatives as well as relations among cocalero movement leaders, local and central state officials, and guerrillas. We will observe a series of strategic alliances, negotiations, manifestations of resistance, and for the most part, a blurring of group boundaries. In the ethnographic analysis of the negotiations following the cocalero marches it became apparent that the state was "a significantly unbounded terrain of powers and techniques, an ensemble of discourses, rules, and practices cohabiting in limited, tension-ridden, often contradictory relation with one another" (Brown 1995, 174). Moreover, the campesinos' feeling of abandonment was shared by local representatives such as mayors and other officials, who blurred the line between the state and civil society by ceasing to identify themselves as agents of the former and becoming active members of the latter.

Putumayan civil society also demanded the state's support in gaining autonomy from non-state armed actors. Coca growers were seeking to free themselves from dependence on illegal armed actors with their participation in civil society and interaction with the state as an active provider of services. When the cocalero movement sought a commitment from the state to allow for its democratic participation, the notion of civil society was imbued with new meaning. In the context of the Colombian armed conflict, the usual boundaries between civil society and the state are blurred; it becomes necessary to reconsider the extent to which strengthening civil society requires autonomy from or opposition to the state. I argue that in conflict-ridden zones, an alternative model is emerging where there is continuity between the state and civil society, each seeking to establish cooperative relations with the other to oppose violence and bring state presence back to areas where it has been wholly or partially absent.

In Putumayo, the Revolutionary Armed Forces of Colombia (Fuerzas Armadas Revolucionarias de Colombia, FARC) acts like a state (Aretxaga 2003) and fulfills the functions of a government by exercising local power and territorial control, regulating the illegal coca market, and enacting laws and norms enforced with strict sanctions. However, the two governing powers that exercise juridical functions in this zone—the local state and FARC—do not necessarily supplant each other. The tension that exists between the state and the guerrillas on the one hand, and between the people of Putumayo and their two "governments" on the other, makes the definition of boundaries between the state and civil society even more complex, as will be discussed. Foucault ([1976] 1994, 1979) emphasizes the generalization of discipline and power to the extent that social subjects appear to be condemned to subjection, and to the extent that political or ideological opposition to the disciplinarian structures is nonexistent. But the cocalero movement challenged and contested campesino subjection to both the state and the guerillas. Throughout this ethnography of the 1996 cocalero movement I have sought to emphasize the agency of its subjects.

Natural Leaders: The Central Actors in the Cocalero Movement

The leaders of the Civic Movement for the Comprehensive Development of Putumayo are the central actors of this ethnography. I interviewed them, transcribed those interviews and their public speeches during various phases of the movement, and used the resulting texts throughout my analysis. Because these leaders wanted the history of the movement to be written, they contributed openly and generously to this work. When this research was published in Spanish it circulated widely in the region and was welcomed as a recognition and validation of campesino struggles (M. Ramírez 2001). Now I wish to give these subaltern and situated actors the opportunity to share their understandings of coca cultivation and armed conflict in

Putumayo with a wider audience. A careful examination of the movement leaders' arguments and discourse is thus at the core of this book.

These individuals are defined in the region as "natural leaders." Huber Ballesteros, a unionist, explained the meaning of this term:

> A natural leader is a grassroots leader who starts in the countryside and stays there. We've all gone through the process, but when we understand what kind of organization we need, and that we need to take up other goals—political and economic goals that may be national in scope—then they say that we're not so natural anymore. But it seems to me that if you're a campesino, then you continue to be a natural leader. You don't become a leader through things like academic studies, although some do study when they have the opportunity. But you continue to be a natural leader not from what you learn in classes but from a step-by-step process of self-improvement. Some go faster and some go slower; some make more progress and others make less, but that's the way it is.[16]

Recognition as a campesino is key to being considered a natural leader: a member of the community struggling to improve the welfare of his or her fellows. As natural leaders attain formal education, they gain access to social and cultural capital that enables them to make connections between local and national struggles.[17] It may seem that such individuals would cease to be considered natural leaders, but as Ballesteros clearly articulates, it is a person's campesino origins and continued campesino identity that gives him or her legitimacy as a "natural" representative of a campesino community.

The leaders of the cocalero social movement were not only campesinos but also colonos and representatives of colonos as a social group. Some came to the western Amazon from other marginalized areas of Colombia where they had also settled as colonos, such as Caquetá in the case of Ramiro Grisales or Arauca in the case of Luis Emiro Mosquera. They arrived in Putumayo during the 1980s, uprooted a second time due to their participation in leftist and alternative political parties. Other leaders such as Gilberto Sánchez had been in the department longer. Sánchez took up a leadership role after participating in government workshops and programs during the 1980s.[18]

Under the National Rehabilitation Plan (Plan Nacional de Rehabilitación, PNR), assemblies called Rehabilitation Councils were established in all the municipalities of the western Amazon and the Baja Bota of Cauca.[19] These councils were to be spaces where government officials and community representatives could sit down together "to channel community demands and assure the appropriate use of resources provided by the Plan for the development of a more democratic political culture and local political leadership" (National Rehabilitation Plan 1994, 14). Local leaders and community representatives participating in the Rehabilitation Councils learned to negotiate with the government and became familiar with participatory democracy and legal ways to defend their rights. The PNR also held skills development (*capacitación*) courses for community leaders. These courses are remembered in the region as one of the great achievements of the PNR because the skills acquired by local leaders allowed communities to communicate their needs and proposals to the government effectively. These new spaces for negotiation with the state and organized civic participation have been a feature of the local political culture since the days of the PNR, and they became central to the 1996 Putumayo cocalero social movement. The leaders' negotiating skills were incorporated into the struggle against crop fumigation and were used above all to pressure the state to meet its constitutional obligations.

What did all of the movement leaders have in common? They rejected the use of arms and sought to increase spaces for popular participation. They had all chosen to participate in politics to lend a future voice to colono campesinos, the department, and the region. For example, Ramiro Grisales was elected to Mocoa's municipal council in 1988 and to the departmental assembly in the 1990s. Gilberto Sánchez was municipal councilman to Puerto Asís starting in 1992. Both of them, and most of the other movement leaders who entered politics, belonged to alternative political parties.

Thus, events in Putumayo led by these "natural leaders" also provide an opportunity to examine how civic movements develop into political and electoral movements. As we shall see, the region has experienced ambiguous political processes, with advances and reversals in degree of autonomy from the traditional parties and from the guerrillas. New forces seeking to find autonomous space within local politics are articulated in accordance with the conjuncture of relations between the regional and national forces that impede or strengthen their attempts. In this book we will closely consider the actions and positions of Putumayo's "natural leaders," who can also be considered local intellectuals (Mallon 1995, 323) or peasant intellectuals (Feierman 1990).

Fieldwork in a Conflict-ridden Zone

I did the bulk of my fieldwork in 1998 and the first half of 1999, working intensively in the Putumayan municipality of Puerto Asís and in the municipality of Piamonte in the Baja Bota region of Cauca. In addition, I spent time in other Putumayan municipalities for purposes of comparison. I returned to Putumayo in 2001 when Plan Colombia—a security and antidrug assistance program funded in excess of $6 billion by the United States beginning in fiscal year 2000—was being implemented, and I visited several times in 2001–8 to monitor its implementation, the responses of coca growers and government officials to its anti-drug, counter-insurgency, and counter-terrorism policies, and the way that the cocalero social movement was adapting to changing circumstances. Between 2000 and 2004 I updated the data and wrote a chapter on the implementation of Plan Colombia. I made further updates in 2006–7.

When I was collecting data in the region early in 1998, the paramilitaries and FARC were in the midst of an intelligence war. Each was concerned that unknown individuals might be informants for the other side and both were carefully monitoring the comings and goings of outsiders in Puerto Asís. To establish a role for myself in the community, I stayed in town with the family of a female anthropology student at the University of Popayán, and introduced myself as the young woman's professor there to supervise her thesis work on the oral history of Santa Rosa, a municipality in the Baja Bota. In this capacity I was able to conduct interviews without raising suspicions that I was a spy or a possible enemy who could use people's words against them. As I mentioned above, most people were ready to be interviewed, believing that the history of their struggle should be recorded and that their points of view on coca should be heard outside the region.

Working with this student, I learned that we had to keep our physical distance from the police station in Puerto Asís to avoid being considered police informants. Even if we had to take a very indirect route to walk somewhere, it was important not to pass by it. I could not visit the jail to interview imprisoned cocaleros or anyone else related to the drug trade, such as drivers or processors, because that would have linked me to them and their activities. We were advised not to raise suspicion by staying in town more than a few months. We were to arrive, do some work, and then leave as people expect researchers to do. I extended my fieldwork to Piamonte in the Baja Bota so as not to spend too much time in any one place.

The Baja Bota is an ideal spot for the study of marginalization because it is peripheral in both national and departmental terms. It shares all of the social, cultural, political, and economic characteristics of the western Amazon, including the dominant presence of FARC guerrillas (who use the area as a refuge due to its extreme isolation) and the intensification of coca cultivation in the last two decades. Although the book centers on the cocalero movement in Putumayo, my research in the Baja Bota of Cauca deepened my understanding of the social movement by providing a basis of comparison.

An additional advantage to working in the Baja Bota as well as in Putumayo was that I was able to observe the attitude of FARC regarding the establishment of the new municipality of Piamonte in 1996. This was the first time the state had attempted to impose civil authority in an area where the guerrillas had theretofore exercised absolute control. FARC had been in the region for several decades and the population was used to seeing the local guerrilla commander as the primary authority in their area. FARC frequently called meetings about local matters that were attended by community leaders and members. The fact that local people freely discussed the outcomes of these meetings helped me to understand their perspective on FARC and its role in their lives. Due to the guerrillas' firm control of the Baja Bota at the time of my fieldwork, there was no paramilitary presence. In this sense the Baja Bota was a safer place to do fieldwork than Puerto Asís. Since the area was not contested, I did not have to worry about being targeted by paramilitaries and had to gain permission to work only from FARC.

Stating my research objectives clearly was essential to my own personal safety. After attending a meeting to discuss planning for the new municipality of Piamonte, I was approached by a member of FARC in civilian clothes. He was a *miliciano*, a guerrilla assigned to intelligence duties in town. "So," he said, "you're the one who's researching the culture of coca for COLCIENCIAS?"[20] When I realized that he knew I was a researcher, I thought that somehow he must know what I was doing and that I should answer his questions. Several people in the area had advised me that this was the best policy. I responded, "Well, the notion that there is a 'culture of coca' is debatable and that's discussed in the research, but I don't see it that way. Do you think there's a new culture that relates specifically to growing coca? Maybe coca is just another crop, another way for campesinos to get by."

My student assistant got nervous and moved away. The miliciano asked me why my friend had left and I answered, "Because she's from Puerto Asís.

You know that people here are very careful about talking to strangers and you haven't really introduced yourself. Also, she'll still be here in the region after I'm back in Bogotá. I can leave when I want to and there's less danger that someone will accuse me of being with one or another armed group. Anyway," I said, "if there's any question about the project I'm the one to ask because I'm the director." He then gave me a copy of a FARC communiqué about their campaign to protect the natural environment. It said that people should not dump chemicals used to process coca leaf into the rivers. He said, "If you or I call a community meeting to talk about these environmental issues they wouldn't come but if FARC calls a meeting they show up. You're an anthropologist. Can you explain why that is?" I hadn't told him that I was an anthropologist so that made me even more convinced that he knew a lot about me. "Well," I said, "people obey FARC because they're the authority here, but I think it's possible to get people together if it's for something that interests them."

He returned to the topic of the chemical waste and pollution produced by processing coca leaf and asked if it was possible to propose a project and apply for funding to promote environmentally sustainable practices. "Yes," I said, "but the proposal would have to come from some organization or institution." The miliciano then asked me why he had not seen me in the eastern part of Piamonte where coca was being mono-cropped. There had recently been a shooting when some of the officials of the new municipal government were visiting veredas to give talks on the municipal land-use plan. I had been traveling with them but when the official was shot the tour was cut short. I told the miliciano what had happened, but he said that the shooting had been investigated and determined to have been an isolated act. "People were angry that experts were being hired from outside the municipality to work in the municipal government," he said, but the problem had been cleared up and now it was safe to go back to the veredas. He was implicitly giving me permission to continue my research. Once I acquired that permission, people were willing to open their doors to me.

When I went to look for my assistant, she warned me that the man had not introduced himself and that you have to know who you're talking to. I told her that I answered his questions because he knew a lot about me. When a local woman came up to us, I asked her who that man was whom we had been talking to and she confirmed that he was a FARC miliciano. The next day I saw the miliciano in the street and I started to greet him, but he turned away after gesturing to me that we should not recognize each other. I had passed the test and he had no further interest in talking to me.

In my fieldwork I utilized the cocalero movement as a central theme and conducted semi-structured interviews of differently socially situated actors (local, regional, and central government officials, coca growers, movement leaders, and others). I used these interviews to describe and analyze these actors' perceptions and interpretations of illegal crops, the movement, the region, and the local and central governments. I collected movement narratives that revealed multiple tensions between the actors. As an ethnographer I analyzed related documents and local texts as social practice in order to demonstrate how discourse structures behavior (Foucault 1971, 1973). I examined newspaper, television, and radio interviews of peasant leaders, government officials, and NGO representatives to reveal how discourse shaped the views of the differently situated actors, including their points of agreement and difference. I also examined written materials, including newspapers, as cultural texts (Gupta 1995).

The Structure of the Book

The first chapter provides a historical outline of the colonization of Colombia's peripheral areas during the twentieth century, revealing that colonos were living in these areas when coca arrived and turned them into cocaleros. This chapter also gives a historical perspective on the arrival of guerrillas and paramilitaries in Putumayo.

The second chapter provides an overview of coca production in Colombia from 1994 to 2006, comparing it with the cases of Peru and Bolivia in order to understand the market dynamics of coca production in a regional context. It describes the unfolding of antidrug policies promoted by the United States, emphasizing how in Colombia the drug war became, in practice, a counter-insurgency war that legitimized state violence. This chapter also describes the process of coca cultivation, harvesting, and processing in local laboratories, and provides ethnographic vignettes of daily life in a region rife with armed actors and drug traffickers.

The third chapter describes the civic movements of the 1970s and 1980s and discusses the movements of the 1990s as predecessors to the cocalero social movement. It discusses how the conversion of civic movements into political movements has become practice in this marginal region, as a way to make demands heard by the central government.

Chapter 4 examines how the constructed marginality of the Amazon region mediates social, political, and cultural practices and affects central government policies. It analyzes the organization of the social movement and its submerged networks, emphasizing the ambiguous alliance between cocalero leaders and guerrillas. The analysis develops the argument that collective identities in the Amazon region are shaped by a sense of exclusion, abandonment and misrecognition by the state.

Chapter 5 relates the principal negotiating goals of movement leaders and maintains that this social movement focused on one fundamental demand: that the Colombian nation-state recognize the campesinos in their condition as social actors rather than criminals and acknowledge their "right to have rights." It also describes the suspension of negotiations, the development of the initial agreement, the nature of the final agreement, and the end of the mobilization. The description of these events provides additional detail for the ethnography of the social movement.

Chapter 6 examines local state formation in Putumayo through the analysis of governance practices of both FARC and the national and local state representatives during the negotiations.

Chapter 7 analyzes the strategies used by movement leaders after the negotiations to continue representing the cocalero campesinos. It develops the argument that the politics of citizenship was at the core of the cocalero social movement and that in this conflict-ridden region a redefinition of civil society is occurring.

Chapter 8 explores what has happened to the cocalero movement and its central demand for citizenship in Putumayo under the strictures of the U.S. war on drugs. Because Putumayo contained 54 percent of the Colombian total of illegal crops in 2000, it became the epicenter of Plan Colombia. Aerial spraying was intensified and alternative development plans began to be implemented as compensation for fumigation and forced eradication.

CHAPTER ONE

History of Colonization, Marginalization, and the State

Guerrillas, Drug Trafficking, and Paramilitarism
in the Colombian Amazon

The Amazon region has been seen by the central government both as a solution to land pressures elsewhere in the country and as a national security buffer zone to protect the country's sovereignty on its southern border. These views of the region have defined state policy toward the Colombian Amazon and fueled the sense of abandonment that drives the region's discourse regarding the central state. This chapter reviews the geographical origins and migration timeline of colonos of Putumayo and the Baja Bota. We will see connections between this process of colonization and other events in the region's history, the popular perception of the state and state formation in the Amazon over the last century.

Several colono identities emerged as a result of colonization. This chapter examines how these identities were constructed both within the Amazon region and in relation to the central government, thus ascribing meanings to the region and its inhabitants that the colonos have simultaneously resisted and reinforced.

The chapter also describes the arrival of FARC in western Amazonia as a result of the violence that swept central Colombia between 1946 and 1966, their arrival in Putumayo in 1984, and their transformation into the authority in the region. It relates the history of coca cultivation in western Amazonia from its beginnings in the 1970s through its expansion into the dominant crop of the 1980s, and the ensuing war between FARC and drug traffickers for control over coca production and marketing. A grasp of the role of both these forces in the region is crucial to understanding how the cocalero movement emerged and operated.

Finally, I track two waves of the paramilitary phenomenon in Putumayo: their arrival at the end of the 1980s, which was linked to narcotrafficking, and their second appearance in 1997 after they had come together under the name United Self Defense Forces of Colombia (Autodefensas Unidas de Colombia, AUC), a political and military group that declared war against FARC. Paramilitarism not only increased political violence in Putumayo but also changed the way its residents related to FARC.

Colonization of the Colombian Amazon:
The Construction of an Empty Territory as a Receptor for Displaced People

The central government, in the hands of the dominant elites that have historically owned and run the state in Colombia, has traditionally classified Amazonia as *baldío* (*terra nullius*, legally vacant and unowned land), implicitly denying the existence of those who lived there and re-designating it as a receptor for people displaced from other parts of Colombia.[1] The colonization of the Colombian Amazon began thus in the late nineteenth century and has continued ever since, mainly by residents of the Andean highlands who left their homes in response to waves of social, political, and economic upheaval in central Colombia. Landless campesinos began to leave the highlands in the 1930s in search of a more stable livelihood on the open frontier. Deprived of their small plots by large landowners, these campesinos migrated to the marginal areas outside the agrarian frontier throughout the twentieth century, allowing elites to sidestep agrarian reform and legitimize the highly concentrated ownership of land that has characterized Colombia's rural property structure.[2]

This migration accelerated in the 1950s due to confrontations between the dominant Liberal and Conservative political parties in the interior of the country, a period known as *La Violencia* or the Violence. These traditional political parties fostered a bloody, vicious partisan rivalry in the countryside through institutionalized patron-client relationships, pushing affected campesinos further and further away from the center. Colonization in the "margins" was later formalized by government settlement programs that implicitly recognized Colombia's structural land tenure problems.[3]

The colonization of Colombia's western Amazon has been so consistent that mechanisms have been established for newly arriving colonos to integrate into the area's social, political, and economic structures. Putumayo's case is one of dynamic frontier expansion in which the state moved into new productive areas while reproducing its institutions and the class structure upon which it was based (Moran 1988). The Colombian political culture also reproduced intense political rivalries, the exclusion of third parties, the dependence of local authorities and political bosses on the central elites, and widespread administrative corruption. However, the state presence was felt only intermittently, and the frontier had "its own simultaneous autonomy, resistance, acquiescence, change, and persistence" (Whitten 1985, 47), as will be discussed.

Colonos have been defined as a contingent population, as people who arrive and leave along with an evolving cycle of commodity booms (rubber, pelts, gold, and most recently, coca) that had little lasting effect on their lives and culture. This construction represents the culture and identity of the migrant population as a cipher: non-native and present in Amazonia only to extract wealth. Coca may seem to be just one more commodity of this kind, but it has had long lasting effects that distinguish it from the others.

The western portion of Colombian Amazonia (the departments of Putumayo, Caquetá, and Guaviare) received the majority of Amazonia's population influx (see map 1). In the 1990s, western Amazonia was highly populated, with 86.3 percent of the Colombian Amazon's total population at a density of 2.5 inhabitants per square kilometer.[4] Colonos were culturally dominant. Eastern Amazonia (the departments of Amazonas, Vaupés, and Guainía), by contrast, was characterized by a predominantly indigenous population, significant urbanization and a much lower population density of 0.1 inhabitants per square kilometer.[5] Guerrilla activity and coca farming were found mostly in western Amazonia.

Marginalization and the Construction of a "Place Outside the Law"

The historically marginal Amazon region can be characterized as an "out-of-the-way place" (Tsing 1994), where the center can solve its problems without having to make structural economic, social, or political changes. In Putumayo, the government added the ascription of a "place outside the law," when coca cultivation—the main agricultural and economic activity of local campesinos—was declared illegal. As increased coca cultivation attracted the presence of the guerrillas, Putumayo came to be represented as a region inhabited by criminals, thus furthering its marginalization.

During a Peace Forum in Puerto Asís, some had stated that "We have gone from being a violent state to being a barbarous state, in some cases with the indifference of the citizenry."[6] Soon afterward, the Mocoa-based Human Rights Ombudsman for Putumayo wrote to then-President Samper saying, "We are attempting to put an end to 'the law of the jungle' where any-one can violate another's right to life and physical integrity because he can be sure that nothing will happen to him."[7]

The views of these government officials evoked historical images of the region that served to "explain" the ongoing violence. The region's barbarity was reified; the area operated under "the law of the jungle"; lack of civility was the norm. Yet the local officials' analysis of the increasing violence was contradictory. While they spoke of the struggle against impunity, their conception of the region as barbarous legitimated the reign of violence. Their very "explanation" justified the Colombian center's view of the region as marginal, either empty or inhabited only by barbarians in their "natural state"—an open invitation to the "civilizing" influence of re-colonization missions.

The departmental government plan for Putumayo 1998–2000, named the Territorial Pilot Plan for Social Peace (Plan Piloto Territorial de Convivencia), described the department as dominated by the coca economy, "an extractive and inequitable development model" (12) within a weak and de-legitimized state, racked by the resulting struggle over territory and generalized violence. This diagnosis deemed the violence "not a conjunctural scenario but an evolving process" (13). The Plan explained that the violence resulted from historical "barbarism" in the Amazon, a longstanding element of the region's historiography, and one which meant, according to departmental officials, "an unviable society without human rights, without respect for rights, and without tolerance," where "democracy isn't feasible" (14–15). The coca economy was analyzed as "a focused strategy" (16) founded on a lawless frontier, implying that certain places in Putumayo were barbarous (Lower Putumayo) while others were not (Upper Putumayo), a representation that will be discussed in the next chapter (Government of Putumayo 1998, 12–16).

Thus, the Amazon region was defined by the central government as a space to be wrenched from the hands of lawless barbarians, conquered, and cured of its criminality and illegality. State repression (aerial spraying, militarization, and dirty war tactics) was legitimized through the construction of "stereotypic and dangerous impressions" (Herbst 1994, 18) of the inhabitants of Putumayo as criminals and guerrilla collaborators.

The stigmatization of this "marginal and peripheral" region and population by the Colombian heartland brought about resistance in the form of protest movements. Here it is worth considering Slater's (1998, 387) assessment that "regional social movements have challenged the existing territoriality of the state and in this struggle new forms of spatial subjectivity and identity have emerged." The cocalero social movement of 1996 challenged the state in this way, as will be discussed further.

Periods of Migration and Regional Origins of Colonos in Putumayo

This section provides a history of colonization in Putumayo and the Baja Bota of Cauca. As will be discussed, coca farming stimulates migration (for example by harvest workers who follow the crops), but is by no means the only cause of colonization in the region.

There have been five distinct waves of migration into Putumayo. Roman Catholic missionaries were the first to attempt to colonize the Colombian Amazon region in a first wave from 1850 to 1946. However, indigenous resistance prevented any permanent colonies until 1887 when a concordat between the Vatican and the Colombian government authorized permanent missions on the Amazon frontier. Missionaries constructed the first roads to the region from central Colombia. They founded towns such as Puerto Asís in 1912, to defend Colombian sovereignty near its southern border and sponsored white settlers in order to "civilize" the territory and provide the indigenous "savages" with a way of life to emulate. Two main expeditions brought colonizers to the Amazon from the Colombian center during this period. The first, in 1890, was intended to extract quinine and the second, from 1903 to 1930, was to gather rubber. The constructed horror of the jungle, of savagery and cannibalism, and its related imagery led the colonizers during the rubber boom of the early twentieth century to ascribe these characteristics to Putumayo and to create a space of death, terror, and cruelty.[8] Extra-legal rights and rules allowing for violence were agreed upon in this context. Today's Putumayans refer to the period of the rubber boom when they attempt to explain the "barbarism" that some state representatives ascribe to the region, as discussed above.

In 1930, a border conflict between Colombia and Peru stimulated further colonization, as the Colombian government established an ongoing military presence to reinforce its sovereignty over the area. Military forces completed roads that had been begun by missionaries years earlier. These included roads from Pasto (in the highlands of Nariño) to Mocoa, Neiva (in the highlands of Huila) to Florencia, and La Tagua to Puerto Leguízamo (see map 3).

The second wave of colonization was a result of La Violencia. Partisan

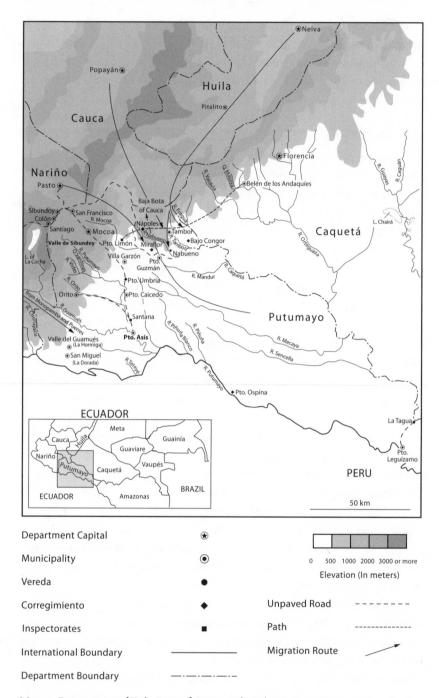

Map 3. Putumayo and Baja Bota of Cauca, migration routes, 1900–1946.

violence broke out as Liberals began to persecute Conservatives during the 1930–46 period of Liberal party hegemony. Conservative Mariano Ospina Pérez won the presidential election of 1946, and during the next four years Conservatives began to persecute Liberals. Social movements initiated during the Liberal regime were repressed and violence intensified. Between 1946 and 1958 political violence was rampant, mostly in Tolima, Huila, Valle del Cauca, Cundinamarca, Boyacá, Antioquia, Viejo Caldas, Santander, Norte de Santander, and the eastern plains (Llanos Orientales) of Arauca, Casanare, Meta, and Vichada (see map 4). The violence provoked a mass exodus from these regions and dramatically increased the population in the Amazon lowlands.

The third wave of colonization in Putumayo took place from 1963 to 1977. In 1963, the Texas Petroleum Company (Texaco) began to explore for oil in the municipalities of Orito, Acae, San Miguel, and Valle del Guamués. State development programs including a project for the colonization of Putumayo were begun in 1964. In 1965, approximately 200 kilometers of roads were built and people settled along them (Alomía et. al. 1997, 17). In the late 1960s, highly productive oil reserves were discovered. During a 3-year period, Texaco drilled fifteen oil wells and built a 310-kilometer pipeline to the town of Tumaco on the Pacific Coast. Petroleum-related activities created high expectations for employment, but only 1,000 local workers were hired (Corsetti, Tommasoli, and Viezzoli 1987, 145). Production was export-oriented. Colonization began in Valle del Guamués and continued in Puerto Asís. Colonos founded today's town centers of coca production in Putumayo, such as La Dorada, San Miguel, El Placer, El Tigre, and Siberia.

A fourth wave of migration took place between 1977 and 1987. Coca cultivation had begun and a coca boom quickly developed. This economic bonanza brought new colonos into the Amazon region and triggered a decline in non-coca subsistence agriculture by established colonos. From this point on, local economic activities were increasingly dominated by the cocaine-driven demand for coca.

Between 1987 and 1996, coca production increased and then stabilized. A fifth wave of migration from the departments of Huila, Cauca, Valle, Nariño, Caldas, and from Ecuador continued to enter the area until 1994. After that, smaller numbers of migrants continued to enter the department, attracted by opportunities for coca production and by increasing activity in the oil industry.

The data in tables 1 and 2, from a 1991 survey of the geographic origins

Area of violence   – – – – – – – – – –

0   500 1000 2000 3000 or more
Elevation (In meters)

Map 4. The geography of *La Violencia*, 1949–1953. (Reproduced by permission from Guzmán Campos, et al., 1980; map 6, p. 97)

Table 1. Putumayo colonos' departments of origin by percentage

Nariño	54.5	(other)	4.9
Cauca	14.6	Caquetá	2.4
Putumayo	8.1	Cundinamarca	2.4
Valle del Cauca	5.7	Meta	1.6
Tolima	4.9	Huila	0.8

Source: Reprinted with permission from Eduardo Ariza, María Clemencia Ramírez, and Leonardo Vega, *Atlas cultural de la Amazonia Colombiana: La construcción del territorio en el siglo XX*. Bogotá: Ministerio de Cultura-Instituto Colombiano de Antropología, Corpes Orinoquia, Corpes Amazonia, 1998.

Table 2. Percentage of colonos' arrival in Putumayo by years

1930–1946	0.8	1987–1986	37.6
1947–1967	23.2	1987–1993	19.2
1968–1977	19.2		

Source: Reprinted with permission from Eduardo Ariza, María Clemencia Ramírez, and Leonardo Vega, *Atlas cultural de la Amazonia Colombiana: La construcción del territorio en el siglo XX*. Bogotá: Ministerio de Cultura-Instituto Colombiano de Antropología, Corpes Orinoquia, Corpes Amazonia, 1998.

of Putumayan campesinos, highlight two phenomena. First, the predominance of migrants from Nariño is striking. The Nariño migrants, who had been small-holders in the highlands and had lost their lands, sought to acquire small pieces of land in Putumayo to call their own. The Nariño traditions they brought with them shaped their perception of the state and, subsequently, the course of the political organizing movements. Second, while the greatest number of migrants entered the region during the coca boom (37.6 percent between 1978 and 1986), large numbers also arrived during the 1947–67 period of La Violencia and during the petroleum exploration that followed. Taken together, these two periods account for 42.2 percent of the sample.

Periods of Migration and Regional Origins of Colonos
in the Baja Bota of Cauca

Like Putumayo, the Baja Bota of the department of Cauca was administered by Capuchin missionaries based in Sibundoy through the Apostolic
Prefecture of Caquetá established in 1905. As in Putumayo, the missionaries began to develop a road system. The road from Belén de los Andaquíes
in Caquetá to Puerto Limón in Putumayo is particularly relevant (see map
3). This road, completed in 1919, cut across the Baja Bota, effectively short-
ening the distance between Florencia, the capital of Caquetá, and Mocoa,
the capital of Putumayo (see map 3). The settlement of Nápoles was established on this road in 1933 by seven families from Huila (R. Ramírez 1991,
35–36). Other families traveled from Huila on the Caquetá River and established themselves near the Tambor and Congor Rivers (see map 5). In time,
the discovery of alluvial gold in the Puerto Limón region became the basis
for an extractive economy. In 1940 colonos from Nariño, Upper Cauca and
Putumayo settled on the Nabueno and Tambor Rivers in search of gold (see
map 3). Another wave of colonization began in the early 1950s, motivated by
La Violencia and other factors. Both earlier colonos and new arrivals began
to move into the interior of the Bota. Others who had initially settled in
Putumayo also began to move into the area. The settlements of La Vega, Piamonte, Miraflor, and Campoalegre were founded by migrants from Nariño,
Huila, and other parts of Cauca. The vereda of Samaritana was founded in
late 1958 by colonos from Putumayo and Nariño (R. Ramírez 1991, 44). The
northern portion of the Baja Bota was also settled by arrivals from Nariño,
Huila, and Putumayo (see map 5). Puerto Limón was the commercial hub of
the area until Puerto Guzmán was founded in 1975 and took over that role.

In the eastern and lower portion of the Baja Bota, on the other hand,
colonizers arrived mostly in the late 1960s, 1970s, and 1980s, and primarily
from the department of Caquetá by way of the Caquetá and Fragua Rivers.
Among the veredas founded by migrants from Caquetá were El Remanso
(1973), Villa Lozada (1977), and El Triunfo (1978). More recent settlements
include Fragua Viejo (1980), Bajo Congor (1982), and Yapurá (1988). Curillo,
the region's commercial hub in Caquetá, was founded in 1965 (see map 5).
Roberto Ramírez remarks on the colonization of the lower Baja Bota, "An
estimated 60 percent of the colonos living in the basin of the Fragua Grande
River (the Baja Bota's eastern border) in 1977 had previously been colonos in
other parts of Caquetá. Since 1982 there has been a general tendency toward

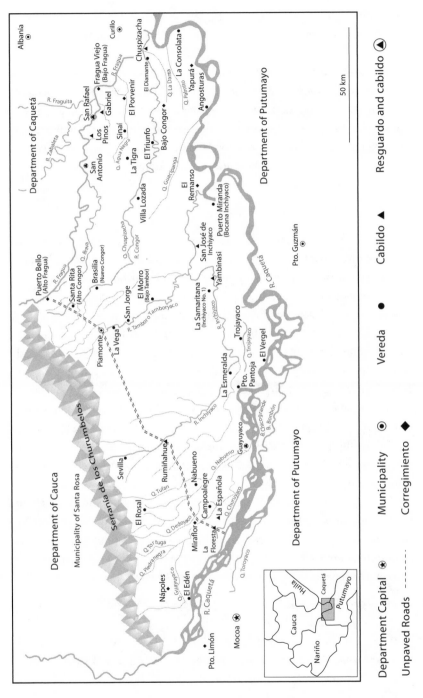

Department of Caquetá

Albania
⊙

Curillo

Department of Caquetá

R. Fraguita

Fragua Viejo
(Bajo Fragua)
Chuspizacha

San Rafael
Gabriel
El Porvenir
El Diamante
La Consolata

R. Zabaleta

Los
Pinos
Sinaí
Yapurá
Angosturas

San
Antonio
Q. Agua Negra
La Tigra
El Triunfo
Bajo Congor

Villa Lozada
El
Remanso

Q. Guaetpanga

Puerto Bello
(Alto Fragua)
Puerto Miranda
(Bocana Inchiyaco)

Department of Putumayo

R. Fragua
Q. Brava
Santa Rita
(Alto Congor)
Q. Chuspizacha

Brasilia
(Nuevo Congor)
R. Congor
San José de
Inchiyaco

Pto. Guzmán
⊙

El Morro
(Bajo Tambor)
Yambinasi

Piamonte
San Jorge
R. Caquetá

La Vega
R. Tambor o Tamboryaco
La Samaritana
(Inchiyaco No. 1)

Serranía de los Churumbelos

Trojayaco
Q. Trojayaco

Sevilla
La Esmeralda
El Vergel

Department of Cauca

Rumiñahue
Pto.
Pantoja

Municipality of Santa Rosa

El Rosal
Nabueno
Q. Nabueno
Guayuyaco

Q. Tufan
R. Inchiyaco
B. Chicogrande

Campoalegre
Q. Dedoyaco
La Española
B. Bombón

Miraflor
La
Floresta
Q. Churuyaco

Q. Tortuga

Nápoles
Q. Piedranegra
Department of Putumayo

Q. Toroyaco

El Edén
Q. Guayuyaco

R. Caquetá

Mocoa
⊛

Pto. Limón

50 km

Department Capital ⊛   Municipality ⊙   Vereda ●   Cabildo ▲   Resguardo and cabildo ◭

Unpaved Roads -------   Corregimiento ◆

[inset map: Cauca, Huila, Nariño, Caquetá, Putumayo]

Map 5. Municipality of Piamonte (Cauca).

intra-regional migration in Caquetá, largely connected to the growing of coca. This has stimulated the most recent colonization of the Baja Bota of Cauca" (1971, 82).

Coca appeared in the Baja Bota during the first half of the coca boom, 1978–82. By the beginning of the second half of the coca boom, 1984–87, it was planted throughout the zone on isolated and uncultivated lands. In the northern Baja Bota it was generally grown on small plots alongside traditional crops, but a coca monoculture had begun to emerge in places like the Lower Congor Valley of the southern Baja Bota.

Colonization and the State in Western Amazonia

It should be reiterated that coca has been cultivated in the Western Amazonian region for over thirty years. Coca was seen by small growers simply as a means of survival, a way to improve their standard of living, a means by which colonos had been able to gain access to basic services which the state has not provided. As a general rule, the state has limited its involvement in the Amazon to establishing basic services for the colonos in or near town centers. The rest of the area lacks adequate basic services such as roads, water, electricity, health care, and education. State development programs have mainly benefited large-scale landowners, who act as agents for the settlement or expulsion of colonos. Many colonos are forced to sell or abandon their plots as a result of bank debts. Colonos experience the loss of their land as an injustice that goes unpunished and as institutionalized violence (Molano 1988). This resentment helps legitimize guerrilla actions that defend colono interests.

Small growers reported that coca provided them with sustenance and work. They stressed the social causes of its cultivation and "relativized" its illegality. In the eyes of the campesinos, growing coca to maintain a family did not make one a criminal. A leader used a metaphor to explain this conceptual relativization of the legality of coca:

> Most people are involved with coca because they don't see any other solution to the social problem of unemployment. Some people are involved with coca even though they don't really want to be, *in the same way that there are people who get involved in the traditional parties without enthusiasm because if they don't join the party they won't get a position, they won't get credit. They [the political parties] are illegal too, be-*

cause they're trading on the people's consciousness, which is a commodity to them. Contraband is illegal material but at the core the problem is unemployment, that's the social problem.[9]

Coca, in the campesino vision, was a crop like other crops, a source of income, comparable to political clientelism, which could also assure one of a job or access to contraband. In the Putumayan context, where employment opportunities were minimal, coca growing was considered legitimate as long as the government was providing no income-producing alternative.

People living in the Amazon were invisible to the state and the colonos had gradually internalized this invisibility. The result was a reconfiguration of the historical construction of the empty territory, the territorio baldio or terra nullius:

> The only thing we need here is government help. I say to mister government man that this is Colombia! We need to be recognized. We need loans, but not from the Caja Agraria [Agrarian Bank], which only lends you money if you have 20 head of cattle. . . . *We ask mister government man to look over here and see that people want to work* and he has to take us into account. This is Colombia too. It's very hard to work with only your bare hands. (Interview of colono Don Juan in Silva 1991a, 42; emphasis added)

Another campesino addressed this concern at a May 1997 forum:

> We can see that the national government has abandoned some regions totally. They think that there are no people here. For example, here in the area of Mandur [in the municipality of Puerto Guzmán] just a few days ago they said there were no people here. We were presenting a proposal for a community project and they said, "What for? Where's that region?" They didn't know where Mandur was and they didn't know that there were people living there because they don't know the area. They don't know anything about our problems. We've been completely abandoned by the national government and that's why we're in this conflict that we're in.[10]

This discourse of state absence in the region has been internalized as a feeling of abandonment that permeates all social strata, extending even to local state representatives such as the mayors: Puerto Asís Mayor Nestor Iglesias declared on a national news program that "We can't go on being treated as fourth- or fifth-class citizens, as if we weren't Colombians," adding "We feel abandoned, seeing that the indifference of the national government places us in the middle of a war that is not our own."[11] After a century of colonization, it has become a shared metanarrative: the state fails to fulfill its *paternal* responsibilities to provide for the people's welfare. This results in poverty and a consequent dependence on illegal crops. It denies them citizenship and thus excludes them from the important inner workings of the central government that determine the region's future. Even worse, it leaves them alone to confront the armed conflict which its absence has promoted.

For their part, national and regional government representatives assert that working with coca promotes a "narco mentality" characterized by individualism and a desire for easy money, that it corrupts social values and undermines the social fabric. This is a stereotyped view of the people in coca-producing regions as violent, rootless fortune seekers who act outside the law in accordance either with their own perverse set of rules, or with those enforced by the non-state armed actors present in the region. This stereotype fails to take into account the long history of colonization in Amazonia and the presence of population sectors that predate the arrival of coca. Thus, in this context it is apparent, as Nugent (1994, 336) has pointed out, that only by conceiving the state and the community as interdependent can it be understood how each of them helps to "create, construct and enable (or not enable) the other according to specific material-political interests and cultural conceptions that are contingent in time and through space." This interdependency is central to understanding the emergence of the cocalero social movement.

The Construction of Colono, Campesino, and Cocalero Identities

Campesinos have been settling in Putumayo for three generations. One generation arrived with children born elsewhere who grew up there and formed a second generation. The third generation are the grandchildren of the original migrants. As Putumayan-born residents, many of this third generation have closely identified with the department and led efforts to improve it. They include both campesinos and others who have left the area to study and then returned.

The distinct waves of immigration in the area's history have settled into layers of society that relate to the region in different ways, both with respect to coca growing and to drug, guerrilla, military, and paramilitary violence. The landowning colonos that formed the earlier migratory waves to Putumayo are known to invest in housing improvements and diversified agriculture. They grow other crops along with their coca, raise cattle and hogs, or engage in other productive activities such as fish farming and handicrafts. These colonos use only family labor to harvest and process their coca, never employing outside help. Other farmers, generally more recent arrivals drawn by the coca, focus exclusively on plots of coca larger than three hectares in size and contract outside labor for the harvest. A government development official coordinating voluntary coca eradication and substitution commented, "We need to distinguish the colono population that has put down roots. Because of their geographic and social situation, they have some potential to recoup their farming operations with legal crops, but they tend to work individually. The younger population tends to resist involvement in social or productive projects. One of their principal characteristics is that they insist on individual problem-solving" (Social Solidarity Network–IICA, 1998, 10).

This official highlighted the need to distinguish between recently arrived colonos and those whose families have lived in the region for several generations, and between individual and community production. Members of the third generation tend to be more aware of the uniqueness of the Amazon than the older colonos, and they have proposed coca substitution projects tailored to the natural environment and well-suited to cooperative enterprise. A local professional and member of this third generation stated, "If we want to participate in the national economy, we have to do it right. A small campesino can't do it. The only way it can be done is to join together through cooperative organization. As a cooperative you can build an agro-industry."[12]

What is clear is that they are colonos or campesinos who grow small plots of coca. Once the state began to fumigate their coca crops and they started protesting the fumigation, they began to identify as cocaleros. It can be argued that the spread of the cocalero identity as a collective marker was a response to indiscriminately repressive antidrug policies. This represented not only their acceptance of being coca growers but also their assumption of the identity ascribed to them by the government. However, they accepted this identity for the purpose of contesting it and manifesting their disagreement with the policies through which the state had criminalized them.

Moreover, it is worth pointing out that the slight difference in meaning between *campesino colonos* and *campesino cocaleros* in and of itself illustrates the ambiguous identity of the social group.

There are also geographical variations of identity: in areas such as Valle del Guamués, colonos are primarily from Nariño and have settled permanently. They strongly identify as residents of the Amazon, as campesinos without regard to origin. In the Baja Bota and in Puerto Guzmán, colonization has been secondary and colonos are for the most part originally from Caquetá. Their identity as migrants is stronger and they maintain their status as colonos, not in the sense of being rootless, but rather as an important marker of identity. Due to its location between Caquetá and Putumayo, the Baja Bota can be seen as a stereotype of the marginal periphery of Colombia, and of the Amazon in particular. In the late 1990s, about half of its population had commercial ties to Mocoa, Villagarzón, and Puerto Guzmán in Putumayo, while the other half did business in Curillo, La Novia, and Zabaleta in Caquetá. People living in the Baja Bota often traveled to Putumayo and Caquetá, but returned home after days, weeks, or even years of being away. Residents of the Baja Bota often spoke to me of the time that they had spent outside the area, but always within the framework of an intended return. The Baja Bota was a base from which they had visited other places, but to which they belonged and would eventually return.

The people of the Baja Bota welcomed new colonos who arrived in search of opportunity. Being an outsider did not present problems, and newcomers quickly become integrated into local routines. Observing that some leaders of the Community Action Committees had only been in the region for two years, I asked them about their acceptance as community members. The answer was always the same: all were welcome, and if a newcomer was eager to work for the betterment of conditions in the community, he or she could immediately begin work with the Community Action Committee. Saying that one was "just passing through" became an identifying marker in the zone, as one community leader made clear at a meeting in Yapurá:

> Most people around here say "Ah! I'm from Valle, I'm from Caquetá, I'm from Tolima, I can't really say why I'm here, and I won't be here too long." Since we're just passing through, we don't take possession of the land that feeds us. We tell people that we're going to be here for just one or two years. Baloney! We're going to get old and die here, but we're supposedly just passing through. I propose that we conduct

a consciousness raising campaign and that we take possession of the land. This land is ours by virtue of the fact that we're living on it and it's our subsistence. That makes it ours. Keep in mind that this is the inheritance of our children. This land is the inheritance that we are going to leave to our children.[13]

Residents of the Baja Bota made it clear that they were settlers and constructed an identity as a people from elsewhere. Having settled in the area, however, they implicitly appropriated it. Because this population had arrived as part of secondary colonizations, settlement in the Baja Bota was characterized by multiple discontinuities and ruptures. Many people did not identify themselves as natives of any place in particular. As colonos, they made a life for themselves wherever they ended up, all the while maintaining their connections to one or more places where they had previously lived.

The inhabitants of the Baja Bota had sought to incorporate their region into either Caquetá or Putumayo beginning in 1955. In 1980 they began to demand a municipal government for this area of lower Cauca and in 1987 they formed a Pro-municipality Committee. This was another strategy in their long struggle for an identity as residents of the Baja Bota. The importance of this demand was demonstrated when it became central to the 1996 cocalero movement. One outcome of the movement for the over eight thousand inhabitants (more than one thousand of whom were Quechua speakers of the Inga indigenous group) of the Baja Bota was that the town of Piamonte was founded that year. At last the government of Cauca recognized their active citizenship in the department; with municipal status, they also gained access to economic transfers from the capital in Popayán. This was a necessary and important step for their inclusion and participation as citizens of Colombia. As Pile (1997, 30) puts it in his discussion of marginalized and excluded territories, a redefinition of the territory was accomplished as a result of popular struggle: "In order to transform its meanings, undermine territory as a natural source of power, and enable territory to become a space of citizenship, democracy, and freedom—within limits."

The Politics of Inclusion and Exclusion: Arrival and Consolidation of FARC in the Amazon Region

The presence of FARC in the Amazon region can be traced back to La Violencia. During the 1940s the persecuted Liberal families began to form armed self-defense groups called *cuadrillas*. In 1949, in Tolima, the Communist Party also organized armed campesino self-defense groups to resist Conservative persecution.[14] These became mobile guerrilla units known as marching columns (*columnas de marcha*). The columnas de marcha began traveling for months at a time, fleeing their persecutors and also organizing themselves into larger bodies. In 1950, the Liberal- and Communist-armed self-defense groups joined forces under a unified high command in southern Tolima, but political and ideological conflicts soon led to a rupture. By the end of 1951, an open war between Liberals and Communists was well under way. In August 1952 the Communist Party called the First National Guerrilla Conference to unify various armed groups into one campesino self-defense guerrilla army (J. González 1992).

The mobile columnas de marcha reappeared as a result of repression under military dictator General Rojas Pinilla (1953–58).[15] Once the military government was deposed, the columnas de marcha again reverted into campesino self-defense groups, mostly in six rural areas in Colombia's geographical center: Marquetalia (Department of Tolima), Riochiquito (Department of Huila), Pato (Department of Caquetá), Alto Sumapaz-Duda (Departments of Cundinamarca and Meta), and Ariari and Guayabero (Department of Meta) (see map 6). They settled lands through a process that W. Ramírez (1981, 204) has called "armed colonization." Ramírez points out that FARC, while a revolutionary armed group linked to the Communist Party, is seen more importantly as a strategic tool for campesino colonization through the expropriation of land in the hands of big capital.[16] The "armed settlers" were campesinos excluded by the traditional party-based elites, expelled from their lands and persecuted by the military because of their Communist affiliation. They were forced to arm themselves in order to defend their lives and their families. In 1958, when the National Front (a negotiated power-split between Liberals and Conservatives) was established, the commanders of the campesino self-defense groups sent a letter to President Alberto Lleras (1958–62), requesting peace and amnesty in accordance with the National Front's stated policy of re-integrating armed groups into civil society, hoping to re-establish their agrarian communities.[17] "Thus the *columnas de marcha* gave way to self-defense zones based on a broad and well structured agrarian movement that would exercise political and military leadership, administer justice, distribute land, and maintain internal control of the settlements" (J. González 1992, 63).

Between 1958 and 1962, new settlers organized themselves into an

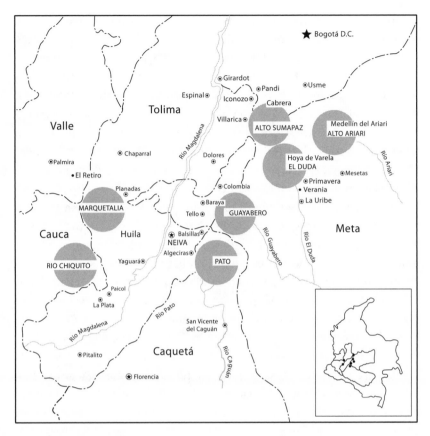

Independent Republics   🔵

National Capital   ★

Department Capital   ⊛

Municipality   ⊙

Vereda   ●

International Boundary   ──────

Department Boundary   ─·─·─·─

Map 6. The "Independent Republics," 1955–1965. (Reproduced by permission from Jairo González, *Espacios de Exclusión: El Estigma de las Repúblicas Independientes 1955–1965* [Bogotá: CINEP], 167)

agrarian union to distribute individual plots of land, hoping to live and work in peace. However, their plan was destined to fail. Conservative parliamentarian Alvaro Gómez accused the settlements of being "independent republics." The government began to see them as "a Communist threat." The success of the Cuban revolution in 1959 prompted the Colombian Communist Party to declare a policy that combined "all forms of struggle," meaning that both legal activities such as electoral politics and illegal activities such as guerrilla activities were legitimate ways to challenge the government (J. Gonzalez 1992, Pizarro Leongómez 1992). Based on this doctrine, the independent rural communities associated with campesino self-defense organizations gradually but openly took on the characteristics of a guerrilla rear guard in the struggle against the oligarchy embodied in the National Front. The government rehabilitation programs initially intended to integrate armed campesino groups into society began to focus instead on political and military control. Repression and violence against the campesinos returned, new armed groups appeared and engaged in banditry, and the expulsion of settlers by large landowners became commonplace.

A dirty war became the daily reality in these regions. Although the National Front had opened a democratic space for the two traditional parties, it precluded alternative political expression, relied on a state of siege to maintain public order (Pizarro Leongómez 1992, 159) and developed ever more sophisticated mechanisms of repression and terror (Chernick and Jimenez 1990, 12).

Communist leaders wanted their party to be able to participate in government, but the existing government neither recognized nor responded to their repeated appeals. Rather, influenced by the prevailing Cold War discourse, it waged a war against the "independent republics" between 1962 and 1965. In 1964 the government launched Operation Marquetalia, a military campaign named after the Communist stronghold that was its target.[18] When the region was seized by the military, the Communists called the Southern Front's First Guerrilla Conference (distinct from the First National Guerrilla Conference in 1952) and announced the establishment of FARC. Military attacks against the "independent republics" continued in 1965 and included an advance on Rio Chiquito and Pato (see map 6), accelerating the transformation of the self-defense forces into guerrilla units. At a subsequent Second Guerrilla Conference in May 1966, Manuel Marulanda assumed command of FARC and further institutionalized its existence as a guerrilla army. Self-defense groups once again became mobile guerrilla units whose goal was to consolidate a revolutionary army (J. González 1992, 67). They began to enter every region of the country. A regional social movement with political goals had transformed itself into a national armed revolutionary movement.

It is important to bear in mind that FARC combatants were campesinos. They presented themselves as such and were perceived as such by the rural population in the areas of their revolutionary activity. FARC earned credibility with the rural population as a result of their presence in daily campesino life. William Ramírez argues, "the personality of this campesino movement cannot be reduced to the ideology or the political interests of the Communist Party, as some attempt to do when they provocatively characterize it as nothing more than the armed wing of that organization. . . . The guerrilla project, as elaborated in the areas under FARC's influence, is more a new form of armed colonization than a political demand to substitute itself for the state and even less for the destruction of capitalism" (1981, 205).

This analysis helps us to understand how armed campesino groups exercised authority in the marginal areas to which they fled. Although this view of FARC as armed colonizers has been criticized (Fajardo 1998), and although FARC developed other interests over time, it is important to note that since its beginnings, FARC's stated aim was to improve the lives of campesinos and to struggle for their inclusion in the life of the nation. Commander Marulanda made this point in a commemoration of FARC's first thirty years:

> We wanted to avoid this confrontation for the good of all Colombians, but we weren't strong enough to do so. Today the military high command, the congress, and President Guillermo León Valencia are completely responsible for what is happening, because they have been mesmerized by their successes in the struggle against "banditry." *To confuse ex-combatants with bandits was to betray a total lack of responsibility and analysis of how we were living in the region when we combatants and the inhabitants of all the regions were working as one so the government would facilitate all kinds of credits and help to improve the conditions of life for the whole community.* With the money invested in the war against forty-eight men in Marquetalia the government could have improved the conditions of life for the people of the region and rebuilt the towns. (Marulanda 1994; emphasis added)

Central government policies that exclude these marginal areas effectively cede them to FARC. The state has responded to socio-economic and political problems in guerrilla-controlled areas with repression, establishing structures that promote state violence over the long term.

FARC history as written by its members sees Operation Marquetalia as a diagnostic event that embodied the monopolistic political behavior of the Liberal and Conservative elites:

> We in Marquetalia were dedicated to creating our own wealth for the good of our families and to supply the people in nearby towns like Gaitania, Planadas, and Neiva. . . . But the policy developed by the National Front . . . labels all of us living in the region as bandits. When we were informed by various very credible sources of the imminent military operation in the region, we addressed ourselves to the whole Colombian people, through some members of congress, to the national government, to the governors, to the Church, to the unions, to the civic movements, to French intellectuals, to the International Red Cross, to all democratic and progressive people. We knocked on every door in an attempt to be heard and thus avoid the war that was to nobody's benefit, especially when we had barely emerged from a long struggle between parties that had caused many deaths and a lot of damage to the national economy. The only entity that heeded our call and tried to visit us, to confirm that we were workers, was the Church, and they were impeded from doing so by the high command. So our efforts to avoid war were in vain. Campesinos from many regions also mobilized, asking for some solution other than confrontation. Despite everything, the government was determined to officially declare war. (Marulanda 1994)

Marulanda reiterated the notion that the inhabitants of Marquetalia wanted to work and live in peace but that their representation as bandits legitimized violence against them, making these goals impossible to achieve. They resented the government's refusal to hear or even see them. The campesinos looked to the state for the satisfaction of their material needs and for inclusion in the national order, but the state was deaf to their pleas. Instead the traditional elites and military promoted violence against them, and a state of generalized violence has existed ever since. These long-standing historical structures must inform any explanation of contemporary political violence in the Amazon region.

The Arrival of Drug Traffickers and Appearance of Paramilitaries in Putumayo

Coca farming first came to Putumayo in 1978. The first variety, *coca cau-cana*, was grown near the Caquetá, San Miguel, Guamués, and Putumayo Rivers, and production boomed for the next five years. Well-protected coca plots were usually located deep in the forest where no state colonization programs were under way. These areas were part of an Amazonian forest reserve off-limits to farming or subdivision. Colonos on these lands, therefore, had no legal titles and consequently no access to bank credit for plantain, corn, rice, and other crops they were growing (R. Ramírez 1998, 98). Drug traffickers provided them with coca seeds and the chemicals needed to process coca leaf into paste. Then the traffickers bought the paste, often bartering goods such as food and clothing: "The people who bought the coca arrived with food and clothing, which they would trade us for coca. They often brought good quality food at good prices" (interview of colono Don Juan in Silva 1991a, 41).

Coca production decreased sharply in the 1980s due to government suppression of drug trafficking. In April 1984, drug traffickers responded to a series of criminal prosecutions by assassinating Justice Minister Rodrigo Lara Bonilla, and prices stabilized (Salgado 1995, 41). As Uprimny (1994, 83) has pointed out, when government repression increases, either some commercial networks are interrupted or the control of certain coca production areas is contested. Nevertheless, the supply is only temporarily suppressed. Market forces stimulate production in other areas and marketing through other networks, and the effects of the repression on the market are rapidly neutralized.

As a result of actions taken by the Anti-narcotics Police in 1987 against the Medellín Cartel in Puerto Triunfo and Doradal in the mid-Magdalena River Valley (Magdalena Medio), cartel boss Gonzalo Rodríguez Gacha chose Putumayo as a location for his highly profitable business of processing and stockpiling cocaine, a new home base for his personal protection services, and a training site for paid assassins (*sicarios*) (Andean Commission of Jurists 1993, 29). Moreover, he developed an extensive area of coca cultivation in El Azul on the Ecuadorian border. He built laboratories with total output of one ton of cocaine per week and two landing strips to receive coca paste shipments from Peru. Local labor and immigrants from all over the country were enlisted in the operation at La Hormiga, La Dorada, and San Miguel (R. Ramírez 1998, 99). A colono who worked in El Azul reports:

Yes, I worked on two farms during the coca boom. On one they paid
us with threats and on the other with *bazuco* [cocaine byproduct similar to crack]. It was Slavery. . . . When this was going on about twenty
or thirty men and women were arriving in San Miguel every day. They
came from all over, *Paisas* [from Antioquia and northern Caldas],
Blacks, Indians, but mostly they were from Nariño. There were always
some strangers there offering work, so you got there and asked them,
"Do you have work?" "Yes, we need eighty workers." "OK, so let's go."
And they loaded them into ten, fifteen, or twenty canoes. From that
moment on nobody could back out. You had to go like I went myself
to the farm in El Azul.

The illegality of coca and the reality of the Amazon as a region beyond
the reach of the state deprived the workers of any protection once they em-
barked on the journey to a plantation. Drug traffickers imposed their own
law and forced people to work. Workers who wanted to be paid off and leave
the plantation risked being killed:

If someone said, "I'm leaving, I need my pay," "Come here," he would
reply. "Everyone who wants their pay raise your hand," and they took
them to the river, made them stand in a line along the river, took out
a machine gun and killed them. They fell right into the water. The San
Miguel River was the cemetery there. They all died: big and small children, women, and men. . . . That's why I ran away from there. I ran
away in the middle of the night with five compañeros. We were in our
underwear; we went as far as a place called Teteyé. . . . We got work
there. (Testimony of a colono in Silva 1991b, 39)

On the next farm where this same colono worked, laborers were paid exclusively with bazuco: "We never got a penny there; we were paid in drugs. If
anyone asked for money they killed them right there and if anyone ran away
they sent three gunmen to hunt them down and kill them. The guy had
twelve hectares and we were his slaves. He got us addicted so we would keep
asking for more" (testimony of a colono in Silva 1991b, 40).

Creating drug dependency among the workforce was a sure way to increase profits and a practice that underscored the popular perception of
Amazon residents as virtually disposable people who could be abused with
impunity.

At first, the drug traffickers collaborated with FARC. Due to FARC's military power, traffickers had to ask for permission to conduct their activities. FARC established the following conditions, which were initially accepted: first, the guerrillas had a monopoly on firearms. Second, coca growers had to pay taxes like any other farmer. Third, the payment of harvest workers with bazuco was prohibited (Molano 1988, 35). FARC won popular support with their prohibition of payment with bazuco. The fact that the traffickers accepted these conditions reflected FARC's very real local authority and extensive territorial dominance.

By 1995 FARC was organized into sixty-two fronts in seven territorial blocks (Eastern, Southern, Magdalena Medio, Northwestern, Central, Northern, and Western). The main front in Putumayo was the Thirty-second Front, which operated near the Caquetá River, Puerto Guzmán, Santa Lucía, Puerto Limón, the upper Putumayo River, the Vides River, La Hormiga, La Dorada, and El Tigre (Valle del Guamués). The Forty-eighth and Thirteenth Fronts were also present in the Putumayo department. The Forty-eighth Front operated in the area of the Guamués and Teteyé Rivers, La Hormiga, La Dorada, Orito, Churuaco, San Miguel, and El Placer. The Thirteenth Front operated in Mocoa, Villagarzón, the Baja Bota of Cauca (the municipalities of Piamonte and Santa Rosa) and part of the department of Caquetá. Together, the fronts in Putumayo and those in the departments of Huila, Caquetá, Guaviare, Meta, and Nariño constituted the Southern Guerrilla Block, one of FARC's strongest military wings due to its substantial revenues from taxing the coca industry (Echandía 1998, 37; see map 7).

After one year of the Medellín cartel's activity under Rodríguez Gacha, El Azul had been turned into a paramilitary base, and a paramilitary group under his leadership called Los Combos "exercised jurisdiction over a large part of the territory, conducting rural patrols and wielding the economic and political power that the drug traffickers had acquired in the municipal seats" (Andean Commission of Jurists 1993, 29). Until 1987, two FARC representatives managed the arrival and departure of airplanes in El Azul and provided traffickers with protection in return for a monthly tax payment (Andean Commission of Jurists 1993, 69). However, this Amazon-wide agreement between FARC and drug traffickers did not last (Molano 1988, 36). At the end of 1987, traffickers killed their FARC "protectors" and war was declared. In an alliance with another guerrilla group in the area, the Popular Liberation Army (Ejército Popular de la Liberación, EPL),[19] FARC attacked the paramilitary base at El Azul in 1988. Los Combos successfully repelled the combined guerrilla attack.

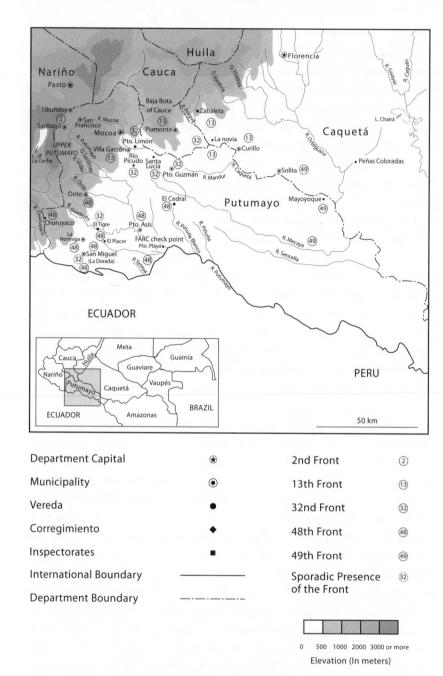

Department Capital	⊛	2nd Front ②
Municipality	◉	13th Front ⑬
Vereda	●	32nd Front ㉜
Corregimiento	◆	48th Front ㊽
Inspectorates	■	49th Front ㊾
International Boundary	———————	Sporadic Presence ⟨32⟩
Department Boundary	—·—·—·—·——	of the Front

0   500 1000 2000 3000 or more
Elevation (In meters)

Map 7. Location of FARC fronts, Putumayo and Baja Bota of Cauca, 1999.

Later Los Combos became known as Los Masetos, a name derived from the narco-backed paramilitary organization MAS (Muerte a Secuestradores, or Death to Kidnappers) operating in the Magdalena Medio region. In 1981, the M-19, a largely urban intellectual guerrilla group kidnapped Marta Nieves Ochoa, a sister of leading drug traffickers in Medellín.[20] In response, Pablo Escobar of the Medellín cartel brought together two hundred traffickers from all over the country to form MAS. Ostensibly, MAS would free kidnapping victims and kill those guerrillas who were directly or indirectly responsible for the scourge of kidnapping (Salazar 2001, 82). MAS also openly and broadly targeted putative guerrilla collaborators.

During the same period, the military in certain regions was promoting and supervising civilian self-defense groups (*autodefensas*) which sought to maintain those areas free of guerrillas and their illicit taxation or protection payments. They were largely financed by drug traffickers who had a vested interest in eliminating the need for these payments. For example, in 1982 army Captain Oscar de Jesús Echandía Sánchez called upon landowners, political leaders, and representatives of Texaco and other businessmen in Puerto Boyacá, a city in Magdalena Medio, to form and finance a self-defense group to fight FARC (Kirk 2003, 108–9). These military and civilian-backed autodefensas were the origins of modern paramilitarism in Colombia.

By the late 1980s paramilitary groups all around the country were engaged in an extermination campaign against the political opposition, particularly against the Patriotic Union (Unión Patriótica, UP, the civilian political party allied with FARC).[21] In Putumayo the paramilitaries also turned on civilians they accused of being FARC collaborators. Los Masetos began to target alleged Communists around El Azul, in nearby Puerto Asís, Valle del Guamués, and Orito. They killed the local leadership of the UP, and the leadership of the Popular Front (Frente Popular, FP, the civilian political party of the EPL), as well as activists in the Civic Movement of Putumayo.[22] These three political groups that were targeted represented the political opposition to incumbent local officials, whom they accused of embezzlement, administrative incompetence, and complicity with paramilitaries. This provoked army and police commanders as well as local civilian authorities to call them "guerrilla supporters," encouraging sicarios affiliated with the paramilitaries to kill them (Andean Commission of Jurists 1993, 70). People in these towns remember their terror at seeing such killers dressed in civilian clothes and riding motorcycles:

The coca boom began in 1978. There were motorcycles all over the place and they didn't respect the elderly. The coca boom lasted until 1982. Until 1983 there wasn't any violence. I treated a lot of people for injuries caused by motorcycle accidents. The other boom was between 1984 and 1988. In 1987 Los Masetos arrived, and they were here until they were driven out in 1991. They were the "black hand" that carried out social cleansing. They killed addicts and alcoholics, people who didn't pay their debts, and guerrillas, or actually the guerrilla "militia," the townspeople who were reporting things to the guerrillas. They killed anyone who went around in a poncho and rubber boots. You couldn't go around like that anymore. They killed a lot of teenagers between 14 and 16 years old back then and just a few adults. We knew how to recognize them.[23]

FARC's Thirteenth, Twenty-sixth, and Thirty-second Fronts attacked for the second time and finally seized El Azul in 1990, killing sixty-seven paramilitaries. So many people were killed that "people living on the banks of the San Miguel River close to what happened say that a large number of bodies floated downstream" (Andean Commission of Jurists 1993, 70). Researchers from the Andean Commission of Jurists found explicit testimony that linked the Masetos to the National Police. A policeman who testified stated that both the police and the Masetos were considered "the law" (Andean Commission of Jurists 1993, 71). After the 1990 FARC attack in January 1991 popular pressure temporarily drove the Masetos out. They left Valle del Guamués in January 1991, Orito in February, and Puerto Asís in March. Townspeople denounced members of the security forces who were collaborating with paramilitary groups and involved in human rights violations (Andean Commission of Jurists 1993, 32).[24] This action is recalled by inhabitants of Puerto Asís as an exceptionally heroic act:

The surviving Masetos took refuge right in town but because of the intolerable things they did they were driven out by the civilian population, a heroic act without any precedent in the country. The last straw was the death of a really beloved man, a butcher. His *compañera* [common-law spouse] bravely denounced the crime publicly and with the help of the parish priests the people gathered in the Church of San Francisco of Assisi. It was Holy Week and the church was packed. From there they sent word to the military and police authorities. Then the victims of the dirty war publicly denounced the indiscriminate killings perpetrated by the Masetos with the acquiescence and support of the police, very fearfully at first, but then with confidence inspired by their unity. Armed with shotguns and machetes, the people gave the police twenty-four hours to remove the Masetos from town or face open and all-out civil war. The police escorted the paramilitaries to the airport within a few hours. (CORPOS 1991, 62)

This event came to symbolize popular empowerment in Puerto Asís. Edilberto Imbachí, an indigenous leader in Putumayo, explained that the paramilitaries were expelled due to their violation of certain accepted norms of daily life:

The most difficult time in Puerto Asís and in all of Putumayo was between '89 and '91. In '91 there was another thing. The paramilitaries were completely confident around here. They killed a drug addict, but this was a well-known drug addict from town. He helped people with their luggage in the terminal and begged a couple of coins. He was a popular figure in town. In this case people protested. They said no more, and the people acted. Then the paramilitaries made another mistake. The Church spoke out about this killing because the Church was playing an important role in trying to control social problems. Anyway, the paramilitaries thought it would be easy to shut the priest up by killing his nephew. Even though the victims weren't from the town, still Puerto Asís had become one of the most violent towns in the country and people were fed up with that reputation so when they killed the nephew of the priest the people rose up. They said "no more; that's enough." They began to identify the houses where the paramilitaries lived and who was funding them. Some 30,000 people rose up and with one mind they burned the houses of the paramilitaries. They identified the mayor as a financial backer of the paramilitaries and burned his house. The mayor wasn't there, but his wife was there and died.[25]

The same indigenous leader explained the consequences of the population's identification of the paramilitaries with the police:

FARC were attacking the paramilitary camps at the same time. The paramilitaries wanted to blend into the population in town but when they arrived they found the guerrillas waiting for them. So the police and the military protected twenty one paramilitaries. They personally escorted them to the airport and put them on a plane. What an outrage! *That's exactly when we were able to prove the way the police and the military were acting in coordination with the paramilitaries. And in '91, make no mistake about it, it was the people who drove the paramilitaries out of Putumayo; they were like police by another name. The police themselves retreated to their barracks because the situation was dicey.* But yes, they did destroy the Department of Administrative Security [Departamento Administrativo de Seguridad, DAS] barracks; it was completely destroyed. And from '91 on, it was another story after that uprising there in the region.[26]

FARC had acted in accordance with the will of the population, who wanted the paramilitaries expelled from the territory.

Since the first colonization of the Colombian Amazon, large landowners and merchants had dealt with the colonos arbitrarily. The drug traffickers of the 1980s and 1990s simply continued this tradition. The debt-for-work system was ubiquitous and highly profitable for the drug traffickers.[27] Staples such as sugar, coffee, and salt were advanced to the colonos, and merchants would be paid after the harvest in the form of coca. The supplies provided in advance were overpriced, but only the lowest possible value was put on the coca. Guerrilla groups were accepted by the colonos due to their support for longstanding but unfulfilled demands on the state for protection, land, credit, access to markets, and social services. FARC displayed impressive local power and authority, maintaining order in Putumayo and other parts of the Amazon by enacting laws and norms backed up by strict sanctions. As a colono states,

> *After the Masetos, FARC arrived and imposed order. They got it right, I mean everything.* No more payment in bazuco, no more gun thugs, no more Masetos stealing chickens. Now you can go to your fields or wherever and nobody will steal anything. They've been struggling with this for a whole year. Everyone here has adjusted to this new situation and we've been very happy, very content. The guerrillas are real men. (Testimony of a colono collected in Silva 1991b, 40; emphasis added)

Convivirs and Colombian Paramilitarism in the 1990s

Academics, NGOs, and popular leaders have considered Colombian auto-defensas to be mechanisms of state terrorism, owing to their promotion by the state and by military officers (Medina, Téllez, and Téllez 1994). In 1995, during the presidency of Ernesto Samper, the state in effect lent its support to paramilitary organizations when it legalized self-defense groups known as *Convivirs*, defined in Decree 356 of 1994 as special surveillance and private security services that function in high risk areas to restore tranquility and to ally themselves with military and police agencies." The decree also stated that through Convivir organizations, "Information networks shall be established in order to identify events that could disturb the peace" (Equipo de Alternativa 1997, 9). The legalization of these organizations created a conduit for the legal purchase of weapons which would then be channeled into other hands. After the inception of Convivirs, paramilitarism intensified and spread throughout the country. In a book written with journalist Glenda Martínez, paramilitary leader Salvatore Mancuso gave a detailed history of how the existence of legal Convivir groups helped him to consolidate his own organization (Corporación Nuevo Arco Iris 2007, 13). Campesino communities that suffered displacement or massacres repeatedly attributed these abuses to paramilitary forces and denounced the army's decision to ignore said activities.[28]

The news media have pointed to the relationship between paramilitary-guerrilla confrontations and the struggle for control over coca production and trafficking.[29] Guerrillas regulated coca production and distribution through the collection of taxes in the affected zones, so these confrontations were both economic and geo-political. Coca money bought continued military strength and thus political control of these territories. The civilian population was not only caught in the resulting crossfire, but was also scapegoated. The guerrillas, paramilitaries, and armed forces all coerced the civilian population into taking sides. Army Major Villamarín referred to FARC: "They intimidate campesinos, expropriate their lands, and force them to work in the 'white gold' business [the illegal cocaine trade] while they involve them in terrorist actions, incorporating them into 'Bolivarian Militias' and the clandestine Communist Party" (Villamarín 1996, 15). This description characterizes campesino coca growers as controlled and terrorized by FARC but at the same time willing to engage in its terrorist activities, and it even implies they were politically motivated to join the Communist Party. It identifies civilians as participants in FARC's auxiliary organizations, which makes them legitimate targets in the so-called drug war. The line between fighting drug traffickers and fighting rebels began to blur.

As the debate over government-sponsored Convivirs developed, newspaper columnist Amilkar Serrano expressed the opinion that "without [civilian] collaboration, the military becomes weak."[30] Serrano listed all the different ways in which the population was collaborating in guerrilla-controlled areas, emphasizing intelligence activities such as sharing information about military movements and enemies within the population. The column also stated that "This is the civil society support that our Security Forces do not have," and that the serious losses suffered by the military at the hands of the guerrillas had to be blamed on "the lack of military intelligence" or "precise and necessary information."[31] The focus was on the importance of Convivir activities in changing the balance of power and making military success possible: "And that is just where the Convivir program plays a crucial role. Through this program it will be possible to reverse the present direction in the relationship between the forces. I see these cooperatives as the base or the rearguard with whose help the armed forces will operate successfully."[32]

The army argued that in order to control the Convivirs, these "security cooperatives" should be directly tied to specific military brigades to consolidate a direct alliance of organized civilian anti-guerrilla forces and the military.[33] Moreover, when their base at Las Delicias in Putumayo was taken over by FARC, military analysts concluded that the principal cause of the military's inability to defend it was the lack of a civilian intelligence network in these colonized areas, where most confrontations with the guerrillas take place.[34]

It becomes evident that the military did not conceive of confrontations with guerrilla combatants as separate from the activities of civilians in guerrilla-controlled regions. The intensification of a counterinsurgency war requires inhabitants to take a stance. Military assumptions about people being "guerrilla collaborators" stemmed from the nature of the regular interactions between FARC and civilians. As a result of these assumptions, the population was targeted for several forms of violence.

In November 1997, the Constitutional Court rejected a suit challenging the legality of the Convivirs.[35] That same year, various paramilitary groups combined into the United Self-defense Forces of Colombia, AUC. While some components of AUC had previously worked to defend private interests against guerrilla incursions, with the formalization of the national AUC, these illegal groups joined the overall anti-guerrilla struggle and assumed military functions normally reserved for the state. In the words of Carlos Castaño, commander of AUC, "This represents a group of people who have not been protected by the state" legitimizing their assumption of state functions to provide "justice" in their territories of influence (in Aranguren Molina 2001, 200). This was the paramilitaries' way of declaring that they were "political subjects" who would thenceforth contest FARC's control of territory. They began seeking control of guerrilla turf, especially where illegal crops were grown. These areas were strategic objectives as sources of financing for the intensifying armed confrontation. Accordingly, paramilitaries made their incursion into Putumayo, Meta, and Casanare in 1997 and by 1998 the consequences were strongly felt in Putumayo, as will be discussed further in chapter 7.

In sum, the guerrillas, military, and paramilitaries have all mediated the daily life of Amazon residents. Campesinos, indigenous peoples, and outsiders in search of a way to make a living have had to cope with and participate in this conflict-ridden situation as well as resist or negotiate with perpetrators of violence.

CHAPTER TWO

Coca and the War on Drugs in Putumayo

Illegality, Armed Conflict, and the Politics of Time and Space

The anti-drug policies of the United States have a bearing on the expansion and contraction of coca cultivation in Bolivia, Peru, and Colombia. These countries have used very different approaches to coca cultivation, though each has been, at some point in the past twenty years, the world's leading producer and processor of the leaf. This chapter analyzes the changing dynamic of Colombia's coca production within the Andean region and specifically on the western Colombian Amazon, especially Caquetá, Guaviare, and Putumayo, where intensified aerial fumigation since 1994 has been unsuccessful in eradicating coca. While cultivation in some departments or countries has been dampened for periods since then, it has always simultaneously increased in other areas. The end result in the Andean region has been only a slight decrease in coca cultivation.[1]

The regulation of the local coca market by FARC, at one point prompting the armed forces to refer to them as "the third drug cartel," has transformed the war on drugs in Colombia into a counterinsurgency war. This chapter gives an account of the steps of cocaine production from cultivation of the leaf through the marketing of the drug. It examines how the assumed link between coca production and violence conceals the ubiquitous political violence in Putumayo. It concludes with an analysis of how spaces are imagined and constructed in Putumayo, in a way that relates to the presence of coca, and how the meanings ascribed to these spaces are reinforced or resisted by its inhabitants.

Colombia in the Andean Region: From Coca Distributor to Main Producer

Different cultures, histories, legislation, and governmental approaches to coca growing in Bolivia, Peru, and Colombia have caused varied results in the international drug war. Bolivia's and Peru's large indigenous populations, for example, contrast with Colombian indigenous groups, who represent only two to three percent of the country's population. At the same time, the internationalization of coca has led to such extensive intervention by the United States in all three countries that their autonomy in dealing with coca as they wish has been compromised. Moreover, coca production and processing in each of these countries is intertwined with the international drug economy. Policies that eradicate coca in one Andean country usually increase its production or distribution in another.

As a traditional indigenous crop, coca has been cultivated in these three countries since pre-Hispanic times. It is usually chewed like tobacco and also can be "boiled, ground, toasted, or used dry; . . . used alone or mixed with other substances; . . . be drunk as a tea or used as an ointment, bathing solution, or in massages, to cure dozens of folk illnesses" (Sanabria 1993, 38). Coca tea is a traditional beverage throughout Bolivia and Peru, and derivative products such as ointments and bathing solutions are common there. In Colombia, coca has traditionally been used only among some of its indigenous groups, such as the Paeces and Arhuacos in the Andes Mountains and the Huitotos and Western Tukanoans in the Amazon. Their use of coca is limited to chewing and to some medicinal applications. Such differences partly explain why coca cultivation is more harshly penalized in Colombia than in Bolivia and Peru, where it is still legal under certain circumstances.

In Bolivia, the coca plant is perceived not only as a natural resource but also as part of the country's cultural heritage. The region of Yungas, north of La Paz, has the strongest tradition of coca production, and it continues to be legal to grow it there. The Bolivian Ministry of the Interior clearly distinguishes between coca leaf and cocaine (Del Olmo 1989, 298), and authorizes a total of 12,000 hectares of legal coca production for legitimate cultural uses such as chewing, tea, soft drinks, and soap. In areas where the Bolivian government does require coca eradication, the process is voluntary, and coca producers are able to negotiate their rate of crop substitution. Moreover, the government has staunchly opposed fumigation with toxic herbicides in recognition of the importance of coca in the local indigenous culture. This sentiment was reflected in the election of Evo Morales, a former coca grower and cocalero union leader of Aymara descent, as President of Bolivia in 2005.

In contrast to the Bolivian approach, Peru's legislation condemns the indigenous tradition of chewing coca leaves and prohibits private cultivation. In eastern Peru, coca was eradicated with toxic herbicides in the 1990s (Sanabria 1993, 238). However, the state does authorize coca cultivation and marketing for medicinal, industrial, and scientific purposes only through a state-owned monopoly, the National Coca Company (Compañía Nacional de Coca, ENACO) (De Rementería 1989, 366–67), regulated by the Ministry of Health (Del Olmo 1989, 291 and 298).

While the Peruvian model is stricter than the Bolivian one, both of these countries, unlike Colombia, offer substantive alternatives to complete criminalization that recognize the traditional uses and cultural importance of coca. Colombia can be further distinguished by the presence of guerrillas who regulate coca production and sales. The Sendero Luminoso (Shining Path) guerrilla group in Peru played a different role vis-à-vis cocaleros than the guerrillas do in Colombia. Between 1983 and 1989 in some regions, the Sendero sided with cocaleros to resist government eradication efforts. However, by the 1990s many campesino populations, including cocaleros, were beginning to organize civilian defense patrols to fight against the Sendero. In any case the Peruvian guerrillas did not regulate coca production as do the FARC. This distinguishing feature in Colombia has led, in sharp contrast, to a blanket stigmatization and criminalization of virtually every aspect of coca production and processing, as will be discussed further below. Despite these prohibitions, Colombia has dominated the coca production market for more than the past ten years.

In April 1998, Rand Beers, director of the Bureau of International Narcotics and Law Enforcement Affairs, said that "The success in sharply reducing coca cultivation in Peru and Bolivia by disrupting deliveries to Colombia changed Colombia from a nation that largely processed and transported cocaine to the leading grower of raw coca."[2] Coca production began to decrease in Bolivia and Peru in 1998, but increased in Colombia by 100 percent in the two years between 1997 and 1999, when overall volume in the region increased. By 2000, Colombia had 73 percent of the world's coca growing area.

The war against drugs declared by the United States operates under the assumption that by reducing the production of coca leaves, cocaine prices will rise, causing consumption to drop. However, when the wholesale price of cocaine was high during the 1970s and the early 1980s, consumption rose and then stabilized. When prices dropped, consumption did not rise and seemed even to decrease (Uprimny 1994, 84). The general strategy of combating coca production in order to diminish cocaine consumption has clearly been ineffective. The United States' Office of National Drug Control

Table 3. Hectares of coca cultivation in the Andean region, 1994–2006

	Bolivia	Peru	Colombia	Total
1994	48,100	108,600	44,700	201,400
1995	48,600	115,300	50,900	214,800
1996	48,100	94,400	67,200	209,700
1997	45,800	68,800	79,400	194,000
1998	38,000	51,000	101,800	190,800
1999	21,800	38,700	160,100	220,600
2000	14,600	43,400	163,300	221,300
2001	19,900	46,200	144,800	210,900
2002	24,400	46,700	102,000	173,200
2003	23,600	44,200	86,000	154,100
2004	27,700	50,300	80,000	158,000
2005	25,400	48,200	86,000	159,600
2006	27,500	51,400	78,000	156,900

Source: Coca surveys by UNODC Illicit Crops Monitoring Programme with the Governments of Bolivia, Colombia, Ecuador, and Peru, June 2007.

Policy (ONDCP) estimated in 2006 that "U.S. retail cocaine prices were about 20 percent *lower* in July 2006 (roughly US$165 per pure gram) than in July 2003 (roughly US$210 per gram), and purity was nearly 25 percent *higher* (about 74 percent vs. about 60 percent)" and that "the price continued to fall through October 2006, when (at about US $135 per gram) it was some 35 percent lower than in July 2003" (Walsh 2007, 7). In its 2007 *National Drug Threat Assessment*, the U.S. Justice Department noted that notwithstanding a high level of cocaine interdiction and seizure in 2005, there had been "no sustained cocaine shortages or indications of stretched supplies in domestic drug [cocaine] markets" (U.S. Department of Justice 2006, 3). After over ten years of counter-drug policies directed by the United States toward the Andean region, the situation has not significantly changed.

Colombian Criminalization of Coca and Implementation of Aerial Spraying

The Colombian National Narcotics Council (Consejo Nacional de Estupefacientes, CNE) is composed of cabinet-level ministers and the law enforcement agency directors and charged with enforcing the 1996 Narcotics Statute (Law 30), a highly repressive law passed by Congress to curtail coca processing (De Roux 1989, 320). Under this law, the CNE was moved from the presidency to the highest levels of the Ministry of Defense and was given responsibility for producing and enforcing administrative decrees regarding crops used to produce illegal drugs (coca, poppies, and marijuana) and for establishing policies and programs to combat production, distribution, and use of drugs. The statute officially differentiates medicines from narcotics, defined as non-prescription drugs that act on the central nervous system and produce dependency.

The law also defines specific violations and penalties for all persons participating in the production of any plant intended for use in the elaboration of narcotics. It prohibits the transportation or processing of such plants, as well as the presence on one's property of landing strips, laboratories, or other facilities for narcotics production. It specifies procedures for the destruction of coca plantations and materials used in coca processing. The law states that those individuals with more than 20 coca plants would be sanctioned with fines and prison. It further stipulates that the cultivation of coca would be permitted only in the context of medical or scientific research and, with regard to a very limited number of plots, for those few indigenous communities for whom the use of coca was an element of their "culture and tradition" (Articles 3–7 and 32). Under the Narcotics Statute, the CNE would promote coca substitution programs in areas where indigenous peoples and colonos had begun planting coca for commercial purposes. Another law in 2000 (Law 599) revised Colombia's penal code to integrate the Narcotics Statute, reaffirmed the illegality of growing coca, and increased penalties for violations.

This law confirmed coca-growing campesinos' perception that state legislation was enacted not for their benefit but rather to target them for persecution:

> But what the government does do is take some young guys and throw them in jail. They have our son over there. They took him away and left us two here alone. And we're old; we're lost without him because he looked out for us. One day he went to the *Caja Agraria* (Agrarian Bank) to see about a little loan. They said they couldn't give him a loan because there wasn't any money. So he came here and said to Papa that he was going to work in the coca harvest. Unfortunately they caught him there harvesting those four coca leaves and look, they have him there almost three months now. And it was barely a quarter of a hectare. Our boy wanted to work; he had attended a course through the National Rehabilitation Plan. (Interview of colono Don Juan in Silva 1991a, 43)

The criminalization of coca cultivation explains why in Colombia aerial spraying of coca plantations is standard procedure, unlike in Bolivia and Peru, which have prohibited it. The fumigation of coca plantations in the Colombian Amazon with the toxic herbicide glyphosate began in 1994 (Vargas 1999, 122) and had increased forty times over by 2006. Although the area of coca cultivation decreased significantly between 2001 and 2003, it stabilized after that time despite a continuous increase in the area being sprayed.

Even though indigenous territories were at first not targeted for coca eradication, their spraying was subsequently made legal.[3] The national crop substitution plan known as PLANTE (Plan Nacional de Desarrollo Alternativo), begun in 1994 as a response to the growing coca economy in the Western Amazon, had an Office for Indigenous Peoples (Plante Indígena) to mediate between the CNE and indigenous populations. Though it protected their collectively owned indigenous reservations (*resguardos*) from fumigation for a time, this office was closed in 2002. In the case of the colonos, there has been no protection from fumigation. Although substitution plans have been offered to small coca producers with up to three hectares of coca, the intensified international war on drugs blurred the distinction between small and large-scale producers, defined as those with more than ten hectares of the crop.[4]

Aerial spraying has given rise to numerous complaints of adverse health and environmental impacts. Residents in the spray zones say that they are frequently exposed to the spray mixture and suffer a variety of ailments as a result. This has been confirmed by emergency health services in the clinics where residents come with their health problems after fumigations take place (Revelo 2001). Concerns have also been raised about the impact that widespread spraying may have on Colombia's enormously diverse and fragile tropical ecosystems as well as on the alternative crops promoted as substitutes for coca.

These health and environmental concerns have been downplayed with arguments that the ill health suffered by many people in the spray zones is caused by generally poor conditions in these areas or by exposure to agricultural and drug processing chemicals, and that glyphosate has been shown to be fairly benign with respect to the natural environment, as reported to the Organization of American States (Solomon et al. 2005). However, no serious health and environmental monitoring has been conducted, nor studies specific and rigorous enough to measure the impact of the kind of spraying being implemented in Colombia. Moreover, the United Nations Office on

Table 4. Hectares of aerial spraying and coca cultivation, 1994–2006

	Spraying	Coca		Spraying	Coca
1994	3,871	45,000	2002	130,000	102,071
1996	18,518	67,200	2003	133,000	86,340
1999	43,111	160,199	2004	136,550	80,350
2000	58,074	163,289	2005	138,775	87,750
2001	94,500	144,807	2006	172,025	77,870

Sources: Data covering 1994–2000 from National Narcotics Directorate, 2001; data covering 2001–2006 from coca surveys by UNODC Illicit Crops Monitoring Programme with the Government of Colombia.

Drugs and Crime (UNODC) reported in an annual survey that aerial spraying caused the forced displacement of populations in coca-growing areas (UNODC and Government of Colombia 2003, 29). To further the negative impact on the affected population, Colombia law stipulates that people displaced by fumigation (rather than armed conflict) are considered ineligible for Internally Displaced Person (IDP) benefits.

History of Coca and Cocaine in Colombia through the International and National Merging of Counternarcotics and Counterinsurgency

Commercial coca growing began in eastern Colombia in around 1975, promoted by emerald dealers who established links with the industry in Peru and Bolivia even before the end of the Colombian marijuana boom.[5] These emerald dealers had connections for marketing cocaine as a result of their experience in the marijuana trade. At first, coca was grown in Iquitos, Peru, by Peruvians, exported as coca paste to Colombia's eastern plains to be processed into cocaine by Colombians, and marketed by Americans.

At the end of the 1970s, Colombian drug traffickers decided to grow their own coca (C. Ramírez 1998, 14–15). At first, commercial crops extended from the tropical Brazilian border region in the state of Vaupés, west toward the headwaters of the Vaupés River and east to Miraflores in the state of Guaviare. Gradually, the cultivation area extended to all the colonized areas in the Amazon Region and to Meta, Caquetá, and, by 1978, to Putumayo (Alomía et al. 1997, 7). The extent of coca cultivation in each of these departments varied according to landholding patterns in place at the time, which in turn reflected the different processes by which the Amazon region was settled during the twentieth century.

In Putumayo, coca is grown predominantly by campesino small land-owners, while in Caquetá and Guaviare there are significant numbers of medium and large landowners and coca growers. In the 1990s, planta-tions of up to three hundred hectares were established and managed by drug dealers in Guaviare, prompting the head of the Anti-narcotics Police, Corneal Gallego, to call the department "an ocean of coca" by 1994.[6]

In 1999 and 2000, while the Anti-narcotics Police increased its fumiga-tion activities in Caquetá and Guaviare, coca production intensified in other areas of the Amazon like Putumayo, which became the leading coca pro-ducer both regionally (50 percent of the coca in western Amazonia) and na-tionally (40 percent of the Colombian total).[7] In 2000, Putumayo became the new focus of aerial fumigation efforts, and production began to decrease the following year.

Whereas coca was being cultivated in six departments in 1994, this num-ber increased to twelve departments by 1999 and skyrocketed to twenty-two in 2000 and twenty-three in 2006 (UNODC and Government of Colombia 2007). Instead of dismantling the chain of coca production, aerial fumiga-tion of coca crops has accelerated the clearing of more and more tropical forest as coca cultivation has migrated throughout the country, causing major environmental damage.

In addition to spreading coca cultivation around the country, the drug war's emphasis on fumigation legitimized the role of guerrillas in rural coca-growing areas. Since fumigation disproportionately targets campesino coca growers, this population sympathized with guerrilla resistance to the government policy and benefited from any protection the guerrillas could offer against it. Territory under guerrilla control increased. Moreover, there is evidence that the military did not have a real commitment to or belief in the effectiveness of coca eradication, but rather aimed simply to attack the guerrillas.[8] The military claimed that the guerrillas had replaced the Cali and Medellín cartels. They took to calling FARC narco-guerrillas, a term first coined in 1984 by Lewis Tambs, then the U.S. ambassador to Colombia (Arrieta et al. 1990, 223), meaning guerrillas who had abandoned their revo-lutionary and political ideology and had to be dealt with as drug-dealing criminals. Colombian Army Major Villamarín provided a very clear exposi-tion of this line of thinking:

> The guerrilla-drug trafficker alliance was forged in the 1970s to meet reciprocal needs of the two parties. They both felt cornered by the

Table 5. Hectares of coca cultivation in Western Amazonia and other departments of Colombia, 1991–2006

	1991	1992	1993	1994	1995	1996	1997
Guaviare	21,400	22,900	24,100	26,300	28,700	38,600	29,000
Caquetá	8,600	8,400	9,300	11,700	15,600	21,600	31,400
Putumayo	2,200	2,400	4,000	5,000	6,600	7,000	19,000
Norte de Santander	—	—	—	—	—	—	—
Bolívar	5,300	3,400	2,300	1,700	—	—	—
Meta	—	—	—	—	—	—	—
Nariño	—	—	—	—	—	—	—
Antioquia	—	—	—	—	—	—	—
Subtotal	37,500	37,100	39,700	44,700	50,900	67,200	79,400
Percentage of total Colombian coca cultivation	100	100	100	100	100	100	100
Total Colombian coca cultivation	37,500	37,100	39,700	44,700	50,900	67,200	79,400

Source: National Narcotics Directorate, *Observatorio de Drogas de Colombia*, Coca Surveys by UNODC Illicit Crops Monitoring Programme.

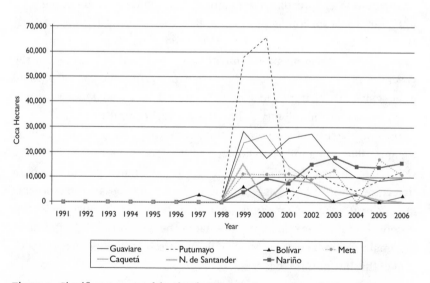

Figure 2. Significant coca cultivation in Western Amazonia and other departments of Colombia, 1994–2006. (National Narcotics Directorate, *Observatorio de Drogas de Colombia*, Coca Surveys by UNODC Illicit Crops Monitoring Program)

1998	1999	2000	2001	2002	2003	2004	2005	2006
26,700	28,435	17,619	25,553	27,381	16,163	9,769	8,658	9,477
39,400	23,718	26,603	14,516	8,412	7,230	6,500	4,998	4,967
30,100	58,297	66,022	47,120	13,725	7,559	4, 836	8,963	12,254
—	15,309	6,280	9,145	8,041	4,471	3,055	844	488
—	5,897	5,960	4,824	2,735	4,470	3,402	3,670	2,382
—	11,384	11,123	11,425	9,222	12,814	18,470	17,305	11,063
—	3,959	9,343	7,494	15,131	17,628	14,154	13,875	15606
—	3,644	2,547	3,171	3,030	4,273	5,168	6,414	6,157
96,200	150,643	145,497	123,248	87,677	74,608	65,354	64,727	62,394
94	94	89	85	86	87	82	75	80
101,800	160,100	163,300	144,800	102,000	86,000	80,000	86,000	78,000

Armed Forces and the guerrillas discovered in drug trafficking a . . . source of income. They agreed with the mafias to protect and defend the coca-growing areas, processing laboratories, and access roads, distracting military operations with the diversionary tactics of irregular warfare. For this they were remunerated by the drug traffickers with money, arms, and logistical support. But as one would expect, this just made Tirofijo [Manuel Marulanda] and the other commanders in the secretariat want to form their own cartel that would generate a very juicy income stream for them. The narco-guerrilla marriage was reconfigured, but the concept was the same. FARC organized another drug-trafficking cartel, hiding behind the Leninist hypocrisy that "The end justifies the means." (Villamarín 1996, 21–22)

Although fighting coca production and trafficking continued to be the official counter-narcotics policy of the Colombian government, supported by the United States, the conflict gradually began to take on the characteristics of a counterinsurgency program.[9] The United States' drug war, too, began to resemble a counterinsurgency war in practice.[10] In early 1998, the *Dallas Morning News* reported that "Clinton administration officials acknowledge they are having difficulty reconciling their current 'hands-off' policy toward the insurgency with their desire to aggressively prosecute a $215 million-a-year international war on drugs."[11] Vargas (1996, 69–70) spells out the political implications of this shift:

1. It conflated the internal conflict with international organized crime, situating the insurgents as enemies of world order based on their ties to the drug economy. They were put on the same footing as drug traffickers.
2. It effaced the fact that the guerrilla involvement was to provide security at the level of raw material production. They were secondary beneficiaries of income derived from an illegal drug trade managed by international crime organizations.
3. Measures such as extradition would in the future be applied to the guerrilla leadership, imposing the framework of international conflict on the Colombian national territory.[12]

By re-framing Colombia's internal armed conflict in terms of the war on drugs, US policy-makers were able to garner support for Plan Colombia, the massive aid package launched in 2000 that centered on the aerial eradication of coca in largely guerrilla-controlled western Amazonia. On August 2, 2002, in the aftermath of September 11, 2001, the United States Congress and the Bush administration openly declared that the war on drugs in Colombia would be transformed into a counterinsurgency war. Furthermore, previous restrictions on the use of anti-narcotics resources were lifted to create one unified front against drug trafficking and organizations classified as terrorist, which included guerrilla groups FARC and the National Liberation Army (Ejército de Liberación Nacional, ELN), and the paramilitary group, AUC.

The Consolidation of Coca Growing and Processing in Putumayo

In late 1989, coca was suffering from intensified government suppression and from damaging plagues. In addition, coca prices dropped, leading to a major economic depression in Putumayo.[13] Until 1990, few agrochemical products were necessary to produce a profitable coca crop. However, coca monoculture, with its resultant pests, began to require increasingly large agrochemical inputs. By the end of that year, infestations of harmful insects had made the continued cultivation of the Caucana variety of coca impossible. In 1992 and 1993, the Bolivian and Peruvian Tingo María varieties were introduced and as a result of their much higher resistance to pests, cultivation was reactivated and production levels increased enormously (Alomia et al. 1997, 18).

Other factors also contributed to this production boom. First, Putumayo's location on the international border expedited rapid coca paste processing and cocaine export. Drug traffickers built mansions in the border area. They did not permanently reside there, but used them for negotiating and conducting business transactions with Peruvians and Ecuadorians.[14] In April 1996, a local newspaper reported that the area around Valle del Guamués in southern Putumayo and just north of Ecuador was developing its own economic role by providing support services to drug traffickers. It had become a bridge for the export of some nine hundred kilos of cocaine weekly, bound for the United States and European markets. These weekly shipments required an investment of about 100 million pesos [US$97,000] for land and river transportation, bribes, mules, and supplies. Much of this money was moving directly into the regional economy of Putumayo, Caquetá, and the Republic of Ecuador.[15]

Second, since FARC's authority to impose norms and wield justice was recognized, its regulation and taxation of coca production, processing, and marketing legitimized the economic activity. In 1998, FARC was taxing small producers 20,000 to 40,000 pesos (about US$14 to $28) per hectare for each coca harvest (forty-five to sixty days apart), depending on the amount of land a campesino had planted. Those with more than five hectares were charged instead in coca paste, by kilo of coca leaf harvested or by kilo of coca paste produced. In one case, the tax came to three kilos of coca paste per harvest on a plantation of twenty-two hectares.[16]

Third, coca turned out to be well adapted to the tropical forest environment, more profitable than other crops, and easy to market. In fact, said the colonos, growing other crops simply benefitted dishonest buyers:

> But what happened? The subsistence food we grow here isn't worth anything. We don't get a fair price. The middleman robs us. He doesn't pay a just price to the campesino who has sweated, who has put his life on the line, who has killed himself. He could be killed by a falling tree, bitten by a snake, or die from disease. All that just so a guy like that can come around and not pay a fair price, not even pay what you need to survive. *We were about to disappear here . . . Coca, on the other hand, was more worth it . . . you could make more, you could dress better, buy better medicine.* (Interview of colono Don Juan in Silva 1991a, 41; emphasis added)

When a family of colonos arrives in the coca region, the men often per-form day labor in the coca fields and women may prepare meals for other workers. Slowly they save enough money to rent or buy a small piece of land, making payments from the money they earn growing coca. Other families may form partnerships to start growing coca right away. Using one of the fol-lowing arrangements, longstanding colonos help new people get settled and integrate themselves into the regional economy even if they own no land:

1. One partner provides land and seeds and another provides labor. Once the coca is harvested the costs of production are deducted and the har-vest workers (*raspachines*) are paid. The resulting earnings are divided evenly.
2. One partner provides land, the other seeds, and together they obtain all other inputs on credit. Both partners work and their earnings are divided evenly.
3. Three people form a partnership. One provides land and the other two provide labor as well as seeds and all other inputs on credit. Once ex-penses are paid their earnings are divided evenly.

Producers usually incur debt. When the product is sold in the form of leaf or paste, they pay off their debts, including the money owed to raspachines, and they are immediately ready to begin a new production cycle. Coca is bought immediately, on site, and for cash. Campesinos do not have to struggle or pay to transport it to distant markets. Coca paste is also far easier to trans-port than rice, plantain, corn, or manioc. Hence, coca production represents greater economic stability for the campesinos and their best opportunity to participate in the market economy.

Coca cultivation has been the dominant industry in the Colombian Ama-zon for the last thirty years. Yet, the poverty of the colonos has deepened due to an inflationary process and the lack of other sources of work. One campesino reacted to the idea that colonos grow coca to get rich: "We've all grown coca and we're all poor. It's true that some people have gotten rich but they're the mid-level buyers or the ones who grow larger amounts of coca."[17] However, unlike other extractive, export-oriented industries in the region such as quinine, rubber, and mining, a portion of coca profits is in-vested in services such as college education, which are not seen as an invest-ment in the region, but which result in improved living standards for colono producers as well as harvesters and related workers. Thus, coca cultivation can no longer be considered a mere short cycle economic activity. Rather, it has become an alternative source of income for a marginal community that has seized the opportunity to challenge that marginality, imposed by the traditional dominant classes, "a rearguard economic activity sufficient to maintain the boundary between productivity and mere subsistence" (Tovar 1993, 27). An entire generation has grown up in the Amazon region whose knowledge of work is limited to the coca industry (Ferro et al. 1999). At a July 2004 workshop with campesino coca growers in Orito, I asked them about the expenses and profitability of planting and growing coca. What followed was an animated discussion about the different varieties of coca that could be planted and the pros and cons of each. They mentioned three varieties: Bolivian black, Bolivian red, and the Peruvian variety Tingo María. Tingo María produces more leaves than the Bolivian black, they said, but the leaves contain less of the active ingredient for cocaine, so more of them are required to produce the same amount of the final product. It was clear that, thirty years after the onset of the coca boom, the campesinos had learned a lot about coca agriculture.

Coca is cultivated and processed in ten of the thirteen municipalities of Putumayo (see table 6), which in 1997 meant that 78.5 percent of the state's population was involved in its production or marketing (Gaviria, Bonilla, and Arenas 1997; and Alomía et al. 1997). Between 1999 and 2001, Orito, Puerto Asís, San Miguel (La Dorada), and Valle del Guamués (La Hormiga) were the primary producers, typically on plots of three to five hectares.[18] As a result of Plan Colombia, coca cultivation began to decrease significantly in Putumayo in 2002.

While local corn reaps two to three harvests per year, Tingo María produces six harvests per year and does not require replanting. The Bolivian black and red varieties of coca produce up to eight harvests a year, but are more affected by pests and disease. A hectare supports twenty to thirty thousand bushes of the more popular Peruvian variety. Coca shoots are planted in rows one meter apart, two or three shoots every eighty centimeters. Fertilizer and herbicide must be applied, and since coca is attacked by worms and fungi, insecticide and fungicide must also be used twice between harvests. More agrochemicals must be used during times of heavy rain. Sometimes coca producers do not understand the distinctions between the chemicals and think they are fertilizing when they are in fact applying insecticides and fungicides. But the crop can be lost if the required spraying, fertilization, and harvesting are not done on time. Caring for coca is extremely demanding. As people say, "Growing coca enslaves you because you can't leave the crop for a minute."[19]

Table 6. Hectares of coca cultivation in Putumayo, 1999–2006

	1999	2000	2001	2002	2003	2004	2005	2006
Mocoa	274.43	510.56	112.00	122.18	91	27	69	145
Orito	9,734.96	10,854.98	7,629.19	1,441.73	352	516	523	1,153
Puerto Asís	11,340.48	13,018.72	8,679.57	2,898.25	1,527	543	1,414	2,509
Puerto Caicedo	3,454.66	4,146.60	2,340.49	708.90	210	141	330	547
Puerto Guzmán	7,986.52	6,153.36	4,184.77	2,494.47	2,297	1,050	1,928	2,118
Puerto Leguízamo	2,622.10	5,368.41	3,831.27	3,186.88	1,454	1,275	2,546	2,562
San Miguel (La Dorada)	8,700.95	7,983.17	4,041.29	902.56	600	194	661	756
Santiago	0	0	10.86	7.55	0	0	3	6
Valle del Guamués (La Hormiga)	14,031.40	16,523.88	9,269.25	1,552.84	850	471	1,033	1,896
Villagarzón	151.49	1,462.69	952.06	410.04	178	169	456	561
Total Putumayo	58,297.01	66,022.36	47,119.75[a]	13,725.40	7,559	4,386	8,963	12,253

[a]Total adjusted to account for an additional 6,069 hectares that, according to the DNE, were missed by aerial photography due to cloud cover.

Source: National Narcotics Directorate, *Observatorio de Drogas de Colombia*.

The Coca Harvest Worker: El Raspachín

Coca must be harvested every forty-five to sixty days, depending on the variety. The first three or four times a crop is harvested from a bush, it is still young and tender, so the leaves must be plucked carefully. During subsequent harvests, the leaves are scraped off by hand, or as people say, "milked" off each branch. The harvest is labor intensive, so temporary harvest workers are employed. Men, women, and children work as "scrapers," or *raspachines*.

During the negotiations following the cocalero movement, raspachín representatives defined three subgroups among themselves. Some harvest workers are migrant campesinos fleeing the poverty of their home regions. Others are seasonal farm workers with harvesting experience in coffee, cotton, or other crops elsewhere in Colombia. Both of these groups hope to remain in the area. The third subgroup consists of migrants hoping to make their fortune and return to their places of origin.

Experienced farm workers say that the coca harvest is more difficult than picking coffee, and that it can take as much as eight months to become a skilled and productive raspachín. The entire hand must be used to scrape the leaves off the branches. Specialized groups of skilled raspachines can work continually by moving from one plantation to another. Because the work is so taxing, the workforce is mostly made up of young people, many of whom lack educational and other opportunities in their places of origin. They may be the children of landless campesinos or unemployed urban dwellers.[20] Raspachines' hands are typically stained from their work. The high concentration of herbicides, fungicides, and insecticides in the coca fields frequently produces skin rashes and allergic reactions.

Some local youth limit their work in the coca harvest to school vacation times, but most adolescents in the region prefer to make money on the harvest than stay with their families and study. For this reason, the school dropout rate has become a big problem among twelve- to fifteen-year-olds and sometimes even younger children. A father of two adolescents who left home to harvest coca told me that he had appealed to FARC to help retrieve them. Some older youths use money from the harvest to return to school. The belief that education is important in order to "become someone" in life

Figure 3. Raspachines harvesting coca. (Orlando Restrepo, Casa Editorial, *El Tiempo*)

Figure 4. A raspachin stripping off coca leaves. (Casa Editorial, *El Tiempo*)

is still strong in the region, and the ability to invest in education is one of the major benefits that coca growing has provided to campesino cocaleros.[21]

An inexperienced raspachín can harvest only twenty-five to fifty pounds, or one to two *arrobas* per day, which will not pay enough to live on. An experienced raspachín working a good crop can harvest up to ten arrobas per day. Raspachines are paid ten percent of the value of their harvest. In 1998 one arroba of coca leaves was worth 12,000 pesos, or US$8.40. A raspachín would be paid 1,200 pesos, or US$0.84 for each arroba of coca leaf harvested, so ten arrobas would pay US$8.40 a day. Buyers come to a road near the plantation to buy the unprocessed leaf.[22]

Home Laboratories for Processing Coca Leaf

Other campesinos make their living by producing paste from coca leaves in small thatch-roof shelters near their houses. These workers use a mechanical chopper to chop one arroba of coca leaf at a time. They add water and one kilo of cement and mix these into a mash. This mash sits for twelve hours, and is then poured into a mixing tank along with five gallons of gasoline, where it sits for another two to three hours. This solution is strained through a cloth to remove the leaves. Ten liters of water and fifty cubic centimeters of sulfuric acid are added, and the solution is then left to sit again until the gasoline and water separate.

The gasoline is then discarded and the water treated in one of the following two ways: (1) one gram of potassium permanganate for each cubic centimeter of sulfuric acid is stirred in for two to three minutes and then the solution is strained again, or (2) sodium hydroxide is added and it is not strained again. Ammonia or sodium carbonate is then added to the remaining solution, which separates into a transparent liquid with coagulates. The mixture is strained through a cloth once more and then cooked. While it is cooking, visible impurities are removed. Cooking continues until all the water evaporates, leaving only an oily liquid, which is then dried in the sun. A woman who works processing coca compares this stage to cooking: "It's like making cheese: If it's too watery you have to cook it more; you have to remove any pieces of grunge or too much water, strain it in a bowl and there it is."[23]

One arroba of coca leaf produces between fifteen and twenty grams of coca paste and each hectare produces approximately five kilos per harvest.[24] In 1998, a kilo of paste was worth 1,200,000 pesos, or about US$840.00. After deducting the cost of materials (fertilizer, herbicide, insecticide, fungicide, processing supplies) and labor, the profit to the campesino grower per hectare was 317,115 pesos, or US$262.00 per hectare per harvest (Sabogal 1998). On a three-hectare plot (the average size in the area), a campesino family was able to make 950,000 pesos (US$665.00) every two months, almost double the Colombian minimum wage that year.[25] Both the campesinos and the raspachines made a basic living. Coca production and processing was and is a continuous productive activity that provides a reliable economic environment for the small producer when other factors do not intervene (Sabogal 1998, 35).

As figure 5 shows, the production of coca paste was most profitable during the first coca boom in 1979–84. Prices fell steadily during that period, though, and then stabilized with some variation in response to externalities including the intensity of government efforts to curb production. Nevertheless, the price paid to campesino producers has fallen over the long term and has shown no signs of recovery, even after the cocalero marches of 1996. Still, coca was and is a profitable crop compared to the available alternatives.

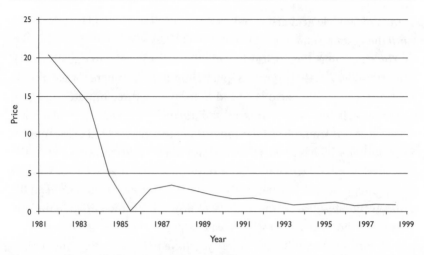

Figure 5. Price paid to producer for a gram of coca paste, in U.S. dollars, 1991–1998. (Reprinted by permission from Sabogal, 1998)

The Local Coca Dealer: El Traqueto

Large-scale drug traffickers run their businesses from Bogotá, Cali, and Medellín but keep representatives known as *traquetos* in coca-producing regions. "You go to Cali or Medellín and there they put you in touch with the boss by telephone. You talk to him and if he likes you and trusts you, then you agree on an arrangement. He calls the accountant and tells him to give you a certain amount of cash. You can't bribe him because you never see him. He's in his office and everything is done over the phone."[26]

In 1998, traquetos would arrive in the region with a lot of cash from drug traffickers—up to 100 million pesos or more (US$70,028 in 1998)—to buy coca paste from campesino producers in the areas designated for that purpose by FARC. During that period, FARC was collecting a tax of 20,000 pesos (US$14) from buyers and 50,000 pesos (US$35) from sellers on each kilo of paste.[27]

Most of these intermediaries were from Putumayo. Because of their family ties, their activities were not condemned. In fact, traquetos were respected. They looked after their home communities, supported local political campaigns and pressured elected officials to fulfill promises. Traquetos themselves have also been elected to political offices such as the municipal council. Locals would not only accept having traquetos in office, but would grant them more legitimacy than they would traditional politicians, as is clear from the following testimony of a political leader in Puerto Asís: "At least they weren't in it to steal from the state, and not to help themselves to municipal resources for personal advantage, since they already had everything they needed. They truly cared about the people and saw their chance to do something from their position on the council" (testimony in Sánchez 1998, 44).

During this first coca boom, local traquetos helped build the regional education center in La Hormiga. Some of them are known to have used political intimidation such as having an opposition member of the municipal council briefly kidnapped during a vote. Because local commerce depends on coca money, however, merchants sought to maintain good relations with the traquetos in much the same way they would pay monthly taxes to the guerrillas.

Local Cocaine Laboratories

Cocaine, the final product, is produced in more sophisticated laboratories funded by traffickers and operated by local personnel. In 1997, a payment to FARC of one million pesos (US$876) was required to establish a new laboratory (Alomia et al. 1997, 25). FARC did not guard the facilities; they only regulated the market. As one former traqueto reported, "The guerrillas just collect taxes. They tax us 40,000 pesos (US$35) per brick and one brick is a kilo of crystal cocaine."[28] The laboratory is organized as follows:

> First of all to work there you organize your setup. The lab has five parts: a mixing tank, a recycling room, a microwave oven room, a kitchen to eat in, and a dormitory, which is hardly used because sometimes you don't even sleep because you have to always be watching what might happen. For example, you might have to get out of there quickly if the army shows up. The mixers work in the mixing tank room; the pressers, who compress the bricks; the filterer, who is in charge of seeing that all the liquids are completely clean and pure and who controls the liquid measurements. There is a person in charge of the supply room, and there is a final presser who makes sure that all the bricks are tight and compact. The liquid is processed for re-use in the recycler. Two people work there day and night. There's also a generator man who's in charge of everything that has to do with electricity and connections, six or more security personnel and one woman, a cook. A laboratory can either be mobile or semi-permanent; semi-permanent for three or four months. After that they have to be moved because by then a lot

of people know about it and it's better to be safe. The crew members are the owner (*patrón*), the general manager: he doesn't do anything but give orders and see that everything is working like it should; the chemist: they bring chemists from the universities in Medellín or Cali; six or seven mixers: they dissolve the merchandise; the oven-tender, the finisher: he finishes the drying just right after it comes out of the microwaves; the pressers, and the wrapper: he labels each brick with tape and a letter. Every patrón has his own letter. That way when they get shipped to the United States or to Europe the people there know who it's from.[29]

Twenty to thirty people can process twenty to fifty kilos of coca in two weeks. Occasionally up to eight hundred kilos of coca are processed in one laboratory. Since the laboratories are located deep in the jungle, people will work nonstop for three weeks, returning home only after the job is finished.[30] The work is very hazardous. As the former traqueto explains, people put their lives at risk:

> I remember one time we were working with like 800 kilos and, well, we were down there and we had a big kitchen; we had a big communications setup and an expert to operate it. He was an army veteran and we had like the latest equipment. He was intercepting all the army communications and all of a sudden he told us that they were approaching where we were and everybody ran and grabbed the most valuable things like the communications equipment; the generator, which is a big heavy machine; the microwaves; and the merchandise. So then when we had almost everything, he said that the patrol was going off in another direction . . . and we put everything back together and kept working. You practically can't sleep. That time we had already gone four days without sleeping. Once in a while they let us sleep like two hours, but without even taking our boots off because you have to be ready at any moment to get out of there fast because the army patrols are always going along the rivers or flying overhead and they can come crashing in at any time.[31]

However, he continues explaining that it is a well-paid job compared with legal work in the region:

> I'm out of that now and I'm working in a business because that's very dangerous and with a family you shouldn't take so much risk. But

look, if you don't have an education they don't pay you any more than 350,000 pesos [US$245] a month to work in a business and you have to put up with a lot of things for that amount of money. But if you go and work hard for two weeks, no matter how bad it is you make at least 500,000 pesos [US$350] or more now, no less. If you work as a manager you make 1.5 million pesos [US$1,050] and up, so . . . don't you think it's worth it?[32]

Illegality is the most important externality in the coca and cocaine economy. Risk adds value to the final product, but campesinos risk little and consequently receive a very small proportion of the final sale price. "Most of the price increase takes place in marketing and distribution in the United States and other industrialized consumer countries where risks are higher" (Thoumi 1995, 135).

Daily Violence in Puerto Asís

A full 71.5 percent of the violent deaths recorded in Putumayo between 1991 and 1998 occurred in its towns (cascos urbanos), and 20.8 percent occurred in rural areas.[33] Eighty-nine percent of the victims were males. Young persons between the ages of fifteen and twenty-four accounted for 30.6 percent of victims, and persons between twenty-five and thirty-four for an additional 27 percent (Revelo 1998). Both drug trafficking and paramilitarism help account for the concentration of homicides in the towns and among young males. The paramilitaries recruit young males in the towns to inform on others, known as milicianos, who have been recruited for guerrilla intelligence operations. Young men choose to affiliate with one or another of these groups for personal reasons such as to avenge the death of a family member, to please or obey another one, or simply to find work in this poverty- and unemployment-racked region:

> Our poverty is crushing. We don't know what course to take and that's one of the main things—that the campesino, the young guy or girl makes bad choices because the paramilitary groups show up, the guerrillas, the army, and you get involved with any of these groups. So who's the soldier? Who's the guerrilla? Who's the paramilitary? He's the brother of the guerrilla or he's the brother of the soldier. He's the guerrilla, the cousin, the nephew. Because of our poverty, because we don't have any decent options, we don't know what to do, so we have

to join one of them in order to survive. So this is one of the situations, one of the tragedies that we see and that has us involved in the armed conflict.[34]

The youth of Puerto Asís are wary. No one can be trusted. It is impossible to know "what that person might be into," one young person told me. "You can't just talk to somebody because you don't know who he or she might be." This is one of the first rules learned in Puerto Asís. One popular adage is "*estar callado y no mirar*" (Hold your tongue and don't stare). This is how the general population deals with the daily specter of violence.

Many of the youth who align themselves with one side or another of the armed conflict belong to families that came to Putumayo to grow coca and are seen as outsiders by those who have lived there for more than twenty years and consider themselves to be more "authentically Putumayan." Even longer-term colonos who are equally involved in the coca economy make this distinction. The following anecdote illustrates the point: A well-known health worker who has lived in Mocoa for over twenty-five years arrived to visit his friends at a house where I was staying in Puerto Asís. After watching the eight o'clock novela (soap opera) with the group, he said, "Well, now let's talk. What 'known' person have they killed lately?" referring to townspeople of over twenty years' standing. The homeowner, a twenty-six-year veteran of the government malaria service born in Puerto Leguízamo answered, "Nobody 'known.'" He went on to tell how a young guy had been killed in the park and he explained who his family was, but made it clear that they were not "known" people. He continued: "That kid must have been involved in something and probably talked too much." It is an accepted fact that being an informant or poking your nose where it doesn't belong may lead to a violent death. In these cases the deceased is usually blamed for his own death, while the passing of a "known" person is often lamented with a proclamation, truthful or not, that "He wasn't involved in anything," and that "They confused him with someone else."

Anybody can become a victim in Putumayo, and people want to know who has died before getting a good look at the body, which usually lays in the street for some time before being retrieved. The local funeral director, who is known as the Vulture (*la Chula*), stays on top of events. She is always aware of the latest death and collects the bodies from where they lay. An air of mystery surrounds her. People say that she has a love for the dead, that she knows who would die beforehand, and that she opens bodies even before they died.

When the prosecutor retrieves a body, he will issue a death certificate and call three or four relatives to testify as to the identity of the deceased, but will not carry out any real investigation. Impunity is the norm.

A generation has grown up in Puerto Asís not only growing and harvesting coca, but also living on intimate terms with death, as this woman explains: "The children go out to see the bodies here, and they get used to it. They expect to hear what happens and to see dead bodies. They aren't traumatized like in the places where it happens for the first time like I saw on TV, what they showed when the guerrillas took Mítu (Department of Vaupés) [in November 1998]."[35]

Violence has become routine. I overheard one teenager say to another in a café, "Tell me who it was so I can blow him away." People would hear bursts of shooting in the street and then discuss them like any other ordinary event: "Fifteen minutes ago there was some shooting around here." If a group is gathered in the street, people assume they are looking at dead bodies. The municipal building's security guard passed me in the street one day and said, "Come see who they killed." When we got close to the cluster of people he had pointed out, we found that they were just gathered around talking to some television actors who were visiting Puerto Asís. In Puerto Asís, places have become markers of violence in the collective memory of its residents: El Billar la 25, a pool hall where the owner's sixteen-year-old son was killed in broad daylight; streets where teenagers were killed because they had walked by and witnessed other murders taking place; the paramilitary gathering spot; the corner where a twelve-year-old boy was found dead, to name a few.

Families who arrived in the zone in the 1950s and 1960s would try to send their adolescent sons to school outside Puerto Asís to spare them from this cycle of violence. One woman said, "Sending my son to study in Popayán is a way to save his life because if he stayed, he'd end up on one side or the other and become a victim of the cycle of retaliation."[36] With the phrase "cycle of retaliation" she referred to the chains of personal revenge-taking that occurs among town residents, even though acts of violence are usually committed at least nominally on behalf of paramilitaries, guerrillas, or drug traffickers. Retaliation and counter-retaliation are a central factor in the generalized violence.

Julia, the wife of the police inspector of the Piamonte corregimiento called Fragua Viejo, told me her family's story when I was there in 1998, a story that illustrates this situation: She was born in Fraguita in the department of Caquetá, but her family settled on a farm in the Baja Bota. Two of her sisters lived nearby and another lived in Zabaleta, Caquetá. Her brother had lived in Bogotá from the time the guerrillas killed her father and other brother "back when the guerrillas executed people without investigating, because now things are different." The brother in Bogotá had fled the area after he had retaliated by killing two guerrillas and could not safely return. When the paramilitaries moved into the southern part of Colombia, he saw an opportunity for further revenge. He joined them and returned to Putumayo as a paramilitary. He visited his sister's farm with some of his new comrades in 1998, but in that FARC-dominated zone, his visit identified her family with the enemy. They were threatened and forced to flee to Mocoa, abandoning their farm after investing fifteen years of work in it.

In his description of life in Puerto Asís, John Harold Agudelo, an UMATA official, told a similar story regarding his family trying to stay out of the cycle of violence:

> My father is a *Paisa* [a person from the department of Antioquia or surrounding areas] and my mother is an *Opita* [a person from the department of Huila]. Yes, I was born in Puerto Asís in '70 and well, it was very nice. We didn't have any problems. I remember I used to play outside the house with toy cars. *You didn't find bodies around, there wasn't anything like that. It was a very peaceful place, but a very neglected place. It's still neglected, but there were no public services then, there wasn't anything. Still, it was peaceful, which is the most important thing.* And when I was about twelve, so in '82 more or less, or in '83, coca arrived, the violence started and our problems began. Then the guerrillas came in. And basically because of so much violence and the way society was really coming apart at that time, young people were becoming guerrillas, sicarios [paid assassins], or drug traffickers. I began to be influenced by it too and I started wanting to get involved in the drug business or to take up arms, like do bad stuff and hang out with bad people, people who came from other parts of the country, sicarios. They got to be your friends, and you started to get to know them, to carry a gun. So my *mamá* and my *papá*, well my family saw this and said, "No. We can't let our son get corrupted like that, get hurt or get into that stuff." So they sent me to study in Cali, thank God, because I don't know if I'd still be here or if I'd be gone, because 80–90 percent of my friends, of the kids I used to play with, have died. The social decay here has been really bad and anyone who was here became a drug trafficker or a paramilitary or a sicario. But all of us who

left have graduated now. We're the first generation of professionals in this place, because this place is very new.[37]

Agudelo blamed the presence of drug traffickers, paramilitaries, and sicarios for the "social decay." Although he mentioned the 1984 arrival of the guerrillas in the zone, he did not group them with the others. This is understandable if we recount the events surrounding the arrival of the first drug traffickers and the first selective massacres in the region. As mentioned in the previous chapter, the guerrillas mobilized against the drug traffickers in support of the campesinos in 1991, expelling the Rodríguez Gacha paramilitary group with the active participation of the population. This event served as a temporal marker in the collective memory of Puerto Asís, and was often cited as an example of the power of popular organization, to encourage people to fight the terror and fear of the new paramilitary presence. The mother of an adolescent boy articulated the distinction made between guerrillas and paramilitaries in the area: "When a boy of that age disappears, the first thing that occurs to you is that the guerrillas took him. A boy in our neighborhood is missing and that's what people fear. If it's the guerrillas, they send you a letter pretty soon saying that your son is OK and then you know what happened. But the paramilitaries come and kill people for no reason."[38]

Although many people have abandoned the area due to the increasing level of armed conflict, there is a generation that does not want to leave the only place they have known, a place where they have struggled for peace:

My family came from far away and stayed here because we liked this land and we grew up here. My papá, for example, I think he'll die here. I doubt very much that my mamá would want to leave either. Actually she'd like to but just because of the violence. She says, "I'd like to get out of here with my children." But everything she has is here, the businesses, the farm, her friends, everything. Imagine leaving everything and starting in a city. There's violence in the city. Not like here, but city life is hard. We'd like to see things resolved here, have peace and be able to work, because we have the most wonderful riches on earth in this zone. That's something that we're aware of. We know that.[39]

Doña Laura was a nurse and pharmacy owner in Puerto Asís who had originally come to Putumayo to work for Texaco in the 1960s. She also favored life in the area: "Despite the fear you live with here, I prefer small towns. You can live a more peaceful life. In Bogotá you have to watch out for thieves and sometimes you have to catch two or even three buses."[40] Laura contrasted the kinds of violence she had to deal with in Puerto Asís with those that take place in big cities where people do not know each other. People in Puerto Asís perceive the urban environment to be even more violent than the daily violence they face. They have developed ways to deal with local violence, and more importantly, they value the fact that an individual can have a place in the community in their town. Doña Laura, for example, helped residents with their health questions and gave injections. Leaving town would be to abandon a life's project constructed around her identity in Puerto Asís. She represents a generation of people who, although not born in the region, define themselves as Putumayan and seek to find meaning in their lives amid the daily violence.

Coca and Violence, Inevitably Linked?

According to data from the Putumayo Health Department (Departamento Administrativo de Salud de Putumayo, DASALUD), homicide was the leading cause of mortality in Putumayo during the 1990s. The general mortality rate per 100,000 inhabitants from homicide in Putumayo increased from 115 to 227.3 in 1991–97, far exceeding the 1997 national rate of 60. When Plan Colombia began in 2000, the homicide rate per 100,000 residents in Putumayo was 180.8 while the national rate was 63. As the plan got under way in 2001, the homicide rate in Putumayo decreased to 98.7, but rose again the next year to 182.7. Within Putumayo, the coca-producing municipalities of Valle del Guamués, San Miguel, and Puerto Asís had the highest rates of homicide mortality in 1991–2002.

The high rates of violent death in the coca-producing municipalities of Putumayo have largely been explained by the national and regional governments as phenomena associated with the coca economy. Thus, the departmental development plan for Putumayo stated that the coca economy is the cause of "the degradation of social values," the violent resolution of daily conflicts, and "the high homicide rate" (Government of Putumayo 1998, 16). Some examples of coca-related motives for homicide are the settling of accounts, the elimination of informants (*sapos* or "toads") by the drug traffickers' strong-arm groups, and the actions of organized crime groups only indirectly related to the drug trade. This assessment recognizes neither the involvement of the civilian population with armed groups in the region nor the alternatives proposed by an organized sector of society to lessen

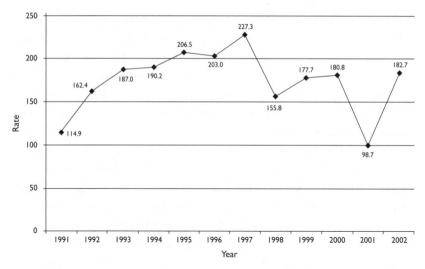

Figure 6. Mortality rate from homicide per 100,000 inhabitants, Putumayo, 1991–2002. (Putumayo Health Department, DASALUD)

the violence. The upturn in violence in Colombia as a whole, says Uprimny (1994, 96), did not have an "unambiguous association" with drug trafficking: "The fundamental problem of human rights in Colombia in recent years has much more to do with the so-called dirty war, the actions of paramilitary groups and death squads." He asserts that the paramilitary groups have acted with the acquiescence of the armed forces. These assertions are relevant to the case of Putumayo, whose inhabitants are labeled not only criminals and drug traffickers due to the illicit cultivation of coca but also "guerrilla collaborators," and therefore fall victim to state violence from both the armed forces and paramilitaries. In short, an excessive emphasis on linking coca cultivation and homicide rates has served to obscure the wave of political violence that followed the arrival of the paramilitaries, who were in large part responsible for the increased violence.

The Politics of Place: Spatial Identity, Stigmatization, and Contestation

Coca cultivation associated with armed non-state actors came to define not only the way the central state represented the Amazon region as a whole, but also the way local state officials and Putumayo inhabitants referred to their own internal differentiated spaces. To examine how the state has conceived of and defined the Amazon and how its inhabitants have responded to this definition, one must look at the "spatial framework" of the state in terms of Lefebvre (1991, 281): as a space within which power is centralized and from which sovereignty is proclaimed over a specifically delimited and defined territory. It is critical to keep this spatial framework in mind in light of the marginality ascribed by the state to this region. According to Lefebvre, the state first defines its area of sovereignty, then establishes spatial differentiations within it, for purposes of control and to set the terms of negotiation with subnational representatives. Finally, it defines a ranked hierarchy of internal spatial divisions, "from the loweliest places to the noblest, from the tabooed to the sovereign" (Lefebvre 1991, 282). Two aspects are important to understanding those spatial divisions. First, dialogue between local powers and the state inevitably results in "uneven and unequal development of social powers and regional spaces" as Roseberry (1994, 359–60) states, following Gramsci. Second, different identities are ascribed to these places, as Gupta and Ferguson (1997, 13) have pointed out:

> Identity and alterity are therefore produced simultaneously in the formation of "locality" and "community." Community is never simply the recognition of cultural similarity or social contiguity but a categorical identity that is premised on various forms of exclusion and constructions of otherness. . . . It is precisely through processes of exclusion and othering that both collective and individual subjects are formed. With respect to locality as well, at issue is not simply that one is located in a certain place but that the particular place is set apart from and opposed to other places.

Seen from the Colombian center, Amazonia is an internally homogeneous region, "the Other Colombia" according to the state, or "the New Colombia" in the discourse of FARC, reflecting its own presence and control. Moreover, it is a region dominated by international drug interests. A more careful examination, however, reveals internal spatial complexity both in the Amazon region and in Putumayo itself. Identities and meanings have been constructed, and ascribed to physical locations, throughout the region's history of colonization. The cocalero social movement emerged in places that had been historically and culturally constructed, not only by their inhabitants but by local, regional, and national perceptions, and mediated by localized hierarchical power relations. These socio-cultural constructions of the region were neither fixed nor presupposed. They changed over time despite certain structural continuities. Different social actors from both inside and outside these spaces confronted one another and engaged in power struggles over the construction or negotiation of identities.

As a result, Putumayo is anything but homogeneous. It is a richly varied and textured territory where subjective perceptions of identity associated with certain places determine social and political practices that imbue those places with particular meanings.[41] The internal spaces and places are hierarchically interconnected rather than naturally dissociated. This interconnection provides a starting point for the differentiation and transformation of spatial identities. Upper Putumayo is constructed in contraposition to Lower Putumayo reflecting historical variables and their respective indices of violence. These comparisons create the basis for their assignment to categories of "civilization" versus "barbarism" or "savagery."

Upper Putumayo comprises the municipalities of Santiago, Colón, San Francisco, and Sibundoy, all located in the Sibundoy Valley, where dairy farming and milk processing are the principal economic activities (see map 2). Historically the valley was the center of activity for Capuchin missionaries, who founded primary and secondary schools that still exist today. Thus the people of the Sibundoy Valley are the most educated in the department and the area is considered "civilized." People in the valley do not identify with the violence that characterizes Lower Putumayo since coca is not grown in Upper Putumayo and guerrillas are not based there. The same holds true for Mocoa, the departmental capital.

Like Mocoa, Villagarzón and Puerto Guzmán are in Middle Putumayo (see map 2). Mocoa and Villagarzón define themselves in contrast to those "violent and barbarous" places known to be dominated by coca. Mocoa was founded in 1780 and was also a center of missionary activity from which the Franciscans set off on expeditions into the Amazon jungle. Many Mocoans can trace their genealogy back to colonial times. They consider themselves natives of Putumayo, unlike the inhabitants of Lower Putumayo, whom they consider rootless migrants. Although coca is grown in Villagarzón, this municipality has a shared colonial history with Mocoa. In the regional imagination, coca and violence do not define these towns. They are considered "civilized" because of their colonial history.

Although it is in Middle Putumayo, Puerto Guzmán shares the characteristics of Lower Putumayo with Puerto Asís, Valle del Guamués, San Miguel, Puerto Caicedo, and Orito. These are coca growing municipalities and home to Fronts Forty-eight and Thirty-two of FARC (see maps 2 and 7). Among them, Puerto Asís, Valle del Guamués, and San Miguel were the most stigmatized as violent and coca-ridden. Orito, on the other hand, was associated with the oil industry. It is home to the regional administrative offices of Colombia's state oil company, ECOPETROL (Empresa Colombiana de Petróleos), and is not stigmatized as coca- or conflict-ridden. These perceptions, however, do not correspond to the area of coca actually under cultivation in the respective municipalities. At the beginning of 2000, Orito had ten thousand hectares of coca, while Puerto Asís had only five thousand. Nevertheless, when I was in Orito preparing to leave for Puerto Asís, virtually everyone I spoke to warned me about the violence there and told me to be careful.

When I mentioned my plans to go to Valle del Guamués, the warnings became dire, since this was considered the most violent area, said to be plagued by rampant "barbarism." As was discussed in chapter 1, the first drug traffickers arrived there in the 1980s to establish their base of operations. *Los Combos*, the first private strong-arm squad in the region, was also formed and began operations there. While it is true that more coca was being grown in Valle del Guamués than in other municipalities (twenty thousand hectares including those in nearby San Miguel), the municipality's reputation also suffered from the many stories woven around coca-driven violence. These stories not only weighed on the department's social memory and molded the identity of Valle de Guamués residents, but also obscured the reality of the political violence that intensified there after 1998.

The municipality of Puerto Leguízamo is somewhat distinct from the others. Like eastern Amazonia, it has a large indigenous population, and as a result inter-group relations are less strained. In addition, it has a military base that people in other municipalities of Lower Putumayo associate with the appearance of paramilitaries in the area. These characteristics distinguish Puerto Leguízamo from the rest of the region, and the military base has prevented significant activity in coca agriculture.

Various municipalities within Putumayo stand in political opposition to each other. Mocoa, for example, is the department's center for traditional Liberal and Conservative Party politics, while alternative political movements have emerged in Puerto Asís. Mocoa and Puerto Asís are also counterposed in that the former is an administrative center, the departmental capital, while the latter is the commercial center for the coca economy of Lower Putumayo. Mocoa's political monopoly was challenged in the 1990s when other municipalities were strengthened by political, fiscal and administrative decentralization. Municipalities such as Puerto Asís, Orito, Puerto Guzmán, Valle del Guamués, and San Miguel, spurred on by their mayors, joined forces to resist stigmatization as coca producers. Together they have resisted their definition by central and regional authorities as violent and lawless spaces, seeking to redefine themselves as sites of citizenship, democracy, and the promotion of peace. At one point, some Putumayan mayors even began to promote the department as a "Territory of Peace," a technique used in other areas of Colombia to assert a community's neutrality in the armed conflict. While I was doing fieldwork, the director of the Presidential Reintegration Program in Mocoa traveled from Puerto Leguízamo to Puerto Ospina in a Peace Caravan to publicize this idea across the department.

In sum, within Putumayo, different areas are seen by Putumayans and outsiders as tied to the coca economy to a greater or lesser degree. These representations generate a series of interrelations, discontinuities, and even confrontations between different areas and their populations. These social phenomena are important factors in the analysis of the territorial space and they will be referenced to the extent that they help us to understand why violence intensified in some places and not in others, why certain civic and social movements emerged or did not emerge in various places, and why local, regional, and national representation was achieved in some places and not in others (Routledge 1993, xv).

CHAPTER THREE

Turning Civic Movements into a Social Movement

Antecedents of the Cocalero Social Movement

The Putumayo cocalero social movement of 1996 was preceded by many civic movements from the 1970s through the early 1990s that made demands on the government for basic needs such as infrastructure, public services, health care, housing, and education. These demands were conveyed through the civic strike (*paro cívico*), a form of protest that emerges around the common demands—generally related to public services or regional development issues—of various social sectors. A civic strike partially or completely paralyzes an area economically in order to exert pressure on state authorities (Giraldo and Camargo 1978, 9). In the case of Putumayo, they were often followed by negotiations with those authorities.

Yet these movements must be seen as more than just demands for better living conditions. The emergence of civic strikes in Putumayo made its residents visible and reiterated to the ruling class and central government the condition of Putumayo as home to a marginal population, an "abandoned" zone that the "development" of the center had not reached, as evidenced by the lack of public services. In this sense, and from a historical perspective, these movements are conjunctural manifestations of a broad *social* movement centered around the demand that the Colombian nation-state recognize Putumayo residents' citizenship and rights. In the words of a department official recalling the Putumayo civic strikes:

> These social phenomena are due to and stem from the vacuum of traditional political leadership. If truth be told, this traditional leadership is oriented primarily to benefit individuals, interest groups, or parties, but with few exceptions there hasn't been representation in Congress or in the departmental or municipal governments that has taken the leadership to truly stimulate the development of the department. Confronting this vacuum and the innumerable problems they

face, the people have taken it upon themselves to organize civic movements that have resulted in very long strikes.[1]

This chapter examines the tendency of some of these local civic movements to become political movements independent of the traditional parties, to seek local and national representation and to make their presence felt at the time of elections. This tendency became much more visible after national reform in 1986, which brought administrative decentralization, the first-ever popular election of mayors, and the emergence of alternative political parties in the regions. The fact that a representative of the Putumayo Regional Civic Movement was elected head of Orito in 1996 gives us the opportunity to analyze a mayoralty that defined itself in contrast to the practices of the traditional political parties. The establishment of the Putumayo Municipal Association provides an opportunity to examine the relationships among Putumayo mayors and between them and the governor, developing the themes of decentralization, local state formation and the department's relationship to the central state. Finally, this chapter discusses the difficulty of maintaining alternative parties whose counter-hegemonic discourse is identified by outsiders with the guerrillas, subjecting them to delegitimization and persecution.

Civic Movements of the 1970s and 1980s

Two civic movements of the 1970s that ended with the burning of the Puerto Asís town hall and the Army's uprooting of the community are retained in the social memory of the people of Puerto Asís and Putumayo. They took place in January and December of 1974 to demand running water, sewers, and roads. During the second of the movements, transportation was blocked, all businesses were shut down for two weeks, and land was seized to build housing in a new barrio called "Salvador Allende," today one of the largest in Puerto Asís. "The repression of these movements was violent," a Colombian human rights NGO reported: "Colonel Rojas, the martial-law mayor, under instructions from the *Intendencia*, treated the protest as an insurrection and according to participant eyewitnesses, five town residents were killed that day" (Andean Commission of Jurists 1993, 25).

Several of the civic strikes in table 7 contributed to the emergence of the cocalero social movement and served as training grounds for its leaders-to-be. Of note are the June 1980 civic strike, the October 1981 mobilization,

Table 7. Collective social actions in Putumayo, 1980–96, including civic strikes, civic strikes with campesino participation, strike threats, campesino and civic mobilizations, civic takeovers, and presentations of petitions

	Action[a]	Municipalities
June 1, 1980	Civic strike with campesino participation	Puerto Asís
October 8, 1981	Campesino mobilization	Sibundoy, Colón, Santiago
October 3, 1982	Civic strike with campesino participation	Whole department
May 28, 1983	Presentation of petitions	Puerto Asís
January 21, 1984	Campesino mobilization	Puerto Asís
August 18, 1984	Civic mobilization and presentation of petitions	Puerto Asís
May 21, 1986	Civic mobilization and presentation of petitions	Whole department
January 25, 1991	Civic mobilization	Mocoa
September 26, 1992	Presentation of petitions	Huitoto Indian reserve
August 18, 1993	Civic takeover	Orito
September 2, 1993	Civic mobilization	Mocoa
January 19, 1994	Civic strike	Puerto Leguízamo
February 12, 1994	Civic takeover	Puerto Leguízamo
April 18, 1994	Civic strike	Puerto Leguízamo
November 18, 1994	Campesino mobilization	Puerto Asís
December 19, 1994 to January 8, 1995	Civic strike with campesino participation	Puerto Asís, El Tigre, San Miguel, La Dorada, Orito, La Hormiga, Puerto Leguízamo
November 20, 1995	Civic strike	La Hormiga
January 4, 1996	Campesino strike threat	La Hormiga, San Miguel

[a]CINEP's databases distinguish between civic strikes with campesino participation and urban civic strikes.

Note: A mobilization is a form of collective social action that lasts for a period of days or weeks in public spaces. It entails a combination of actions including marches, mass meetings, rallies, sit-ins, and other public demonstrations. It may coincide with a significant date that commemorates a notable past event (Archila et al. 2002, 261). A civic mobilization (*movilización cívica*) is a mobilization in the context of a civic strike. Both campesino mobilizations (*movilizaciones campesinas*) and campesino strikes (*paros campesinos*) generally involve travel by campesinos from their *veredas* into nearby town

Opposing Agency	Demands	Participants
National government	Public services, roads, health care	Campesinos
Departmental government	Public services	Campesinos
Departmental government	Public and social services, roads, credit, housing	Campesinos
Municipal government	Human rights, paramilitary presence	Campesinos
Departmental government	Credit, markets, roads, public services, education	Campesinos
National government	Markets, land, roads, public and social services	Campesinos
National government	Roads, social services	Campesinos
None	Killing of 7 people accused by Army of being FARC	Residents
National government	Ethnic rights	Indigenous people
Municipal government	Water, sewers	Residents
Municipal government	Water, electrical power	Civic movement members, residents
Municipal government	Water, electrical power	Councilors, teachers, Civic movement members, residents
Departmental government	Against removal of mayor	Residents
Municipal government	Against mismanagement, for public services	Councilors, teachers, residents
National government	Environmental: glyphosate	Campesinos, residents
National government, ECOPETROL	Environmental: Glyphosate, regional development, roads, peace, royalties, regional dialogue	Campesinos, residents
National government	Noncompliance with 1995 La Hormiga Accords	Residents
National government	Noncompliance with 1995 La Hormiga Accourds, Glyphosate, regional development	Campesinos

centers (*cascos urbanos*) for the purpose of presenting demands to government representatives. The town's usual activities may be suspended, forcing stores, schools, and government offices to either close or focus on the campesinos' demands. A civic takeover (*toma cívica*) refers to the peaceful occupation of public and/or private institutions in a town for a limited period of time (Archila et al. 2002, 261). The public presentation of petitions (*petitorios*) to government or private entities sometimes take place without accompanying protests, mobilizations, or strikes.

Source: Centro de Investigación y Educación Popular (CINEP), *Database of Campesino and Indigenous Struggle and Displacement 1980–1997*.

and especially the twenty-day civic strike in October 1982. This last strike is remembered in the region because all social sectors participated in its marches: the Church, teachers, students, businesses, the general population, and ECOPETROL workers through the oil workers' Unión Sindical Obrera (USO). This broad coalition demanded construction of the Mocoa-Pitalito highway, health care services and facilities, public services such as municipal electricity, credit, housing, and improved living conditions in general. They were given two generators from the Colombian Institute of Electric Power (ICEL), and they prompted the start of a Putumayo hydroelectric interconnection project.[2]

In early 1986, local leaders began to pull together to form a still-recalled civic movement, "a pluralist entity situated above party politics and fighting for adequate provision of public services and development of regional roads" (Andean Commission of Jurists 1993, 27). The movement began to garner support from leftist parties, civic and social organizations, and progressive individuals from the traditional parties. After the successful May 1986 mobilization and following the presentation of petitions, this civic movement showed clear signs of becoming a regional political alternative. In 1988, the movement formalized into a party named the "Popular Civic Movement of Putumayo" as a vehicle for political action.

The Civic Movement of the 1990s:
Predecessor to the Cocalero Social Movement

As was discussed in chapter 2, beginning in 1990 there was a significant increase in coca cultivation in the Western Amazon, and an increase in fumigation as part of the "war on drugs" financed by the United States. In January 1991, the National Narcotics Council (Consejo Nacional de Estupefacientes, CNE) authorized the use of the herbicide glyphosate in aerial spraying. In 1994, spraying in Guaviare was intensified and by November "Operation Termite," a fumigation program run by the National Police to eradicate coca, was in full swing.

People in the region took note when that same year, President Ernesto Samper stated in his inaugural address that there would not be a single coca plant left on Colombian territory when he completed his term. President Samper's reputation was badly damaged by evidence he had received drug money for his campaign, and he was under particular pressure internationally. By late 1994, Operation Resplandor, a program imposed on Colombia by the United States government, was under way. It was designed to eradicate illegal crops by means of chemical spraying, again targeting coca growers over the large marketing networks (ILSA, CINEP, and Revista Colombia Informa, 1995). The Samper government's determination to demonstrate its commitment to the anti-narcotics fight left no room for limitations on scale or exceptions to aerial spraying.

The same year, campesinos of Putumayo and Guaviare began to denounce the use of glyphosate, saying that it affected not only illegal crops but others as well, and that it was harmful to people. A local newspaper carried a front page story headlined, "It's Raining Glyphosate," informing its readers that the "glyphosate war" was intensifying, as "the government has announced that it will continue with eradication of illegal crops."[3]

There was little environmental regulation, protection or oversight of fumigation at this time, though Resolution 0001 of 1994 included several guidelines.[4] The Environmental Ministry proposed a regulation for "the establishment of environmental monitoring teams in every region of the country affected by narco-cultivation to ensure that the application of herbicide is done within the technical parameters and environmental conditions specified for these activities," but these teams were never used.[5] At the same time as the increased fumigation efforts, the government was preparing to launch a social investment program called the National Alternative Development Program (Programa Nacional de Desarrollo Alternativo, PLANTE). It was founded in October 1994 by the National Council for Social and Economic Policy (Consejo Nacional de Política Económica y Social, CONPES) to "use social investment to complement forced eradication campaigns in order to prevent, curb, and eliminate the growing of illegal crops." The program would be "limited to areas with a campesino economy, where projects are formulated and executed with community participation to create opportunities for legal income generation, improve quality of life, protect the environment, and promote ethical and cultural values conducive to social harmony" (CONPES Document 2734, 1994). Activities would begin in 1995, with eradication coming first, followed by gradual crop substitution. Although PLANTE was conceived in terms that earned the support of the local population, its application earned the sincere criticism of cocalero campesinos, as shall be seen below.

During a mobilization in Puerto Asís in November 1994, campesinos denounced the use of glysophate. The national government ignored them, instead taking the stance reflected in this newspaper article: "The civic strikes

Figure 7. Indigenous people and colono campesinos during the 1994 civic strike in Puerto Asís. (Jorge Parga, Casa Editorial, *El Tiempo*)

of the last few days in Miraflores and Puerto Asís were organized by drug traffickers and guerrillas working together." It explained that these organizations "were interested in preventing an attack on one of the most important fronts in the international narcotics trade." The director of the National Police "denied that the substitution of another substance for glyphosate was being considered in the campaign to eradicate illegal crops," and added that "the operations to destroy these plantings will not be suspended . . . The operations to destroy coca crops in Guaviare and Putumayo with glyphosate will be intensified in the month of January."[6]

In December 1994 and January 1995, over the Christmas and New Year's celebrations and traditional annual carnival, more than five thousand campesinos and indigenous people mobilized in a civic strike in Puerto Asís, Orito, San Miguel, and Valle del Guamués (La Hormiga) (Peñaranda 1996, 27). The campesinos protested fumigation and demanded implementation of the social investment plans developed by PLANTE and the Social Solidarity Network (Red de Solidaridad Social).[7] They also demanded projects in road-building, electrification, education, and health, which would be chosen by municipalities and funded by petroleum royalties. Most importantly, they demanded a peace process that would involve the population.

This December–January strike became national news, but whereas the local press had stressed the social problems behind coca cultivation, the national press had a different take. On November 22, 1994, Pasto's *Diario del Sur* ran the headline "Puerto Asís: Fumigation Cannot Eradicate Injustice," while in Bogotá, *El Tiempo* published an article titled, "Guerrillas Behind Strike in Putumayo."[8]

Strike leaders demanded that a national government commission come to La Hormiga to negotiate within forty-eight hours. When no government commission arrived by January 5, the strike continued. *El Tiempo* reported the torching of an ECOPETROL facility; blocked or closed highways including the main one from central Colombia to Mocoa; the 52 billion pesos (US$50 million) fiscal deficit; and a teachers' strike in Putumayo, all under the headline "Campesino Attack on ECOPETROL Complex in Putumayo." In short, it described utter chaos, closing with the subheading "Violence and Drug Trafficking" and this report:

> The roads that foreigners opened in this territory more than twenty years ago in a search for oil are clogged with brush. The people of these settlements expected these new roadways to rescue them from their oblivion, but they are waiting still. Abandonment is so familiar to the residents of Putumayo that they are convinced that they constitute a "huge environmental reserve." It is difficult to get to the region or to get out of it. Many give up on the idea when they consider the mudslides that block the highway almost daily. On other days of civic strikes the campesinos themselves come out to block traffic in the name of some demand. The only people who move freely are guerrillas and drug traffickers. In the roadless expanse, criminals have taken advantage freely of the contiguity of the two countries [Colombia and Ecuador] to avoid being brought to justice. . . . All its natural wealth, the beauty of its mountains and valleys, and its potential mineral wealth remain to be discovered. But Putumayo is considered a territory of misery, violence, and drug trafficking.[9]

The press describes the Putumayan population as accustomed to abandonment in a geographically and symbolically isolated region, where civic strikes only bring increased isolation as "the campesinos themselves" block entry into the zone. It feeds the image of an uncivilized region where drug traffickers and guerrillas find fertile ground for their lawless activities, utterly losing from view the people who were repeatedly asking the federal government to make its presence felt, seeking dialogue and *concertación* (cooperative effort).

On January 6, a Carnival day, Putumayo was still paralyzed by the civic strike. An article reported that when two hundred fifty soldiers approached the occupied ECOPETROL facility at Churuyaco in helicopters, "the demonstrators pulled out white handkerchiefs, sang the national anthem, and one of them threw a molotov cocktail. The flames and the fear that the oil tank would explode provoked a stampede of thousands of demonstrators."[10] There was significant discussion later among march leaders about who had thrown the Molotov cocktail, as it was not part of the plan, but it coincided nevertheless with a shift in the national approach to the situation: "The peaceful demands of the movement, its civic character, gave way to militarization of the conflict after the government sent a contingent of a thousand soldiers who cleared the demonstrators out of the oil facility, and after guerrillas shot down a fumigation helicopter and attacked the jail in Mocoa, freeing a number of campesinos detained when the demonstrators were driven from the oil installation" (Peñaranda 1996, 27).

The state's commitment to a repressive response was confirmed, legitimized by violence in the region and the presence of guerrillas, who were accused of being behind the strike. Minister of the Interior Horacio Serpa asserted that "campesino movements are part of the guerrillas' plan for destabilization" and exhorted the citizenry: "Don't let yourselves be manipulated or reduced to incivility and don't give any space to drug traffickers or subversives."[11] This discourse, centered on guerrillas and traffickers, left no room for the civic nature of the movement to be validated. Accordingly, the state's counteroffensive made no distinction between guerrillas and civilians. The guerrilla attack on the Mocoa jail was an isolated incident, but in the context of the civic strike it reinforced the armed forces' belief that the campesinos were insurgent allies, which justified their mobilization of counterinsurgency troops.

Meanwhile, the national government requested "normality" while it sent a commission to La Hormiga to negotiate the campesinos' set of demands. The commission met with the strike committee for four days and reached an agreement, thereafter known as the La Hormiga Accords, which "made a complete return to normality possible" (Ríos 1997, 29). José Noé Ríos, who chaired the commission, relates:

When we got to La Hormiga we found out that *dark forces* had informed the mayor that if the commission had not arrived by 2:00 p.m. he should leave the area. We were also informed that *intelligence had discovered that people other than the strike leaders had plans to commit terrorist acts that same day*. Our arrival immediately calmed the situation. I think that we were just what the situation called for and we were right on time. (Ríos 1997, 167–68; emphasis added)

Ríos evokes the images of terrorism and "dark forces" that have for so long informed the government's policy in the region, casting the commission as a civilizing, savior figure. Still, he recognized the civic essence of the strike, insisting that even though civic strikes are "usually fomented and frequently infiltrated by radical and insurgent forces . . . normally [they] have popular support and the support of the organized community" (Ríos 1997, 81).

The La Hormiga Accords obtained government commitment to infrastructure projects that had been demanded in previous strikes, including a Pasto–Mocoa electrical cable and the provision of electricity to La Hormiga, Orito, and La Dorada. They also laid out plans for an environmental feasibility study for an Orito–Monopamba highway, which would shorten the distance between Orito and Pasto from twelve hours to six hours. The Accords committed ECOPETROL to the payment of royalties, participation in community development programs, and help in maintaining the La Dorada–La Hormiga–Yarumo road. Finally, they provided for improved educational and health services in the towns involved in the strike. Regarding the issues of fumigation and alternative development programs, the Accords stated that eradication of illegal crops had to conform to Narcotics Council Resolution Number 0001 of 1994, which stipulates a procedure to protect traditional crops from glyphosate, and most importantly, restricts aerial spraying to coca crops of over two hectares.

Decentralization and Political Representation: Civic Movements as Political Movements

Before the 1968 Constitutional reform, political and administrative functions were highly centralized in Colombia. The reform maintained the overall political centralization but established measures for administrative decentralization, including the transfer of legal authority and resources to subnational entities (departments and municipalities) and revenue-sharing for health and education programs. The decentralization process intensified under President Belisario Betancur (1982–86). He established Regional Councils for Economic and Social Planning (Consejos Regionales de Planificación Económica y Social, CORPES) in 1985 to decentralize state investment (Huertas, Pressacco and Puente 2000) and made political changes to meet the demands of local and regional movements. Law 78 of 1986 established the popular election of mayors, who previously had been appointed by governors. This change was intended to open up new spaces for citizen participation, strengthen local institutions, and "guide the expanded participation" (Gaitán 1988, 63). These decentralization measures did in fact empower local and regional governments. The changes meant that "[Now] the people have their mayors and municipal councils as interlocutors and reference points of political power" (interview with Ballesteros, January 27, 1998).

Colombia took longer to decentralize at the departmental level, however. In the 1980s the Colombian Amazon was still made up of territorial subdivisions called *intendencias* and *comisarías*, administered by the central government's Ministry of the Interior and Justice until 1975, when an Administrative Department (Departamento Administrativo de Intendencias y Comisarías, DAINCO) was established for this purpose. At the local level these territories, including the intendencia of Putumayo, were managed by presidential appointees.

In 1991, a new constitution changed this panorama. Intendencias, dependent on the central government for all political and administrative matters, became departments, equal in status to all others. The transfer of administrative powers and resources to the departments was reinforced. Popular election of departmental governors was introduced. The new constitution also emphasized citizen participation as key to the success of decentralization. "Social participation became an essential mechanism for the public relationship between the state and society" (Restrepo 1995, 57). The legislation that followed the 1991 Constitution, such as Law 134 of 1994, established formal mechanisms for citizen participation including popular referenda, recall of elected officials, the Constituent Assembly plebiscites, and municipal hearings open to the public. These mechanisms would be used by the citizens of the new Department of Putumayo to express their demands on the state.

Parallel to first stages of decentralization, the administration of President Belisario Betancur was in negotiations with FARC. In 1984, the two sides signed the Uribe Accords, which were intended to lead to a cease-fire, truce, and eventual peace. This process led directly to the formation of a new political movement in March 1985 — the Patriotic Union (Unión Patriótica, UP). The UP was established by FARC and other leftist parties and movements, seeking "a democratic opening that will guarantee the right of an opposition movement" to engage in "popular participation in decision-making by the state" (FARC 1998c).

The UP garnered impressive results in the 1986 national election, gaining three senators, nine representatives, and a presence on 150 municipal councils. It was established as an important political force, especially in the country's least integrated departments (Gaitán and Ospina 1992, 132). The UP gained strength in Puerto Asís, while another leftist party, the Popular Front (Frente Popular), gained strength in Orito and in Valle del Guamués (Andean Commission of Jurists, 1993). Also in 1986, its first year of existence, the UP suffered a wave of assassinations that was unleashed nationwide. Three hundred of its members were killed that year in this dirty war.[12] Such killings were also directed at community leaders and campesinos involved in civic movements. In Putumayo the persecution extended to the Popular Civic Movement of Putumayo and to community leaders whom others associated with the left because their proposals diverged from those of the traditional parties (Andean Commission of Jurists 1993, 27).[13] The first popular election of mayors in Colombia took place in 1988, and two alternative party candidates were victorious in Putumayo: Alirio Romo Guevara of the Popular Integration Movement (Movimiento de Integración Popular) in Puerto Asís and Servio Tulio Garzón of the Popular Progressive Alliance (Alianza Popular Progresista) in Orito. These mayors represented political forces that had arisen largely in peripheral regions as a result of the continual civic movement activities since the 1970s. These parties' mere existence, let alone their electoral successes, enhanced Colombian democracy by changing the rules of the game in a country so long dominated by the two traditional parties. They also altered access to power, allowing members of civic and community organizations to participate directly in political decision-making without having to depend on a political patron or sponsor.

In the words of Patriotic Union leader Bernardo Jaramillo before his assassination in 1990: "I believe the direct election of mayors is the most important democratic gain that the people have won, because it has to do with this type of new democracy that we are proposing . . . Decentralization has enabled people to see a direct connection between the most mundane problems they are experiencing and our national problems" (Harnecker 1989, 89–90).

A regional civic leader commented on civic movements' conversion into political movements and the struggle of these movements to maintain independence vis-à-vis the traditional Liberal and Conservative parties:

> After the strike of 1982 a political movement was organized in 1986. In 1988 this movement [the Popular Civic Movement of Putumayo party] won several seats on the Municipal Council and Intendancy Council [now the Departmental Assembly]. I myself was here [in Mocoa] heading a list of candidates and we won two seats and I became president of the Municipal Council. In [the 1982] strike we didn't have an organization with political goals, strictly civic. But afterwards the people said, "Man, we struggle here for stuff but when the elections come, the same faces always show up to make the decisions and take the powerful positions. So let's participate." The party grew after that, but we saw that maybe alone we wouldn't grow much, so for the '90 elections we made the Popular Convergence coalition and won a seat in the House, with Liberal support. Some of the Patriotic Union leaders who were in the Civic Movement didn't like the Convergence because it had that Liberal sector, so they split off . . . and formed another political movement, Campesino Unity [Movimiento Unidad Campesina] in 1990. They continued their political work as Campesino Unity and won several mayoralties and council seats.[14]

The organization of alternative parties reflected a push-and-pull relationship with the Liberals and Conservatives, and also delineated different geopolitical spaces within Putumayo. Luz Angela Flórez, a 1986 civic mobilizations' leader, and a member of Mocoa's political class, who opposed the Conservative and Liberal parties, was elected to the Intendency Council in 1988 and ran unsuccessfully for mayor of Mocoa in 1990. In October 1994, a representative of the Campesino Unity Movement, Jairo de Jesús Casanova, was elected mayor in this party's cradle and stronghold, Puerto Guzmán. The New Colombia candidate, Miguel Ángel Rubio, became mayor of Puerto Leguízamo. Ramiro Grisales, a campesino colono leader, native of Puerto Guzmán and member of the Popular Civic Movement of Putumayo party, was elected to the departmental Assembly as a UP candidate that same year. In 1996 he became part of the Campesino Unity Movement in Puerto Guzmán and later helped lead the cocalero social movement. In Orito in 1996, the locally organized Orito Civic Movement and Putumayo Regional Civic Movement succeeded at electing Luis Alfredo Urbano as mayor to replace Conservative Wilson Antonio Robles, who had been stripped of his office for corruption.

Other mayoral and council candidates switched from being Liberal or Conservative to represent these new parties, and later switched back. Former Puerto Asís mayor Romo Guevara, for example, became a Liberal Party candidate for the Departmental Assembly for the October 1997 elections. In Mocoa too, which has a reputation among community leaders for being dominated by traditional parties and opportunistic political maneuvering (*politiquería*), an alternative party was formed in 1994. The Putumayan Community Bloc (Bloque Comunitario Putumayense) won a seat on the Municipal Council but lost its bid for the Departmental Assembly. This movement began to lose strength and ended up playing coalition politics with the traditional parties in Mocoa.[15]

This tension between building and maintaining an autonomous alternative political party that represents the region's people, and the tendency to establish coalitions with the traditional parties in hopes of attracting more voters, is a structural characteristic of politics in the region. Inherited loyalties to Liberals or Conservatives and the dominant clientelism are inescapable structural pressures. These are reinforced by the persecution political leaders receive when they identify with a more broadly representative alternative, becoming associated in consequence with the Communist Party and FARC. The conformation of a "political field of struggle" (Bourdieu 1994) between different ideological forces is distorted by the violent exclusion of parties that seek to promote interests beyond the status quo.

Former Puerto Leguízamo mayor Miguel Angel Rubio commented on the origins and repression of some of Putumayo's alternative political movements:

> At first we operated as the Patriotic Union on a departmental level, with two council members in Puerto Leguízamo, seats that we held until the year 1991. In 1992 the repression became so suffocating that that had to change. For example, in Puerto Asís and Puerto Guzmán we couldn't participate as the Patriotic Union, so we participated as the Campesino Unity Movement. The Civic Movement is new, because there had been civic movements before, but the one with our goals [the Putumayo Regional Civic Movement] started at the end of 1994

and beginning of 1995. This situation isn't unusual for the traditional parties; they know that although the name is different, the ideas are the same. That's why there has been trouble.[16]

Local leaders depended upon a political culture of resistance to counter the traditional parties' domination through exclusionary practices, clientelism, and political machinery. This culture of resistance became a counter-ideology and was condemned and repressed as such by elite forces. Political positions are subjective, articulated contingently in an attempt to construct political and ideological hegemony, yet subject to the ambiguity and antagonism of social and political practice in the department. Actors may be Liberal, Conservative, or independent depending on conjunctural demands, and may assume different political positions for different electoral periods, or simply to survive.

The work of civic movements striving to become political organizations to represent the regional population's interests has been translated into social practice, confirming that "the political is one of the possible forms of existence of the social" (Laclau and Mouffe 1985, 29). Thus we have been able to observe the emergence of a new social movement in the Western Amazon—civic movements that open diverse political spaces, generate multiple demands, and question the traditional political parties, all while seeking the recognition and power necessary to intervene in the hegemonic discourse of the central state.

The Case of the Mayor of Orito

Luis Alfredo Urbano, a local strike leader and member of the Orito and Putumayo Regional Civic Movements, was elected municipal councilor in Orito in 1994 and mayor in June 1996. One of the mayor's distinguishing characteristics was his fifth-grade education. Formal education, though highly valued, is not easily accessible in the region. Mayor Urbano, who described himself as "a campesino and a victim of the lack of educational opportunity," was a good example of this reality. In a published interview he stated that "I didn't want to be mayor because I haven't studied. I didn't have the opportunity to go to school and learn municipal administration" (*From the Fields to City Hall: A* Campesino *Who Became Mayor of Orito without Wanting To*; interview by L. Ramírez in *Así es*, 1998). Locals know that a lack of education can lead to poor administrative practices, which is the reason new municipal officials often request training in terminology and procedures of both the central government and development agencies. Mayor Urbano's administration focused on education, he said, and he "spared no effort to ensure that teachers were always paid and that the town's children could have the opportunities that I didn't get" (interview in *Así es* by L.Ramírez, 1998). A political actor whose experience was garnered from his leadership in civic movements, Mayor Urbano challenged the political representativeness of the traditional parties, party-based continuity, and the prerequisite of formal education, i.e. cultural capital. He was elected instead because he possessed political capital, founded in his reputation and credibility with the population (Bourdieu 1994, 92).

Upon his election Urbano declared that "[My] administration will be based on the demand that the national government comply with the agreements reached as a result of the past civic strike [La Hormiga Accords]." He argued that Orito could make progress on this basis, since he was committed to the people and would provide the community with resources that other politicians had used for their own personal gain.[17] Early in his term, Urbano commented on his position with regard to the traditional parties:

> People say that we haven't done anything because we don't have the support of the politicians. But to tell you and everyone the truth, we've made a lot of progress with projects in many veredas, and that's good for me and for the Orito Civic Movement. . . . As a result of many broken promises we've learned that the community must help with the execution and supervision of projects, and that whoever manages the funds has to make them pay off. They can't be stealing them. This proves once again that we don't need political bosses to do what needs to be done. (Interview in *Así es* by L. Ramírez, 1998)

Urbano and the civic movements he was part of defied the hegemonic political culture of clientelism by performing governmental functions with community collaboration rather than the help of a national-level political party, patron, or established machinery. Despite this independence and his political capital inside Putumayo, however, the Mayor lacked the traditional cultural capital he needed to compete within the political and legislative machinery beyond his region. This factor and his limited education forced him to hire a Liberal politician as his advisor, a man who had participated in monitoring for the implementation of the 1995 La Hormiga Accords. The advisor took advantage of the Mayor's confidence to engage in the kind of corruption endemic to Putumayan politics, such as forging Urbano's signature to steal funds earmarked for the purchase of several generators. As a result, Urbano was jailed.[18]

One civic leader referred to the persistent political clientelism as a key political structure in the region when he described how the guerrillas, another important external factor for local mayors, sometimes boycott elections: "Here there is an old politics of clientelism and people vote for whatever might offer them something. It's difficult for other political proposals, and above all, people who might have a tendency to vote don't do so because in some zones the guerrillas don't let people vote. So the people who have economic power, political power, always win."[19]

Indeed, guerrillas in these regions do exert significant pressure in various forms on local politics. They monitor mayors to prevent deficient or corrupt administration and are known to punish offenders. They frequently demand 10 percent of the municipal budget as a *vacuna* (literally "innoculation," or protection money). When this happens, mayors feel that they have no choice but to embezzle and turn over these funds, making the town the ultimate loser. FARC has expressed theoretical support for decentralization and the popular election of mayors:

> It is precisely by reversing the direction of local administration that this enormous machinery of clientelism and corruption protected by impunity can be dismantled from the bottom up. . . . Local power is the exercise of positive freedom, consecrated as participation in the 1991 Constitution. . . . In other words, that the people participate in the ideal of the general good, in the administration of the city, neighborhood, town, vereda, or corregimiento, exercising power for the common interest. . . . Local government should provide appropriate mechanisms for the election of the best and most honorable individuals to administrative positions, people who will govern in defense of the common good. (FARC 1998a)

Yet FARC hinders the people's ability to elect the best public servants when they boycott elections (prioritizing instead their military-strategic position) and threaten, tax, and pressure mayors. Representatives of the Colombian Federation of Mayors met with FARC Commander Marulanda in La Machaca in May 1997 and told him that despite their neutrality in the conflict, they had been unfairly accused by both guerrillas and paramilitaries. Marulanda responded, "Mayors can't remain on the sidelines because paramilitarism is a problem for the state. . . . They cannot be neutral when faced with these

murders and massacres. They should condemn and pursue these groups."[20]
Although FARC's Marxist discourse indicates support for the struggles of the
oppressed classes, it does not in practice support political alternatives that
emerge from the population.

The national press had its own take on FARC's relationship to local
mayors. In a May 1997 article titled *The Guerrillas' Mayors*, the news weekly
Semana reproduced a military intelligence document indicating that 138
mayors including those of Puerto Guzmán, Orito, Puerto Asís, Puerto Caicedo, and Puerto Leguízamo were working directly with guerrillas.[21] Despite
regular interaction with local mayors in the areas under their influence, the
guerrillas have not in reality made life easier for these leaders: FARC's mixed
message lauds them one day as representatives of the people and condemns them the next as representatives of the central government. In Mayor
Urbano's case, "working" with FARC took on the following form on one occa-
sion: the guerrillas held him and his administrative aide for twenty-two days
for alleged mismanagement of funds. "Once we were detained, they told us
that we had a lot to answer for in terms of squandering and accounting for
public money. I said that I would respond because I needed to clear everything up." The mayor suspected that his political enemies were behind this
detention: "We've always had people who want to sully the image of the administration. They act hypocritically, making accusations against us so the
guerrillas will think that we're corrupt paramilitary collaborators while leading the army and government to believe that we're guerrillas or guerrilla collaborators. None of it is true. We have our own ideas and we know very well
that we are bringing changes with a true Christian spirit and nothing else"
(interview in *Así es* by L. Ramírez, 1998).

The larger context of the conflict between paramilitaries and guerrillas
amplifies the power of rumor and gossip in the region, changing the nature
of daily communication. Because armed groups in the region use local informants to maintain control, it is easy for a person to finger a personal
enemy as a "collaborator" by going to the guerrillas or army and providing
information, true or not, that will damage them. Mayor Urbano continued:
"Now that we've been released there are new rumors. Some say that it was
a staged kidnapping, and according to others we went to get guerrilla training. I'm sure that if people spent their time doing useful things instead of
inventing these stories, there would be more business in the municipality
and there would be more jobs for people developing the region" (Interview
in *Así es*, by L. Ramírez 1998).

In another example, former-Mayor Rubio of Puerto Leguízamo describes

how personal conflicts and political rivalries are routinely resolved by manipulation of the official oversight agencies and armed actors:

> I don't think that Putumayo's problem is so much the guerrillas or the
> paramilitaries. The problem is the political opposition that tries to get
> the other guy out at whatever cost. So one of the weapons they use is if
> they can't get at someone through the Comptroller's office, if they are
> conniving, and if they can't get them through the Prosecutor and all
> those agencies that can be used to harass them, then they try to con-
> nect them with one of the actors in the conflict and I can tell you this
> from experience. They accuse me of being a guerrilla so I have prob-
> lems with the paramilitaries, and they accused the mayor of Valle del
> Guamués of being a paramilitary, so he had problems with the guer-
> rillas. As far as I know and can tell, in both cases it's false.[22]

In sum, the change to popular election of mayors brought with it far
greater access to power for the local population. Yet this access has come
with costs. As Mayor Rubio pointed out, any mayor in Putumayo has a really
serious problem: he is the enemy of the army, the guerrillas, *and* the paramilitaries. The change has also produced new local practices in dialogue
with the armed conflict—practices which mediate all social and political relations in the region.

The Municipal Association of Putumayo

Faced with the situation described above and wanting to have a voice at the
central level, the thirteen Putumayo mayors of the 1995–98 term formed
the Municipal Association of Putumayo in March 1996, "to lobby the central
government for large regional development projects that would bring economic and social benefits to the region, which has been ignored by national
administrations as they come and go."[23]

Like Luis Alfredo Urbano, these mayors did not consider themselves
to be like other politicians who "come and go" without discernable effect,
but rather they felt untainted by the political practices of previous mayors.
This self-image reflected a loyalty to the people who had elected them over
any political party, a change consistent with the still relatively new popular
election of mayors. They promised to lobby the state directly for development projects without political or clientelist intermediation. In the words
of Mayor Rubio: "We founded the Association because there are regional

projects that someone should present, that someone should follow up on, that someone should be shepherding through the bureaucracy."[24]

After the founding of the Association, it was largely inactive for the remainder of the 1995–98 term because of other demands on the mayors' time and because of the difficulty of bringing together the diverse agendas of Upper, Middle, and Lower Putumayo. When the mayors all left office in April 1998 (due to term limits), they were able to dedicate time to reviving the Municipal Association. This second effort was led by the Lower Putumayo mayors (Puerto Leguízamo, Valle del Guamués, Puerto Caicedo, Puerto Asís, Orito, San Miguel, and Puerto Guzmán) with the participation of the mayor of Villa Garzón in Middle Putumayo. Mocoa's mayor had to withdraw from his initial participation due to accusations of pursuing personal interests and ignoring the Association's policies. The Upper Putumayo mayors (Santiago, Sibundoy, Colón, and San Francisco) were invited to participate, but declined. In keeping with the historical differences between Upper and Lower Putumayo, the Association's director explained that these areas are "culturally different."[25] Contrasts among different geographical and cultural spaces within Putumayo once again emerged, challenging the construction of the regional identity sought by the mayors. Mocoa's civic movement was also aloof from the Regional Civic Movement because it did not identify with the regional focus.

Without Mocoa, the Municipal Association included eight municipalities, towns that shared a common cultural identity and political agenda. Coca was grown in all of them, a fact that fundamentally marked their identity in contrast to Mocoa, Upper Putumayo, and the Colombian center (which viewed them with skepticism for this same reason). In the words of a Mocoa resident: "Mocoa officials don't acknowledge coca as a local problem, though this city has indirectly benefited from it. Mocoa can't claim to be clean. That's the hypocrisy of our city. Mocoa's history rests on a traditional veneer but only in appearances. At heart they are libertines and they will live off whatever they can. Still, there's a cultural clash with Puerto Asís."[26]

By banding together, the mayors of Lower Putumayo achieved a counterhegemonic discourse opposing the national hegemony, negotiating directly with state bodies like PLANTE without the mediation of old-style, revolving-door politicians. They opened an office in Bogotá, establishing an ongoing visible presence in the national capital that became a symbol of their insistence on recognition as legitimate, popularly elected public officials and

Colombians with citizenship rights. After two years of work the Putumayo governor and national senators and representatives began to sense that the Municipal Association was slipping out of their political control. The Association's direct dialogue with the central government cast doubt on the governor's relevance and his commitment to the region. Indeed, the Association did not consider the politicians elected to national Congress from Putumayo to represent them. Likewise, it saw the governor of Putumayo as an "other" in opposition to whom it defined its own political identity.

Implementation of the La Hormiga Accords: PLANTE, the Putumayo Regional Civic Movement, and the Lead-up to the 1996 Cocalero Marches

The La Hormiga Accords of January 1995 established a commission to monitor implementation of the commitments it contained. This La Hormiga Accords Monitoring Commission, composed of four community and four national government representatives (plus alternates), first met in Orito in late February 1995. The civic strike's leaders continued their work at this meeting, during which the governor of Putumayo and the mayors of San Miguel, Orito, and La Hormiga also joined the Commission. Around this same time, the Civic Movements of Orito, Puerto Asís, Puerto Leguízamo, and the Campesino Unity Movement of Puerto Guzmán joined forces with the Putumayo Regional Civic Movement to fight fumigation on a united front. One of problems these groups had throughout the monitoring process was with the implementation of the PLANTE program. Created amidst the war on drugs, PLANTE was oriented toward eradication as a precondition for alternative development programs. It initially focused on towns and veredas "that don't plant illegal crops as part of a broader production system . . . commercial growers of illegal crops are excluded."[27] PLANTE's first director was Héctor Moreno Reyes, who promoted punishment of the small coca producer throughout his tenure. In his words, "Illegal crops are not legal, no matter what their size . . . although they argue that poverty is the fundamental factor that explains why campesinos participate in illegal cultivation" (Moreno Reyes 1997). To accept this explanation, argued Moreno Reyes, would mean accepting that the end justifies the means. "Drug trafficking is caused by greed," he said, "which also affects the campesino." Although Moreno Reyes said that only marketing and processing, not production, would be penalized, he also insisted that "The concept of gradualism in eradication of illegal crops does not exist in Colombian alternative development policy," and that "only when the campesino, indigenous person, or colono has abandoned his participation in growing crops will it be possible for him to have access to PLANTE benefits." He maintained that glyphosate, rather than those who process coca, had been demonized.[28]

One of the PLANTE benefits was supposed to be access to credit for campesinos through the Caja Agraria (Agrarian Bank). While PLANTE announced that in 1995 it released "366 million pesos [US$350,239] in credits to small producers linked to agro-industrial production whether or not they grew illegal crops," an article six months later told a different story: "PLANTE? We're still waiting: campesinos say no help yet."[29] The latter article concluded, "It seems that the state has little or no interest in Putumayo. The poverty and needs get worse with every passing day."[30] Campesinos complained of the endless red tape and requirements of the Caja Agraria, including land titles and cosigners, which many of them lacked. Most people who received credit were not involved directly in coca growing. At one point in Puerto Asís, residents were saying that the loans had been granted to purchase taxis in urban areas. According to one PLANTE worker, the failure of the Caja Agraria credit program was due to "the lack of community involvement." He explained:

> If PLANTE had done things right, the credits wouldn't have been given to just anybody, but only through Municipal Rural Development Councils [Consejos Municipales de Desarrollo Rural, CMDRs] or Campesino Associations. . . . First require them to organize, to get together and propose a productive project. . . . Either with the CMDR approving the projects or with the loans given to campesinos known to participate in community life, who act as citizens, who are involved in collective processes. If it had been like that, then things wouldn't have ended up like they are now.[31]

PLANTE's success was also sabotaged by corruption and cronyism. Local government officials, in keeping with the clientelist culture in the region, diverted funds intended to finance crop substitution for their own benefit or to people not engaged in coca growing. Such corruption is fed by the generalized feeling of abandonment by the state: when state funds *do* show up in the region, it is seen as a fleeting opportunity to be taken advantage of, leading to diversion of the resources and distortion of policy. Moreno Reyes himself saw this tension between central and local government officials as one of the reasons for PLANTE's shortcomings: "Some government officials, despite the efforts of the president, [have] not want[ed] to fulfill their responsibilities to the initiative" and explained that "almost 70 million pesos [US$66,985] never reached their intended recipients. The campesinos ended up with nothing because some state officials decided to use the money for other purposes with no concern for the needs of the rural population and with no regard for the state's objectives."[32]

Moreno Reyes's positions and priorities for PLANTE angered campesino cocaleros. In a letter from the leaders of the Putumayo Regional Civic Movement to President Samper on December 26, 1995, they informed him that the Movement "was organizing and preparing for a second strike and of course in solidarity with other departments." The reasons they listed for taking this step were displeasure over noncompliance with the La Hormiga Accords, fumigation, a lack of respect for the people's sovereignty, raids on campesino dwellings and lands, damage to the Amazonian environment ("the lungs of the world"), death threats against movement leaders, and PLANTE's noncompliance with the CONPES document and Narcotics Council Resolution 0001 of 1994. Tensions between PLANTE and the Monitoring Commission and Putumayo Regional Civic Movement reached a boiling point by early 1996. At a January meeting in Mocoa with representatives of the Ministries of Interior, Education, Health, and National Planning, the National Institute of Highways, and the Colombian Institute of Electric Energy (Instituto Colombiano de Energía Eléctrica, ICEL), the Monitoring Committee took an inventory of the projects completed in Putumayo one year after the La Hormiga strike. Displeased with the results, the Commission requested that the agreements regarding regional infrastructure improvements not be forgotten. It stressed the need to optimize PLANTE programs requesting "more clarity with respect to its benefits, conditions, and total value for each campesino or colono who decides to stop working with illegal crops" as well as a designated person at each Caja Agraria office to provide information on PLANTE.[33]

Comments by Moreno Reyes that month in *El Tiempo*, under the headline "Dark forces behind Putumayo Strike," also angered local leaders: "According to the director of PLANTE, 'Small rural producers would strike under pressure from guerrillas and drug traffickers,' and the Commission members did not really represent the people since they 'are not campesinos; one of them is a lawyer and another is a teacher.'"[34] Moreno Reyes delegitimized the lawyer and teacher as mediators between the campesino movement and central authorities, because as "peasant intellectuals" (Feierman 1990) they diverged from the stereotype of colonos as poor uneducated campesinos. In addition, he linked strike leaders to guerrillas and drug traffickers with statements that put them in danger of army repression. (Strike leaders José Portilla and Colombia Rodríguez were subsequently murdered, in January and February of 1996, respectively.) On March 22, the Commission sent Moreno Reyes a letter informing him that they had unanimously decided to break off dialogue with PLANTE.

Government fumigation plans continued undeterred, however, and on March 30 the television news program *TV Hoy* announced that Putumayo would be sprayed with glyphosate. Organization for a second strike continued, since to the campesino cocaleros it seemed that a strike was the only way for their voices to be heard, their demands met, and their situation recognized by the central government. A correspondent reported in the local newspaper *La Nación*: "After hearing news [of the spraying], residents and colonos of San Miguel are indignant and in a state of alert for a regional strike. The great majority of them depend on illegal crops. The Association of Community Action Committees indicated that they would not allow a single hectare to be sprayed."[35] The article reported the opinion of the Municipal *Personero* (Ombudsman) of San Miguel, Carlos Virgilio Castro, who said that a second regional strike would do irreparable damage to merchants and haulers and to oil drilling, since equipment and wells were potential targets of the strike. Moreover he called attention to the question of law and order, stating that it would be even more serious, since guerrillas based in the area would take advantage of the situation. Castro called upon the central government to provide a prompt solution to the pressing problems, particularly with regard to the La Hormiga Accords.[36]

At this juncture, the fragmentation of the national government was clearly visible. The regional prosecutor recognized the campesinos as the agents of the strike, with the guerrillas based in the area potentially "taking advantage" of the situation, while Hector Moreno Reyes and others in the center characterized the strike movement as a result of pressure from guerrillas and drug traffickers. Ultimately, in the face of a publicly looming strike, the central government decided to continue with repressive strategies, delaying distribution of PLANTE resources and further promoting aerial spraying.

CHAPTER FOUR

The Cocalero Social Movement

Stigmatization and the Politics of Recognition and Identity

The ubiquity of FARC in Putumayan daily life was a key aspect in the organization and unfolding of the cocalero movement. This chapter begins by describing the factors that led to the cocalero marches themselves, mobilizations that began in the veredas and moved on to occupy the urban centers for over a month. It also analyzes the relations between FARC, the leaders of Community Action Committees (Juntas de Acción Comunal or JACS, the basic entities of social organization in rural areas at the community and vereda levels) and the cocalero social movement leaders, in order to understand how these networks made the movement and the negotiating power of the population possible despite FARC's authoritarianism.[1]

In addition, this chapter examines the emergence of a collective identity (Melucci 1988; Laclau and Mouffe 1985) linked to the cocalero campesinos' collective action in pursuit of their recognition as social actors. This examination comprises two central arguments. First, the longstanding historical construction of marginality in Amazonia is used to justify and legitimize repressive state policies in the region. The military's actions and discourse, analyzed in this chapter, make the hegemonic perception of this marginal and excluded "other" quite evident. The refusal of the state to include cocalero campesinos in its polity was what most galvanized their movement. The campesino cocaleros' rejection of their own exclusion catapulted the emergence of a cocalero identity and social movement, making it clear that localized responses to the hegemonic state are shaped by the extent to which the people in those locations contest or resist its authority and ascribed meanings (Gramsci [1944] 1992; Roseberry 1994).

Second, the cocalero colonos in Putumayo and the Western Amazon deployed a "politics of recognition" (Taylor 1995) throughout the preparations, actions, and aftermath of the 1996 uprising. They contested their stigmatization as illegal actors and temporary migrants in search of easy money.[2]

Instead, the cocalero campesinos defined and presented themselves as Colombian citizens, internal migrants (colonos) seeking to work and improve their standard of living, who were at the same time residents of Putumayo, Caquetá, and Guaviare.

I argue that the notion of citizenship mediates the paradoxes within the cocalero movement, which derives its identity not from its opposition to the state but from the social and political exclusion of its members *by* that state.[3] The state's misrecognition (Taylor 1995) and abandonment of the campesino cocaleros were therefore important precursors to the identity formed through the cocalero social movement.

Finally, it is important to point out that the construction of the colono/cocalero campesinos' collective identity was affected not only by the identity ascribed to them by broader society, but also by the identities ascribed to them by other social groups within the region. The analysis in this chapter makes it clear that spatial categories affect the articulation of identity, concretely in relation to those meanings ascribed to rural and urban spaces within regions.

Conditions Leading to the Launch of the 1996 Cocalero Marches

In late 1995 the Samper administration was engaged in a frontal assault on drugs, the effects of which were felt in Putumayo immediately. Deep dissatisfaction with PLANTE among campesinos and government noncompliance with other parts of the La Hormiga Accords meant that planning for another strike was gaining momentum.[4] The government, meanwhile, continued down a road that would virtually guarantee this strike would in fact take place, and with more popular support than ever.

Since 1987, the National Narcotics Council (Consejo Nacional de Estupefacientes, CNE) had regulated the production, distribution, transport, and use of chemical products used in the processing of coca. These chemical precursors were acetone, chloroform, ethyl ether, hydrochloric acid, toluene, acetic anhydride, urea, diesel fuel, and kerosene. In its May 13, 1996 Resolution Number 0001, the CNE put new limits on the sale of gasoline and cement, the two main precursors to coca paste, in Guaviare, Caquetá, Putumayo, Vaupés, Vichada, and Meta. Registration was required for any sale of cement exceeding 600 kilos or gasoline exceeding 220 gallons. Also, a sales receipt and registration document were required to enter Putumayo with said quantities of these products. In June 1996, five municipalities in

Putumayo—Puerto Asís, Valle del Guamués, San Miguel, Orito, and Puerto Caicedo—were subjected to strict surveillance and control by police and national army officials, upsetting their populations.

The effects of Resolution 0001 of 1996 were immediately felt in the western Amazon. The construction sector was hurt and municipalities saw reduced tax receipts from the sale of gasoline, normally a major source of municipal income. Moreover, gasoline and cement prices nearly tripled. The governor asked the central government to make an exception on cement, arguing that it was needed to build schools and health centers, but the request was ignored.[5] Small coca producers were affected the most. Unlike drug traffickers, they lacked the resources to obtain gas and cement by bribing public officials. To a significant extent, the economic hardship caused by this regulation sparked the outbreak of the cocalero social movement.[6]

On the same day and at the request of military leadership, President Samper designated all municipalities in Guaviare, Vaupés, Meta, Vichada, and Caquetá as special law enforcement zones due to the "criminal and terrorist organizations . . . undermin[ing] public safety and harmony" in the region (Decree 0871 of May 13, 1996). This designation triggered curfews, checkpoints, and restrictions on movement (Decree 0717 of April 18, 1996).

Even though Putumayo was not declared a special law enforcement zone, people in the area believed that it had been. The fact that Putumayo shared the same problems as the other departments, and its contiguity with those departments, established a metonymic relationship that convinced Putumayo residents they were subject to the law. In my fieldwork, every person asked whether Putumayo had been declared a special law enforcement zone answered affirmatively. The municipal councilors of Caquetá began a campaign of "NO to Special Law Enforcement Zones and YES to Special Social Investment Zones," sending the message that, faced with the repressive actions of the state, the people of the region would mobilize and express their needs.[7]

Meanwhile, two new military operations, Plan Condor and Operation Conquest, were under way. As explained by the President in July 1996: "Plan Condor was intended to destroy crops and laboratories, seize chemical precursors and interdict commerce. . . . In the development of this plan through the month of June this year, we have confiscated three times more drugs and twenty-five times the amount of precursors. We have destroyed twice the amount of crops. The operation has cost drug traffickers about 400 million U.S. dollars." He described Operation Conquest:

This is the most important anti-narcotics operation carried out in the world. We seek to destroy more than 27,000 hectares of coca, which is 70 percent of the coca cultivated in Colombia and approximately 15 percent of the world total. The Armed Forces and Police will carry out an anti-narcotics operation in an area of Guaviare where nearly 60 percent of the illegal crops in Colombia can be found. About 3,000 Army, Navy, Air Force, and Police personnel will participate. Our goal is to begin a series of massive cleanup operations in order to sweep drug trafficking out of strategically located zones. This operation combines vital elements such as intelligence, communications, and rapid response capability.[8]

President Samper continued, "We are spending almost a billion dollars annually on this struggle, of which we receive less than 15 percent in foreign assistance. When it comes to the fight against drug trafficking we respond only to the pressure of our own convictions." Addressing the campesinos, he said "We are counting on you to continue forward. Welcome to Condor and Conquest."[9] It was evident from the president's comments that he was ignoring the concerns expressed over the previous year and a half by campesinos regarding the serious shortcomings of the PLANTE program and the fumigation of their crops. He maintained that the anti-narcotics fight was unrelated to pressure from the United States.[10]

At an international seminar on illegal crops held the previous year in Bogotá, campesinos from Guaviare, Putumayo, and Caquetá had agreed to mount coordinated demonstrations if fumigation were initiated in any one of those three departments. The launch of Operation Conquest in Guaviare triggered a campesino march on July 15 of 1996 to protest the special law enforcement zone, the widespread fumigation, and related army abuses.[11] In turn, support marches were begun in Putumayo on July 25 and 26, 1996, near the towns of Orito, La Dorada, La Hormiga, and Puerto Asís. In Caquetá, where the anti-narcotics police began fumigation in Remolino del Caguán on July 22, marches were held a week later.[12] Likewise, in the Baja Bota of Cauca, marches to Miraflor and the neighboring department of Caquetá began on August 4.

La Nación reported the marchers' arrival in Santuario, Caquetá:

Five Thousand Campesinos in Santuario. The inspectorate of Santuario on the Florencia-Montañita highway was transformed overnight. Its usual tranquility gave way to the presence of thousands of

Figure 8. Cocaleros' strike in Guaviare. The poster says, "In solidarity with Guavare. Putumayo: We're here. Caquetá: We're here. Huila: We're here. Cauca: We're here." (León Darío Peláez, Casa Editorial, *El Tiempo*)

campesinos from every corner of Caquetá. They built crude shelters of bamboo and plastic along the highway, in pastures, on soccer fields, and in the park, awaiting just one government response: "There will be no fumigation." The first demonstrators arrived last Tuesday morning from Alto Orteguaza, farm workers from San Antonio, Getuchá, Milán, Grenario, and from various veredas in Solano. People from Unión Peneya, Solita, and Maticurú arrived yesterday. Others are expected from Caguán, Puerto Rico, Curillo, and Valparaiso. Five thousand farm workers have arrived in just two days, and their leaders expect that number to double today. Entire campesino families have left their farms and plots, traveling to Santuario on the Orteguaza and San Pedro Rivers. Others have traveled by land, hundreds of them arriving on foot yesterday from all points in the region.[13]

By August 2, "At least ten thousand campesinos from Lower and Middle Caguán joined the ongoing protests in Cauca and Putumayo over the fumigation of illegal crops."[14] As the movement erupted, PLANTE director Hector Moreno Reyes declared outside forces responsible for it:

The situation that has been created in Guaviare, Putumayo, and Caquetá is not a direct consequence of the manner in which the program
is being carried out. It is fundamentally a predictable reaction on the
part of the forces and interests affected and threatened by the actions
that the government is taking in these regions. . . . The campesinos
in these places are no more than hostages to guerrillas and drug traffickers, and they have no alternative but to obey them. . . . As long as
that situation continues, the farm workers will continue to criticize
PLANTE. . . . The principal obstacle to the success of this substitution
program is the idea that drug traffickers are invincible.[15]

The Armed Forces and Operation Conquest:
Legitimizing the Exercise of Violence

Though Putumayo had not been fumigated, its movement leaders strongly
identified with the struggles in Caquetá and Guaviare and were doing everything possible to avoid similar treatment at home by the national government. Police authorities in Putumayo said they were surprised by the demonstrations, since the government had not announced fumigations there,
nor declared it a special law enforcement zone. Indeed, the police gave
this as one of their reasons for believing the movement was sponsored by
"narco-guerrillas," the military's term for FARC.[16]

The central government's and armed forces' idea that the guerrillas were
behind the movement continued to pervade and inform their decisions.
General Bedoya, who was directing military operations in the zone at the
time of the marches, further complicated the situation by equating FARC
with drug-trafficking. He complained that the government gave insufficient
support to "large operations against FARC, like Operation Conquest. We
have a new tragedy, the result of bad government, of an unwillingness to
make the political decision to eliminate the problem of drug-trafficking."[17]
From the general's point of view, the priority of Operation Conquest was to
fight the insurgency. Illegal crops—President Samper's stated target—were
secondary.

General Bedoya asserted that the mafia lent money to cocaleros to plant,
harvest, and process coca and that once the loans came due, "these migrants
from every part of the country have no way to respond and are trapped, kidnapped by FARC, which forces them to promote strikes like those we are see-

ing." He maintained that repressive military measures were necessary "to protect the people who are prisoners of the mafia. They are slaves, moved around like herds of animals by FARC terrorists" (Padilla 1996, 18–20). This analysis denies the campesinos any agency or independent initiative, comparing them even to animals—a depth of dehumanization that legitimized their exploitation and exclusion from civilized society (Leach 1972; Sibley 1995). As hostages of FARC, the General said, they should "accept the help of the Army to flee from FARC abuse" (Padilla 1996, 18). Thus, the armed forces proceeded to forcibly evacuate 150 people from Guaviare in military aircraft to Villavicencio in the department of Meta, their supposed place of origin. According to the General, this evacuation, along with the destruction of crops and laboratories, was a step toward putting 100,000 cocaleros out of work in Guaviare, Caquetá, and Putumayo: "When the work dries up, they will have to leave just as they arrived, because to cite the case of Guaviare, less than 2 percent of the residents were born there. We are helping to relocate them" (Padilla 1996, 19). General Bedoya also employed the hegemonic discourse of environmental protection to eclipse the needs of Putumayo residents with those of the Amazonian forest: "What we need to do is try to save the forest that the narco-guerrillas are destroying with chemicals used for coca" (Padilla 1996, 20). The military was portrayed as a savior that would take control of the area "after decades of official abandonment," in order to "prevent the guerrillas from earning $6 billion a month by processing ten tons of cocaine" (Varela 1998, 21). Bedoya's July 1996 statement to the press clearly reflects his vision: "We're going *to take back this territory* that is flooded with illegal crops. The government and the armed forces are going to *combat this scourge. This is a war and we're going to win it*."[18]

Over time, this narrative of a "conquest of the Amazon" came to dominate, direct, and legitimize the repressive measures and violence of the armed forces. A negative collective identity as a social group outside the law was imposed on the cocaleros. They were "the mafia's masses, sponsored by the FARC Cartel" (Padilla 1996, 18). With cocalero campesinos configured as criminals dedicated to illegal activities and therefore politically, socially, and economically marginal with respect to the center, the movement could and would no longer be seen from the center as the essentially campesino phenomenon that it was.

This configuration of the Amazon region as full of migrants and criminals under the orders of the guerrillas echoes the historical period in which the region was represented by Spanish conquistadors as inhabited by savages. In both periods, an "indomitable" people must be overcome and "normalized." This interpretation of phenomena and its evocations of collective historical memory influence the manner in which violent events are generated, confronted, and understood (Aretxaga 1993; Coronil and Skurski 1991; Feldman 1991; Taussig 1987).

Civilized, Orderly, Clean Towns Versus the Polluting Countryside

One of the principal objectives of the campesino marches was to enter urban centers and departmental capitals to negotiate with politicians or officials with decision-making power. To the military and some town residents, the marchers posed a threat that "barbarism" from the uncivilized and marginal borderlands could overwhelm the "civilized" center. For other town residents, the presence of campesinos inspired solidarity based in the awareness that the region ultimately shared a common destiny.

Take the example of the approximately ten thousand campesinos who were in Santuario, Caquetá, for over two weeks in July 1996. General Nestor Ramírez explained why he prevented them from crossing a bridge into the center of Florencia, the department's capital: "I'm fulfilling my constitutional responsibility. I'm protecting the property of the citizens of Florencia, of the decent people. . . . I'm not creating obstacles; I'm not closing down roads. I'm placing some limitations on the violent elements so that they will not so easily violate the rights of others."[19]

A campesino marcher stated forcefully at the bridge:

> We're not here to cause any disorder. Our goal, or the goal that I've heard all the participants express, is, *we march to demand our rights*. We march to claim what is ours. We are not marching to demand the end of fumigation; if maybe that is the way many people have interpreted this, no. The majority, maybe all of us, agree that coca should be stopped; we say so. [We are demanding] that there be guarantees of other work for people in the countryside, just like for people who are working in town. We people, *we all need our rights, so what we are demanding is our rights*.[20]

The interviewee emphasized that the marchers were demanding their rights as campesinos, but even more so as humans, contrasting them with the townspeople whose rights, he says, *are* respected. By counterposing the countryside to the city in this way, he contrasts the "uncivilized" nature of

Figure 9. Closed bridge preventing cocaleros from entering the town of Florencia, Caquetá. (Felipe Caicedo, Casa Editorial, *El Tiempo*)

the former with the "civilization" of the latter in an example of the pervasiveness of the state's marginalizing discourse. Another campesino explained:

> We want to enter Florencia so we can sit down with a representative of the central government, or so the President will address our concerns and really approve what we are demanding. They should tell us that they'll go ahead and give us the credits. That INCORA and the Caja Agraria are going to determine the campesinos' needs and give them credits. . . . They've told us a lot of lies and every time they lie to us they start [political] campaigns. They inflict military repression on us like now in Lower Caguán. We can't work, we can't even sleep.[21]

Another voice during the march was reported in *La Nación*:

> The protest is to tell the Interior Minister, the Defense Minister and the Anti-Narcotics Commander that they can't do away with coca because that's the only means of subsistence that we have and they haven't provided alternatives. We're just going to march, we're not going to close the roads or provoke any disorder, but if the national

government doesn't listen to us, we'll have to protest in some other way. We need them to come and negotiate so we can move forward with these demands.[22]

The armed forces continued to repress with their own, official version of events, as stated by General Nestor Ramírez:

> The masses are being forced by FARC to move around, obstructing highways and traffic. Therefore we have to act. In the case of Santuario we must act to defend the rights of the good citizens. Unfortunately, other people's rights, the rights of some people who are poor, but nonetheless are engaged in illegal activities like drug trafficking, well, their rights are in the middle. But the serious thing is not these people, but the people who are manipulating them, the people behind them who represent greater interests, large sums of money, the cartels: the FARC Cartel, the Cali Cartel, and other cartels.[23]

Major General Mario Galán Rodríguez concurred: "The strike in Putumayo is unquestionably being led by FARC Fronts Thirty-two and Forty-eight, which have forced the campesinos to come out and protest against the government. The campesinos don't know why they're in these protests, and the terrifying thing is that they've been compelled to leave their farms . . . the only interests at stake here are those of the narco-guerrillas, and those interests are purely economic."[24]

The marchers were seen as ignorant, "out of place" off their farms, and basically disposable, rejected based on certain classificatory schema in the sense described by Mary Douglas (1966): they had to be excluded so that the hegemonic structure could maintain its power and impose symbolic order.[25] If the campesinos had been let into the towns, they might have symbolically contaminated the "good citizens" inside with their incivility.

While the armed forces tried to impose this view of the marchers as a malignancy, some inhabitants of Florencia disagreed. One resident said, "I think they should [be able to cross the bridge] because they're also human beings and have a right to live. We should see if an agreement can be reached, because the campesinos shouldn't be manipulated like that. They should be treated with solidarity."[26]

In Mocoa, the culture clash with rural campesinos caused a significantly higher tension level. Marchers from Puerto Guzmán and Piamonte, in the Baja Bota, began arriving on August 7. In an article titled "Cocaleros Rule in Mocoa," a journalist residing in the Putumayan capital related:

Thousands of coca growers have taken over the Municipal Building and the offices of eight government agencies, consolidating control of this town that they have occupied for twelve days. There is no Army presence in the city and the police are in their barracks. The civil authorities are nowhere to be seen, hence the population remains subject to the orders of the campesino leaders—a situation that has again been described as a mass hostage-taking. The campesinos are enforcing harsh measures to control the population, including mandated business hours, the paralysis of transport and restrictions on people's freedom of movement. The measures ordered by the strike's Central Committee are obligatory, enforced by groups of strikers armed with knives and clubs who patrol the streets aggressively.[27]

A Mocoan described his experience: "Beginning yesterday, nobody travels in any vehicle in the streets of Mocoa, not even a horse-drawn wagon. . . . Until yesterday Mocoa was an oasis of peace and tranquility; now we're in a crisis. The common people of a city that is the definition of peaceful, very conservative, very tied to their traditions and customs, are under lots of stress and full of fear."[28]

Police Commander Colonel Orlando Díaz explained this fear to national radio reporters: "The population is in terror because no coca is grown in Mocoa. We can say that campesinos and guerrillas have taken more than 23,000 people hostage in the municipality."[29] Fear of the marchers became a basis on which to construct a negative stereotype of the campesino cocalero, and once a person or group is constructed as a "bad object" (Sibley 1995, 15), people want to distance themselves from it. However, once the townspeople's initial fear of the marchers was overcome, they began to see them as fellow human beings in crisis, trying to express their needs. After the first confrontations between the Police and campesinos, preventing entry of the latter into town, a group of Mocoa residents interceded in their favor:

The Mocoa Pro Strike Committee was formed in order to receive and welcome the people that had come from Puerto Limón, Puerto Guzmán and Caquetá. The army was concentrated in Villagarzón, intending to keep the marchers back, but the Conciliation Committee helped them to continue through. Some people in Mocoa mediated between the Government and the marchers; together with the mayor, the ombudsman and the attorney general's representative they reached agreements to avoid further confrontations.[30]

A journalist described ambivalence and evolution in the attitudes of the Mocoan townspeople:

> At first people formed an anti-strike committee but others talked to
> them, so the committee and the idea of opposing the strike disap-
> peared. Townspeople were afraid of the marchers, but they were also
> convinced that the strike would benefit them as well. Radio Putumayo
> began to broadcast interviews with strike leaders and authorities. The
> station was trying to show the human side of what was happening in
> order to discourage panic and confrontation in town. Soon the people
> of Mocoa began to help the marchers out. But the people at the radio
> station were accused of abetting the strike.[31]

In sum, the marchers explicitly stated that the goals of their mobilization
were peaceful: to negotiate with local functionaries and the central government, not promote coca growing as such. They explained they felt obligated
to grow coca for their subsistence, placing responsibility for their precarious socio-economic situation on the Colombian state and its failed strategies. The Putumayan campesinos' presence in the towns and their counter-
interpretations to official versions of the regional situation provoked both
fear and supportiveness in the department's urban dwellers, whose ambivalence in itself reflected the limited resources in this marginalized zone.

The Politics of Recognition and the Emergence of Collective Identities

> Our identity is partly shaped by recognition or its absence, often by
> the misrecognition of others, and so a person or group of people can
> suffer real damage, real distortion, if the people or society around
> them mirror back to them a confining or demeaning or contempt-
> ible picture of themselves. Nonrecognition or misrecognition can
> inflict harm, and can be a form of oppression, imprisoning some-
> one in a false, distorted, and reduced mode of being.
>
> —Charles Taylor, "The Politics of Recognition"

A politics of recognition that occurs through the relational construction of
identities between groups played a central role in the cocalero social movement. An analysis of the imposition of meanings by one group on another
group is fundamental to the understanding of the collective identities the

cocaleros emerged. The meanings that define group members are recognized as identifiers either because they have been either imposed on them by others, forged by themselves, or both (Young 1990). In the case of the people of Amazonia, the most powerful "others" in identity formation are representatives of the central state.

Young extends her analysis of the social group to the point of saying: "Sometimes a group comes to exist only because one group excludes and labels a category of persons, and those labeled come to understand themselves as group members only slowly, on the basis of their shared oppression" (1990, 46). Wendy Brown (1995, 73–74) similarly argues: "In its emergence as a protest against marginalization or subordination, politicized identity thus becomes attached to its own exclusion both because it is premised on this exclusion for its very existence as identity and because the formation of identity at the site of exclusion, as exclusion augments or 'alters the direction of the suffering' entailed in subordination or marginalization, by finding a site of blame for it."

In Amazonia identity stems from abandonment by the state as is evident in the following statement: "This is one of the most remote zones of the country. We are ignored. The only thing you see here is isolation and abandonment by the government. The state doesn't even want to see progress in Amazonia. Being in Amazonia is equated with being backward." [32]

This disaffective discourse is internalized and becomes a constituent part of the subjects' identity and particularly of their subjection. In a context of exclusion and misrecognition of the inhabitants of Amazonia by the state, a mirror image is established within which "an identification" takes place, as described by Lacan (1977, 2), transforming them into political subjects. [33]

In the realm of subjectivity, what an individual feels or experiences is what becomes real (Gianni 1997, 134). When individual self-realization is precluded, antagonism toward the "others" who impede that goal may surface and be expressed violently. It can be argued that campesinos and colonos of Colombian Amazonia share a representation of "contingency and incompleteness" pointed out by S. Nugent (1993, xxi) in reference to campesino communities in Brazilian Amazonia. [34] Furthermore, campesino cocaleros suffer a distorted representation as rootless migrants looking for a fortune in easy money in order to return to their regions of origin. The state does not even recognize them as residents of the places where they live and work. The feeling of denigration, negation, and invisibility permeates the cultural and political discourse used in the region, as reflected in a letter to the Ombudsman's Office from the campesinos of the vereda Villanueva in the jurisdiction of Mayoyoque in the municipality of Puerto Guzmán, Putumayo:

> Gentlemen of Corpoamazonia, of the Ombudsman, agriculture, how are we campesinos going to survive if the government fumigates everything we have? Along with the illegal crops, they also fumigate the legal ones. We're suffering from hunger. Our pastures have been fumigated along with the plantain, the yuca, the corn, the rice. *We campesinos what we want to do is make the government understand that like you we to are humans, that we are also Colombians that like you we have children to.* The only difference between your children and ours is that your children will never be herd to say I'm hungry like we hear a lot from are children after the fumigation and the only thing we can say is the plane truth that the government did away with evrything.[35]

The central government's categorization of Putumayo and the Baja Bota of Cauca as a red zone (*zona roja*), or conflict-ridden area, just furthered the state's absence in the minds of local leaders, since national and regional politicians and public officials were afraid even to visit. A community leader of the Baja Bota explained: "Traditional politicians don't show their faces here because it is a zona roja, a zone of conflict." Another added: "And this is not the first or only time that it has been labeled a zona roja, so that doesn't bother us. We are proud to live in this area."[36] The advisor to the Interior Minister commented: "The thing is that this is still seen as a war zone by the armed forces, by the guerrillas, and by the paramilitaries."[37] The stigmatization of the area's inhabitants as violent, and the fear that this reputation inspired, was one of the stereotypes that the campesinos fought.

State violence, exclusion, stigmatization, and marginalization of the inhabitants of western Amazonia, and the global importance that coca cultivation acquired with the war on drugs, combined to create a cocalero campesino social movement to demand the presence of the state as partner in promoting community-centered development of economic alternatives to coca cultivation. A leader describes these demands and how they transformed into the mobilization:

> The communities wrote to the Presidency, the Solidarity Network, the Ministries of the Interior, of Agriculture, of the Environment, etc., re-

questing meetings. They never received one positive response to their concerns, to the voice of the community. So this lack of dialogue, the authorities' deafness to the problems that the community wanted to address convinced the community that this was a dead end. We felt that we had no option but to organize the municipalities to confront the problem in another way.[38]

Paradoxically, the Colombian government did not decide to enter into dialogue with the movement until the expansion of coca cultivation increased the pressure on it in the United States's certification process.[39]

The Civic Movement for the Comprehensive Development of Putumayo and the Consolidation of the Cocalero Social Movement

The campesino movement of the 1994–95 civic strike experienced some fissures that resulted in spotty participation among municipalities: "People talk about Orito [the protest in 1996] and La Hormiga [the 1994–95 protest]," explained the leader of the Putumayo Regional Indigenous Organization (OZIP) after the 1996 strike. "We [Civic Movement leaders] tried to dialogue with the negotiating commission of that time to strengthen their hand, not undercut them, but maybe they didn't see it that way. . . . It was a struggle, a real process, that year and a half that I'm talking about, to determine how to unify that movement."[40] The Putumayo Regional Civic Movement, which began preparations for the second civic strike against fumigation in 1995, was determined instead to involve all of Putumayo. It began by identifying community leaders such as JAC members, teachers and health workers, since development issues were becoming increasingly important to their agenda. The goal was to build a social movement among all thirteen of Putumayo's municipalities, indigenous groups, campesino coca growers and harvesters, and leaders from other sectors as well. They would form a single movement:

> We decided that all the leaders of Upper, Middle, and Lower Putumayo would meet together. At this meeting the leadership broke with the Civic Movement of Orito, Valle del Guamués, and San Miguel, and with Campesino Unity of Puerto Guzmán, and formed the Civic Movement for the Comprehensive Development of Putumayo. The movement was organized by vereda. Leaders were chosen for each vereda and financial contributions were pledged or made by all present. Orito, Valle del Guamués, and San Miguel were the most experienced.[41]

The Civic Movement for the Comprehensive Development of Putumayo set out on a "unified struggle" to bring together all the department's ethnic, political, and social movements and to collaborate with movements in Caquetá, Guaviare, and Meta, where illegal crops were also cultivated: "We discussed a national mobilization so that the House of Representatives would meet in order to address this matter as a social problem affecting the country. . . . We wrote a very ambitious document and we were aware that it was utopian; we were saying that we needed to mobilize at least a million campesinos in Colombia to make the state understand that this was not a criminal problem; it was a social problem."[42] Movement leaders sought to illustrate the magnitude of the coca problem by proposing a National Forum (Mesa Nacional de Concertación) to analyze state policy on crop substitution. This forum would seek broad agreement on solutions.

On August 15–17, 1995, a department-wide seminar on illegal crops was held in Puerto Asís. On August 18, the participants sent a document to President Samper that contained a basic proposal for a community-centered dialogue on the problem of illegal crops. After the seminar, the leaders held a forum in Puerto Guzmán for the broader population to discuss the problem and to inform them about the outcomes and proposals that came out of the seminar.

Within this national perspective and with department-wide ambitions, Civic Movement leaders set about organizing the local campesino populations:

> At first we organized it through the inspectorates . . . [which] would call the veredas together. In the meeting of veredas we would just deal with the presidents of the JACs. Then as soon as this group was briefed, there were three- or four-day workshops . . . on the whole problem, the whole situation that was coming. They [the presidents of the JACs] went and they led their workshops as they understood things and then we would get the reports. . . . Among the most important things we were looking for was that they didn't respond to the campesinos' questions but rather that they would bring questionnaires with them to find out about the strengths and weaknesses of the people, because we were going to go vereda by vereda. . . . Sometimes forty of us would go and sometimes one would go alone. They would tell us that three veredas were meeting in different places, so one guy would go here and one there. That's how we divided ourselves up.[43]

These workshops were financed by cocaleros themselves. They emphasized the importance of unifying the civic movement throughout the department, and reached Upper Putumayo municipalities not previously identified as coca-producing, such as Sibundoy, Santiago, San Francisco, and Colón. The workshops raised consciousness about fumigation and the national and international contexts surrounding illegal crops. OZIP leader Edilberto Imbachí explained that through these workshops, "The people began to realize that . . . the problem of illegal crops went beyond the borders of Colombia, [that] it was not a Putumayan problem," and that a real solution needed to involve not only Putumayo but Caquetá, southern Bolívar, and Guaviare. "But we have the same problem in Peru and Bolivia. So we said that we needed a large mobilization in order to be taken seriously."[44] The workshops also prepared campesinos for the hardships of mobilization.

> First we took up a collection. That is, *the problem was illegal crops and we were going to finance the solution with illegal crops, too. That's what we had to do.* We set a monetary assessment per hectare. We already had . . . first, an operating proposal, and also the political proposal that we were going to put on the table. The people agreed to take to the streets. Logically we had arranged that not everybody could come out, some people would have to stay home, at least one person on each farm. But another team would be on the farms collecting food, firewood, meat, everything to sustain a strike, because we would call the strike for an indefinite period. We wouldn't lift the strike until we had negotiations. We told the people that it would be very hard because the *state has always responded militarily to political proposals from the national periphery and that it would not surprise us if that happened, if their human rights were disrespected from start to finish.*[45]

The movement sought to inspire vereda residents' informed, voluntary participation in the mobilization. Their desire for genuine community participation remained constant at each phase of the mobilization and in the follow-up activities afterward. The movement's leaders did not want to reproduce the negative practices of the dominant political culture, but rather to distinguish themselves by way of inclusion so they would not become "a head without a body."[46]

Campesino Organization in the Marches: Community Action Committees, FARC and the "Obligation to March Voluntarily"

The 1996 cocalero movement was not exempt from the tensions, pressures and ambiguity that characterized social and political practice in Putumayo. Like the civic and political movements before it, it struggled with issues of autonomy vis-à-vis both the traditional parties and armed groups in the region. It became clear during the movement that there was a strong, active connection between campesinos and guerrillas in the region. However, analysis of the degree (if any) to which the former were "puppets" of the latter (as many in Bogotá chose to believe) revealed a far more complex and mutually-independent dynamic than one would conclude from *El Tiempo* headlines like "Guerrillas Responsible for Strike in Putumayo."[47]

The ambiguity of the FARC-campesino relationship is captured in the words of one farmer: "We were obligated to march voluntarily." While the impetus for the marches came from the campesinos themselves, and from their leaders who were increasingly angry about the implementation of La Hormiga Accords, FARC played a significant role in the organization as well. Just as they wielded power over much of the daily life in areas of Putumayo they controlled, so too did they influence how the Movement prepared and executed the mobilization. FARC supported the marches, but in an authoritarian manner. Rufina Jamioy, an indigenous Inga woman from La Floresta vereda in the Baja Bota said she almost had to go to Morelia, Caquetá, on orders of FARC, "because we weren't working. We were going to go but we begged them because of the small children and in the end they didn't send us. Some girls went to talk to soldiers and FARC pulled them out of the march as a punishment."[48] Albeiro, a JAC leader from the vereda La Consolata in Piamonte, commented: "It's FARC that has oriented us. They are responsible for the organization's progress. The guerrillas help people organize and promote the coordination of the JACs. The guerrillas establish order in the region and they are obeyed. And the community has become aware of the necessity of organizing itself."[49]

However, to call the cocalero movement the result of guerrilla activities or of campesinos' fear of FARC is to gloss over the population's will and capacity for negotiation. The reality was that, faced with the prospect of fumigation decimating their livelihoods, the campesinos had an endogenous motivation to organize, as well as the desire and capacity to participate in negotiating regional development plans and policies. This motivation was encouraged and channeled by FARC.

The extensive informal networks of the JACs were put to use by movement organizers, and they became the primary unit of organization for the mobilization. One campesino described how in the process, the JACs "took responsibility for what needed to be done in each vereda."[50] According to the Ministry of the Interior's 1996 JACs database, there were 824 individual JACs registered in Putumayo that year, with a total membership of 34,693. The JACs not only facilitate social and political relations among the people, but also the government, political parties, and FARC establish working relationships through their contact with the leadership of these committees.

Within this dynamic, the population's own needs and previous struggles enabled it to create a space to negotiate with the guerrillas as illustrated by the examples below. While FARC's role included setting the start times of marches, the campesinos did not always follow obediently. For example, when the marches were set to begin in the Baja Bota, FARC determined that the veredas would head for Caquetá and Putumayo, which some of them did. However, other veredas were opposed to leaving Cauca because their agenda included pressuring the central government to create a new municipality around Piamonte in the Baja Bota, and they saw the marches as their best opportunity to do so:

> We were never advised by the guerrillas; what we did was based on the convictions of our own leaders. As I was telling you, the guerrillas opposed us in the strike because they wanted us to go to Putumayo and Caquetá. We didn't do that, we said that we had to keep our fight in Cauca and they disagreed with us. No, there was no confrontation. They just stopped helping us. . . . There wasn't any discussion about it, they just sent word that they weren't helping us with a "let's see how you do" attitude. They thought we were a weak group. Both the guerrillas and the government thought that since it was such an isolated zone, our strike was going to fail. And it was one of the best strikes there was. It had a national impact due to it being peaceful, because of the quality of the negotiators, and because of the things we gained in the negotiations.[51]

It is important to note that in some sense, Castillo saw the government and the guerrillas in the same light. Both the state and the guerrillas predicted that the strike would fail. Both defined the area as isolated or marginal; the guerrillas implied that the people there could exercise power only by uniting with Caquetá and Putumayo. Both were proven wrong. The movement kept its autonomy and won a victory with the establishment of the Municipality of Piamonte.

The naming of march leaders in Putumayo in 1996 was another illustration of civil society's relative autonomy in relation to FARC. "The guerrillas named some people and civil society named other people to lead the marches, so they opposed [FARC's] orders," explained Ana Beiba Rincón, women's representative to the march's follow-up committee.[52]

A campesino woman from the Baja Bota commented on the FARC's role in organizing the movement:

> Let's say coordinators, not directly, but yes, they were working with us there. They took charge of forming the committees, they saw who would distribute the supplies, and they also requested help from Popayán. Baby formula for the children was sent over from there, and they organized who would prepare it for the children. Every day the children got formula. If they hadn't been there maybe things wouldn't have been as organized as they always were, because you know sometimes when there are things like that, someone wants more than the others, and problems come up. Even with them, there were fights sometimes. After three days, when the people were set up with their shelters, then they arrived and organized how we were going to build the shelters.[53]

Rufina Jamioy told me her first impressions of the strike at the gathering place for the Baja Bota. She recalled the arrival of the first marchers in front of her house, carrying a Colombian flag as an affirmation of their citizenship. There was a man "who was in charge. He was ugly and skinny and the women all commented, 'All those men letting themselves be led by just one guy!' He wanted to see us all working, digging latrines, carrying firewood, cooking, or serving. He didn't want to see anybody being idle."[54] This man, identified as a member of FARC, organized the security guards, drivers, curfew, food distribution, and animals. He took care of the marchers' health needs, even obtaining refrigerators for the vaccines. He established order in general.

FARC established some of the basic overall rules for the 1996 marches, envisioning a disciplined environment where their authority was recognized. They prohibited coca production during the marches, regulated commercial activity, and set the amount and collection method for a tax on campesinos. Fifty thousand pesos (US$25) per hectare of coca were to be given to the JAC finance committees to form march committees. Some JACs collected 600,000 to 800,000 pesos (US$300 to 400) to fund the first days of the march. The head of finance in each vereda would provide the JAC chairperson with data on the money collected, collection methods, and the relation between each person's contribution and his or her economic situation. In some cases, the tax was unrelated to the amount of coca a family cultivated: "They had to donate. The JACs took a quota, say 10,000 pesos [US$5] per family. That adds up, and they would buy an animal, for example. Then because the number of people kept growing and they all had to eat, in the end the people who had so many head of livestock had to contribute. . . . They had to, for better or worse."[55]

Twenty percent of funds collected were channeled to the Central Organizing Commission, made up of one leader from each of the nine municipalities. This commission was "like a JAC, with a president, a treasurer, a controller to provide oversight, and a secretary to keep records."[56] A second coordinating committee, made up of a president chosen by each vereda, facilitated communication between the Central Organizing Commission and all the veredas. Within the veredas also, committees were established to provide support to the higher leadership bodies on needs such as security, finances, transportation, health, food supplies, and rented equipment.

Eight to twelve people were designated to stay at home in each vereda, working to send food and other supplies to the marchers: "Then people were chosen to stay on, per organizing committee plans . . . in each vereda to guard the houses and buildings, to make the rounds, and to feed the animals."[57] In the Bajo Congor vereda of Piamonte, one man who stayed recounted that his team of twelve people also guarded valuables stored in the school, and that they would meet to take meals together.

On site with the mobilizations, task forces were set up to meet specific needs. Certain people from each JAC were selected to ensure hygiene while others performed security functions, guarding the town centers and keeping potential saboteurs out of the march. Others from each vereda were responsible for seeing that people had medical supplies, which were distributed to the committees by the Central Organizing Commission. Albeiro, the La Consolata JAC leader, described his experience:

At the time of the marches, we were discussing whether we would participate, and we did go with our families after a lot of deliberation. One hundred seventy of us went to Mocoa and Villa Garzón from Yapurá, La Consolata, and El Palmito. They sent us supplies from La Consolata, and we also received supplies in Putumayo. I was working on the equipment committee. I would count the people I was in charge of and collect the supplies. It went so well that we brought supplies back home with us. They sent us dried beef, honey, rice, plantains, etc. We received total support. It didn't go so well for the people in Caquetá. There were deaths, disorder, hunger, and confrontations.[58]

The transport task force conducted a census of boats, outboard motors and fuel in each vereda to make sure that all useful equipment would be available to the communities. Food task forces instructed each person to bring his or her own plates and silverware, while vereda leaders arranged the food shipments and provide stoves. "They told us to bring food supplies from each vereda and also to contribute livestock. Each committee had to bring meat."[59] A campesino from Puerto Asís told me that people with ten cattle had to contribute one; people with twenty had to contribute two; and those who refused to participate had to contribute five.[60]

FARC also contributed significantly to food and supplies for the march: "The guerrilla army was living right together with the marchers and was giving them meat. Eighty five cattle were slaughtered and there was enough meat thanks to the guerrillas' help."[61]

As a merchant in Puerto Asís commented, "The strike was very well organized." On July 28, the Civic Movement for the Comprehensive Development of Putumayo issued these guidelines to organize the daily life of the campesino occupants and their hosts in the towns, down to the smallest detail:

1. Granary owners will be permitted to receive shipments on Fridays. All sales will take place on Saturdays and Sundays from 6 a.m. until 2 p.m. They will be closed the rest of the week.
2. Two pharmacies will be open 24 hours a day from Monday to Saturday. Pharmacies will rotate this responsibility. All pharmacies may open for business on Sundays.
3. Juice will be sold by street venders every day from 6 a.m. to 2 p.m.
4. Sales of bottled gas will not be restricted, but at no time will sellers be authorized to raise prices. Any violation will be punished by permanent closure.

5. Bars, soda fountains, and pool halls will be closed at all times.

6. Restaurants will be open for business on Saturdays and Sundays from 6 a.m. to 2 p.m.

7. Gasoline stations may also do business as usual.

8. Larger retail establishments will be open for business on Saturdays and Sundays from 6 a.m. to 2 p.m.

9. Bakeries will be open on Saturdays and Sundays from 6 a.m. to 2 p.m.

10. Butchers may do business on Saturdays and Sundays.

11. Court sessions and the prosecutor's office will function as usual.

12. Auto and tire repair shops will do business as usual.

13. Effective immediately, explicit authorization is required for any and all vehicular and motorcycle traffic.

14. The offices of the Caja Agraria will remain closed.

15. Telephone offices will function as usual provided that needed services in support of the civic strike are available.

16. Traffic permits will be granted to supply trucks, gasoline tankers, and people with medically certified health needs.

17. Personnel will be relieved only on Monday, Wednesday, and Friday, from 8 a.m. to 10 a.m.

18. It is recommended that each community bring necessary provisions such as plantain, yuca, firewood, etc.

The local daily reported: "The campesinos now residing in Mocoa are ruling the city. They decide what establishments can open, what foods should be contributed, and what penalties should be imposed on those who do not cooperate in meeting the needs of their movement."[62]

Even Eduardo Díaz, a central government official, was impressed by the organization involved in maintaining such a long mobilization. "The organizational level of the rural people, of the campesinos, is very high," he commented, elaborating,

> The way they mobilized, the way they organized the building of their shelters in Orito, the way they took control of Puerto Asís, Mocoa, all testify to their very high level of organization, a military kind of organization. For example, it was surprising to see how they assigned the streets, with the kitchens serving as barricades and with an eating space behind each kitchen. There is no doubt in my mind that this was due to the influence of FARC's military experience.[63]

The guerrillas' daily activities in these border regions made them social actors who could intervene in the civic strikes, help the campesinos, and magnify the impact of the marches by organizing the campesinos to stay mobilized for months at a time. By lending this logistical support to the cocalero movement, FARC helped strengthen the movement leaders' negotiating position vis-à-vis the state, and its own position vis-à-vis the campesinos as a defender of their rights. Eduardo Díaz acknowledged the organizational skills of the campesinos and spoke of "FARC's influence," rather than claiming that the movement's accomplishments were wholly due to FARC's military organization. In this sense he accurately recognized an important aspect of the cocalero marches of 1996—the campesinos' agency.

CHAPTER FIVE

Negotiations with the Central Government

Clashing Visions over the "Right to Have Rights"

What surprises me is the bravery of certain people there in such a complicated situation, negotiating in the presence of the drug-traffickers, the guerrillas, the social protest movement, the repression against the movement.

— Jaime Navarro, advisor to the interior minister
for the 1996 Putumayo negotiations

This chapter is a detailed ethnography of the negotiations in Putumayo following the 1996 marches. It explores the meaning of cocalero campesinos' insistence on dialogue with central government representatives and their determination to exercise participatory democracy, a basic principle mandated by the 1991 Constitution.[1] The demand for negotiations and signed agreements in Putumayo revealed a profound popular desire for civil, social and political citizenship rights.[2] It was a struggle to open democratic spaces under the adverse conditions of a region dominated by armed actors and the criminalization of coca growers—factors that combined to repress and silence popular expression. In Putumayo, where a sense of extreme exclusion is a defining identity trait, the struggle to construct citizenship is a struggle over the "right to have rights."

The fight for meaningful citizenship and the implicit redefinition of the political culture have been seen as characteristic of Latin American social movements (Foweraker 1990 and 1995; Harvey 1998; Alvarez, Dagnino, and Escobar 1998). This certainly was clear in the demands of the cocalero social movement.

In the case of Brazilian urban social movements, Dagnino (1998) examines how new forms of collective action have contributed to the redefinition of the political and cultural dimensions of the struggle for democrati-

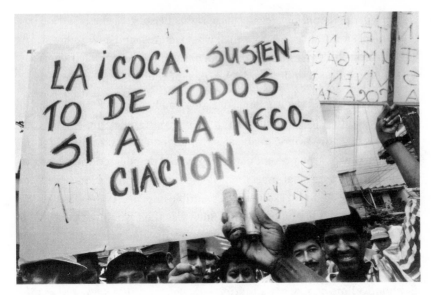

Figure 10. Poster stating, "Coca! A Means of Support for All, Yes to Negotiations." (Jorge Parga, Casa Editorial, *El Tiempo*)

zation and argues that an alternative conception of democracy is effectuated through a redefinition of citizenship and of its central referent, the notion of citizenship rights. These new social movements demand the radical transformation of political institutionality, i.e., a redefinition and a new delimitation of "the political." Dagnino (1998, 50) argues that "The redefinition of the notion of citizenship, as formulated by social movements, expresses not only a *political strategy* but also a *cultural politics*" (emphasis in the original). In defining this new citizenship, Dagnino understands the notion of "rights" as presented in the concept of the right of new social actors, of the excluded, to have rights and the need for society to "learn to live on new terms with these emergent citizens."[3]

Hannah Arendt (1949, 30) introduced this concept in her article, "The Rights of Man," a reflection on the concept of human rights in light of the thousands of stateless refugees in 1945–50 postwar Europe, officially categorized at the time as "displaced persons":

We only became aware of the existence of a right to have rights (and that means to live in a framework where one is judged according to actions and opinions) and a right to belong to some kind of organized community, when there suddenly emerged millions of people who had lost and could not regain these rights because of the new global political situation. . . . Before this, what we must consider today as a "human right" would rather have been thought a general characteristic of the human condition which no tyrant could take away.

Arendt noted that the existence of rights had been transformed from an a priori condition to a demand. In this same vein, reflecting on the characteristics of Latin American social movements, Foweraker (1995, 113–14) concludes that "in the present context of partial democracy, the best working definition of a social movement is a popular organization which can make plausible claims to exercise a perceptible impact on the extension and exercise of the rights of citizenship." Such was the case in the post-march negotiations, which provided a medium for campesino participation in collective and participatory decision-making; this participation had a catalyzing effect, thrusting the cocalero organizations into public view as a social and political movement. The movement's *politics of influence* and *politics of reform* (Cohen and Arato 1994, 526) were at the core of the campesino demands to negotiate with the central government, participate in the reform of state institutions, and help set policies for the region.[4] A focus on the agreements and disagreements among and between the cocalero movement leaders and the regional and central governments provides us with a prime opportunity to understand local perceptions and expectations of state policy and legislation from an ethnographic point of view.

This analysis of the 1996 negotiations takes on greater significance if we view it in light of the crisis of hegemony that the Colombian political regime has suffered since the 1980s as a result of the United States' war on drugs.[5] Never was this crisis more evident than during the presidency of Ernesto Samper, due to the accusations that his political election campaign had been partly financed by drug traffickers. The intensification of fumigation and the government targeting of coca growers promulgated during his administration were, among other things, forms of posturing for the United States.

At the same time, the fumigations and related activities contributed to the growth of a large cocalero campesino social movement that revealed the complete lack of state planning for alternative production by this group. The social movement delegitimized the central state in the eyes of the people of Putumayo. More and more campesinos questioned the trustworthiness of the state and began to participate in protests. At the same time, the movement demanded a greater and more effective state presence in the area. The interaction of the social movement with the state was not only central to the construction of its identity but was also a strategy to expand the state's presence in the region. Moreover, the cocalero campesino social movement demanded inclusion through close collaboration in a joint effort (*concertación*) with government agencies, Taking the above considerations into account, the beginning of the 1996 Putumayo negotiations must be seen as far more complex than just a demand for improved living conditions. The negotiations created a space for the campesino cocaleros to confront identities and demand that the state recognize Putumayo's history of violence, displacement, and abandonment by the ruling class, and acknowledge the economic and social structural causes of coca cultivation. The negotiations were also a site of confrontation where the government's framing of coca growing as primarily illegal and criminal clashed openly and fundamentally with the campesinos' experience of it as a means of survival given the absence of other options for sustainable development.

Perspectives on the Arrival of the Cocaleros and Ensuing Confrontations

Within a week of the start of the 1996 strike, an estimated 32,000 demonstrators had arrived in Orito, Valle del Guamués (La Hormiga), and Puerto Asís, with thousands more in Mocoa and a few other towns in Putumayo, and several thousand in Miraflor in Cuaca (see map 8).

Upon their arrival, campesino leaders and the representatives of eighty Puerto Asís JACS met with the governor of Putumayo, the mayor of Puerto Asís, and the Putumayo police commander, but this meeting resulted only in a reiteration of the campesinos' desire to negotiate directly with the central government.[6] While the governor announced that the 32,000 marchers were ready to stay for as long as necessary until this demand was met, entire families continued to arrive daily to join the other protestors.

Just as the campesinos were received with some ambivalence by their "hosts" in town, the crowds of marchers also met with divergent reactions from the security forces, the governor, and local government administrations.

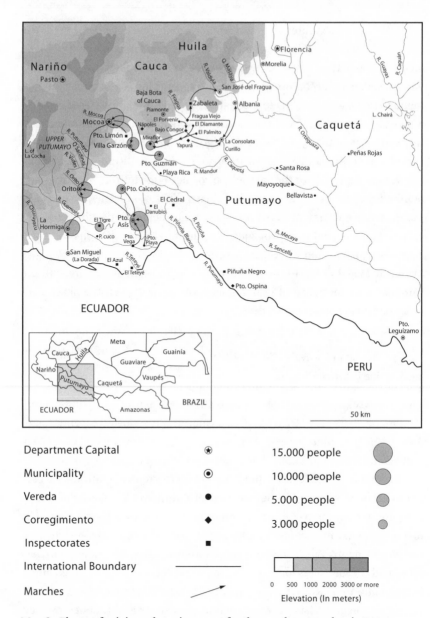

Map 8. Places of origin and staging areas for the cocalero marches in Putumayo and Cauca.

The Army and Police

On July 28, two days after the strike began, there was a confrontation between fifteen thousand demonstrators in Puerto Asís and a unit of the National Police that had been brought in from outside the department. The police attempted to clear the demonstrators from the town center, where they had put up their tents. Police used tear gas and fired into the crowd repeatedly to force the demonstrators to retreat. One campesino was killed and two were injured; a lieutenant colonel was cut with a bladed weapon. These aggressive tactics were consistent with statements made by national police authorities as soon as the marchers arrived in Puerto Asís: "The Security Forces are determined not to allow the demonstration to proceed."[7]

The national security forces considered the campesino mobilization to be an illegal form of pressure on the government that violated the Constitutional limits on peaceful public demonstrations. In a letter dated July 29, 1996, from General Mario Galán, commander of the Army's Third Division, to the governor of Putumayo, the general expressed the Army's doubts about the movement's legality. Article 23 of the Colombian Constitution allows for "respectful petitions" to be presented to the government, but the army believed that such "demands had not been officially presented" by the campesinos, "who instead were seeking to pressure the government with their march." The army also maintained that "the demonstrators [had] confirmed that they were intimidated by armed parties [FARC] into gathering at the various locations, and they [had] been forced to stay in these places against their will." In the view of the army, this coerced gathering was a violation of Article 24 of the Constitution, which allowed for freedom of movement for all citizens. The army also maintained that meeting the campesinos' demands would require changes to existing narcotics legislation, and that their blocking of air and land transportation was a violation of human rights.[8]

The police in Putumayo similarly perceived the marches to be part of the "narco-subversion's civic strategy" to force the government to stop fumigating, an attempt "to portray this scourge as a social rather than a criminal problem."[9] In a letter to the governor analyzing the security situation in the department, the Putumayo police commander interpreted support for the protest by the commercial sector and drug traffickers as a defense of their own business interests, "since fumigation hurts them the most." He predicted an attempt by the demonstrators to cut off transportation in and out of Putumayo and characterized the "guerrilla occupation of Mocoa" as "an attempt to destabilize the national government." He further denounced an attack on the San Miguel police station by demonstrators, terrorist actions against the petroleum infrastructure and public transportation, and FARC checkpoints along roads connecting Valle del Guamués (La Hormiga), San Miguel (La Dorada), Orito, and Puerto Asís.[10]

On August 2, campesinos tried to occupy one end of the Puerto Asís airport runway in order to halt domestic air travel, but were prevented from doing so in a violent clash with national police. Two campesinos were killed, one disappeared, and thirty-two were injured.[11] Armed Forces Commander Admiral Holdan Delgado stated in *El Tiempo* that the forces under his command "had used only tear gas to quell the disturbance," and that he "had no information [indicating] that they had to shoot." He indicated that the situation was beginning to calm down but reiterated that a major military effort was required because the population was under pressure from FARC: "They are trying to create an environment of fear and shoot someone so they can blame it on the Security Forces."[12] *El Espectador* reported:

> What had been considered a hypothesis was borne out yesterday with the death of two people and the injury of twenty-six, the result of an exchange of fire that lasted about an hour *between the supposedly unarmed campesinos of Putumayo and members of the Security Forces.* Last night the central streets of Puerto Asís were a virtual battleground between FARC guerrillas and members of the Military Police. When the Security Forces tried to prevent an incursion of a large body of demonstrators onto the airport runway, guerrillas hiding among the protesters opened fire against them. The guerrillas were shielded by the civilians whom FARC instigated to commit terrorist acts.[13]

The labeling of the "supposedly unarmed campesinos" as agents of FARC completely denied them their own agency. The armed forces' "hypothesis" had become a self-fulfilling prophecy: in their view, the military was smack in the middle of a counter-insurgency war as soon as the campesinos arrived in town. The police commander in Putumayo, Orlando Díaz Plata, explained the situation similarly: "The campesinos didn't want to strike, but they were forced to. Where could these 30,000 people have come from, who are occupying several towns? They say that FARC Fronts 32 and 48 have been in charge of organizing the strike since January last year [1995]."[14]

A spokesperson for the armed forces in Puerto Asís misinterpreted another aspect of the marchers' demands: "What they are asking for is very unlikely, because they are talking about not fumigating illegal crops, which would mean legalizing this activity."[15] Finally, the security forces continued to deny the Putumayo campesinos their roots in the area by characterizing them as migrants. In the first few days of August, the army forcibly evacuated dozens of campesino mother and child demonstrators to their supposed "home" in Nariño, just as they had done with the Guaviare demonstrators who were sent to Villavicencio, Meta, in July.[16] Strike organizers interpreted this action as a military tactic against the campesino movement.[17]

The Governor and Mayors

While the security forces made it clear that they wanted to end the occupation of Puerto Asís as soon as possible and by repressive means if necessary, the governor and mayors of Putumayo sympathized to a much greater extent with the demonstrators' demands. Once the marches began, Governor Fuerbringer and the mayors urgently demanded a central government commission.[18] A few days later, there were disturbances in Puerto Asís "only a few hours after a desperate Governor Fuerbringer graphically told Interior Minister Horacio Serpa that he did not intend 'to put up with any more of this shit. It's so tense that something very serious could happen at any moment.'"[19]

Local authorities such as the Puerto Asís mayor Alcibiades Enciso and Governor Fuerbringer supported the demonstration and interpreted it as: "to some extent justified by the difficult conditions that the government maintained in this region for years before the decentralization process began, when they gave us many new responsibilities, but not the tools to fulfill them."[20]

The Puerto Asís mayor Enciso advised the campesinos and put the town hall at their disposal at the beginning of the occupation to help them present their demands to the government. He also expressed his position in favor of a peaceful resolution:

> That is the goal: you are here to negotiate. You have an organization and you should establish a commission to speak to the central government. I see the situation differently from the way the army and the police describe it. I see the thing from a different point of view. I would like to tell the government that this is bad. I say this as a civilian

local official—because to me the most important thing is to settle this peacefully; it shouldn't be settled by force. I wouldn't like to see the municipality militarized, because that would have consequences for us. We can work this out with a good dialogue. But above all, we must all act in a disciplined way. I'm convinced that everything is going to work out peacefully.[21]

On July 7, 1996, Enciso opined to an evening news show that "The strike is a symptom of the deep needs of Putumayo's campesinos." The Valle del Guamués mayor Felipe Guzman explained, "Some say that drug traffickers and guerrillas in the department are instigating these disturbances, but we mayors aren't certain of that." The Puerto Leguízamo mayor Miguel Ángel Rubio added: "The solution to this problem is political, not military. To find a solution there should be negotiations with the organizers."[22] Seeing no other short-term solution, the mayors lobbied strongly for negotiations. A letter sent to Serpa by five Putumayo mayors on August 3 made this explicit (see appendix 1).

Governor Fuerbringer reiterated to the press that the disruption to law and order was a result of the central government's refusal to send a negotiating commission. On August 4, he and Putumayo's nine mayors traveled to Bogotá to hold an emergency meeting with Serpa.[23]

Meanwhile, the armed forces complained that the governors and mayors "had impeded their efforts to control the area and disperse the demonstration for a week." General Mario Galán, commander of the Third Army Division, sent a letter to Enciso after some confrontations between civilian and military authorities complaining of the lack of cooperation from the mayor.[24] A journalist commented that "the passive attitude of the officials was portrayed as an attempt to garner political favor with the population and derive resources from the central government."[25]

Pressure on the Oil Infrastructure: The Staging of a Negotiation Site

In Orito, protestors paralyzed ECOPETROL's oil pumping station. A national newspaper presented the act as a decision they made "in view of the fact that the national government has sent no sign of willingness to dialogue" and warned that the "occupation of the ECOPETROL installations in Orito would take the trans-Andean pipeline out of service. Every day the pipeline carries forty thousand barrels of crude to the port of Tumaco, where it is loaded onto tankers for export."[26] Ten days later, *El Tiempo* reported that "production was paralyzed, falling by 3,200 barrels daily" due to several cocalero occupations and acts of guerrilla sabotage against the oil pipelines.[27] Army and police defenders of the ECOPETROL installations were reinforced with additional personnel brought into the area. Thus Orito became strategic to the demonstrators. As the most heavily guarded site in Lower Putumayo, it was the only place where the military could guarantee the safety of a negotiating commission.

The confluence of coca cultivation, the guerrilla presence, and active oil wells in Lower Putumayo commanded government attention. This difference between Putumayo and Guaviare or Caquetá, neither of which had an oil industry presence, resulted in less intense fumigation for Putumayo. Its residents and those of the Baja Bota repeatedly told me that if it were not for oil in the area, the central government "would not even bother to look at us."

The central government ultimately decided to open negotiations in Orito, which would also help it protect oil company interests. The Orito ECOPETROL Club served as a site for negotiations. The Army provided a security perimeter so the government commission could feel relatively safe, although demonstrators and guerrillas continued to exert pressure with threats against them and attacks on the oil pipeline. The Orito mayor Luis Alfredo Urbano would lend important support to campesino negotiators, in his dual roles as mayor and Civic Movement leader.

The Reluctance of the Central Government to Negotiate on Campesinos' Terms

On August 1, 1996, the Civic Movement for the Comprehensive Development of Putumayo sent a document entitled "Reality and Alternatives to the Social Problem of Illegal Crops" to the interior minister. This was their response to a demand made by him and by the military for a "wish list" before the negotiating commission could depart for Orito on August 5. This initial document expressed four fundamental premises that would later become central to negotiations.

> We campesinos of Putumayo want to make a positive contribution to the search for mutually-agreed and viable solutions that will definitively resolve the problematic condition of the small agricultural producer. We propose the following:

1. Social recognition of the overall problematic of illegal crops along with the design of comprehensive substitution policies in consensus with communities.
2. The formulation of a sovereign policy on illegal crops.
3. The designation of communities with illegal crop problems as special social investment zones.
4. A clear and precise differentiation between campesino coca growers, drug traffickers, and guerrillas.[28]

The document asserted that "the problem of crops classified as 'illegal'" is the result of "the phenomenon of the economic, social and agro-economic crisis, produced in turn by state policies related to the development of the regions colonized by campesinos."[29] It stated that the campesinos had arrived in Putumayo as a result of the political violence of the 1950s, and that the law unfairly made "the only income-producing product" in the area illegal. To treat the problem as a criminal matter—"proceeding with force and repression"—they said, "would deepen rather than resolve the conflict." The Civic Movement wrote that campesinos experience fumigation as a form of violence, and that a state anti-drug policy of fumigation would "require the campesinos to move on, taking the problem with them, but not offering any fundamental solution." Finally, the movement evoked the constitutional principle of cooperative and participatory decision-making and action (*concertación*).

The "Reality and Alternatives" document detailed specific demands with regard to comprehensive agrarian policy, electrification, roads, health, education, housing, human rights, telecommunications, and land-use planning. It demanded human rights guarantees and introduced the need for international oversight to ensure compliance with agreements. The interior minister responded to these requests by stating "We will not travel to negotiate with the demonstrators because at least six of the points they are requesting violate the law and the Constitution."[30] After an emergency Security Council meeting he declared, "The Executive is open to seeking solutions to the Putumayo conflict, but solutions based on violating or negotiating the laws are unacceptable."[31]

Finally, after an August 4 meeting in Bogotá between the Putumayo governor, mayors, and Horacio Serpa, it was announced that a commission would travel to Orito for *conversations*, but not negotiations. The government's justification for this distinction was that the Putumayo strike leaders were outside the law: "The government made it clear that agrarian reform, health issues, electrification, and the protection of human rights can be discussed, but under no circumstances will any decriminalization of illegal crops be negotiated."[32] In addition, Serpa complained on national television that no agenda had yet been established for discussions of the social aspects of the campesinos' situation: a paradoxical statement since the campesinos considered recognition of the social nature of the problem to be prerequisite to the negotiation of any specific remedies.[33] At the same time, President Samper stated that "In many ways I appreciate the social realities that have driven the campesinos to express their grievances."[34] The concept of the "social aspects" of the situation was an ambiguous formulation wielded in accordance with the needs of the speaker and the moment.

The Negotiating Teams

An eighteen-person central government team traveled to Putumayo on August 5 with orders not to negotiate on any point concerning eradication or fumigation of illegal crops, but to reach whatever agreements were possible on the provision of services and the construction of infrastructure projects already budgeted for.[35]

The representatives for the campesino negotiating team were elected by the leaders of the Civic Movement and the JACs. The larger body of campesino protestors demanded additional representation as the following testimony explains.

> The Orito negotiating team was selected by the Civic Movement for the Comprehensive Development of Putumayo. There were 600 [more] people from Puerto Guzmán, and they joined with Puerto Limón and Santa Lucía to make a total of 4,000. They demanded the right to elect a representative to the talks themselves. They didn't allow the car to set off from Mocoa without him and they threatened to turn back the car if it didn't take him. They called the mayor to ask his permission, and that's the way it got done.[36]

In the end, eighteen representatives were elected for the campesino team: one or two from each municipality plus two indigenous representatives and four Civic Movement leaders. Luis Emiro Mosquera, head of the Civic Movement, was chosen as the general coordinator. The Civic Movement leaders also recruited several key departmental, religious, and NGO workers to advise the team and sit in on negotiations.

The local and departmental governments participated as a third party. Their team was made up of the Putumayo Governor Jorge Fuerbringer Bermeo and the seven mayors from Middle and Lower Putumayo (Orito, Villagarzón, Puerto Caicedo, Puerto Guzmán, Puerto Asís, Puerto Leguízamo, and Valle del Guamués).[37] The first negotiating meeting was held in Orito on August 6, 1996.

Central Aspects of the Negotiations: The Abandonment of the State

The Civic Movement leaders opened the negotiations with a presentation on the history of colonization in the region, to lead their audience to an understanding of why coca had become the most important local crop. They began by describing the colonization of the Amazon that resulted from Colombia's internal conflict during La Violencia and the massive campesino migration because of a deficient agrarian system and lack of land for small shareholders. They pointed out the dearth of government policies specifically tailored to and appropriate for the Amazon. They explained their own understanding of their regional identity within the Colombian nation-state, molded by the armed conflict and the consequent arrival of the internally displaced population, reflecting the region's stark marginality in relation to central Colombia. They submitted a draft proposal for an agreement with the government that implicitly demanded recognition of the structural problems underlying the phenomenon of coca growing: "The state and government understand that the existence of small coca growers is a legal problem with serious social and economic implications and that it is motivated by historical and structural social factors."[38]

The government commission rejected the opening text proposed by the campesinos for several reasons:

> First we got into a discussion over whether illegal crops and fumigation were the result of state abandonment. This was something that we weren't going to agree on, but that was the explanation they were proposing, and the explanation that we put forward was very similar, but the inverse to theirs. . . . Precisely because there is no state, drug traffickers and coca networks finance the development of this type of economy . . . A stronger state presence is not what the drug traffickers *or those who depend on them* want. They're going to move to other zones anyway, where they can do their work without having to

worry about anyone bothering them. Based on these two explanations, we weren't going to agree on which came first, the chicken or the egg.[39]

The government team counter-proposed their own opening text: "One of the reasons for the establishment of a regional economy in Putumayo based on the production of illegal drugs is that large drug trafficking networks use their enormous resources to stimulate this production."[40] It was neither social history nor a lack of appropriate government policy that promoted coca cultivation, but rather the power of drug-trafficking money.

The government draft went on to indicate that this dynamic "has therefore caused large migrations to urban centers and rural zones, and the opening of new areas to colonization. This, combined with precarious state presence and lack of appropriate development policies, has made planning and adequate attention to the growing demand for services and social infrastructure difficult, increasing the levels of poverty, social decay, and violence."[41] Government representatives wanted the scant state presence in the region to be viewed in light of the overwhelming wave of colonization that had reached the area. In words of presidential representative Eduardo Díaz:

> Public investment was relatively small and now too, it is relatively small in terms of the population there, which overwhelms any possibility of state presence. The colonization is wildly active, so it is really impossible to be everywhere. . . . People of every imaginable description are arriving and leaving at all times for many different reasons; it is very unstable. The truth is that you get to the zone one day and the next day there's another colonization going on further downstream with new demands for schools, for health services. It's like a teeming mass of humanity.[42]

Díaz went on to explain the role of FARC in the government's understanding of the Putumayo equation:

> I think that what FARC were essentially defending was the status quo, because things are very convenient for FARC just as they are. They can collect their coca taxes and as long as no other force is present they have no competition from the state or from any other leadership. So in that sense, FARC doesn't want things to change, they want the settlements to remain isolated. That way they can move around like they do, control coca production, collect taxes. Those things strengthen them.[43]

The president's advisor asserted that the lack of state presence in the Amazon region was utilized by and benefited illegal forces such as drug traffickers and guerrillas, so much so that they would promote this very absence. His understanding failed to account for the encouragement that FARC had given to campesinos to demand state presence and accountability (as will be discussed in chapter 6), let alone the clear support of FARC for the 1996 Civic Movement marches and social demands made of the state.

Cocaleros: Only Negotiating Partners, or Social Actors Too?

Just as the central government and cocaleros differed over the structural causes of coca growing, they had distinct conceptual frameworks regarding whether cocaleros should be considered social actors. In their proposed agreement, the campesinos insisted, "It is the responsibility of the national, departmental, and local governments, along with the organized community, to make common decisions that will assure comprehensive processes of regional development to complement crop eradication and substitution. In this sense, the small grower who participates in voluntary eradication and substitution *is a social actor and a legitimate negotiating partner in the search for comprehensive solutions.*"[44]

The government representatives, on the other hand, continued to put the law before economic realities, denying the campesino cocaleros social agency because of the illegality of coca growing:

> In a country like Colombia there are certain laws that we must obey, let's be clear on that . . . Colombian policy toward the drug problem, toward narcotics trafficking, would not be negotiated. One of the elements of that policy, specifically Law 30, tells us that anyone who grows coca is committing a crime. . . . There are things here that we can discuss . . . for example, *the idea that the small grower is a valid negotiating partner in the search for comprehensive solutions, but in what way? Dr. Díaz told you a moment ago that that was completely acceptable, [although] not as a social actor but as a valid negotiating partner, because the recognition of a social actor can't be based on the fact that that social actor is committing a crime.*[45]

Although it would seem that to speak of "valid negotiating partners" also implies a social recognition of the cocalero campesinos as distinct from guerrillas or drug traffickers, an overt acceptance of them as social actors was impeded by national and international political forces that were insisting on immediate, non-negotiable eradication. The Colombian armed forces, attorney general, and PLANTE director, as well as the United States, all accused the central government commission in Orito of negotiating with criminals. The Interior Ministry advisor Jaime Navarro explained:

> At that time it was being said that it was obviously a social problem, and the discussions that we had on the phone with Serpa were like, "Be very careful! Don't let anything happen that looks like an amicable agreement, like gradual eradication. The term *gradual* should not appear anywhere. Nor the term *social recognition*." It was clear that we should not use those words but we should make them happen. That was the problem. Serpa knew that it was a social problem, and that the solutions would be gradual.[46]

According to this statement, for political reasons the Samper administration was unable to take certain positions openly. This put them in the ambiguous position of recognizing the campesinos as legitimate negotiating partners but not as social actors.

The same political pressure caused even the term "negotiating partner" to acquire a criminal connotation in the minds of some branches of the government. Local government officials began to worry that they might be subject to investigation for aiding "criminal" campesinos through the negotiations. Indeed, the Lower Putumayo mayors' August 3 letter to Serpa addressed this issue in its final point (2c; see appendix 1). Just after that letter, a group of mayors also met with the Attorney General to ask that they "not be drawn into any criminal investigation."[47] *El Tiempo* carried this headline: "Mayors: 'We are neither subversives nor drug traffickers,'" and reported that the mayor of Puerto Asís, Alcibíades Enciso, had this to say as he left the meeting: "We came to tell Attorney General Valdivieso that we are neither subversives nor drug traffickers and to request that his office be impartial when they receive reports from army and police generals and colonels stationed in Putumayo. We make this request because it is not true that we belong to the guerrillas. We're 'between a rock and a hard place.'"[48] Indeed, while the president's negotiating commission was doing its work in Orito, the attorney general Alfonso Valdivieso's office was simultaneously investigating the organizers of the Putumayo marches "for their criminal associations."[49] Valdivieso was "insisting on the need to fully investigate the circumstances leading to the protest."[50] On August 6, *El Espectador* reported that "an anonymous group of prosecutors arrived in Puerto Asís on Saturday to determine whether or not there is evidence to warrant a formal investigation against [Civic Movement leader] Gilberto Sánchez, who was an agitator in the events leading up to Friday's disorders. Charges to be considered could include sedition, rebellion, and terrorism."[51]

There was a generalized fear in the region of being tried and punished for growing coca, a fear that was understandably rekindled by the August investigations. Nevertheless, as one campesino commented, "The state can call them all criminals, but since it can't imprison all of them, it will have to accept that they are not."[52] To the campesinos, recognition as social actors in daily practice meant the construction of an identity as a distinct group, independent of guerrillas and drug traffickers, that in spite of or perhaps because of its disadvantages within the national system, deserved a voice in regional policy making. One sign carried by the marchers said, "Ignorant Campesinos? Bull. We're Audacious!!" Juan Carlos Palou, a Solidarity Network official during the 1996 cocalero movement and subsequently director of PLANTE said, "The cocalero campesinos have demonstrated that they are a very powerful social force able to put both the government and the state in a very tight spot."[53]

To be denied any role except "valid negotiating partner" by the government felt to the campesinos like a deprivation of their agency, their group status, and their active participation in policymaking. It seemed to be simply a continuation of the state practice of setting policies and designing coca eradication programs without consulting them, a strategy that had led to failure of substitution projects in the Amazon in the past. Yet, this refusal by the government to openly recognize the cocaleros as social actors allowed it to save face vis-à-vis both international players and certain of its own branches. Designation of the campesino cocaleros as valid negotiating partners legitimized the government's decision to sit down and dialogue with them. It demonstrated interest in small growers, yet distinguished them from the high-volume drug traffickers who deserved a harder line.

Gradual versus Total Eradication

An important aspect of the cocalero campesinos' petition to be recognized as social actors was their willingness to eradicate coca as a sign of good faith and as a basis for potential partnership with the government. A community spokesperson made this clear: "We have said that we are inclined to participate in voluntary crop substitution without having to be coerced. So if we have expressed the intention to do this voluntarily, why can't we be interlocutors in order to speed up the process of finding an overall solution? Why isn't that possible if we are not defending drug trafficking here?"[54]

The debate over recognition of the campesino as a social actor and the relationship of this decision to the illegality of coca cultivation implicitly brought up conflicting models of gradual versus immediate coca eradication. For the government, it was "urgent to eradicate and replace illegal crops and the coca economy completely and definitively. We must establish and execute comprehensive projects, programs, and actions directed toward the harmonious development of a Putumayo without coca, supporting a viable and sustainable economy of solidarity."[55] The central government commission maintained that eradication was non-negotiable, and it had to be complete and definitive. Gradualism was not an option, and campesino acceptance of this fact was a prerequisite to any agreement on projects for alternative crops.

The campesinos also recognized that it was "legally, socially, environmentally, and economically pressing to completely eradicate illegal crops and their economies, and to lay the basis for the development of a Putumayo without coca that supports a viable and sustainable economy of solidarity through comprehensive substitution programs."[56] The campesino leaders, however, did not believe that such language precluded gradual eradication of coca. In fact they clearly stated, "Based on voluntary eradication, it is the government's responsibility to provide colono and indigenous small growers with productive, legal, income-producing, and environmentally viable options that will enable them to overcome the negative conditions that led to the establishment of illegal crops."[57] The implementation of such options would take time—and thus, a necessary gradualism in the eradication of existing coca crops. In the words of one community spokesperson during the negotiations,

> Why can't they understand that this substitution should be gradual? Think about the government's response and the plans they propose. How can they tell us that if we can borrow several million, two or three million pesos to plant rubber, that the campesino would have to eradicate his crop, and wait seven years until he can harvest rubber? Would the government also lend the campesino what it takes to support himself for those seven years? No, we are saying that the substitution

should be gradual in the sense that when the alternatives presented to the campesino begin to produce income, they will also be an example to convince more campesinos to eradicate their crops.[58]

Campesinos maintained that they needed time to see the results of an economic alternative before committing themselves to eradicating their coca crops entirely. In "Reality and Alternatives," community representatives had included a proposal for the creation of a revolving fund to provide cash for the purchase of food crops. This idea had been floated by the campesinos since the time of the La Hormiga Accords. In the negotiations, campesino leaders attempted to get the state to commit to providing resources for this kind of project until they could reach self-sustainability: "The problem is, if we don't take care of [the revolving fund] it will be because there is not a real willingness for substitution. So I ask you to help us find viable means for substitution. Let's not commit ourselves to fantasies and end up believing in them."[59]

The growers' willingness to participate in substitution would not be sufficient to achieve it. The state too, would have to show a commitment and play a prominent role in any viable substitution process. A Civic Movement leader commented: "We agree to the substitution of these crops, but by means of serious commitments fully complied with. Otherwise, sooner or later, we would just be transferring the problem somewhere else."[60] Colombia's long history of violence and displacement led the campesinos to believe that the government did not take them seriously and might not keep its promises. They clearly placed the burden of proof on the government, carefully conditioning their willingness to give up their coca livelihood right away:

> In that sense we are saying, in terms of a gradual substitution, that if the alternative presented to the campesino is credits for the purchase of seed corn, for example, and due to the circumstances the government agrees to purchase the harvest—because that is another problem—then new outside markets open up, well, *if after eight months we see that the state is holding up its end of the bargain, then we will comply because the state is complying.*[61]

The government held to its staunch position that total eradication would be a sine qua non of any deal. At the beginning of the negotiations, this position was so radical that the commission purposely ignored a part of the La

Hormiga Accords, reinforcing its reputation for untrustworthiness among the campesinos. The president's representative Eduardo Díaz considered this prior agreement—not to fumigate crops of under three acres—to have been a mistake, commenting to me, "It contradicts the state's principle that we must do away with coca." Referring to the Accords, he said: "With the fumigations being pursued in Guaviare, one of the complaints that people made was based on the commitment made in the previous agreement of 1994, and '95, that crops of less than three hectares would not be fumigated. We entered these [1996] negotiations on the basis that this time coca eradication is non-negotiable, not like two years ago [referring to the negotiation of La Hormiga Accords]."[62]

From the central government's point of view, the specter of large-scale drug trafficking power lurked behind every concern that the campesinos expressed, limiting the trust it could place in them. This, along with the impossibility of negotiating on issues of fumigation or gradualism, prevented the kind of direct dialogue that would otherwise have been possible. Over the course of the negotiations, however, the government began to distinguish clearly and publicly between a policy of voluntary eradication for small growers and forced eradication by fumigation for large plantations. In the words of Eduardo Díaz:

> The fact that we are sitting here stems from the realization that on one hand we have the problem of the campesino grower and it calls for different measures than the problem of large plantations. That's clear to us; that's why we distinguish between forced eradication and voluntary eradication accompanied by a crop substitution process. . . . We're trying to eliminate an economic interest that has been growing nationally and regionally through the production and trafficking of illegal products. Yes, it has its network and its presence here, but that doesn't mean that the campesino growing one or two hectares is a drug trafficker. The government does not believe, has not believed, and will never believe that the problem of the campesino grower is the same as the problem of the drug trafficking mafia. The government has that perfectly clear, and that's why there is a PLANTE for the campesinos but a law enforcement approach for drug traffickers. This should be understood.[63]

While agreeing with this distinction between the small grower and large plantation owners, the campesino delegates wanted the draft agreement document to exclude any distinction between forced and voluntary eradication. They proposed the following text: "A program for the gradual replacement of illegal crops will be implemented in parallel with and simultaneous to the formulation of a medium-term development plan to substitute an economy based on legal, productive, and income-producing crops for the economy based on illegal crops. . . . A national institution and process of concertación will be established for this purpose."[64] The establishment of a national concertación process was intended to continue what was begun in the negotiations. It would be a way to guarantee the campesinos' inclusion as citizens with a right to participate in the making of policies that affected them.

Suspension and Redirection of Negotiations

Unable to gain unambiguous recognition as campesinos and colonos who grow coca, as social actors distinct from drug traffickers and guerrillas, the Civic Movement representatives suspended the solution-building process by walking out of negotiations on August 9, 1996. This move took the government negotiators by surprise:

> Eduardo Díaz and the members of the government commission at that time thought that the campesinos were also very worn out, that they would get tired and give up. . . . Emiro [head of the Civic Movement] announced that negotiations were breaking down, and that was going to be that, and Eduardo Díaz said, "Well let them break down then, because really what is going to end this, is that it will become exhausted and cave in on itself." "That's not true," Emiro responded, "If you want to see how much the campesinos support this process and how this process is going to continue, we'll show you." Nobody believed him. But the next day more than 100 vehicles full of people from La Dorada, La Hormiga, and San Miguel appeared in Orito. It was impressive. It impressed Eduardo Díaz.[65]

At the breaking point of the talks, government representatives tried to redirect the discussion, taking refuge in the simpler matter of providing services: "The people of Putumayo are interested in solutions: roads, electrification, schools, health, education, credits, access to markets, and the infrastructure of Putumayo. That's why we came here."[66] In fact, the commission officials had come prepared with a repertoire of services from within their respective departments, in hopes of coaxing an agreement out of the movement negotiators. At the same point, García chose to relate an anecdote, perhaps paradoxically: "There are many people involved with illegal crops in Colombia who tell us, 'I don't want credits. Build a road and I can take care of myself.'" García's understanding of this comment was clearly mediated by his view of coca as an economic activity with negative effects on the people: he interpreted it as the campesino's desire to break out of coca growing with or without the state's help, "because in all this time, illegal crops in Putumayo have not stimulated development. On the contrary, they have stimulated tremendous social division and disintegration."[67]

The vice minister Echeverry then exaggerated the Civic Movement leaders' resistance to limiting the talks to infrastructure, to the point of distorting their negotiating position: "The movement insists that they are not interested in a comprehensive agrarian policy, in electrification, roads, health, education, housing, human rights, telecommunications, or land-use planning. Instead the movement starts from the premise that Colombian legislation on the control of narcotics must be changed. This commission regrets that position, and understands that what this movement and its organizers are asking for is a legislative reform process that is the responsibility of the national Congress."[68]

In reality, however, García was reacting to a structural problem in Amazonia, as important to many campesinos as the issue of credit: the lack of roads to transport agricultural products to market. García had not understood that the campesinos were demanding a comprehensive solution to the agrarian problem that would lead to a solid alternative economy.

During the August 9 walkout, a campesino spokesperson, frustrated by the lack of agreement after three long days of negotiations, pleaded with the government team as he got up from the table: "Really listen to us, because it doesn't serve any purpose if we just explain our views and you just explain government policies, and in the end everything is the same. We need to produce something jointly."[69]

The Comprehensive Emergency Development Plan for a Putumayo Free of Coca

The government commission returned to Bogotá as soon as the negotiations were suspended, but Serpa did have three representatives stay on to see whether they could restart the dialogue. They were Jaime Navarro (Serpa's advisor), Eduardo Díaz (director of the Solidarity Network and presidential representative), and Fernando Salgado (Health Ministry representative). Díaz described this trio's mission at that juncture: "I stayed there with a Health Ministry official because I had talked to Serpa and Serpa told me, 'Do everything you can.'"[70] The leaders of the Civic Movement for the Comprehensive Development of Putumayo responded to the overtures of these three officials by proposing a change in the negotiation agenda to analyze the human rights situation first, then the public order in the zone following the campesino mobilizations, and leaving the question of illegal crops to be discussed third, since this was the topic that had caused the negotiations to break down.[71]

While the government commission had been willing to negotiate on human rights from the start, branches of the government had taken contradictory, confusing actions and positions in this regard. The attorney general's office expressed an intention to protect the respect for life, yet opened investigations on movement leaders that put their lives in danger. The armed forces had declared the movement illegal in an effort to justify their repressive measures against campesinos. Moving human rights to the top of the agenda, therefore, "saved the dialogue" according to the press.[72] Negotiations with the three officials reopened on August 10 after one day of suspension and based on the movement's proposed new agenda. Above all, the negotiators sought to keep the previous disagreements in mind to find a shared conceptual framework for the problem of illegal crops. Eduardo Díaz explained: "First we generated a very simple document stating that we were producing a joint plan for a Putumayo without coca. Even though the mobilization continued, we were working under the understanding that would be an agreement."[73]

This goal of a "Putumayo without coca" provided the parties with the foundation for an agreement. While they had different ideas about how to achieve it, the government and campesinos shared this goal. The Civic Movement proposed the creation of a development plan that would specify steps needed to substitute other crops for coca. A local official and advisor to the Civic Movement explained the origin of the idea for a new development plan: "I proposed to Emiro that the text of a comprehensive development plan be negotiated. Both parties, the Civic Movement and the state, readily accepted the idea. The departmental government was not happy that another development plan was being written, because they had already written one. The campesinos proposed that the department not be in charge of carrying the new plan out."[74] Jaime Navarro described the jurisdictional dilemma: "We can consider the plan, but there is a legal problem. There is already an authorized Putumayo Development Plan. . . . drawn up by the Departmental Assembly, the body that has legal standing to establish development plans, so we would have to find a way around that. The point is how to avoid confusion of two different departmental plans."[75]

To help avoid this confusion, the campesino negotiating team proposed the name Comprehensive Emergency Development Plan, and described their vision of it as a "departmental emergency plan with comprehensive programs and measures for the harmonious development of a Putumayo without coca, sustained in an income-generating economic model of solidarity with the additional resources required to carry out the necessary administrative measures."[76]

Governor Fuerbringer believed that "the majority of the campesinos' demands were included in the existing departmental plan, called the 'Public Awareness Campaign for the Development of Putumayo.'"[77] Movement leaders, however, felt that the idea of this new plan was more positive because it responded directly to the people's demands and allowed for community participation. Eduardo Díaz concurred that the formulation of a new, more participatory development plan was valuable in the context of the negotiations: "My approach in the negotiations was that we were working against drug trafficking. That's why the development plan provided a path to a Putumayo without coca. Now, *how* can we eliminate coca? That's the tough part."[78]

The agreement to create this joint plan did not promise a differentiated approach to the small grower, nor did it recognize the historical nature of the agrarian problem, but the vision of a Putumayo without coca did allow the parties to reopen negotiations. It provided a cooperative means to a shared ideal of an end. The title that the movement and government commissions agreed on—"Comprehensive Emergency Development Plan for a Coca-free Putumayo Sustained in an Economy of Solidarity"—allowed them both to cry victory while providing a viable platform for moving forward with negotiations.

Shaping of the Initial Agreement

Once the parties agreed on this conceptual approach to the coca problem in Putumayo, they drafted an initial document designed to overcome the differences that had led to the earlier breakdown of negotiations. It read as follows, with paragraph numbering added:

(1) The establishment in Putumayo of a regional economy principally based on the production of illegal crops has resulted in large scale migration to urban and rural areas and the opening of widespread areas to colonization, increasing social decay and violence.

(2) As a result there is an urgent legal, social, environmental, and economic need to eradicate and replace illegal crops and completely and definitively restructure the economy in order to establish the basis for and execute a Comprehensive Emergency Departmental Development Plan through integrated projects, programs, and actions directed toward the harmonious development of a Putumayo without coca based on an income-generating and sustainable economic model of solidarity.

(3)(a)Voluntary eradication and substitution of small plots of illegal crops is viable through a united effort involving campesinos, colonos, indigenous people, the government and international partners.

(3)(b) In order to assure the success of this Voluntary Eradication and Substitution Plan for small-scale illegal crops and the consolidation of the campesino economy, it is necessary to clearly define the areas of agricultural and forest industry production and areas of environmental production, as well as timetables, resources, procedures, controls and monitoring mechanisms. This coordinated effort is intended to preclude factors that might lead to the continuity, reproduction, or expansion of the illegal economy.

(4) In this sense, small growers involved in the voluntary, total, and definitive eradication of illegal crops and the substitution of legal crops are valid and necessary interlocutors in the formulation and implementation of comprehensive solutions.[79]

To avoid the chicken-and-egg problem of the first negotiating session, the parties ultimately agreed not to specify the underlying causes of coca cultivation in the first paragraph of the agreement. The campesinos rejected the government's suggested language on drug traffickers and considered its omission to be a victory:

Here in the case of Putumayo, that's not the case. Here the campesinos help each other, but not with resources from drug trafficking. Here the campesinos give one or two hectares to new arrivals, who have gotten here just by stubborn determination. And in case that isn't enough, they give them seeds, or at least they front them the seeds until the land produces. I think it's significant that we've eliminated that term [drug trafficking networks].[80]

Movement leaders had wanted to name both "civilian authorities" and "international partners" as their collaborators at the beginning of the document's third paragraph on cooperation:

Why civilian authorities? As we were saying yesterday, we're not interested in leaving these negotiations committed to a policy of war. We want to leave these negotiations committed to a policy of peace, a civilian policy. That's why we say "civilian authorities." And why international partners? Because this special plan, this Emergency Plan, requires resources. And the resources that it requires, let's be clear, may be more than the state can provide. So we can make use of international support because the problem is that big.[81]

The Movement wanted the state to commit itself to a policy of peace in the region via mention of "civilian authority," so that campesinos could deal directly with state representatives and without the Army's intermediation. They wanted to stop the war that had been declared against them by the military. The presence of international partners, which was the only part they succeeded at including in the paragraph, would also serve to put their plight in a more civilian and less repressive context.

While the campesino leaders clearly desired an international presence in the area, there were some aspects of past multilateral plans that they did not want repeated. Indeed, the discussions for the drafting of the rest of the third paragraph revolved directly around a program that the United Nations had sponsored in the region in the early 1990s. This program had concentrated its efforts exclusively in clearly defined "coca areas." A member of the campesino negotiating commission explained why they objected:

And what happened? . . . It's unjust that in those areas where campesinos have obeyed the law despite their abandonment by the state, they should continue to be ignored by the state. It's like saying that you should engage in illegality if you want to get a response from the government. We don't believe that we should create divisions among the campesinos by paying attention to some and abandoning others.

Really, we should look at the specifics of the terrain in order to avoid development plans that threaten to destroy the environmental potential here. . . .[82]

Campesino leaders proposed to delimit areas for environmental protection or production, crop substitution, and agricultural/forest products, and to specify the types of projects that could be carried out in each of them. Areas that met the environmental needs of other productive ecosystems would be protected, and development projects for residents of these areas would have to be environmentally appropriate. The campesinos' greatest victory was won in the fourth paragraph, where they were recognized as "valid and necessary interlocutors" in the creation and implementation of practical solutions to the coca problem in Putumayo. While their value in this sense would seem implicit in the very fact that they were jointly negotiating a document—any document—with the central government, the exact final language nevertheless had a very powerful symbolic importance to them. While it did not explicitly recognize them as "social actors," it did so implicitly. Their input was finally considered "valid," even "necessary," and they were helping to define and implement comprehensive solutions.

The drafting of the first four paragraphs of this initial agreement in Orito allowed movement leaders to begin to think about lifting the strike. However, the importance of this language was clearer to movement leaders than it was to other campesinos, who were more concerned with specific demands for services. A few of their posters expressed this: "Thirty Years of Oil Extraction Here and the People without Roads, Electricity, Plumbing, Schools, Credit, or Hospitals," "We Demand Compliance with the Accords: Health, Education, Roads." One march participant told me, "The first page of the initial agreement was key for the Civic Movement and for civil society. The rest of the agreement is a response to the demonstrations: roads, bridges, electrification, etc."[83]

Final Agreement and End of the Mobilization: Two Perspectives on Its Achievements

The second part of the initial agreement established twelve working groups made up of "community representatives and central government officials with decision-making authority" to deal with the lack of public services in Putumayo and to come up with solutions. The understanding was that once the work of these groups was done, the strike could be lifted.

Figure 11. Cocalero campesinos demanding a state presence. The central poster says "Piñuña Negro. We demand a solution to the problems of the campesinos of Putumayo. We want peace." (León Darío Peláez, Casa Editorial, *El Tiempo*)

This agreement reflected the campesinos' two main concerns: first, they needed a true commitment from the government to work alongside them and support them with resources until solutions were actually implemented. Second, they wanted to use the 1991 Constitution to exercise their freedom of expression without suffering military abuse and—a hotly debated point which the campesinos managed to get included—to require the government to keep its word. This initial agreement was signed on August 11 and the working groups started meeting right away. A new wave of central government representatives from various national institutions including the Interior, Agriculture, and Health Ministries, PLANTE, INCORA, and the Solidarity Network traveled to Orito for this second stage of negotiations.[84] Conscious of the complexity of the task that lay before them and of their responsibility to the cocalero campesinos, Civic Movement leaders, for their part, continued to seek the technical support of local officials as expert advisors. This second phase lasted one week, during which the twelve working groups were consolidated into eight (listed in appendix 3). Though the discussions were heated at times, they were fruitful.

Outside the negotiating spaces, however, conflict and confrontation continued between the cocaleros and the military. Two fragmentation grenades were detonated on August 13, one at a campesino security post in Orito and the other in the middle of a tent encampment. Two campesinos were killed and thirty-two were injured (CINEP and Justicia y Paz 1996, no. 1, July–September). Movement leader Luis Emiro declared that the initial agreement would be respected and negotiations continued, but he requested that the government investigate this attack on the civilian population apparently intended to hinder the process.[85] Emiro's statement reaffirmed the campesinos' overarching desire to come to an agreement and avoid further conflict and violence. They expressed regret for the sabotage of the oil pipelines "because such acts do not reflect the civic character of the mobilization, nor its orientation."[86]

The discussions and work of the Human Rights Working Group that week largely centered around fears among movement participants that they themselves would be targets of threats and reprisals. Leaders and demonstrators requested that the Presidential Advisor on Human Rights set up a government hotline for the use of strike leaders and participants. They also requested a review of all the human rights violations that had occurred in the context of the mobilizations and amnesty for employees who had missed work because of the strike. The Civic Movement displayed interest in both defending freedom of expression and in the struggle against impunity, so at the signing of the agreements they demanded that "officials be sent to take appropriate steps, together with civil, military, and judicial authorities in regard to concrete cases [of threats, disappearances, and murders]. In these cases the ombudsman and the district prosecutor will be asked to act as well."[87] Despite their fears and sacrifices, the campesinos continued their strike and their negotiations on forming substantive agreements.

By August 18, the working groups had reached and signed specific agreements (summarized in appendix 3) that, combined with the language of the initial agreement, constituted a final complete understanding between the two parties. This document, the "Comprehensive Emergency Development Plan for a Coca-free Putumayo Sustained in an Economy of Solidarity," was signed August 19, after twenty-five days of striking. By signing this document, the parties publicly committed themselves to comply with and implement its contents. They also pledged to engage the community, NGOs, professional groups, and civil society in an ongoing monitoring process through a commission that would provide follow-up and report on implementation. This signing signaled the end of the Orito negotiations and enabled organizers to lift the strike.

When news of the Orito agreement got out, Mayor Urbano issued a decree (Decree 25 of August 20, 1996) officially recognizing August 19 as the anniversary of the day of the signing, the welcome end to a strike that had cost the department millions of pesos.[88] The decree distinguished the day as a historical referent, a culturally appropriated symbol of the Movement's negotiating strength, and the state's acknowledgement of Movement leaders as legitimate campesino representatives and negotiating partners. To this day, Orito sponsors a celebration every year on August 19.

The agreement had great symbolic importance for the Civic Movement. The cocalero campesinos' had gained a new identity through their increased awareness of their own organizing capacity and power to exercise collective pressure in demanding citizenship rights. Jaime Peña, mayor of Piamonte and a member of the Inga indigenous group, referred to the cocalero movement as an identity marker for the region's colonos: "Before the marches, the colonos didn't have an identity, but now they do, even though they don't have a long history in the territory like ours. But they weren't going to sacrifice sixty days for nothing. As a mayor, I have to say that I have a lot of respect for the 1996 agreement."[89] This newfound identity lasted beyond the immediate follow-up to the 1996 agreement. In May 1998, for example, when a commission of JAC leaders occupied the Ombudsman's office in Bogotá (see chapter 7), the campesinos spoke with pride of their participation and resistance—during a month of well organized protests. One of them declared, "It doesn't matter if they spray. We've shown that we're prepared to confront whatever happens."[90]

While the final agreement represented a clear success to both of the negotiating teams, it seemed to have two different meanings to the respective parties. The interior minister stated to the press that "the fumigation of illegal crops was not negotiated in the agreement signed with the coca growers of Putumayo on Sunday in Orito." He added, "The government takes its responsibility very seriously. We intend to eradicate illegal crops in this country, a non-negotiable step toward our fundamental goal, which is to be a nation without coca."[91] A campesino representative's statement, however, illustrated their own understanding of the outcome: "In order to avoid fumigation or any other method of forcible eradication of illegal crops, we agreed with the government on a voluntary plan for crop substitution."[92] The government's position that fumigation had not been negotiated and was indeed non-negotiable, and the campesinos' position that they had achieved agreement on a plan for voluntary eradication to the exclusion of forced eradication, enabled each side to claim victory. It allowed work on the implementation of the specific agreements to go forward. However—though this was not so evident in the afterglow of the successful agreement—it was also a sign of intractable differences between two distinct perceptions of the coca problem: that of central government hardliners versus that of Civic Movement leaders.

Effective Citizenship: "The Right to Have Rights" and the Opening of Democratic Spaces by the Cocalero Social Movement

The successful resolution to the long strike and arduous negotiations had not only a significant effect on the cocalero campesinos' understanding of their own power, but also concrete policy implications for the entire nation that year. Arturo Ospina, Solidarity Network official at the negotiations, noted that because of the campesino mobilization, "The 1997 [national] budget came out differently. Instead of the usual congressional and political process within state institutions, all those marches changed some of the budget's priorities."[93] The marches affected appropriation of state funds by taking the process out of the hands of clientelist politicians. The Civic Movement was exercising a *politics of influence* (Cohen and Arato 1994). The cocalero movement was the first to address the issue of coca agriculture as a social problem that merited the attention of the state and international community in defense of fundamental rights. It can take credit for the adoption of such discourse by government officials.

Holston and Appadurai (1996, 197) have noted that in the emerging democracies of the developing world, "Rights are conceived of as aspects of social relatedness, rather than as the inherent and natural property of individuals." A right is a demand on society for the fulfillment of the basic necessities and interests of its members rather than something possessed by some and not by others. They also indicate that as social movements concentrate on the demand for citizenship rights and broaden the concept of citizenship to new areas of social, cultural, and economic life, they also create new *sources* of citizenship rights. For example, they can stimulate or influence changes in the constitutional principles or legal norms necessary to define and protect these new rights.

The Colombian Narcotics Law was not reconsidered as a result of the cocalero movement, but the government did agree to take a differentiated approach toward growers of up to three hectares of coca than they did with larger producers. This triggered other concrete policy changes. After the campesino mobilizations, PLANTE made an about-face and established that "its principal responsibility was to recognize the campesino, indigenous, and colono social problem that is generated by the cultivation of illegal crops." Juan Carlos Palou, the second director of PLANTE, explained how this goal was to be pursued at the Environmental National Congress in 1998:

> The first task is to identify the target population defined as those campesino, colono, and indigenous communities whose *histories, trajectories, and traditions* demonstrate that they have resorted to illegal crops as a result of the agrarian crisis that has affected Colombia or due to implacable economic realities. Once these communities are identified, it is necessary to develop with them a clear and certain willingness to abandon those crops and to develop legal economic alternatives. Reciprocity between the state and these communities is a necessary and ineluctable condition for the intervention of PLANTE and its ongoing work on a given project.[94]

In this statement, the new director of PLANTE respected the 1996 cocalero movement's insistence that the central state recognize coca agriculture as a social and economic problem, not a criminal matter. The recognition by PLANTE and Solidarity Network officials of the campesino problem and their new non-punitive approach to coca agriculture were definite achievements of the cocalero movement. The cocalero movement engaged in the *politics of reform* which entailed the creation of political subjects who opposed existing state policies and demanded a role in the development of new ones. Jaime Navarro summed up the effect of the movement: "Whatever happens, we can say that the mobilizations definitely caused us to rethink PLANTE."[95]

At the same time, the agreement also included a commitment to improving basic necessities (listed in appendix 3). Instead of referring to this type of accord as "laundry lists" of demands that do not lead to concrete solutions, are seldom met and therefore tend to demobilize movements, I concur with Alvarez (1997, 109) when she points out that when excluded groups demand infrastructure and public services they are in fact demanding "the right to have rights," "not just to social services but to human dignity, cultural difference and/or social equality." A protest sign in Puerto Asís expressed this idea: "Vereda Alto Piñuña Blanco joins the movement with strength and dignity to demand that the government recognize and respect campesino rights." Another sign was equally clear: "We too are Colombians. Why are we ignored? We need a better future for our children. We deserve to be heard."

In the last analysis, the Civic Movement demanded inclusion in the nation-state and the participatory democracy that it promotes, but to which Putumayans have not had access. Theirs was a demand for access to new democratic forms and new manifestations of citizenship. It entailed the democratization not only of the political regime, but of society itself, in opposition to cultural practices that reflect exclusive and inequitable social relations. It questioned the assignment of roles in a predetermined social order and demonstrated the fundamental nature of citizenship as a *politics of culture* (Alvarez, Dagnino, and Escobar 1998). Through their demand for access to the constitutionally guaranteed civil right of citizen participation, cocalero movement leaders acquired the power to contest the government policy of indiscriminate crop fumigation, which itself ran counter to democratic principles, and gained recognition as "legitimate and necessary interlocutors in the development and implementation of comprehensive solutions."[96] Furthermore, the quest for citizenship rights by Civic Movement leaders also included a demand for protection from the arbitrary exercise of state power, such as persecution of movement leaders by the armed forces and the kind of delegitimization that the cocalero and previous movements in Putumayo had been subjected to. In this conflict-ridden region, the right to life and the right to peace had to be explicitly fought for.

CHAPTER SIX

Competing States or Competing Governments?

An Analysis of Local State Formation in a Conflict-Ridden Zone

Philip Abrams (1988, 77) has called attention to the way the claimed autonomy and integration of the state conceals both "the real history and relations of subjection" and "the existence of connections and conflicts" behind "an ahistorical mask of legitimating illusion." Abrams conceives of the state as "an ideological project" intended to legitimize domination, and its "illusory" image of cohesiveness as a disguise of the real institutional disunity and its internal and external relations, which are in fact "a field of struggle." He emphasizes that only when the association between the idea of the state and its instruments of legitimization (such as armies, prisons, or taxation) "is broken do real hidden powers emerge. And when they do, they are not the powers of the state but of armies of liberation or repression, foreign governments, guerrilla movements, soviets, *juntas*, parties, classes" (Abrams 1988, 77). Taking further Abrams' argument, Aretxaga (2000, 53–54) alerts us that "to investigate the power of the state as a mask is to investigate the political fictions we live by," and to examine "the power of its magic" or its "fetish-power" in Taussig's terms (1992, 113). In this same vein, Coronil (1997) has analyzed the magic ascribed by both ordinary people and powerful elites to the wealthy petro-state in Venezuela throughout its political history: a magical state perceived to be leading Venezuela into modernity and miraculously providing welfare to its population.

These conceptualizations of the state provide a theoretical paradigm that serves to demystify the state's expression of power at the local level and reveal it as a process in formation. It enables us to analyze the state's concrete policies and institutions and the sometimes inconsistent ways they interact, and to be aware of the hidden powers that influence and define public decisions. If we take into account that the "myth or illusion" of a cohesive state is constructed by those subjects within whom the state lives (Sayer 1994), we must see the state as a structural effect and stress the study of those discourses, beliefs, and social practices that concretize it and confer power on it (Foucault 1973, 1994; Mitchell 1991, 1999; Aretxaga 2000, 2002; Trouillot 2001).

The presence of state institutions and apparatus in Colombia has been said to be differentiated and uneven (González, Bolívar, and Vázquez 2002). While the state's authority and control of territory are contested in marginal regions, official institutions do exist and representatives of the state do work directly with regional communities to provide services. This chapter seeks to deepen this analysis by examining the meaning that the state acquires as a provider of services in Putumayo, a marginal region whose residents resent the state's historical abandonment and demand that it fulfill its "paternal" obligations. This chapter also examines the process of local state formation in a region where the presence of illegal crops and non-state armed actors alters the rules of the game and leads to extra-legal forms of authority. Local state construction in such a region is a complex phenomenon involving several factors. First, the government in Bogotá seeks to control or "conquer" this region where the war on drugs is seen as a permanent condition. Left to itself, the region would revert to a Hobbesian "state of nature" but the state fights to bring it back to the central "civilized" order. Second, this process is complicated by the contradictory approaches to the local coca economy taken by different central government bodies, creating the kind of "field of struggle" described by Abrams. Third, for its part, the local government identifies with the cocaleros and feels rejected and ignored by the central state. Finally, FARC performs some state functions by providing some services, while supporting the population's demand for increased state presence at the rhetorical level. This makes it one of the "hidden powers" that must be considered in the process of state formation.

By examining the contentious 1996 negotiations more closely, this chapter also casts light on regional perceptions and conceptions of state, fragmentation within it, and the struggle of movement leaders to try and use it to gain autonomy from FARC. The autonomy of the cocalero social movement must be understood as it both coordinates with and opposes the hegemonic state and other dominant groups in the region. Having emerged in response to the state's stigmatization of campesinos for growing coca, the movement contested state policies. At the same time, campesino leaders sought long-term support from the government in order to achieve status as legal actors and citizens, a first step toward autonomy from the influence of FARC, paramilitaries and narco-traffickers.

Implementing Techniques of Government: FARC Authority in Putumayo

FARC's diffuse and not highly institutionalized power has encouraged the population to accept its disciplinary micro-practices (Foucault 1979), which have been integrated into the campesinos' subjectivity and rooted in their local culture. These governmental practices afford FARC a type of oversight capacity that, nonetheless, does not strip state institutions and regulations of their own authority.

The guerrillas use the JAC network to further their control of the population at the local level. In the 1990s, in order to control the flow of people in and out of the area and avoid paramilitary infiltration, FARC asked coca producers and harvest workers in the veredas of the Baja Bota to affiliate with the JACS. To join a JAC, a campesino had to produce a *cédula*, or national identity card. No other document would do. FARC gave people without cédulas a deadline to acquire them and register.

This is one of numerous examples of FARC's adaptation of state-imposed requirements. Instead of trying to institute its own form of identification, they relied strictly on the central government. Growers were responsible for delivering lists of all the harvest workers working for them, along with their cédula numbers, to the appropriate JAC, and the Committees were instructed to provide membership lists. This registration process provided both a measure of control over the population and an accurate population census.[1] People who could not show at least one year's residence in the area and who had neither land to work nor a cédula were forced by FARC to leave (for the most part, this group consisted of migrant raspachines). Due to the paramilitary threat, FARC was not allowing new people into the region. FARC also controlled the movement of people between towns and veredas, curbing the ability of hostile groups to deliver information that might hurt them or the campesinos.

If someone wished to buy land in the area, he or she had to obtain FARC's permission. The guerrillas would approve or disapprove the sale depending on what was known about the buyer. Since there was so much population movement in the zone, many residents did not even know each other. Campesinos would say of potential buyers, "They know who is who, while we don't know who they are." Campesinos supported FARC's control of movement because they were terrified of paramilitaries entering.

The guerrillas established the following additional regulations:

1. Control of river traffic. In Puerto Amor on the Caquetá River, I observed this sign: "Fronts 32 and 49 prohibit river traffic from 6 p.m. to 6 a.m. Fine 500,000 pesos [US$250]. FARC-EP."

2. Certain public establishments had to close at a given hour and not admit minors. The entry of minors under fifteen years of age to pool halls was subject to a fine of 20,000 pesos (US$10). Discotheques could open from Friday through Sunday.

3. The consumption of alcohol was prohibited from Monday through Friday and festivities could not continue into Monday. Those seen drinking at prohibited times were put to work repairing roads or sweeping streets. The mayor of Piamonte, for example, was punished and put to work sweeping the town.

4. Control of automobile traffic. No one could drive after 10 p.m.

FARC kept tight reins on local police inspectorates to the extent that in some of the most remote places they would require the inspector to obtain their authorization before carrying out his official functions. For example, there was a debate among the dozens of JACs in Piamonte some time after the cocalero marches over whether to allow recently appointed police inspectors to do their work. The guerrillas were promoting the creation of Conciliation Committees within the JACs to carry out functions such as tax collection, animal butchering, and removal of corpses. A few months later, the police inspectors in the corregimientos of the Baja Bota resigned on guerrilla orders, leaving only the Piamonte inspectors on the job. One of the inspectors explained that the guerrillas "did not want any state presence."

The guerrillas explained to the outgoing inspectors that they might be called back to service in the future, but that if and when this occurred, they would be employed by the JACs, not the National Police. In a sense, FARC was sending the message "you work for us" to these policemen, though they declined to govern explicitly, operating instead behind the scenes. These events illustrate how FARC suppressed certain government functions. They had the capacity to directly supervise inspectors, but preferred to dismiss them because they wanted no state presence in the area. They proved that it was they who established discipline and order (state-like authority), while continuing to allow the state to provide other community services.

FARC supported decentralization and the campesinos' demands for state services and infrastructural development. FARC also promoted citizen participation in the planning and execution of projects to benefit the region as a tenet of their overall political stance:

Popular local control is an alternative form of participation in civil society that affords the people an opportunity to denounce the reigning
clientelism and corruption and to move toward the solution of their
most deeply felt needs and problems. For this very reason citizens
have the political obligation to exercise it, in order to be really free. . . .
Local power should contribute to the stabilization and adaptation of
localities seeking to construct a collective identity within the framework of their given local diversity. It should help prepare the people to
come to terms with social change, always seeking the common good,
the basis of all republican legitimacy. (FARC 1998a)

Rather than seek to substitute itself for the state as a service provider,
FARC supported the idea that the state should serve the people and be
answerable to them. This concept was also reflected in the FARC approach
to public administration at the municipal level. The mayor had to produce
an administrative plan, implement projects, and present reports to demonstrate that funds had been used to benefit the community, not squandered
or mismanaged, assuring that community needs were being served. In the
same vein, FARC supported the civic strikes demanding that the state meet
its obligations, and audited the state's compliance with its responsibilities.
Thus it was not so clear that FARC completely opposed state presence and
investment in the Amazon region.

In the words of Comandante Joaquín Gómez of FARC's Southern Block,
"FARC supports the civilian population in its fight against corrupt elements,
because we have nothing to defend but the interests of the population." Regarding FARC's seizure of the Delicias military base in Putumayo and their
imprisonment of sixty soldiers in August 1996, he declared, "Ours was an act
of solidarity against the inhuman, repressive, and punitive treatment being
meted out to the campesinos in the south of the country [during the cocalero movement], whose only crime was to demand that the state fulfill its
obligations" (ANNCOL 1998, 3).

While FARC exercised its authority to maintain order, control, and discipline in the region, it did not attempt to be a state within a state for Amazonian residents. In a published interview, FARC Commander Manuel
Marulanda Vélez defined their presence as "a government within the government."[2] Although FARC orders were obeyed, they were often resisted,
challenged, and negotiated by the population, which continued to demand
a state presence in the area. FARC's actions did not always negate the ability

of those impacted to react or act as individual or collective subjects. The JACS were spaces for negotiation with the state and with political party leaders, but above all with FARC. The people of the region negotiated with FARC as an institutional authority, recognizing their governing role.

This dynamic recalls Foucault's analysis (1991) of the art of governing, or "governmentality." Foucault called attention to the importance of understanding "the survival and limits of the state on the basis of the general tactics of governmentality," meaning that the techniques of government are today "the only real space for political struggle and contestation" since "it is the tactics of government which make possible the continual definition and redefinition or what is within the competence of the state and what is not" (1991, 103). In the case of marginal territory in Colombia, control of the population was contested. As Marulanda's quote clearly illustrated, FARC was more interested in its ability to govern and control the population than it was in replacing the broader role of the state. FARC's relationship with the campesinos was ambiguous; it simultaneously promoted participatory democracy and exercised authoritarianism. This was the core of the guerrillas' double discourse: by proclaiming themselves defenders of campesino interests, they legitimized both their military actions and their authoritarianism.

The State's Focus on Sovereignty over Meeting Social and Economic Needs

Jaime Navarro, advisor to the Interior Minister, commented that from the government's perspective, FARC had "controlling authority" in the region, while the mayors had authority, but not control. Although the central state was present in the form of official institutions, its capacity to govern was challenged: "There is no single set of rules. Everything is mediated and negotiated with the other sources of power that are present there."[3] As governing powers, both the state and FARC exercised jurisdiction in the zone, and neither seemed to supplant the other. The region faced "an excess of statehood practices" in the sense expressed by Aretxaga (2003, 396): "too many actors competing to perform as state."

For central government officials, the needs of the population and the proposals of local officials to address the region's social and economic problems were subsumed by the problem of security and the push to recover state sovereignty through military control of territory. These goals were in turn framed by the discourse of the war on drugs, since FARC was defined as a drug cartel. Navarro added "More than state construction, what needs to be done in these regions is the construction of sovereignty. Once sovereignty is constructed, the state can be constructed on that basis."[4] Navarro emphasized the spatial aspect of the sovereign state and its control over a defined territory, echoing Lefebvre's (1991, 281) "spatial framework" of the state discussed in chapter 2. In the same vein, Navarro reflected the view of the Amazon as a marginal region that first had to be incorporated into the "civilized" nation—where the rule of law was hegemonic and not subject to other "uncivil" arrangements—by the proper exercise of sovereignty, over both the international borders that divide Colombia from other countries and over internal, FARC-delineated borders. Hector Moreno Reyes, the PLANTE director during the 1996 marches, similarly maintained that the government needed to make its presence felt before he could concern himself with PLANTE's projects in the borderlands. This perspective would become even more dominant as the paramilitaries consolidated their presence in the region; Plan Colombia began to be implemented in 2000; the antiterrorist struggle took priority after 9/11; and coca growing came to be viewed solely as a source of financing for terrorism. The structural economic, social and political reasons for peasants to resort to illicit crops were given no further consideration (see chapter 8).

The Role of Hidden Powers during and after Negotiations

When negotiators met in Orito to try to solve the coca quagmire in the region, dynamics of influence and behind-the-scenes pressure on both parties began to be visible. The Civic Movement leaders lacked autonomy vis-à-vis FARC and also began to pose a political threat to the department's traditional political players, who reacted by sabotaging their progress. These politicians employed strategies including even manipulation of FARC to thwart their competition, as recounted by the Mocoa Hospital director in this story:

> An election period was coming. Dr. Galarza [a DASALUD official in Mocoa], had been advising the [campesino leaders] on health issues and began to dream of a possible candidacy for governor. The leadership and assistance [Galarza and I] had given to the mobilization had given the campesinos a lot of confidence in us. [The Civic Movement leader] Luis Emiro was very generous in recognizing the very practical help we had provided there, so Dr. Galarza really had developed a very good

image. But he had enemies here among the political class, among the most recalcitrant Liberals, and they found a way to get him kidnapped by FARC, accusing him of being a large landowner, of having pocketed funds from the regional lottery, when really the lottery Board of Directors was made up of the Governors. But around here, you know, they manipulate information. . . .[5]

In this example, damaging charges against Dr. Galarza were fed to FARC by the Civic Movement's political enemies, the traditional "recalcitrant Liberals," so that their candidate would be kidnapped. Dr. Galarza was released after fourteen months in April 1998, a few weeks after the gubernatorial election.

The central government team, for its part, had to conform to the internationally imposed parameters of the war on drugs, with pressure from both the Attorney General's office and hardliners in the Colombian military. These factors compromised the government's ability to support the campesinos in formulating the Comprehensive Emergency Development Plan.

A Solidarity Network official described the specter he perceived lingering behind the cocaleros at the negotiations:

> They were speaking in the name of a civic movement and yes, the Civic Movement exists, but we all know that behind the Civic Movement there is a lot of pressure from armed actors in that region. What we were seeing from the point of view of our side, of the state, was that their positions were very closed, not very spontaneous. It was they— not we, who were representing the state—who were very cautious about what to write, what to sign, what commitments to make. Our efforts really reflected a tremendous political will to try to resolve the problem. . . . In this case the state was well represented. In contrast, we believe that the community representation was not so clear because they were not campesinos. That is, yes they were campesinos, but they weren't really representing themselves there, as spontaneous or traditional movements made up of grassroots campesino organizations normally do. They were representing interests and receiving instructions. If we messed up, it could have cost us our jobs or some administrative sanctions, but they . . . were under great pressure from armed groups, both the guerrillas and the drug traffickers. . . . They could never make any decision, they had to check on every word and double check it to be sure, because they were risking their lives.[6]

The government commission hardliners could not escape the belief that the campesinos were controlled by FARC or traffickers. This impeded their ability to see movement leaders as they were struggling to be seen. The meticulousness over decisions that Ospina observed in the cocalero negotiators may have been more a reflection of their desire to include the broader campesino community than it was an effect of FARC intervention. Campesino leaders saw an opportunity in the dialogue to gain further autonomy from the very actors the government feared were behind them, by winning concrete state support that would supplant FARC's and traffickers' roles in their lives. However, as Civic Movement leaders gained recognition and momentum, the friction between them and some of these groups increased. In the words of Eduardo Díaz:

> We began to meet in Puerto Asís with the [the follow-up committee to negotiations], and this definitely generated a conflict between [Movement leaders] and the guerrillas. This [friction] was clearly expressed, not only with the guerrillas, but with the departmental and municipal authorities also, because to some degree [the leaders] were setting themselves up as the people in charge in Putumayo. . . . They were creating a political space for themselves at the expense of the Liberal Party, the Conservative Party, the mayors, the guerrillas, at everybody's expense, and with the support of one sector of the government that was giving them what they asked for. Not giving them everything, but giving generously.[7]

Jaime Navarro concurred. He indicated that after the negotiations, it became clear to him that FARC had never liked the signed agreement, since it implicitly recognized the Civic Movement leaders' own decision-making power. He appreciated the importance of the role the state could play in providing the region's inhabitants with public services responsive to their needs, and in so doing, gain ground against FARC.[8] Yet his team also was constrained. Díaz recounted the pressures on central government officials:

> President Samper had to be careful because of the political situation at that time. There were coup rumors, and this was a very delicate topic because it was about illegal crops, and any agreement with them might have shed a very negative light on the President and on the country. . . . [The attorney general] Valdivieso was in Washington and I was in Putumayo. Well, at that early stage of the negotiations, the

Figure 12. Cocalero campesinos against the United States' war on drugs. The poster at the right above the cow says, "We voted for Samper, not for the DEA." Written on the cow: "If they spray me I die." (Jorge Parga, Casa Editorial, *El Tiempo*)

text, I obviously had to clear it with Serpa [the interior minister], but you're not going to believe this. Serpa, in order to avoid disputes, had to clear it with Valdivieso, because the Attorney General's office had said that we were negotiating with drug traffickers. Whenever we were ready to sign something, we knew that without Valdivieso's approval they would immediately open an investigation on us for making commitments and signing an agreement with criminals.[9]

As a program of the presidency, the Solidarity Network had to be focused as much on highlighting a "Putumayo free of coca," which had earned the administration legitimacy in the cocalero negotiations, as it was on substantive implementation of its commitments in the Orito Agreement. The central government as a whole was not focused as much on structural solutions to the social, economic, and political problems of Putumayo as on achieving quick eradication, so it could be recertified by the United States.

In sum, hidden powers exercised their influence on the two negotiating parties both during and after the 1996 Orito discussions. FARC ultimately opposed the locally-initiated Comprehensive Emergency Development Plan, creating one of the difficulties the Civic Movement would face in drafting and implementing it.

The government, perceiving the movement's deflating efforts, attributed this dynamic to FARC control and further intensified repressive actions such as aerial spraying. Unfortunately, the divergent interests of the state and the guerrillas ended up coinciding to prolong Putumayo's marginality and frustrate the population's desire to replace the coca economy with productive alternatives.

Fragmentation of the State: Internal Divisions among Government Negotiators

Divisions among the local, regional, and national representatives on the government delegation were clear from the moment the Orito negotiations began. A Solidarity Network official explains:

> The way people arranged themselves around the table mirrored the sectors that were participating. On one side of the table were the campesinos' representatives in all their varieties and subgroups. And the [central] state representatives sat on this side, but sometimes the departmental officials sat on this side and sometimes they sat on the other side. And the mayors sat on the ends. . . . But the curious thing was that sometimes the departmental officials sat on one side, when essential things were being worked out, things that everyone agreed on, but when it came time to take responsibility, they would switch sides. So it was very ambiguous.[10]

Jaime Navarro added:

> One day I had to say to the governor, "Governor, which side of the table are you on?" And he got furious . . . then he said to me, "Why are you asking me that?" So I told him, "Because your staff is on the other side of the table, but you're here with us, planning how to make proposals, how we are going to negotiate. But then we get to the table and we find out that they already know our negotiating plans. So which side of the table are you on?"[11]

The local and regional authorities' ambivalence towards the national representatives was obvious. They could choose to support the central government officials and identify with the state, or they could identify with the social, economic, and political problems of the region, thereby supporting the cocaleros. Their past experience led them to view the central government officials to be outsiders: "A stranger is neither friend nor enemy, and because he may be both" (Bauman 1990, 145). Unlike local officials, central government officials are removed from the reality of life in the zone and as a result, they are oblivious to the effects of some of their decisions.

A local official describes how he and the group of regional officials in general experienced their position between the central government and campesinos:

> I was the hospital director, and the others there were from other institutions. That's just what we needed, that we would fail to defend the region, that, as advisors to the campesinos, we would advise them poorly and let them be tricked! The [government's] idea was that we would help the government negotiate the cheapest possible settlement. *But we are also Putumayans. The conditions in the region are painful for us, too. We also feel the lack of so many things.* But that was the government's mentality, trying to manipulate the negotiations. *They never took a magnanimous attitude.*[12]

In Rincón's words, we see the emergence of a regional identity constructed on the basis of social contestation and confrontation (Fox 1985).

Government divisions existed not just between national and regional officials, but also among central government entities themselves. The contradictory positions of the armed forces, the attorney general, and the negotiators were perhaps the most stark example, but fragmentation could be seen even between development institutions. Official representatives of the Solidarity Network wanted to work with the campesinos "to demonstrate that voluntary eradication was possible."[13] The network's director, Eduardo Díaz, understood that winning the confidence of the campesinos would also mean victory over the drug traffickers and FARC. Jaime Navarro, the Solidarity Network representatives, and other officials at the table who had a work history in the region, wanted to reach an agreement and forge closer ties with the campesinos in order to neutralize the support guerrillas were providing them. Díaz explained: "Our strategy was to achieve an alliance between the campesinos of Putumayo and the authorities, at least the national ones or the ones we were representing. And we had a strong interest in allying ourselves with them, in demonstrating that with an alliance basically between the campesinos and the government, it was possible to construct a different Putumayo. . . . To the guerrillas this alliance is a disaster, but that's our goal, to win over the campesinos."[14]

On the other hand, as a presidential crop substitution program, PLANTE was caught up in the discourse of the war on drugs, criminalizing coca growers and avoiding efforts to define any free-standing comprehensive social or rural development program. As Jaime Navarro described, "PLANTE was completely off track. They had no proposal to work with the people. . . . Hector Moreno insisted that eradication was a precondition for PLANTE to act, so its role was to moralize, to preach to the campesinos that they should abandon their illegal activities and take up legal activities. Only then would PLANTE support them in those legal activities."[15]

Tensions Stemming from the Decentralization Process

The 1991 Constitution recognized departments, districts, municipalities, and indigenous territories as territorial entities and granted them powers, among others, to receive a share of the national revenue, levy taxes, and to administer the resources necessary to carry out their responsibilities. Law 60 of 1993 mandated that funds transferred from the central state to municipal governments be used almost exclusively for education, health care, potable water, and sports and recreation, leaving only a small portion available for other uses. These limitations were imposed in order to create an incentive for local administrations to generate their own revenues. Decree 5367 of 1994 assigned responsibility to the National Planning Department for distributing resources and administering municipal participation in central government revenues.

Tensions inherent to this decentralization process also came to light during the negotiations. Mayors carried their own frustration with the central government because they felt that in this process, "responsibilities were decentralized but resources were not."[16] They felt left in the lurch by "decentralized" problems without solutions, with important funding decisions still being made by the National Planning Department. Jaime Navarro clearly explained this dynamic:

> [The mayors] say, "We are elected by the people; we have to respond to our communities and our communities are not receiving anything. Our own resources and the appropriations we receive are insufficient. We know that a lot of resources are distributed by the central gov-

ernment through the co-financing of specific projects, and that the National Planning Department determines the priorities for such programs, or they are determined through negotiations in Congress. So we are not obliged to support the central government's positions." That's true, because the central government doesn't appoint them and they aren't directly answerable to it. But the central government tells them, "This year you have to make such and such an investment.". . . *It's a dependent decentralization. Planning is done at the central level, these emergency priorities are set at the central level, and the responsibility is passed to the regional entities. . . . So they don't really have any autonomy.*[17]

The "dependent decentralization" described by Navarro led local officials at the Orito negotiations to demand state services, along with adequate funding to carry out the projects in their municipalities. The ongoing power of the National Planning Department in setting budget priorities helps explain the mayors' ambivalence towards central government officials: they depended on but at the same time felt mistreated by them.

A further complicating factor was that the new departments and municipalities created in the 1991 Constitution were marginal areas, almost by definition lacking the revenue collection infrastructure needed to provide them with adequate locally generated funds. Navarro explained: "There are no property taxes. Industry and commerce: what is that? Maybe in Puerto Asís. Apart from that, there is nothing. They live off transfers from the capital."[18]

Despite local complaints about decentralization, the Putumayo mayors and governor acknowledged the state's presence in the form of infrastructure projects, and gave the central government credit for helping previously abandoned communities in this regard. In evaluating the 1996 Orito negotiations, the governor concluded that the government had, for the most part, stood behind projects sponsored by co-financing funds and programs "that were already in progress [or] on the verge of beginning."[19] Co-financing funds were basically central government programs that required a municipal contribution of 15 to 20 percent of the total cost of a project. Although these matching funds were hard to raise, and the level of central government financing obtained was less than expected, the mayors agreed that projects linked to these funds were effectively supported, and that the funds "became the greatest central government contribution to isolated communities abandoned during previous governments. With the help of the four co-financing funds, social projects have been developed."[20] While the government's investments were recognized, the region's dominant narrative remained one of state abandonment and neglect. The Puerto Asís mayor Nestor Hernández Iglesias expressed his lack of confidence in government agencies in Putumayo, saying that "experience has taught us that they are ineffectual."[21]

The Paradoxical Construction of the State

Various dimensions and faces are entailed as a result of the powers, discourses, and practices that cohabit within the popular concept of a single entity, the state (Herzfeld 1992; Brown 1995). The contradictions, ambivalences, ambiguities and paradoxes observable in both the practice of public officials and in its popular representation all contributed to the idea of the state in Putumayo and to the ways people subjected themselves to or resisted it. Subordinate populations use forms, images, symbols, or hegemonic organizations to confront, understand, accommodate or resist their domination (Roseberry 1994). In the words of Sayer (1994, 389), "The polysemic, ambiguous, contradictory quality of these putative state forms, even as they oppress, they also empower. It is not a question of either/or but both/ and." By examining the state's practices in Putumayo we gain insight into its paradoxical construction in the popular imagination. While cocalero campesinos in Putumayo appealed to the state for solutions to their problems, they also accused it of being repressive and menacing, pursuing policies that encouraged violence in the area. On the one hand, the state treated cocaleros as criminals, and sponsored military abuse of human rights that attempted to silence their social and economic demands. On the other hand, it provided services and institutional space for citizen participation. The state was feared but its protection was sought.[22]

In the case of Putumayo, a bipartite understanding of the state makes it comprehensible, but only to the extent that it can be both good and bad at the same time. Campesinos from the Villanueva vereda in Mayoyoque, municipality of Puerto Guzmán, sent this letter to the national ombudsman:

> What we want is that the government understand our needs, that please, before combating, or in other words eradicating illegal crops, first *provide* our community with alternative possibilities for work. We wonder what the government wants to do to our country with this

fumigation. *All the government is accomplishing is creating more hunger and violence because we can all understand that hunger breeds desperation and in a hungry and desperate country violence will always follow.*[23]

The repressive state responsible for enforcement of the laws against coca is rejected, and the service-providing state is forcefully invited. The campesinos believed that the least the Colombian state could do was provide them with alternative opportunities for work, a means of sustenance to replace coca. In the region's collective memory, the government has never been able to provide necessary services to the population. Two banners at the 1996 civic strike read: "Our need for public services makes us strike," and "The government is forcing us to strike." The discourse of state abandonment provided an impetus for people to make demands of the state, wait passively for their basic needs to be satisfied, and then blame the state's inaction for their deplorable situation and their reaction: the strike. A third banner read, "We are a peaceful people waiting for solutions." From the strikers' perspective, the state should have been providing for the people's needs.

The Putumayan discourse fetishizes the state as a paternalist entity with magical protective powers. If it would only intervene and exercise its paternal functions, it could change the course of history for the region and its inhabitants, i.e. its children. In this view, the paternal central state is expected to somehow resolve all the people's problems.

Although this kind of relationship with a state may result in dependence and disempowerment, in the case of Putumayo it has to be recognized that state-sponsored citizen participation had an empowering effect on cocalero campesinos in the midst of armed conflict. Passivity produced by the paternalist relationship with the state was transformed into participative dialogue demanding political and civil rights, and social rights such as education, health care, roads, credit, and coca substitution projects. The population commanded the presence of this "participatory" state where they could have a say, a platform for their struggle against stigmatization as "violent" people who acted "outside the law." In sum, the cocalero movement entailed a process of popular reconceptualization of the state, leading to one in which the people could fully participate. Movement leaders described their central goal as "to construct a new state," seeking to contest campesino subjection by both the state and the guerrillas.[24]

CHAPTER SEVEN

From Social to Political Leadership

Gaining Visibility as Civil Society
in the Midst of Increased Armed Conflict

After the August 19 signing of the Orito Agreement, Putumayans were beginning to see the possibility of a change in their established relationship
with the country's power centers. Paradoxically, the campesinos' role in the
massive transnational problem of coca was what had finally enabled them
to participate in the development of policies and projects. There was now
some hope that they would be included and considered legitimate citizens
instead of marginalized and stigmatized. A local official called this "a historic moment."

Various authors have pointed out that Latin American social movements
often become stronger after successful negotiations with the state (Foweraker 1995; A. Scott 1991; Cardoso 1992; Jelin 1987; Davis 1989). Central state
institutions offer material resources. While it might seem reasonable to
think that the use of these resources might result in the co-optation of a
movement, such a conclusion would be overly simplistic. More accurately
in the case of the Civic Movement, its new posture could be described as a
strategic orientation towards institutions, the objective of which is to gain
a role in the state's decision-making machine at both the institutional and
political levels. Movement leaders placed great importance on the follow-
up meetings with national officials after the Orito Agreement, reflecting a
strategy of "permanent negotiation" common among social movements.
"Once negotiation is routinized, the state looks less an enemy of the social
movements" (Foweraker 1995, 101).

Once the government recognized the Civic Movement as a representative entity of the campesino cocaleros, its leaders shifted their emphasis
to ensuring the Movement's continued momentum. One Civic Movement
leader expressed his intentions: "We have to maintain movement unity.

That's what will enable us to get Putumayo out of the mess it's in, because if the movement falls apart, you'll never see another mobilization or such popular support, and the people will never trust us again."[1]

While the text of the Orito Agreement emphasized the participation of campesino cocalero leaders in formulating the Comprehensive Development Plan, both the government and campesinos began to focus afterwards on the degree of state compliance with the specific services it contained. This chapter discusses the Movement's scrutiny of government compliance and the debate over what technical assistance and local knowledge would be used to formulate a structural solution to coca cultivation. I argue that the Civic Movement's most important achievement was that its leaders were able to contest their criminalization and assert a new Putumayan citizenship by working hand in hand with state officials.

The chapter further examines how the Civic Movement sought out international allies for the conservation of the Amazonian ecosystem and biodiversity as well as for the defense of human rights. It details the Movement's turn to politics and the obstacles it faced from both of the non-state armed actors in the area, FARC and the United Self-defense forces of Colombia (AUC). Lastly, the chapter recounts the consequences of the AUC's arrival in the region and the population's response. As the armed conflict intensified, civilians increasingly began to demand autonomy from the armed actors and sought to gain visibility as a civil society. I argue that in a conflict-ridden region the boundaries between civil society and the state are ambiguous and that civil society emerges as an argument against pervasive violence.

The Base Group and Follow-Up to the Orito Agreement

Once the government and Civic Movement leaders agreed upon making a joint "Comprehensive Emergency Development Plan for a Coca-free Putumayo," they arranged a follow-up meeting for September 17 in Puerto Caicedo. The Orito Agreement had provided for a "base group" committee of "community leaders, technical personnel, professionals, and government officials committed to regional development and recognized by the community" to spearhead this process. The Base Group was charged with "the task of identifying development problems and their solutions, and future promotion of the Plan."[2]

The national government committed to financing the logistical needs of the base group for the six-month period between November 15, 1996 and

May 15, 1997.[3] It drew up a formal employment contract through the Solidarity Network to hire the key Civic Movement members of the base group to outline the development plan. This paid employment and additional institutional support was crucial to the Movement's ability to carry on after the mobilization was over. In this respect, its work with the central government strengthened the Civic Movement. A Solidarity Network official in charge of Putumayo community-government relations commented:

> The Base Group . . . could say, "There are these proposals; you help us so we can help you." They seemed strong and not afraid of confrontations. We felt that we were with allies, with serious people. When the Base Group got to work and made a proposal—it's a group of fifteen people—one felt that they were taking us seriously because they would say, "Our current allies are the head of Plan Sur and the Solidarity Network. We're allied with the national government."[4]

The base group's community representatives were to be elected from among recognized leaders of the campesino communities, ensuring an organic connection between the group and its constituents. This community-based leadership was critical to Civic Movement leaders, because, in the words of one, "If the community doesn't understand the agreement, we run the risk that it will fail." In fact, the base group maintained a strong, effective community voice throughout its existence. For example, Ana Beiba, the women's representative, was elected among thirteen female candidates (one from each municipality) by one hundred independent women grassroots leaders. She explained that though "The Civic Movement represented the marches, it didn't represent the Base Group." While there was some tension between the Civic Movement and independent grassroots candidates during the base group elections, the Movement clearly dominated. Nine of the eleven municipal representatives in the Group were Civic Movement leaders. From the population's and even the government's point of view, the community sector (thirteen community leaders, the women's representative, and the indigenous representative) was, in practice, the core of the base group.

At the same time, the Civic Movement leaders were conscious of their limitations with regard to the skills, knowledge, and technical expertise needed to formulate a successful plan. The Education Working Group (created by the Orito Agreement) had proposed the creation of a University of Valle del Guamués, Orito, and San Miguel to help rectify this lack of training in generations to come. In the meantime, the leaders proposed hiring three renowned experts on Amazonia as professional community advisors: a sociologist, a development economist, and an agronomist. However, these three experts declined to participate, and ultimately just one lesser-known sociologist was hired as an advisor to the community sector.

Base Group members were supposed to assume their positions officially and start work at the September 17 meeting. However, the central government representatives failed to appear, angering the community representatives and local and regional authorities who awaited them. The meeting was cancelled. Movement and community leaders expressed their dismay and disappointment:

> It worries me that the government is so indifferent to this process, that they're not interested in peace negotiations. It could be such a beautiful, participatory moment, to negotiate our development democratically. We mustn't waste this opportunity.[5]

> This is giving the government a golden opportunity to use the words of the Constitution to build real democracy, participatory democracy. But if there is no responsiveness, then unfortunately we see social pressures, mobilizations, and the rest."[6]

The central government communicated its intention to keep its commitment to the Orito Agreement but took its time getting ready, in large part due to the inefficiencies of its own bureaucracy. The first follow-up meeting finally took place a month later, October 17–18, 1996. The national delegation was chaired by Orito veterans Eduardo Díaz and Jaime Navarro of the Solidarity Network and Interior Ministry.

The Base Group was formalized at this meeting and three commissions were established to provide follow-up on specific areas of the Agreement. The First and Third Commissions would primarily monitor and work out the details of infrastructure commitments already made by the central government, while the Second Commission—the only one staffed by Civic Movement employees—would finish the coca-free development plan.[7]

Debates between the Civic Movement leaders and central government representatives on the Second Commission continued to reflect their different visions and priorities. While the state remained focused on achieving complete coca eradication as quickly as possible, the Civic Movement employees emphasized a participatory, gradual process aimed at a complete overhaul of agriculture in Putumayo. They wanted to work not only with the base group but also with

> the communities and social actors of the department as a way to bring a new methodology to the community in organizational terms and in terms of their participation in the decisions being made by different state bodies. Again, this matter of the agreement isn't just about the agreement. The problem is how the community influences the decisions that are made, how the community participates and how we can create a new cultural approach to the general problem here. And when I say general problem I'm referring to the squandering of community resources, of public funds. This isn't just a responsibility of government officials; it's also a responsibility of the community. . . . [We need to] change the mentality of the people.[8]

The initial proposal for the campesinos to eradicate their coca voluntarily, made during the Orito negotiations by the First Working Group and adopted by the Second Commission established by the base group presupposed subsidies and the guaranteed purchase of alternative crops. They proposed credit at an annual interest rate of 15 percent with a two-year grace period on principal and interest, to be made available to forty thousand small and medium property-owning families in Putumayo, cocalero or otherwise, to cover "improvement plans" for each of their farms. The credit would come from a new six-year Agricultural Emergency Fund financed through the national budget and other existing sources. The fund would also provide harvest insurance and subsidized lines of credit, crop purchase, and transportation, such as hiring vehicles to transport harvests from the field to markets in Nariño, Cauca, and Huila.[9]

In addition, the campesinos wanted free technical assistance from the municipal, departmental, national, and international agricultural bodies. They wanted to strengthen the Municipal Units for Technical Assistance to Agriculture (Unidades Municipales de Asistencia Técnica Agropecuaria, UMATA) by increasing their funds from municipal budgets to cover technical assistance for introducing alternative crops.[10] Regarding sustainable production, they proposed to "establish cooperative forest and pasture-development enterprises with the assistance of national budget allocations and international partners." For wage-earning coca harvest workers who did not own land, the campesinos proposed a six-month Emergency Plan through the Solidarity Network for rural and/or urban job development, with an emphasis on forming co-operatives and micro-enterprises.

As far as coca was concerned, the campesinos' willingness to begin voluntary eradication was contingent on the declaration of a "social and political emergency" in the department of Putumayo. This declaration would significantly speed up their ability to launch alternative projects by eliminating many of the legal steps required to register them with the National Planning Department's Project Bank (Banco Nacional de Proyectos de Planeación Nacional).[11] In short, the Civic Movement leaders' stance in the Second Commission reaffirmed and reiterated the campesinos' reluctance to turn over their means of subsistence without having any concrete alternative in place. While they agreed that eradication must be a central aspect of the plan, they were adamant that it could not be the only goal.

The central government, meanwhile, insisted that the Commission should focus on how to eradicate coca as quickly and efficiently as possible, a process to be supported only by delayed access to credit. The Solidarity Network proposed a manual eradication program that would pay campesino landholders 10,000 pesos (US$9.57) a day to eradicate coca. Depending on the size of the plot, the days allotted for this work would be 37.5 days for the minimum of one hectare, 75 days for two, or 112 days for the maximum of three. Once eradication was under way, an UMATA agricultural technician would visit the plot to help the family fill out an application for credit for a substitution project. This would begin a "preparatory" period of about two months, between eradication and credit approval, during which time the campesino would receive a subsidy of 750,000 pesos (US$717.70) for monthly living expenses and be expected to prepare the land for a new use. A campesino with three hectares could get 1,870,000 pesos (US$1,789.47) through this program.

The campesinos had a number of problems with this proposal. First, two months was too long for them to wait for funds to begin crop substitution. Based on their past experiences with the inefficiency of the Caja Agraria, many believed that the wait would in fact be longer. Second, monthly living expenses of 750,000 monthly subsidy or 375,000 pesos a month for the manual eradication of an hectare (US$717.70 or US$358.85) were not enough to sustain a family. Finally, and perhaps most importantly, the proposed program required participants to show formal title or a valid purchase agreement for their land, which many lacked. One movement leader expressed frustration over the government's single-mindedness: "We have to think about measures that will help us begin to build an alternative econ-omy. If PLANTE reduces things to a credit policy, it's because they don't understand the problem. Credit is only one element, *just one tool out of many that would be needed to begin to build this alternative economy."* [12]

Despite the ongoing debate over content, Civic Movement leaders consid-ered the very process of elaborating the Development Plan an achievement of their social movement that both responded to and defined itself in rela-tion to state actors in the region. Indeed, one of their objectives for the plan itself was to increase the community's influence over the state in regional policy. Popular leaders continued to prioritize social representation in the plan and popular participation in its execution over more technical policy proposals for new income-producing projects. One commented,

> We have two alternatives. Either some geniuses come here and make a plan for us without even considering whether we back it or we can all participate in designing a plan for the agricultural sector. . . . Based on my experience, the most important thing is that the process not be directed from above, that the process take place with the partici-pation of all the sectors involved who want to help make change in a region like Putumayo. . . . It requires very good information, and to be very realistic about the conditions and characteristics of the depart-ment. CORPOAMAZONIA could have this information, also the Minis-try of Agriculture, URPA, ICA, and CORPOICA. These are the agencies in the department, and with their help we would be evaluating, taking a snapshot of the agricultural sector in Putumayo. [13]

One thing that both parties recognized by October 1996 was that the vision for the plan was clearly very ambitious, and that its stated goals would be difficult to achieve. Even environmental and agricultural scientists were not clear on how to achieve an "economically productive and sustainable economy of solidarity" in the Amazonian ecosystem. With the complexity of the problem at hand and the desire of the Civic Movement leaders to com-bine expert advice with genuine community participation and buy-in, they had their work cut out for them in the next six months.

Failed Cooperation Between the Base Group and Local and Regional Authorities

Civic Movement leaders were constantly striving to prove their ability to get the campesinos' demands met (their *capacidad de gestión*; Foweraker 1995,

76) through continuous negotiations with government representatives.[14] However, they were ultimately unable to reach their goals. Each person I interviewed provided me with a different reason for this. According to the Solidarity Network representative for Putumayo:

> Local officials didn't show interest in working with them. I never sensed any commitment from them. In fact I sensed a lot of bureaucracy from them, a lot of cronyism. I think that we from the national government were very alone in [the process], even though there was an Agreement. The Network provided some funds, and CORPOAMAZONIA provided office space, some computers, and the telephones, but not any professional assistance. There was a lot of discussion over logistics, and the logistics weren't working out well.[15]

According to local and regional authorities themselves, they were ready to assist the base group, but were never called upon to do so. The CORPOAMAZONIA director Ignacio Muñoz insisted, "The social movement generated fear in the institutions. All of us officials were careful to respond to them and to keep appointments."[16] Muñoz continued:

> The Base Group was made up of natural leaders, but they didn't have a methodology or the kind of direct experience needed to formulate a development plan for each municipality. They took on a major commitment that they weren't well prepared for. They depended on an advisor who had experience in social programs, not in planning. They didn't have a methodology that would lead to defined results. Municipal officials from the Base Group regional delegation were invited to Bogotá, and they went, data in hand, but the work didn't get done. A laundry list of needs doesn't produce a plan.[17]

Governor Fuerbringer did not hide his opposition to the Comprehensive Emergency Development Plan. As he stated publicly at the first follow-up meeting on October 17, he believed that the plan was incompatible with current municipal and departmental governance, as well as with the existing Departmental Development Plan. The governor was neither alone nor totally unrealistic in his reservations. Muñoz complained that once the work of the Second Commission got under way, the community sector of the base group seemed to *want* to work on their own and actively resisted coordinating their plan with the existing national, departmental, and municipal development plans. The local mayors, who had long supported the Civic Movement, also chose not to work with the base group because they felt that as the local authorities they should lead the development process in their own municipalities.

The central government representatives had not anticipated these jurisdictional problems and were not as convinced that the various plans were incompatible. For example, Diego Orozco, the Regional PLANTE Director for Putumayo, pointed out that the Departmental Development Plan had been designed from the reality of Mocoa and failed to cover the needs of the department's coca-producing areas. Others discredited the governor's position, pointing to political motivations. Dr. Galarza, DASALUD official, suggested that one of the reasons for the governor's opposition to the new plan was that departmental assembly deputy Ramiro Grisales of the opposition Campesino Unity Party (also active in the Civic Movement and the base group) was becoming too popular and powerful. The traditional parties, including the Governor's Liberal camp, feared that political gains by Campesino Unity would follow as a consequence.[18] The indigenous representative to the base group, Edilberto Imbachí, observed the region's congressional representatives' unwillingness to participate in a national concertación proposed by campesinos protesting in Caquetá, and explained it the same way: "And they opposed [a national concertación] just out of political jealousy, because that large mobilization produced other figures, people who could enter electoral politics given the right moment. The leaders of the Civic Movement came on the scene and were very prominent at that time, and they were seen as a third force outside the two traditional parties, and quite a threat to them."[19]

Ana Beiba Rincón, the women's representative to the base group, commented to me that both the governor and mayors at first used the base group "for self-promotion," but later left the group in the lurch. Imbachí admitted that this dynamic did in fact eventually contribute to the group's reluctance to collaborate: "There was only interest in working with the national rather than the departmental government because the governor was seen as a political opportunist."[20]

Well-founded or not, the governor's opposition to the new development plan and the political motivations of local and regional authorities contributed heavily to the ultimate demise of the project. Despite several regional workshops with the communities, and a trip to Bogotá to consult with area specialists, the base group's work was never well coordinated with the local and regional authorities, and its hired technical help proved insufficient.

After their employment contract expired in mid-1997, the base group delivered a document to the Solidarity Network written by their sociologist advisor, but this document did not propose concrete technical solutions nor did it reflect the work the group had done in the community. The base group's community sector asked to continue working on the plan, unpaid. They requested travel allowances, office space, and secretarial support to complete matters left unaddressed in their document such as indigenous issues, higher education, petroleum activity, biodiversity, and the environment. They complained that "there had not been adequate specialized technical assistance for the satisfactory formulation of the plan" and that their discussions with the municipal, departmental, and national governments had not included "the process for developing the plan, its contents, its programs, etc."[21] Moreover, they faulted the government for failing to apprise the communities of the development process. The Civic Movement advisor Marino Rincón explained:

> The money that the government provided for the consultants was very little, 1,200,000 pesos [US$1,148] a month in all. Not what a highly qualified consultant should have to be able to focus on the plan . . . so the Base Group didn't find the technical consultants to finish the plan and it was just what they did themselves in some workshops. Plan Sur and the government intentionally assigned the Base Group the responsibility and then didn't offer the technical assistance needed to produce the plan. This was a tactic to wear them out and avoid making a commitment. The result was that they produced a theoretical framework; they set the context, but made no further progress.[22]

The requests of the Base Group Community Sector were denied by the government, and work on the Comprehensive Emergency Development Plan ended there. Jaime Navarro gave the work of the base group mixed reviews. He pointed to the movement's concrete achievements in Putumayo. The group had registered more people in the health system, gotten more teachers into the schools, and obtained improvements in the educational infrastructure, some new roads, and more electricity including generators for some towns. "Yes," he said, "its goals were good ones; yes, it was on the right track." Overall, however, he considered it "a shame that the Base Group had failed to develop the opportunity that they had in their hands."[23]

Luis Alberto Correal, the Solidarity Network's Putumayo official, pointed out that the principal goal of the Civic Movement leaders was to "strengthen the group. They tried to begin their work by conceptualizing a very different approach to Amazonia, something alternative," before proposing concrete activities or programs in detail.[24] In this sense, the movement leaders managed to impose the contextual framework they had proposed during negotiations on the region's discourse for a time. However, Correal agreed that the specific mission of drafting the plan ultimately failed. In the words of Eduardo Díaz, Base Group members "weren't capable of bringing together the authorities," and "we also failed. So the group just became fifteen people that we were helping to finance."[25] Arturo Ospina commented that "if we're going to see the Putumayo agreement in terms of infrastructure, the state has fulfilled 95 percent, and they still say that the state didn't come through, it did, but you know we haven't solved the problem. That's the tragedy for all of us who were involved."[26] Thus, in terms of the overall success of the 1996 Orito Agreement, the officials' consensus was that most of the central government's concrete promises were kept but that attempts to resolve the central issue—how to replace coca as the region's economic engine—had failed. Yet at least on some level, perhaps finding an alternative to coca cultivation was not the central aim of the social movement. Their exercise of citizen participation and their ability to gain international recognition and support were also driving forces behind their motivation to press on.

Putumayan Citizenship: Contesting Illegality through Participation

Civic Movement leaders were presented with an opportunity to move their struggle forward within the framework of participatory democracy, the central notion behind the actions of state institutions. The political appropriation of constitutional rights and particularly of the principles of citizen and political participation was the only discernible legal strategy for advancing the cocalero movement for social emancipation, as a response to intensified criminalization and repression of anti-drug state policies. The proposal for the Comprehensive Emergency Development Plan for a Coca-Free Putumayo established that it would be "based [in part] on the design and execution of *an education and training plan for the New Putumayan Citizen.*"[27] In calling upon the national government to collaborate in solving Putumayo's problems, the Movement stated:

> In this situation we speak as Putumayan citizens first, without any kind of political preference, without sectarianism. *We are simply ex-*

ercising our citizenship rights, on a moral basis and in solidarity. We know that it is the general population that is most negatively affected. We ask the national government to lend us a helping hand to surmount the complex set of problems that define our situation. If that does not happen, this will soon become a breeding ground for illegal and disruptive acts, and profoundly negative and undesirable consequences will follow.[28]

Calling oneself first a citizen of Putumayo of course reflects identification with one's birthplace or current place of residence, but above all, it reestablishes one's contract relationship with the state.[29] In identifying first as citizens and second as Putumayans, the Movement was constructing citizenship, defined by membership and a sense of affiliation where none had existed before, or at least none that had ever been made explicit or recognized as such. Implicitly, the campesinos were claiming to belong in the region, contradicting their reputation as rootless migrants. This demand for "membership" was an exercise of a *politics of citizenship.*[30] The people sought to be recognized by the state as a distinct group with a voice to represent them and with the right to define policies, along with the state, that would benefit them as residents of Putumayo.

As Hall and Held point out (1989, 181), the state must intervene to assure an appropriate conception of citizenship. The Civic Movement leadership sought this intervention, warning in fact of "illegal and disruptive acts" if a hand was not extended to them. Self-affirmation as Putumayan also meant compelling the state to address the department's demands. Movement leaders believed that for crop substitution to succeed, the political will had to originate with the state.

If citizenship and public identity are to be seen as social relations continuously open to interpretation and negotiation (Tilly 1996), it is important to understand the significance of the phrase "Putumayan citizen" in the context of the war on drugs and counter-insurgency war. Recognition as citizens means visibility as a differentiated group; it means an identity *other than* collaborators of the guerrillas or the drug traffickers. It was the beginning of the construction and strengthening of a positive identity with the support of the state. It was clear during the Civic Movement that FARC supported these demands, which suggests that FARC's presence in the region had not led to the population's rejection of the state's presence. On the contrary, Putumayans demanded respect for the 1991 Colombian Constitution:

Law 30 may say that it is illegal to plant coca, but the national constitution says that when the government is going to make a decision that
will directly or indirectly affect the population, that population should
be consulted. Why isn't *that* being recognized? What we are asserting
here is a constitutional right that is ours. If we are going to talk about
the law, well that's the highest law of the Republic. So we're not sug-
gesting that anybody break the law or even change the law.[31]

Through citizen participation, cocaleros also sought to contest the illegality of their situation. As Putumayan citizens, they wished to act within
the law, and further, to bring the law to life through the use of existing legal
mechanisms. This use of the law empowered them in their fight to secure
inclusion in the nation-state. It moved them toward recognition and participation as a differentiated social group with roots in the region, and with a
voice to defend their rights as small growers of coca.[32]

Internationalization of the Civic Movement

The Civic Movement not only worked on a regional and national level, but
also sought allies outside of Colombia. The changing nature of modern
campesino movements due to globalization became evident in the cocalero campesino social movement. The transnational issues of environmental conservation and international human rights were added to the campesinos' list of concerns. As Kearney points out: "There is a corresponding
displacement of political activities by post peasant subalterns into other
political arenas and an enactment of them not as domestic party politics but
as new social movements, which often displace the sites of political work
from the space of the nation-state to international contexts in which non-
governmental organizations are playing growing roles" (1996, 133).

In the search for international recognition, the worldwide interest in the
Amazonian ecosystem provided a way for the Civic Movement to insert itself
in the global context, expanding campesinos' claims "from land as an economic asset to land as but one kind of value within a much larger panoply
of generalized value" (Kearney 1996, 184). In Putumayo, this demand was
expressed in the campesinos' argument that they should play a central role
in the recovery and maintenance of their local ecosystem, and that since
Amazonia is the patrimony of all humankind, that they should also have
cooperation from international bodies: "Everyone talks about the lungs

of the world but nobody says how they're going to help save these lungs of the world. I think [we should do this] with international participation and cooperation in the conservation of the ecosystem in Putumayo and in Amazonia, but working directly with the community through its organizations."[33]

The campesinos' role as protectors of the environment had been expressed at various times. In the Orito negotiations, one movement leader said, "If we take this road, . . . we will also be helping [President Samper] so that the whole world doesn't take away his visa, because if he destroys the forests that are left in the world, nobody will let him in.[34] He'll be persona non grata in the whole world, and that wouldn't be good for us."[35] The discourse of environmental conservation also served the campesinos as a weapon to convince the government to sign the Agreement.

A prominent indigenous member of the Civic Movement and the base group's community sector advisor were invited to Washington in March 1997 for the Third Forum on the Amazon organized by Amazon Alliance.[36] The Alliance's focus is conservation of the Amazonian environment. It favors strengthening regional indigenous movements based on the idea that indigenous people are knowledgeable about Amazonian biodiversity and its management. The Movement leaders began their presentation on the Orito Agreement with the words "There are about 200,000 of us coca growers in Putumayo."[37] By starting in this way, they sought to make small producers visible, distinguish them from drug traffickers, and expose the social problem behind coca growing. They appealed to the Forum for support, presenting the campesinos' desire to protect the Amazonian ecosystem as a reason for making "an economically productive and sustainable economy of solidarity" the centerpiece of their proposed Development Plan.

Another issue that helped the Movement garner global attention was the human rights situation in Putumayo. The successes of the Movement also had begun to cause a backlash from various other regional powers, resulting in rampant death threats and assassinations, as will be related below. With the encouragement of local officials and civic leaders, representatives of the Inter-American Human Rights Commission traveled to Putumayo on December 4, 1997. They met with municipal authorities and members of the Departmental Human Rights Committee, founded in 1994 to formalize the defense of human rights in the department.[38] At this meeting the committee leader and Civic Movement leader Gilberto Sánchez requested that the Commission recognize "the necessity for the establishment in Puerto

Asís of a more permanent international oversight body, since there are violations of international humanitarian rights."[39] Sánchez commented that "The colonos are seen as potential insurgents and this means that the violation of human rights will only intensify." He provided a number of examples of army abuses against campesinos accused of being guerrillas, asserting that "These were not isolated cases; this is the policy of the armed forces." He continued: "One or two months ago, in this very compound, a major with the Twenty-Fourth Brigade, based in Putumayo, stated clearly that the norms of international human rights did not apply to Colombia's internal armed conflict. The colonel later apologized for the major's assertion, but there has been no noticeable improvement in the treatment of civilians in keeping with human rights norms."[40]

By placing the development plan within an environmental discourse and invoking international human rights law, the Movement was able to transnationalize the relationship between the Colombian state and its marginalized citizens, a strategy that gained visibility for the cocaleros not only as social actors but as state subjects who were being denied their rights and subjected to political persecution.

Struggling for Political Representation: The Civic Movement Caught between the Guerrillas and the Paramilitaries

By the time the Putumayo civic strike ended, Civic Movement leaders had achieved significant prestige in the region. People were beginning to talk of the movement as the people's representative. Fals Borda (1990) and Bejarano (1998) have pointed out the tendency of Colombian social movements to turn into political parties because of delegitimized traditional politics. Fals Borda's view of this phenomenon is a redefinition of what is political and implies the construction of a new political culture, while Bejarano sees a crisis of politics and a crisis of identities in need of new points of reference. This dynamic became evident in Putumayo when traditional parties began to fear that the movement might become a political force strong enough to elect national congressmen. Indeed, its leaders had proposed morphing into a political movement with an eye cast on the October 1997 elections for governor, mayoralties, municipal councils, and national congress. Jaime Navarro commented: "In the discussions we told [Civic Movement leaders], 'Don't make the development proposal a government program, a program for electoral politics.' Because the elections were coming and we knew that they were thinking that way; it seems that that was what they actually wrote, a political platform, not a development plan."[41]

The Civic Movement's reputation as defender of campesino interests and its strengthened negotiating position vis-à-vis the state had been achieved in part as a result of FARC's support for the cocalero movement during the marches. This logistical support also evidenced the power of the guerrillas in the region and increased FARC's own political visibility in Putumayo. Paramilitary groups reacted to this reality by announcing their own incursion into the zone, a decision that would dramatically change the political landscape in Putumayo.

Reports from the third national summit of the AUC in November 1996 described this plan: "The Department of Putumayo is another priority. It is urgent that we allocate men and supplies to this mission. The guerrillas have been able to create a parallel government there, which is very dangerous for the nation."[42] Paramilitary forces aligned with AUC in Urabá and Córdoba issued the following communiqué in April 1997 in the municipality of Carepa, with a copy delivered to the Puerto Asís and Orito municipal councils:

> In evaluating the question of law and order in Putumayo, the Central Command of our organization has determined that the guerrillas operating in the region are responsible for the violence. These guerrillas have the logistical support of some mayors and public officials who use a portion of their official budgets to finance subversion.
>
> We have therefore given serious consideration to making our presence felt in Putumayo, first of all in the places where the conflict is worst, such as Puerto Asís, whose mayor is the principal instigator of guerrilla activities, where people allied to our organization have been assassinated, and where additional assassinations are expected.
>
> Accordingly, we declare the mayors of Puerto Asís and Orito to be military targets due to their intimate connections with the guerrillas. The same goes for candidates in the upcoming elections who have guerrilla support, since FARC has immediate plans to capture mayoralties and municipal councils in areas where they exercise a certain degree of control.
>
> We will not repeat our past mistake of seeing individuals who don't have clear commitments to the subversives as military targets. Our mission now is selective cleansing.[43]

Civic Movement leaders began to receive threats. Accusations by the paramilitaries that they were guerrillas disrupted both their work on the Development Plan and their individual political aspirations. On February 15, 1997, Civic Movement leaders met in Bogotá with President Samper, the Solidarity Network director, head of Plan Sur, governors of Caquetá and Putumayo, interior minister, and representatives of the Caquetá and Cauca campesino movements.

The purpose of this meeting was to discuss compliance with the Orito Agreement, but movement leaders also used the opportunity to denounce the imminent arrival of paramilitaries in Putumayo. The Interior Ministry and the Civic Movement jointly organized a Regional Forum on Peace and Human Rights to be held in Puerto Asís on May 7–9, 1997. Luis Emiro Mosquera opened the May forum with these words: "The Civic Movement for the Comprehensive Development of Putumayo will make its presentation in the faith that *honest dialogue will not be a cause for any grave accusations against those with the courage to speak out, nor the taking of lives* of those who express their own opinions on the problem of violence, or who propose strategies for us to find our way out of this painful labyrinth."[44]

The movement leaders were capitalizing on their new, hard-won relationship with the state to demand that it protect their basic rights: the rights to self-expression, physical integrity, and protection of their lives. It was significant that the leaders felt the need to demand these basic rights explicitly and publicly: it can be argued that, in the midst of the conflict, in a zone contested by multiple armed actors, the construction of citizenship became a form of resistance. The leaders were in the throes of another dirty war of a type common in Colombian history, wherein alternative political leaders who begin to gain power are not just caught between irregular armed forces such as FARC and paramilitaries, but also often subjected to pressures and repression by government forces. The Civic Movement's working relationship with the central government, as well as regional and local officials, was therefore providing them a modicum of protection at this time.[45]

Paramilitary threats and accusations that people were guerrillas were made against leaders of the cocalero movement; a local priest who had spoken out in favor of the campesinos; and the mayors of Puerto Asís, Puerto Guzmán, and Orito.[46] Some of the cocalero leaders in Caquetá and Guaviare had in fact been killed.[47] Campesinos used the Forum to denounce these threats and also complained of harassment and accusations by the army:

I want to seriously object to the army's actions against the civilian population, against us, the campesinos living in the backcountry, all kinds of people abandoned by the government. After the strike they sent an army captain who was like the Military Police around here, around the Carmelita vereda going toward Teteyé. . . . They came around to the houses, at four or five in the morning saying, "Open the door, guerrillas, open the door. Where are the guerrillas? Where are the arms? Where is this? Where is that?," pulling the people out to beat them, stomp on them, hit them with the butts of their rifles. The fact is, Colonel, we campesinos don't know anything about arms. OK, maybe a machete or a shotgun, things we use to do a little hunting, but we don't know anything about rifles.[48]

Civic Movement leaders used the Forum to recount their activities before and during the marches, and their subsequent work as the base group. Their presentations were rooted in an analysis of the national and international structural problems that needed to be considered in order to replace illegal crops and achieve peace in the region. They identified four central problems, the solution of which constituted their political platform.

The first problem was "restricted democracy." Movement leaders used this phrase to denote a situation where "political and ideological thought differing from that promoted by the dominant class is described as dangerous and those who express it are considered enemies to be fought or even physically annihilated." The second problem was "the concentration of the best land in large and unproductive *latifundios*." This explained the campesinos' expulsion from their places of origin and their appearance in Amazonia as colonos in search of land. The third problem was "the advantages of the minority over the majority," such that "the latter are not consulted when fundamental decisions are made." The final problem mentioned was "the application of economic, political, and social measures recommended by foreign governments." The movement maintained that "the government of President Samper should provide a sovereign solution to the problem of campesino and indigenous coca growers. International participation in this matter should be limited to the adoption of measures to control consumption."[49]

The main presentation concluded that "a process leading to peace requires profound economic, social, and political changes and the practical application of the rights of citizens. Respect for human dignity is absolutely fundamental." Discourse around coca cultivation and its gradual replacement began to shift from a social and economic perspective toward a political framework focused on peace and democracy.[50]

The Civic Movement was now faced with the dilemma of how much to move from social representation toward political representation. FARC was complicating matters on this issue. While they had promoted the campesino mobilizations, they would not permit the Civic Movement to free itself from their control. FARC not only began to label the campesino leaders on the Solidarity Network payroll as "sellouts" for developing the plan, but also prohibited participation of Civic Movement candidates in the October 1997 elections which, they said, "had ceased to be a democratic conquest and become a deceptive way for the dominant classes to perpetuate control" (FARC 1998b). Moreover, FARC called for abstention from voting, and intervened to prevent the election from taking place. This met with various reactions:

> Whether or not the guerrillas had any interest in politics, in a political solution to the conflict, the fact is that the campesinos and all the poor were practically begging Luis Emiro, who had been the leader of the marches and of the process, to run in the elections as a candidate for the House. There was a consensus in the department that if he ran for the House he'd win with a landslide. The surprise was that Luis Emiro didn't run, because FARC didn't permit him to. It was a big contradiction.[51]

On September 18, 1997, a regional newspaper carried the headline, "318 out of 354 Registered Candidates Withdraw" after FARC sent a letter to the candidates demanding their immediate withdrawal.[52] On October 1, the same paper announced that "The threats of FARC's Southern Bloc have been extended in the last twenty-four hours to all citizens of the municipalities of Middle and Lower Putumayo who participate in the next elections as poll workers."[53] Two days later, an article titled "In Putumayo, Fourteen Towns Surrounded by FARC" reported that the electoral process was in danger where the guerrillas had a permanent presence "and the presence of military forces is not assured." It was also reported that it was the governor's duty to evaluate the situation and decide whether to postpone the elections.[54]

The Civic Movement leaders withdrew to work clandestinely, within the framework of the political culture of marginality. They felt that their lives were in danger from both the guerrilla and paramilitary threats. This fear was understandable in light of their historical memory. In September, the movement organized an open meeting in the Puerto Asís Municipal Park to explain their withdrawal to the campesinos of Putumayo. Luis Emiro Mosquera publicly recalled the history of the dirty war against alternative political parties like the Patriotic Union and the Communist Party. He described the state as a repressive institution that provided him no protection when paramilitary threats to his life were ubiquitous. All the Lower Putumayo candidates participated in this meeting, explained the lack of guarantees for their personal safety, and called for the postponement of the elections. They emphasized issues of peace, violence, and democracy and began to distance themselves from the government institutions with which they had been working:

> When I say democracy I'm not talking about the right to vote. I'm talking about economic democracy, social democracy, and political democracy. . . . How can you talk about peace in a region or in a country like this with the enormous inequalities that we have? Right, but there we find all of those at the highest levels of government talking about peace. What they forget is that the problem of violence is a result of the historic irresponsibility of the people in power . . . and now they come and say that the cause of the war is the existence of the guerrillas, when the reality is just the opposite. In this country the guerrillas exist because of the injustice and repression against the unarmed people.[55]

FARC's contradictory stance, claiming to be true defenders of participatory democracy while operating in an authoritarian fashion against the population, triggered diverse reactions within Putumayo. While the Puerto Asís mayor supported the election postponement, Upper Putumayo mayors did not, indicating that "The elections are the only way to demonstrate to the violent actors that the civilian population does not share their bellicose ideologies and they are tired of the wave of psychological terrorism that has swept through the entire department of Putumayo and increased in the last few months."[56] In the Baja Bota of Cauca, where the first two mayors of Piamonte had been named by decree, the community demanded that the guerrillas authorize elections for October of 1997. A municipal council member explained: "Finally, after many discussions, meetings, demands; after much dialogue, the elections will be held. The leaders and everyone at the meetings have agreed on the importance of being a municipality now, and on the disadvantage we had because there weren't popular elections. They [FARC] accept that and will let the election happen."[57]

The competition between the government and FARC for influence over the Civic Movement intensified during the election period. As Eduardo Diaz describes:

> This was an intense struggle. They [the Movement leaders] were operating clandestinely but they were against the elections. We had met earlier and it was like, we put our cards on the table. They told me no, we're not in favor of the elections. They produced a document signed by the mayor of Puerto Asís; they had gotten people inside the municipal administrations and from the different sectors of the community to produce a document saying that there shouldn't be elections in Putumayo. Well, it was signed by the mayor of Orito, the mayor of [Valle del Guamués] Hormiga, the mayor of Puerto Asís, the mayor of Mocoa. So I was given the hot potato, to go there and make sure that there were elections. They said there can't be elections because there was a guerrilla threat. They never even started with the discourse of the 1970s, that the elections were illegitimate. More or less what they said was that because of the guerrillas' threats they were obliged to protect the community, to protect the lives of the people, and a few mayors acceded to that. So I just went right to Puerto Asís and Mocoa as a pre-election delegate and I argued the point in public with the mayor of Puerto Asís over the radio.[58]

Ultimately, the central government decided to carry through with elections, which generated conflict with Civic Movement leaders:

> And afterwards I had a lot of conflicts with them. The elections, for example: when they decided not to run in the elections I was convinced that Luis Emiro was headed for the House; that he had it lined up. But as the elections got closer they had major conflicts with FARC, the mayors, the traditional political leaders of the area, because they had promoted themselves as a strong independent force with a lot of possibilities in the region. Unfortunately though, in my opinion they submitted to FARC.[59]

The elections were finally held with unsurprisingly minimal turnout, as described by Nestor Hernández Iglesias of the Popular Alliance Party, who was elected mayor of Puerto Asís for the term from 1998 to 2001: "In the case of Puerto Asís, 207 [votes], and I was elected with 103. In the case of La Hormiga only seven votes; in San Miguel there were less than fifty, and in Puerto Caicedo there were also just two hundred votes. That helped us in the sense that with so few votes we are not committed at all to the traditional political class or to any other pressure group."[60]

Paradoxically, the guerrillas' election boycott was an advantage to the mayor. Due to the low turnout, he was elected without having to make any commitments to the traditional political class, and he was therefore able to govern with a certain degree of autonomy. One council member in Puerto Asís reported, "The guerrillas called a community meeting, which was attended by about two hundred people, and they told them that the election was invalid and that they were going to install a mayor. But they didn't. The elected mayor is still there."[61] The mayor's activities continued to be monitored by FARC, but he was allowed to govern, reiterating that FARC's authoritarianism was contested.

Paramilitary Terror and the Response of the Armed Forces

In mid-November 1997, graffiti appeared on walls in Puerto Asís and La Hormiga saying, "Death to guerrilla collaborators. For social cleansing. Sincerely, *Los Paracos* [a commonly used slang word for paramilitaries]."[62] In Zabaleta, Caquetá, other graffiti appeared in November 1997 saying to "Prepare 90 coffins." These messages announced the arrival of the paramilitaries, who had begun to recruit intelligence operatives to compile lists of supposed guerrilla collaborators. Being put on one of these lists virtually guaranteed a violent end. By late November, there had been at least thirty-nine murders in Valle del Guamués and San Miguel (La Dorada). On January 1 and February 15, 1998, there were twenty more deaths and eleven reported disappearances.[63]

The link between the paramilitaries' arrival in the region and the increase in political violence is illustrated by data on human rights violations in Putumayo from the second half of 1996 through the end of 1998. During this period, paramilitaries were responsible for 81 percent of the violations, the Armed Forces for 7 percent, and FARC for 6 percent, with 5 percent unattributed. The types of violation were as follows: threats from one of the three armed groups (60 percent, the most common type by far), murders (15 percent), injuries (8 percent), injuries or deaths caused by explosions

(3 percent), disappearances (3 percent), torture (2 percent), kidnappings (1 percent), and coerced interrogations (1 percent).[64] The civilian population was caught in a web of confrontations between guerrillas, paramilitaries, and the army.

Paramilitaries arrived in Putumayo en masse during the January 6, 1998, celebration of the Carnival of the Epiphany. A local journalist told me: "Thirty-eight *Rápido Ochoa* and *Rápido Magdalena* [two bus companies] buses of paramilitaries arrived between January 4 and January 17, 1998, during the Epiphany Carnival season. There were about 240 names on their list, and they killed 180 people between the end of January and the end of March that year."[65]

People in Putumayo were deathly afraid of paramilitaries arriving in search of "guerrilla collaborators" and people "involved with the drug trade" to kill. After all, virtually anyone could become a target for FARC "collaboration" or drug trade "involvement" in an area with strong FARC presence and an increasingly dominant coca economy since the 1980s. The AUC general commander in Putumayo told *Semana* magazine: "We're barbarous? That's a concept that I'm not going to get into. What's important to me is that all the dead are guerrillas or their collaborators."[66] The following testimony by a local pharmacy owner illustrates their fear:

> Sales were down from April to August 1998. They rebounded in August, September, and October. People outside town had been afraid to go out because the paramilitaries had roadblocks. They waited there, lists in hand. They pulled out the people they recognized and killed them. This was the fruit of their intelligence work. Coca harvesters, guerrillas—they've killed a lot of them. Before it was just a few but now it's a lot. They kill bazuco dealers, degenerates, thieves, guerrilla collaborators. They threatened a woman friend of mine who sold vegetables and I guess bazuco too. Her body was left in the road with the warning, "For Disobedience." You just don't know what people may be involved in; it's very easy to end up on their list.[67]

The paramilitaries mounted roadblocks all along the road from Mocoa to Puerto Asís to stop buses. If they found any passengers on their list, they would kill or take them away. One of the notorious roadblocks during the time of my most intensive fieldwork (January 1998–August 1999) was set up in February 1998 on the road from Puerto Asís to the nearby airport. The airport is located next to a military base, but the passive attitude of the military toward the paramilitaries let their activities continue undeterred. Both groups were feared without distinction. Town residents did not leave the center and campesinos stayed in their own veredas.

Residents of Puerto Asís, Valle del Guamués, and San Miguel internalized the fear inspired by the selective killings that were becoming more frequent and more numerous. People learned to keep to themselves. They tried to remain inconspicuous by not talking to anyone or having too much to do with any other person or thing. Uncertainty and dread overcame people, who were so cut off from events that rumors became the closest connection they had to what was actually happening. A 1997 mayoral candidate in Puerto Asís described the situation: "Rumor kills. Rumor constructs its own reality; it creates facts."

One example of how rumor played a central role in the life of the zone began on February 25, 1999. A Hercules aircraft was seen landing at the military base in Puerto Asís and a rumor spread that it carried away about four hundred paramilitaries. "You feel at peace. You don't have that constant fear and it's like a weight is lifted off your shoulders," said Doña Laura, the pharmacy owner. She decided to keep the pharmacy open late that night. New rumors the next day said that the paramilitaries had not left, or that they had been relieved by others, or that they were hiding, hoping to draw out the guerrillas and catch them by surprise. From one day to the next what had been a sense of relief became an intensified fear of imminent danger. Embroidered facts, stories woven around bits of information: these were the most powerful source of reality.

Doña Laura also told me of her fright when a woman came to tell her that her husband had been shot. She hurried to the hospital and to the morgue, but he was not there. It was only a rumor. She cried as she reported this and added that she had been obsessed with her husband's safety since, that she could not bear to have him out of her sight. She would have dreams about his being shot in which she was trying to calm him.[68]

The specter of death was everywhere in Puerto Asís. Anyone could have been the next murder victim. The newly elected mayor Nestor Hernández Iglesias traveled to Bogotá in late January 1998 to report on the situation: "Witnesses of the selective massacres have been systematically murdered, and state authorities have ignored information provided to them that could have prevented their deaths."[69]

In response to these charges, the commander of the Army's Twenty-fourth Brigade, based in Putumayo, claimed that "These crimes were committed by the guerrillas, who also plotted to attribute them to the paramilitaries and sully the reputation of the army by association."[70] He stated that there had been no massacres in Putumayo and that only twenty-three deaths by firearm had been recorded, a figure considered normal in the region. The Ministry of Defense took a similar approach, announcing that "The Prosecutor's Office has dispatched an investigative unit to Puerto Asís to establish the truth of the crimes alleged by the mayor and determine the nature of the homicides in order to distinguish them from those that occur in the normal course of events in the area."[71]

Mayor Iglesias responded "What the Government says, through the Minister of Defense when he speaks of 'normal deaths'—those are not normal deaths. They are violent deaths that are an everyday occurrence in Puerto Asís, but they can't be normal in a society like ours."[72] The homicide data on motive assigned 79 percent of deaths in the area with "no cause" or motive, illustrating the authorities' accommodation to and virtual acceptance of generalized and indiscriminate murder. The next largest category was that of people killed as a result of political participation, representing 9 percent of the total (CINEP and Justicia y Paz 1996–98). The normalization of violent death in the region made the paramilitaries' work easier, yet it was something the civilian population could not accept and fought against.

Mayor Iglesias also denounced the presence in Puerto Asís of a paramilitary group led by the drug trafficker Gustavo Gómez, "an emissary of Carlos Castaño," the AUC's commander-in-chief.[73] Despite this information, General Nestor Ramírez, commander of the army's Third Division, insisted, "I have no evidence that they were paramilitaries, nor that there were multiple killings on the same day."[74] He sidestepped having to consider the reported deaths as massacres, legally defined as the killing of more than three people in a single incident. He promoted the idea that the deaths were a "settling of accounts" among drug traffickers, to be expected among "criminals and gangsters." The armed forces maintained a representation of the coca-producing regions as rife with criminality due to the presence of traffickers and guerrillas, legitimizing their own role in state terrorism through the active and passive assistance they provided to the paramilitaries.

On January 9, 1999, twenty-eight people were massacred at El Tigre in San Miguel.[75] On February 23, a forum on public security was held in Puerto Asís. The new army commander declared the term "paramilitaries" a misnomer, since it implied a connection to the military, and suggested the term "self-defense forces" instead. He also stated that he had no evidence that they were present in Puerto Asís, utterly ignoring the El Tigre massacre. On May 18, reports of more killings—fifteen deaths over the previous weekend—came from La Hormiga. While the municipal secretary raised the possibility of paramilitary responsibility, the army lieutenant Barbosa maintained that the inevitable correlation between coca and violence "did not rule out the idea that the deaths had been the result of confrontations between drug traffickers and coca harvest workers."[76]

Meanwhile, the paramilitaries continued to use terror tactics against the population in their drive to dominate territory. The AUC entered Valle del Guamués (La Hormiga) to take control on November 7–9, 1999, killing twelve people in the vereda of El Placer. They then moved on to La Dorada, where they gathered the population in the park, held them there for four hours, and then announced that they had come to kill guerrillas and their collaborators. They selected six men from the crowd and killed them. From La Dorada, they traveled to the veredas of Las Brisas, El Empalme, and El Vergel in the rural outskirts of La Hormiga, where they killed seven more people. When they arrived back in La Hormiga, they murdered four more— a total of twenty-nine people in three days.[77]

The population felt powerless. At five o'clock in the afternoon, Puerto Asís suspended all commercial activity and the town center was abandoned as residents sought refuge in the private sphere, at home behind closed doors. Campesinos did not leave their veredas. The danger and chaos at hand led people to accept the new political and social order that the paramilitaries would install.[78] Puerto Asís merchants had appealed to the regional prosecutor when they were first threatened, but ultimately had to accept the paramilitaries' conditions: "We've been victimized by the terrorist actions of a group of paramilitaries who call themselves the Self-Defense Forces of Colombia [AUC]. Those of us who have resisted this extortion and their threats of punishment for non-payment have been forced out of business."[79] In July 1999, paramilitaries called local merchants to a meeting to inform them that they were not going to kill any more of them, but since they were going to protect the people they needed funds and were going to "request" a one-time payment. They would "take care of anyone" who did not pay.[80] FARC, for its part, made it clear to the campesinos that they could not defend them from the paramilitaries. "In war," they said, "lives are lost. People must be prepared to pay the price."

In Putumayo the line between civilians and combatants was blurred. Residents of Puerto Asís reported that army troops had acted as paramilitaries, and that they had recognized soldiers participating in paramilitary massacres. It has been demonstrated that the paramilitaries function with the assistance of the armed forces (Human Rights Watch 2000), and in Putumayo the close ties between these groups have been denounced since 1998 as "a national policy of state terrorism,"[81] which serves as a reminder that such terrorism can become "an intrinsic part of the contemporary exercise of power" (Aretxaga 2000). From the other side, AUC commander Carlos Castaño asserted in an interview that campesinos "live one day as guerrillas and the next as campesinos." He also declared that guerrillas sometimes operate in civilian clothing and that civilians cooperate with guerrillas due to intimidation. Meanwhile, community members were seen among the paramilitaries accusing other residents of being guerrilla collaborators, furthering the complex entanglement of civil society in the conflict.[82]

Just like their electors, local mayors were residents of the region and felt unsupported by the central state, or at least by certain branches of it. In an interview, the Puerto Asís mayor Hernández Iglesias identified as a member of civil society rather than a state representative, saying, "It seems that the government never understood that some day civil society was going to make itself heard, and now that's what we're doing." He went on: "It's the *state itself, through its Armed Forces*, that denied the charges [referring to his report on paramilitary murders]. They didn't want to hear or try to deal with it."[83]

The fear of paramilitary reprisals did not lead most people to assist the paramilitaries or the army in the anti-guerrilla struggle, nor did it lead to unconditional support for the guerrillas. Instead, the residents of Putumayo tried to defend their lives as best they could without fully identifying with any one of the armed actors.

The Rise of Civil Society: Citizens Demand Peace and the Defense of Life

Increased political violence starting in 1997 forced the leadership of the Civic Movement to turn away from their focus on proposals for alternative crops and focus instead on the defense of basic human rights like protection of life: "Civil society in Puerto Asís, like in the rest of the country, has resolved to come out against violence. . . . It's necessary to emerge from indifference and inertia, from the insularity and fear induced by the actions of armed groups. This is fundamental. Collective fear mustn't transform the isolation of the individual into the isolation of all."[84]

The movement had a clear desire for the assistance of the civilian government in stopping attacks on them by the paramilitaries and armed forces. Campesinos demanded that government agencies comply with their assigned functions and also sought support from state entities such as the Personero Municipal (Municipal Ombudsman) which were specifically established to promote community participation.

As a result of community complaints of mistreatment by state representatives and the security forces in particular, the central government created the position of Human Rights Delegate for Putumayo in 1997. The post was based in Puerto Asís. Germán Martínez, the Personero Municipal at that time, took this office on May 29. Martínez, born in Caquetá to colono parents, played a very important role in establishing and engaging in dialogue with civil society: "The people have come to understand that peace is not just the silencing of the guns. They can see that peace is also the contribution I make as a citizen, the responsibility that I should assume in the community. A lot of space has opened up with this understanding. People are talking, discussing the issues."[85]

Martínez was critical of the government's and armed forces' military approach to the Amazon, saying: "They've wanted to deal with the social and ecological conflict by military means, thinking that they can solve the problem in the south of our country by stationing anti-guerrilla brigades or battalions or building military bases there. . . . What's really going on is a big social conflict that needs to be resolved." Understanding the problem, he maintained, required "getting close to the people."[86] Martínez repeatedly supported the actions of the people caught in the middle of the armed conflict, including various events they staged to make themselves visible as a civil society and denounce the human rights violations they were experiencing.

On February 13, 1998, residents of Puerto Asís demonstrated in the streets against the government's cynicism in calling the recent wave of deaths in their region "normal."[87] That month, they held a two-day Forum for Peace, attended by the mayor, governor, and representatives from the related central government bodies. This forum produced a demand for "armed actors [to] assume their responsibilities with regard to international humanitarian law and human rights by ceasing all attacks on unarmed parties. It is likewise hoped that the authorities will assume their responsibility to protect all residents of the department."[88] It also requested a presidential commission to investigate the recent murders and end impunity. On April 6, campesinos marched again in Puerto Asís with white flags to symbolize their desire for peace and safety.

It was a May 28, 1998, demonstration in Bogotá, however, that most emphatically marked the emergence of Putumayan civil society on the national scene. Five hundred JAC leaders from veredas in Puerto Asís, San Miguel, Valle del Guamués, Puerto Caicedo, and Orito denounced the entrance of paramilitaries into the zone, the collaboration of the armed forces with them, and the subsequent wave of murders. They demanded the protection of human life, a prerequisite for the defense of democracy in Putumayo. In the words of one leader:

> First of all, I want to say to the compañeros from all over Putumayo that during our stay here in Bogotá we've written an important page in history. If we're trying to demonstrate the immense sacrifice that we've made to leave our families and our work in the region for three days, we're also setting a very clear precedent for our country and the world to see. For a long time in Putumayo we've heard rumor after rumor of paramilitary murders and massacres to come. We're here to reject the return of terror that we see approaching.[89]

The demonstrators simultaneously occupied the interior ministry, Ombudsman's Office, PLANTE headquarters, Solidarity Network, and the offices of the Colombian Conference of Bishops, chanting, "If there's no right to life why work the land? If there's no right to life what good is money?" A campesino pointed out the paradox: it was precisely the threat to their lives that had motivated people to organize. "People organize out of necessity. When you see four friends die for no reason, then you organize because you could be next. Senseless killing doesn't help the nation."[90]

On June 4, 1998, the campesino representatives in Bogotá, called the Committee of Putumayans for Life, met with President Samper to highlight the same denunciations they had been making all year. The President signed an agreement creating two new commissions. One would investigate and report on the accusations made by the Committee regarding death threats and assassinations, and the other would bring together "broad sectors of Putumayan civil society, local, departmental, and national government agencies, the Church, and human rights organizations . . . to protect the lives and physical integrity of the department's residents."[91] Movement leaders demanded that the process involve the participation and supervision of an international body, but this demand was not met.

The cocalero campesinos of Putumayo had commanded their country's attention and secured a national investigation into the facts of recent murders despite the "disorganization, lack of solidarity, minimal participation in community affairs, internalization of violent models of communication and human interaction" that one departmental government advisor ascribed to them.[92] In these achievements, campesinos clearly demonstrated their capacity for organization and solidarity, facing death threats against themselves and opting for peaceful and effective resistance.

Redefining Civil Society in Conflict-Ridden Putumayo

In general, the dichotomy between the state and civil society is central to the very meaning of the latter term. For Nielsen (1995, 42) and many other political theorists, civil society refers to a social and economic project that may consist of practices, codes, organizations, or institutions, as long as they are distinguished from both the state and the private family sphere. Cohen (1995, 37) defines civil society as "a sphere of social interaction distinct from the economy and state, composed of associations (including the family) and public spaces." Others (Bejarano 1992 and 1995; Bonamusa 1997; Keane 1998; Lechner 1996) further limit civil society to entities not only independent of the state, but also outside the reach of political parties. In all of these definitions, autonomy from the state is a necessary precondition to a strong civil society. Associated with individual freedom, civil society is thus defined in opposition to state power. Sometimes it is reified as a homogeneous collective agent combating a demonic state (Hann 1996).

Gupta (1995) has proposed that the division between the state and civil society be reanalyzed within specific cultural and historical contexts since its accepted analysis is a reflection of the European historical experience, which should not be adopted and applied universally. Accordingly, the term bears redefinition in the context of Putumayo in the mid-1990s when the reestablishment of working relationships between the state and communities became key to both government agencies and the people of Putumayo as they sought to strengthen themselves as a visible civil society. The marginality and armed conflict of Putumayo makes the autonomy and oppositionality of civil society in relation to the state unclear at best. We can identify neither the differentiation nor the confrontation between the state and civil society that we need in order to distinguish the latter. Rather, the boundary between them is diffuse.

The tension in Putumayo between the state and guerrillas and between the people and each of their two "governments" makes definition of this boundary even more complicated. When popular organizations defined themselves as part of civil society, as the citizens of Puerto Asís did in their 1997 letter to the interior minister, they felt the need to explicitly counterpose their identity to those of the armed groups, projecting an image of themselves as legal actors: civilians affected by (but not participating in) the armed conflict.

Referring to the conceptual opposition between the state and civil society, Walzer (1991 and 1995) argues that civil society requires political agency in order to function, and that in this sense the state is an indispensable agent. Although civil organizations may resist the organizational impulses of state bureaucrats or challenge state power, the political power of the state is needed to redistribute resources and to subsidize associative activities, particularly when those organizations benefit from outside resources. Such is clearly the case in Putumayo, where campesinos were making continuous demands for the benefits of state protection and other public services.

This very call for state action was one of the Civic Movement's central demands. Like the new Putumayan citizenship discussed above, new forms of collective citizenship were emerging and defining a local civil society in opposition to both the repressive state and non-state armed actors. This civil society sought strength in constitutionally-guaranteed spaces for democratic participation, and in some cases, in political representation. It emerged in Putumayo in response to the stigmatization of its population as violent and criminal; it sought to re-establish a sense of "moral community" by establishing interrelated, cooperative organizations. In one example, the cocalero movement demanded such moral imperatives as the rights to life and human dignity. The exercise of citizenship mediated between the state and this emerging, redefined *civil society*.[93]

CHAPTER EIGHT

Plan Colombia and the Depoliticization of Citizenship in Putumayo

The cocalero movement and its aftermath revealed three new realities: first, Colombia had become the principal Andean producer of coca for drug trafficking, a distinction it has maintained from 1998 to the present. Second, coca was grown mostly by campesinos on small plantations, so there was a need for new policies directed specifically to them as opposed to drug traffickers. Third, coca cultivation had begun to fuel the armed conflict, in particular once paramilitaries arrived in Putumayo in 1997 and the AUC began to contest FARC's control of illegal crop-growing areas. These regions were strategic objectives as sources of financing for the intensifying armed confrontation.

President Andrés Pastrana (1998–2002) launched the first version of Plan Colombia in December 1998 "as a policy of investment for social development, to deactivate the violence and for the construction of peace" (Observatorio para la Paz 2000, 167). It was explained that drug crops would be dealt with in different ways depending on their origin, purpose, and scale of cultivation, and that plans for social investment would above all be directed to small growers. When President Pastrana presented Plan Colombia in October 1998, he indicated that "Many studies demonstrate the geographic co-occurrence of drug crops and guerrilla presence. This leads one to presume that the guerrillas and drug trafficking are inseparable, although that has not been demonstrated. One could say that their coexistence is a function of the inaccessibility of the zones in question; of a kind of authority exercised by the insurgents that coincides with drug production, even if it is not a cartel; and of the public and private corruption that facilitates this co-occurrence."[1] Pastrana maintained that FARC should not be defined as narco-guerrillas. In this same speech, he declared that he agreed with the insurgents on the need to construct a common agenda for international assistance to the peace process. Pastrana initiated peace negotiations with FARC in January 1999 on the basis of these common positions.

Pastrana described this first version of Plan Colombia as a "Marshall Plan" for the economic and social development of southern Colombia, hoping that the international community would respond to the devastation caused by drug production and trafficking as it had to the devastation of Europe in the Second World War. While originally described as Pastrana's national development plan, Plan Colombia was in fact substantially transformed within its first year as a result of U.S. pressure. A year after he had introduced the plan, President Pastrana presented it as *A Plan for Peace, Prosperity, and the Strengthening of the State* "to ensure order, stability, and compliance with the law; to guarantee effective sovereignty over the national territory; to protect the state and the civilian population from the threats of illegal armed groups and criminal organizations; and to break the existing ties between these groups and the drug industry that supports them" (Contraloría General de la República 2001).[2] The plan became a military strategy to break up alliances that were said to be destabilizing the state and threatening continental security. In this reformulation, social investment projects took a backseat, as the strengthening of state and governmental institutions—code for the counterinsurgency struggle—were considered a prerequisite to their success (Observatorio para la Paz 2000).

In 1999 the six-year budget for Plan Colombia was set at US$7.5 billion. Colombia would provide $4 billion and the international community, including the United States, would provide $3.5 billion. Of the funds provided by the Colombian state, $3.09 billion was to come from the general budget and $1.774 billion from new sources dedicated to Plan Colombia: internal debt incurred through the sale of Peace Bonds, loans from the Inter-American Development Bank, and other international credits.

In July 2000, the Clinton administration moved a special supplemental appropriation of $1.3 billion through the U.S. Congress toward Plan Colombia. The bill included $860 million for Colombia, $180 million for several of Colombia's neighbors, and $260 million for the counter-drug efforts of several U.S. agencies.

Of Colombia's share, 60 percent ($519.2 million) went to the armed forces and 14 percent ($123.1 million) went to the national police for helicopters and equipment. Colombia's navy received funding to expand its river program, and the air force got new OV-10 and AC-47 aircraft (Center for International Policy 2000). The centerpiece of Plan Colombia, referred to as the "push into southern Colombia" (mainly Putumayo and Caquetá departments), was the creation of a new counter-narcotics brigade within the Colombian Army composed of two new counter-narcotics battalions and one that had been established in 1998–99.[3] Equipped with 45 helicopters, advanced communications and intelligence-gathering equipment, training, arms, and ammunition for light infantry, the 2,300-strong brigade would pave the way for mass coca fumigation in Putumayo department, which by 2000 had become the main producer of coca in Colombia. The remaining 26 percent of Plan Colombia's funding ($217.7 million) was allocated to socioeconomic programs to be administered by the United States Agency for International Development (USAID): alternative development (8 percent), displaced population (4 percent), defense of human rights (6 percent), judicial reform (2 percent), strengthening the rule of law (5 percent), and measures promoting peace (1 percent).[4] One of the goals of these programs was to ameliorate the human consequences of the military's anti-drug activities.

Since 2000, successive Plan Colombia aid packages have maintained their focus on security. In any given year, between 68 and 75 percent of the aid has gone to the military and police. Despite calls by some members of the U.S. Congress to spend more on social programs, President Bush's proposed budget for fiscal year 2006 maintained the high proportion of funding for military counter-drug efforts in Colombia. The funds for social and economic aid came from the International Narcotics Control budget of the State Department, further reflecting Plan Colombia's drug-control orientation.

Putumayo presented an ideal scenario for the central mission of Plan Colombia: coca cultivation supported an estimated 30,000 small producers with one to five hectares of coca each, as well as a floating population of raspachines (harvesters) estimated at 50,000. By 2001 it was estimated that 78.5 percent of the department's population was involved in the production and marketing of coca, 20 percent of which was the floating population (ANUC Putumayo 2001). Moreover, the guerrillas and paramilitaries were by then competing over territory and over control and regulation of the drug trade such as the ability to collect extralegal "taxes" (*gramaje*) from residents. In this context, the intensification of the aerial fumigation policy promoted by the United States was an easy sell.

What happened under Plan Colombia to the cocalero movement in Putumayo and its demand for citizenship? As was discussed in chapter 7, at the end of 1997 and early 1998, when the paramilitaries entered Putumayo en masse and committed selective killings and massacres such as the one at El Tigre, the principal Civic Movement leaders were forced either to leave the region, join FARC, or face assassination. The persecution of movement leaders during these years resulted in their virtual disappearance from the social and political scene, weakening the Civic Movement and effectively driving it underground. By November 1999, internal displacement had intensified as a result of confrontations between the AUC and FARC to such an extent that the Solidarity Network was designated as a state institution to attend to the needs of the displaced. In ten years of fulfilling this role, the Solidarity Network was unable to carry out any other socioeconomic projects.[5]

The CMDR's Response to Plan Colombia and Its Negotiations with FARC

As the aerial fumigation policy promoted by the United States intensified, the credible threat of fumigation characterized the coercive nature of the state's presence even more effectively than increased militarization. In response to imminent, intensive fumigation in 2000, the inhabitants of Putumayo proposed social pacts for the manual eradication of coca. The initiative for these pacts originated in the Puerto Asís Municipal Rural Development Council (Consejo Municipal de Desarrollo Rural, CMDR), with the participation of municipal leaders, government officials, the mayor, the governor, and others. Puerto Asís Mayor Manuel Alzate, who took office in 2000, describes the initial reaction to Plan Colombia in Putumayo: "We started to work very closely with the director of CORPOAMAZONIA and with the CMDR, which was also very active at that time. We thought it would be possible to submit a project proposal to the national government and to the embassies, particularly to the United States embassy, demonstrating that manual eradication was another approach, that fumigation was not the only strategy possible."[6]

The CMDR of Puerto Asís played a fundamental role in formulating a proposal for negotiating manual eradication as an element of a broader set of social agreements that would form an alternative to the fumigation promoted by the United States. By April 2001, local CMDRs were clearly perceived as a valid platform for organizing around municipal investment priorities and as a forum for dialogue with the local and central state to convey campesino proposals. Local officials also counted on CMDRs to coordinate activities and provide security when they ventured into the veredas. It had become clear to the cocalero campesinos that one of their most important goals was the decriminalization of coca cultivation. In a context of intensi-fied violence and political persecution by paramilitaries, legal and above-board work like that of the CMDRs gave them the political space to continue with their struggle for recognition as legitimate social actors and valid inter-locutors in negotiations with state representatives.

The National Association of Campesinos (ANUC), which had not partici-pated in the organization of the cocalero movement and was not allowed to participate in the negotiations, came to fill the leadership vacuum left by the Civic Movement in Puerto Asís in 1997–98. Beginning in 1999, Éder Sánchez, the principal ANUC representative in Putumayo, had promoted the strength-ening of the Puerto Asís CMDR. This was in keeping with ANUC's national policy on CMDRs, which from their perspective were "a response to the lack of political space for coordinated participation of campesino organizations and the rural population in the planning, design, execution, and oversight of municipal programs and projects for rural development" (ANUC 1998, 10).

FARC criticized the CMDR of Puerto Asís for working too closely with municipal authorities and ANUC for being totally co-opted by the state. Moreover, they accused the CMDR leadership of working in the interest of paramilitaries. This accusation should be put into context. In July 2000, ad-vancing paramilitaries were continuing to target the municipal centers of the coca growing zone. Puerto Asís had been taken first, in 1998. Orito, La Hormiga, and La Dorada had followed. Paramilitaries took Puerto Caicedo and Villagarzón in April 2001 and by October of that year they were expected to arrive in Puerto Guzmán at any time. When I visited Puerto Asís in April 2001, just after the Puerto Caicedo incursion, I was told that when the para-militaries had entered town they came with a list but did not carry out any massacres. Instead, they called upon people one by one, and depending on their evaluation of an individual's closeness to the guerrillas, they either dictated the conditions that would allow him or her to stay in town or they ordered him or her to leave. It was clear in 2001 that the guerrillas controlled the countryside while the paramilitaries held almost all the towns. Thus the mere fact that the CMDRs met in the towns was enough to associate them with paramilitaries. FARC's condemnation of the CMDRs presented a further example of their distrust of any autonomous campesino organization suc-cessful enough to challenge their authority.

Early in 2000 the paramilitaries killed two JAC presidents and one cam-pesino leader who had been active throughout the formation of the CMDR in Puerto Asís. The territorial division between the guerrilla-controlled countryside and the urban spaces controlled by paramilitaries was stark. The civilian population was trapped, unable to move freely between these antagonistic spaces, and the campesino movement was thus immobilized. One woman campesino leader described the situation: "We can't speak out for the movement now. We don't have the freedom to demand our rights."[7] Éder Sánchez, the leader of ANUC in Putumayo, commented:

> Everybody, including the CMDR presidents, began to say, "We won't go back to town, they're slaughtering us. So the CMDR began to suffer a setback, but we continued to insist on the fulfillment of the people's social needs. We continued to pressure the mayor and the institutions, something that nobody else was doing. Everyone was saying, "They don't come to the veredas any more, our presidents aren't making any demands." So there was a crisis in the CMDR, but we persisted until July [2000], when the guerrillas killed Uvaldo. The problem is that the paramilitaries had killed the presidents; the guerrillas said that we were infiltrated by paramilitaries; the others said that we were guerrilla collaborators; and then the guerrillas called us paramilitary collaborators. So with Uvaldo's death all our work came to an abrupt end. We issued a communiqué saying that as of that moment all CMDR activities were suspended. Our work stopped and now we're trying to regroup.[8]

The paramilitary advance continued. On September 24, 2000, one month before the local and departmental elections, and amid sharpening territorial clashes between FARC and paramilitaries, FARC declared an armed strike (*paro armado*) in Putumayo. During a paro armado, guerrillas occupy access roads and prohibit all traffic into and out of town centers. The principal strike demands were that the state "take heed of our rejection of Plan Colombia and immediately respond to our non-negotiable demand to rein in the paramilitary groups that have sown terror here in the south."[9] This was the primary condition for lifting the strike, which lasted almost three months until mid-December 2000. The civilian population tired of the prolonged paro armado and ultimately rejected FARC. Unlike the 1996 strike, when FARC and the population stood together against fumigation, the paro had not stemmed from any popular needs or demands. Rather, it seemed that FARC was using people to further its own military agenda. The strike was lifted even though the government had not met a single one of FARC's demands.

Figure 13. Graffiti in La Hormiga: "No to Plan Colombia." (Casa Editorial, *El Tiempo*)

In the elections of October 2000, ANUC director for Putumayo Éder Sánchez was chosen by the campesinos as candidate to the Departmental Assembly, largely in recognition of his work with the CMDR. His candidacy was another example of the use of political representation to continue the work of social movements and organizations. He recounted:

> Secretly [because FARC had prohibited participation in the elections] we decided to participate on October 29, and we decided that the CMDR would take the risk despite all the problems, because it was already functioning [again]. We presented two lists, and the head of one of them was elected. I got two hundred votes out of a little more than three hundred for the assembly, so the process is alive. So, since that had worked out, we decided that it was time to regroup, not as a CMDR now, but as a campesino organization. We're going to change the name but the leaders will be the same. From the assembly the work is better grounded . . . and we are generating participation from the municipal council and since we have a representative we will promote the process here in Puerto Asís. That's more or less the story of the CMDR.[10]

We again see a "chameleon" survival strategy here: organizational names and identities were changed as needed to advance the campesino movement. Feeling betrayed by FARC's lack of support for their organizing efforts, campesino leaders liquidated the CMDR and resisted FARC demands. Four months later Éder Sánchez won a seat in the departmental assembly.

FARC responded by proposing an association of JACs that would imitate CMDR organizations but be under guerrilla control. It would be centered in the inspectorates and corregimientos of Teteyé, Bocanas del Cuembí, Comandante, Piñuña Blanco, Puerto Vega, Alto Cuembí, Villa Victoria, and La Carmelita, covering about seventy veredas in all. However, campesinos did not respond positively to this proposal and instead rallied around the CMDR demand of "No to fumigation; Yes to gradual manual eradication" to form the basis for a proposed social pact to guarantee manual eradication. The CMDR delivered this proposal to Puerto Asís Mayor Manuel Alzate, who began his lobbying efforts. The mayor described the process:

> On July 25, 2000, Dr. Gonzalo de Francisco, a PLANTE official [the presidential advisor for social peace and citizen security] and twenty-three central government officials came to Puerto Asís to speak about the implications of Plan Colombia. We presented them with a document stating that we wanted a Putumayo without coca: No to fumigation and Yes to manual eradication.
>
> He told me that the president would accept manual eradication but only if the people produced a document expressing their wish and intention to eradicate coca. That's how this process of manual eradication began, and we are now completing one year of it. The 148 veredas in Puerto Asís signed the declaration of intention; they have not been fumigated and we hope that they won't be.[11]

Mayor Alzate signed the first eradication agreement, called the Social Agreement for Voluntary Eradication and Alternative Development, in the corregimiento of Santana on December 2, 2000. He then called the other newly elected mayors together to encourage them to pursue agreements in their municipalities to head off the imminent threat of fumigation. However, FARC forbade such agreements, giving the mayors pause. Meanwhile, the U.S. continued to exert a great deal of pressure for fumigation. Between December 22, 2000, and January 12, 2001, widespread aerial spraying damaged coca crops as well as commercial and subsistence agriculture in the municipalities of Valle del Guamués, San Miguel, and Orito.

In October 2000, the Colombian president's office had projected that Plan Colombia would displace 209,779 people from Putumayo: 11,047 indigenous people, 158,732 colonos, and 40,000 raspachines.[12] Indeed, the first U.S. appropriation for the plan included US$15 million to assist families displaced as a result of the policy. These projected displacements ultimately said more about government policy than about the population's real readiness to move. In fact, the expected exodus did not materialize. In 2000, a total of only 9,714 people of an estimated population of 323,549 were reported displaced from Putumayo—5,497 into Ecuador and 4,217 into the Colombian interior. By August 2001, an additional estimated one thousand people had fled from the intensifying conflict, particularly from Puerto Caicedo and Villagarzón (ANUC Putumayo 2001). The 10,714 total displacements (versus the 209,779 predicted) resulted not just from the implementation of Plan Colombia, but also from the armed conflict. For example, confrontations between guerrillas and paramilitaries in October 2000 displaced five thousand campesinos seeking "to flee the crossfire, the indiscriminate massacres, and the pall of hunger hanging over lands that had once fed them."[13] For the most part, however, Putumayan campesinos were determined to stay in the region and find alternative means of support beyond the unstable coca economy. They continued to defy the central state's stereotypes of them as rootless migrants in search of easy money.

With aerial fumigation under way, the campesinos decided to defend their social pacts for voluntary eradication and established a negotiating process with FARC. In the end, FARC had managed only to delay the official process, as the eradication agreements were already signed. Campesinos were committed to eradicate their coca crops within one year from the first disbursement of state resources, which would consist of 2 million pesos (US$861) for food security in the form of livestock, agricultural inputs, tools, and the like. Meanwhile, medium- and long-term alternative projects would be designed to follow this first step. While these pacts were originally proposed by people in the region, they gained government support because of the urgency for eradication imposed by the United States' war on drugs.

As they had at the 1996 negotiations, the campesinos proposed a two- to five-year period for gradual eradication of coca with increased aid for food security, which they requested in cash rather than commodities. This way they could decide themselves how to invest the assistance. Above all, they requested a revolving fund or some other mechanism to ensure a viable market for their alternative crops. The government, however, continued to insist that food security assistance be in the form of goods rather than cash to avoid the potential for its diversion into illicit activities.

The government representatives delegated to finalize and sign these pacts imposed their own non-negotiable terms. The very word "pact," they said, implied the formalization of an agreement already reached. No new negotiations were admissible. They also explicitly threatened the campesinos with fumigation if they did not sign. Ramiro Grisales, a Civic Movement leader, criticized the government's intransigence at the Puerto Guzmán signing.

> GRISALES: It seems to me that if two people want to negotiate, then
> they should listen to each other, not try to impose their will. . . . The
> government is not operating in a cooperative fashion here. . . . We
> don't want to dupe the national government, we want this to be a
> serious thing and to make it a serious thing we need much more
> time for crop substitution. We have always spoken for a Putumayo
> without coca, for a sustainable economy [referring to the Orito
> Agreement]. Have any of you who have come here, if you were among
> the 29,000 that were in Mocoa [in the 1996 civic strike], have they
> given you any of what they agreed on after the strike?
> VOICES: No.
> GRISALES: I want the government to understand that we respect the
> institutions of government, but we don't want to be the ones to
> suffer the impositions of the North Americans. This is our country;
> we were born here. We have the right to participate in the resolution
> of our problems.[14]

As in 1996, the central demand was for genuine negotiations in which the proposals of both sides would be considered. Nevertheless, the state refused to negotiate the pace of eradication. The campesinos felt that the state was unwilling to hear them and unwilling to abide by the 1996 agreements. Even the infrastructural improvements and services provided since that time were not part of a coherent departmental or regional development plan. The campesinos wanted the state to demonstrate political will, to make a real commitment to the community, and to work alongside the cocaleros toward structural solutions to the problem of the coca economy. Instead, eradication pacts were unilaterally imposed under conditions dictated by American anti-drug policies, effacing the spirit of the manual eradication plans that the residents of Putumayo had first proposed.

Fumigation and forced eradication, central topics in 1996, continued to be major issues. This fundamental divergence between the cocalero campesinos and the state deepened as the state continued to align itself with the policy of forced, immediate eradication of coca.

Manual Eradication and Splintering of the Civic Movement

By June 2001, thirty-one social pacts for eradication had been signed by campesinos representing eight hundred veredas and approximately twenty-five thousand families. Two other social pacts were signed in July 2001 with indigenous communities. One, called Root by Root (Raíz por Raíz), covered 7,186 families in twelve indigenous groups. The other involved the 1,134 families of the Kofán people.

Nine of the thirteen Putumayo municipalities were covered by these pacts: Mocoa, Villagarzón, Puerto Guzmán, Puerto Caicedo, Puerto Asís, Puerto Leguízamo, Orito, Valle del Guamués, and San Miguel. The campesino pacts were financed by the Peace Investment Fund (FIP) created to administer Plan Colombia resources. PLANTE was responsible for technical assistance under the leadership of Gonzalo de Francisco, the presidential representative for social peace and citizen security.

The indigenous pacts, on the other hand, received funds directly from USAID, which began to work in Putumayo with funding for Plan Colombia in April 2001. USAID had signed an $87.5 million, five-year contract with Chemonics International, Inc., an international development company based in Washington, D.C., which was to administer and oversee alternative development activities in Putumayo and Caquetá, the site of Plan Colombia's "push into southern Colombia." The FIP and Chemonics in turn subcontracted with Colombian NGOs to implement the pacts in different communities: Vida y Futuro (Orito and San Miguel), Fundaempresa (Puerto Asís and Puerto Leguízamo), Fundación Restrepo y Barco (Villa Garzón and Puerto Caicedo), Codesarrollo (Valle del Guamués), Fundacomercio (Mocoa and Puerto Guzmán), and CECOIN/CORFAS (Puerto Guzmán, Mocoa, and Villa Garzón). Chemonics also subcontracted the indigenous organization Fundación ZIO-AI to implement the agreement with the Kofán people. The signing of these pacts staved off fumigation in Putumayo for six months, which did not please the U.S. administration. A news article in St. Petersburg, Florida, reprinted in *El Espectador*, stated: "According to U.S. and Colombian officials, a $1.3 billion U.S. plan to assist in the war against drugs in Colombia has come up against a serious obstacle in recent weeks. President Andrés Pastrana has refused to permit further fumigation with herbicides in the south of Colombia, which is the heart of coca production in that country. . . . Pastrana is under enormous pressure to stop the fumigation." The article quotes a researcher and frequent U.S. government advisor to the effect that "Pastrana's change of attitude came as a great surprise and alarmed many in Washington."[15] The Colombian government was caught between domestic pressure to suspend fumigation and focus on increased social investment and pressure from the U.S. to continue spraying. Faced with accusations that Plan Colombia was being thwarted, de Francisco responded that, "Under no circumstances does the government intend to stop fumigation," explaining that the suspension in Putumayo had been due only to weather conditions. He added that the government also wanted to give alternative development and social programs time to get off the ground before resuming forced eradication, and pointed out that fumigation continued in other departments such as Tolima, Santander, the south of Bolívar, and Guaviare.[16]Aside from an oblique reference to "allowing time for alternative development programs," de Francisco made no mention of the manual eradication agreements in Putumayo. A PLANTE official directly involved in these pacts stated that the struggle to position them as a policy alternative to fumigation would have to take place in Washington:

> The American congress began to ask that the strategy of the agreements be explained to them, so we went to Washington to explain it. Then some NGOs appeared also wanting an explanation, and three weeks ago, eighteen U.S. Senate staffers came to see how the agreements were working. So the agreements themselves are getting a lot of attention. At first USAID saw the agreements as a government issue, but when they saw how things were taking off, they came and asked, "How much money will be needed? . . . We've been able to show the United Nations that 83 percent of the coca grown in the country is in plots smaller than three hectares. . . . [This] would radically change the policy, because there would be very little fumigation. Now we have another much stronger argument, which is that drug traffickers don't invest in the crops any more.[17]

The national government had to seek strategies to impede fumigation. One of these strategies was to work with U.S. Senators who were not convinced of the efficacy of investing in fumigation. On the floor of the Colombian Senate, Senators Rafael Orduz and Juan Manuel Ospina challenged the fumigation strategy. According to Orduz, "It seems that the cure is worse than the disease. There is evidence that it affects human health, damages the environment, and leads to displacement. For these reasons some of us oppose fumigation as a solution."[18] Senator Orduz also pointed out that just as there was no monolithic position on spraying within the Colombian government, there were differences of opinion within the U.S. Senate as well. Colombia used these differences to moderate the strictly repressive policy with a strategy that recognized small growers as distinct from drug traffickers, whose activities it would continue to target uncompromisingly.

At the same time, the European Union began to show interest in financing alternative development programs within the Plan Colombia anti-drug package. At the third meeting of the International Support Group of the Peace Process in Colombia, held on April 30, 2001 in Brussels, the European Union committed 335 million euros (US$300.5 million) to various alternative programs, some of them "representing a substantial development model permitting them to improve their living conditions."[19]

In the October 2000 elections, the governors of Putumayo, Nariño, Huila, Cauca, Caquetá, and Tolima had all been elected with the support of independent political forces. They formed a "Southern Alliance" of governors who agreed that the coca problem was not just about stopping fumigation, but also about implementing an alternative regional development model, an approach that could imply taking into consideration an agrarian reform. This group traveled to the United States in March 2001 and to nine European countries in April 2001 to present their proposal for a Southern Project of "No fumigation and more funds for social investment."[20]

The six governors asserted that this Southern Project was a peace plan that should be submitted for community consultation. They objected to the fact that Plan Colombia had been formulated and imposed without input from the people directly affected or from local or departmental authorities. They considered the plan dead on arrival. Their Southern Project ruled out aerial spraying of crops and proposed a combined manual eradication and alternative development program. The governors' unified position clearly illustrated not only divisions within Colombian government, but also the lack of understanding in Bogotá of reality in the southern region. Their proposal demanded decentralization in the sense of regional participation in national policy-making, in keeping with the central points of the 1996 cocalero negotiations.

While the manual eradication pacts slowed down the pace of fumigation, they also contributed to the disintegration of the regional cocalero movement. Local, short-term, and partial agreements diverted attention from the comprehensive and department-wide dimensions of the problem. Though the pacts contemplated medium- and long-term projects for 2001, almost the whole year was devoted to the delivery of food security resources, an emphasis that the PLANTE representative in Puerto Asís considered to be a political error. While new productive projects had been prioritized in all the social agreements, they were now addressed only secondarily. While the Civic Movement had promoted campesino participation at every stage of their negotiations and in formulating their development plan, the central government was now imposing concrete plans and projects without any community participation. Taken together with the escalation of the armed conflict, these developments made it clear that the negotiating power of campesino organizations had diminished substantially since the 1996 Civic Movement.

USAID's Counterproposal to Manual Eradication

The manual eradication pacts challenged both the fumigation policy and the overall position of USAID. According to the United States General Accounting Office, USAID's activities were based on the theory that "without interdiction and eradication as disincentives, growers are unlikely to pursue legal employment or to abandon more lucrative and easily cultivated coca crops in favor of less profitable and harder to grow licit crops. Furthermore, alternative development, interdiction, and eradication efforts must be carefully coordinated to achieve mutually reinforcing benefits" (U.S. General Accounting Office 2002). In keeping with these policy guidelines, alternative development programs were implemented only as compensation for fumigation and forced eradication. In and of themselves, they were not a strategy for combating coca cultivation either financially or politically.

Simultaneous to the implementation of the alternative development program funded by Plan Colombia and managed by USAID, PLANTE continued to implement coca substitution agreements. However, Colombian government officials were unsure whether all the coca in the Putumayan areas covered by the agreements would be eradicated voluntarily by the end of July 2002 as had been projected. In response to this situation and to the suspension of aerial spraying for almost eight months, USAID decided in September 2001 that the voluntary eradication program was not working. Though USAID had promoted the strengthening of PLANTE in 2000, it now saw PLANTE as too weak an institution to receive and manage its funding. It established a new eradication program called Local Initiatives for Alternative Development and Early Eradication (Programa de Iniciativas Locales para el Desarrollo Alternativo y la Erradicación Temprana, PILDAET) with no

Figure 14. Aerial spraying, a central policy of Plan Colombia. (Casa Editorial, *El Tiempo*)

participation from the Colombian government. USAID resources no longer passed through government bodies such as FIP or PLANTE. The PILDAET program was implemented over the following three years.

Although the early eradication initiative was supposed to arise from within the community, participating veredas had to commit to eradicating all of their coca before receiving project financing. No time period was specified; eradication was to be accomplished immediately. Moreover, in contrast to the PLANTE agreements customarily signed with individual families, PILDAET agreements were signed with whole veredas. Eradication was to be carried out in "representative and verifiable areas" (PLANTE 2001), meaning in areas not controlled by non-state armed actors. This requirement reflected the need of the U.S. government to evaluate the success of the eradication program quantitatively through the number of hectares where coca was fumigated or eradicated.[21]

At the end of July 2002, the Pastrana administration announced the termination of manual eradication agreements. The first year's aid budget had not been fully distributed, and the medium- and long-term development agreements had not been completed. When President Álvaro Uribe Vélez came to office in August 2002, he intensified fumigations, allowed a higher concentration of glyphosate in the spraying formula, and declared fumigation non-negotiable. In December 2002 Uribe's government eliminated PLANTE. The Uribe administration clearly prioritized counterinsurgency operations to break the link between drug trafficking and the guerrillas over development planning.

The Depoliticization of Citizenship

Beginning in January 2003, Chemonics operated without any official oversight. Campesinos were left to interact with private contractors and NGOs intent on meeting their own goals, effectively exposed to the pressures of global anti-drug policy without the benefit of any intermediation by the state.

The implementation of Plan Colombia precluded any possibility of negotiating or financing gradual eradication as the 1996 cocalero movement had conceived it: a component of a comprehensive alternative development plan. Global anti-drug policy is unidirectional in that it is often imposed without the consultation of local governments or civil society in affected regions. This reinforces pre-existing constraints on attempts by the marginalized population to make itself visible through demands for citizenship rights, and makes it even harder for people to define their citizenship in civic, political, social, and cultural terms. Given this series of events, it is indispensable to analyze the relative weight of the different components of citizenship in Putumayo and how the campesino movement goes about demanding them (Marshall 1965).[22] All of the armed actors are present in this space: the police, armed forces, and those who exercise private justice—the guerrillas and paramilitaries. Political democracy is threatened, since the two latter armed groups interfere with the citizenry's access to representation. The function of the central state as a provider of services in the region and its role as an interlocutor with the campesinos is limited.

An undemocratic and authoritarian framework is beginning to close off the spaces for political participation that the cocalero campesinos opened only relatively recently. How can campesinos explain the failure of their projects? Who can they hold responsible? Will the campesino movement be depoliticized in the absence of the state?

As illustrated in figure 15, Plan Colombia has given rise to a multiplicity of campesino associations registered with the Putumayo Chamber of Commerce to present the type of alternative production projects required by USAID. One consequence of Plan Colombia is that campesinos in Putumayo have prioritized their demand for social rights—understood as access to alternative productive projects and economic well-being—over their demand for civil and political rights. In so doing, they have made them-

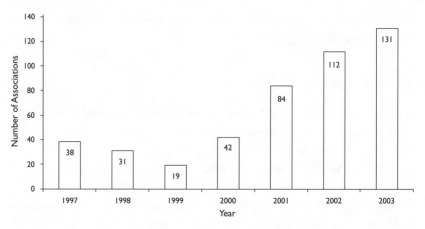

Figure 15. Campesino associations registered with the Chamber of Commerce in the Department of Putumayo, 1997–2003. (Chamber of Commerce, Puerto Asís, Putumayo, 2003)

selves subject to clientelist control mechanisms and authoritarian manipulation by the NGOs that administer available resources.[23] The retreat from demands for civil and political rights intensified with growing militarization and the complete loss of autonomy from the United States with regard to anti-drug policy that has taken place under Uribe's administration and Plan Colombia. The Colombian state has lost its sovereignty in this policy area, and the government has effectively lost interest in developing a comprehensive policy for alternative development. As the anti-terrorist struggle took precedence, coca came to be viewed solely as a source of financing for terrorism; the social and economic problems of small growers were given no further consideration.

In this newly militarized context, civil society in Putumayo could not exercise its political rights. Putumayans lost their civil rights, too, particularly after the implementation of Democratic security, a policy that ironically defined security as "a product of the collective effort of the citizenry: it is the responsibility of all" (Presidencia de la República and Ministerio de Defensa Nacional 2003, 17). The population was expected to support government authorities, the justice system, and the military in order to strengthen democracy and the rule of law. Democratic security openly presupposed civilian involvement in security functions through the establishment of informant networks. Campesinos could be labeled "terrorist auxiliaries" if they did not collaborate as military informants. The negation of meaningful citizenship in favor of a military role resulted from the identification of campesino cocaleros as subjects of the anti-drug policy. Their "right to have rights" was negated. Aerial fumigation of the zone, intensified year after year (see table 4 in chapter 2), was an assault on the fundamental human rights to health, a decent quality of life, and the enjoyment of a healthy environment. It was also a violation, in the words of the Defensoría Del Pueblo (2001, 9), of "the obligation of the state to provide special protection to vulnerable or marginalized groups" as required by article 13 of the 1991 Constitution (Constitución Política de Colombia 1991, 15). The demand for the right to make a living became central, and given the non-negotiability of fumigation, the central goal of Putumayo campesino organizations became access to financing for alternative productive projects that would allow them to survive under these new adverse conditions.

Is a Cross-Border Cocalero Social Movement a Possible Alternative?

From its inception, the Civic Movement leaders sought to forge a "united struggle" that would bring together different ethnic, political, and social movements around their shared problems of state abandonment and its consequences in the region. Movement leaders also sought to unite at a national level with representatives of other departments in order to discuss agrarian reform as well as municipal and departmental planning. Their goal was to devise comprehensive and regional, rather than isolated and local, solutions to the problem of illegal crops. Finally, they made contact with coca producers in other countries, holding the first of several international meetings on illegal crops in June 1995 with growers from Bolivia, Peru, the Colombian departments of Guaviare, Putumayo, Huila, Caquetá, Vichada, Cauca, and the area called the Sierra Nevada de Santa Marta. A second international meeting was held in August 1996 to reconsider the problem in the context of the 1996 cocalero movement. In 2001 the cocalero movement of the western Amazon sought to link up with campesino and indigenous movements for the decriminalization of coca and to promote respect for its ancestral uses. Such movements have gained strength in other regions of Colombia and in neighboring countries.[24] The assumption of a collective identity as cocaleros led to a resurgence of the movement and to a new transnational paradigm.

In May 2001 the Bush administration launched the Andean Regional Initiative (ARI) for regional cooperation against drug trafficking. A U.S. State Department fact sheet stated that "the Andes continue to produce virtually all of the world's cocaine, and an increasing amount of heroin, thus representing a direct threat to our public health and national security."[25] According to this document, Peru, Ecuador, Bolivia, Venezuela, and Colombia shared characteristics such as weak democratic institutions, corruption, and political instability that contributed to the consolidation of drug trafficking, which in turn distorted their economies and discouraged legal investment. It further states that all aspects of the drug trafficking problem must be addressed regionally rather than separately by country.

Faced with the challenges posed by the Andean Regional Initiative, Colombian campesinos were determined to strengthen cross-border cooperation with their counterparts in Peru and Bolivia to resist repressive policies against coca growing. It was clear to coca farmers throughout the Andes that an attack on small growers would not end drug trafficking. Before becoming president, the Bolivian cocalero leader Evo Morales said, "Even if they do away with coca, that won't stop drug trafficking. You can't demonize the coca plant. You have to demonize those who abuse it."[26] At the end of 2001, the leaders of the cocalero movement in the western Amazon who had survived the dirty war began to return to the struggle "after having hidden under the bed in fear for some years."[27] Now that the question of coca growing was being addressed at a regional and global level, they proposed the formation of a broad Andean movement of people unambiguously self-identified as campesino coca growers.

The central paradox underlying the cocalero movement was clearer than ever, now in a transnational context: it was the campesinos' cultivation of coca that had drawn the central government's attention to their plight. This activity now facilitated their linking up with other campesino movements in the Andes, strengthening their movement in general. While cocalero movements grew stronger in Bolivia and Peru, the Colombian situation was dramatically different. Although the movement did not disappear with the intensification of the armed conflict and the war on drugs, it was severely weakened. Movement leaders in Colombia sought support from the Peruvian and Bolivian movements through their participation in the Andean Council of Coca Producers (Consejo Andino de Productores de Hoja de Coca, CAPHC). However, while the central aim of the Peruvian and Bolivian movements was to differentiate the growing of coca for traditional and commercial uses from its use in the drug trade, the core demands of coca growers' organizations in Colombia were the cessation of aerial spraying and recognition of small-scale coca growers not as criminals but as social and economic actors with legitimate needs for alternative development of their regions.

Epilogue

At the end of the first phase of Plan Colombia in early 2006, the Chemonics International development agency completed its contract with USAID on alternative development in Putumayo. After decreasing between 2001 and 2004 due to the alternative development program and aerial fumigation, coca cultivation was beginning to rebound. The alternative development program had been intended to complement forced eradication, and the success of both strategies was measured by the total area of land where coca had been eradicated. There had been no attempt to create or implement a comprehensive alternative development program such as the one promoted by the Civic Movement in 1996 to address structural problems of the peasant economy like poverty, unemployment, and lack of educational opportunity, or to provide access to land, credit, or technical assistance, though it is precisely the lack of these inputs that drove peasants to cultivate coca. Most importantly, an opportunity had been lost to generate the kind of links between the state and civil society that could have legitimized and expanded the state presence in this marginal region and helped make the peasants of the region visible as social actors.

Reduced coca cultivation in Putumayo went hand-in-hand with increased cultivation in the Pacific coast area and other parts of neighboring Nariño as well as in the departments of Meta, Guaviare, Córdoba, western Antioquia, and southern Bolívar. The drug economy once again demonstrated its flexibility in response to drug war policies. New areas for cultivation and new transportation routes were quickly established.

At the close of the first phase of Plan Colombia, both the Colombian government and the U.S. Congress began to reevaluate aerial fumigation as a central strategy for crop eradication, each for its own reasons. For the U.S. Congress, several factors came into play. The United States had made a significant investment in Plan Colombia with limited results, and the war in Iraq was requiring ever greater resources. In addition, the Democratic majority elected in November 2006 was not fully behind the Republicans who had controlled Congress and the White House during the first six years of Plan Colombia (2001–2006).

In Colombia, meanwhile, aerial fumigation continued and small growers were still considered criminals. In 2007, 153,100 hectares were sprayed and coca was manually eradicated on 66,300 hectares for a total of 219,400 hectares, the highest since 1994. Paradoxically, the total area of coca cultivation increased by 27 percent from 78,000 hectares in 2006 to 99,000 hectares in 2007, an area nearly equivalent to the total area of coca under cultivation in 2002 (UNODC 2008). In late 2004, a new program of forced manual eradication was added as an additional component of the war against drugs. It was carried out by mobile eradication teams, rather than willing campesinos. This new element was closely tied to negotiations for the demobilization of paramilitary forces, a process initiated through an agreement with the national government in July 2003. By 2005, fourteen thousand paramilitary troops had been demobilized and "reinserted" into civilian life. As of October 2006, some 2,325 people were participating in 75 mobile eradication teams operating in 18 departments (Acción Social 2006).

Opposition to aerial fumigation and forced manual eradication as well as demands for alternative development have continued to spread, not just in the western Amazon but wherever coca is grown. For example, in May 2006 there were demonstrations by campesino cocaleros in Nariño, Meta, and Cauca. At the same time, the number of forced manual eradication teams has grown. In August 2007 it was reported that "3,100 men comprising 100 teams [would be] sent to areas including Putumayo, Meta, Guaviare, and Nariño."[1] In February and April 2008, about eight thousand peasants occupied the towns of Puerto Valdivia, Tarazá, and Nechí in southwestern Antioquia. Their first action lasted for a month and the second for two weeks. While this mobilization of campesino cocaleros resembled that of 1996 in the western Amazon, their central demand was for the departure of manual eradicators from the region. The campesinos complained that the antinarcotics police who accompanied the eradication teams had militarized the area, producing a great deal of tension and some acts of violence in areas whose inhabitants had already suffered from abuses by military forces. They also objected to the devastating effects of forced manual eradication, a process by which crops are eliminated in their entirety while the government provides for no alternative production or means of sustenance.

Just as they had in Putumayo in 1996, the coca growers proposed an agenda for negotiations with the government that involved gradual voluntary eradication within a comprehensive alternative development plan that included subsidies and investment in productive infrastructure. While the campesinos demanded negotiations with the government and expressed their wish for government assistance in transitioning away from growing coca, the police insisted that the march was being held "at gunpoint" under FARC orders.[2] Violent confrontations broke out two weeks after campesinos occupied the town centers, leading to several deaths and continued charges that the organizers were allied with the guerrillas or that guerrillas were participating in the marches. Detractors of the mobilizations continued to accuse the FARC of instigating them, while campesinos themselves demanded to be seen as small independent growers with critical economic needs who wanted to participate in devising legal, sustainable solutions.

With the help of ANUC, peasant associations in Putumayo's thirteen municipalities united in 2002 to form the Putumayo Coalition of Campesino Organizations (Mesa Departamental de Organizaciones Campesinas del Putumayo). They sought to continue negotiations with local and central government representatives and to monitor and assess Plan Colombia. In August 2006, when Chemonics had ended its programs and the second phase of Plan Colombia was getting under way, the Coalition organized a three-day-long departmental assembly where the historic marches and proposals of 1996 were recalled and re-evaluated. Local, regional, and national government representatives were invited to attend and debate the proposal for a new Comprehensive Development Plan for Putumayo. Several mayors and local officials, the governor, and the two Putumayan representatives to the lower house of Congress attended. The mayors and local officials expressed their interest in supporting the proposal and indicated that "the problem of drug trafficking would persist without an effective agrarian reform policy."[3] One of the peasants' objectives was to establish a direct relationship with the presidency's Alternative Development Program and USAID, without the intermediation of NGO contractors. They argued that the NGOs, rather than peasants, were benefiting from the existing arrangements, and they reiterated their readiness to devise alternative policies and programs for Putumayo with the support of local government representatives.

The Putumayo Coalition of Campesino Organizations also spoke out in an October 2006 letter to the president in which they said that "the solution to the problem of coca crops in the department and in the country will necessarily require changes to agricultural, environmental, and anti-drug policy."[4] They also opposed "handouts" (*proyectos asistenciales*) and stressed their willingness to actively participate in reformulating policy. Delegations of campesino leaders traveled to present their proposals for a new anti-drug strategy and alternative development program to the president and other central government officials.

The campesinos felt that little attention was paid to their demands. They held two other peaceful mobilizations against fumigation and forced eradication in Putumayo, the first in January and the second in March 2007. One participant commented about the March mobilization:

> First 150 families came out and then gradually more came out, but they did so peacefully, so the government would see that we are not violent like they say we are, that we're peaceful and want to show the government that. That's why we came out peacefully. We were with the mobilization for two weeks. We demonstrated because the constitution gives us the right to demonstrate. The mayor and the merchants helped us with food for these people.[5]

In March, the Putumayo Coalition of Campesino Organizations issued a public communiqué reaffirming their autonomy from armed groups and their identity as a differentiated social group: "We are not being pressured or assembled by any illegal armed group; thus we hold the national government responsible for the safety of the women and men campesinos leading and participating in this mobilization."[6]

Despite the peaceful intentions of the campesinos, an armed conflict had been escalating for several years. While peace negotiations got under way with the paramilitary AUC, an offensive supported by the U.S. involving nearly twenty thousand troops was launched in May 2004 against the FARC in the southern departments of Caquetá, Guaviare, and Meta. Its main objective as described by President Uribe was to defeat the FARC by attacking its longtime strongholds and capturing its leaders. Uribe's Plan Patriota stressed the need to "conquer" and seize control of this territory from the guerrillas, recalling General Harold Bedoya's conception of the 1996 offensive known as Operation Conquest. The population resented the militarization of the region. Many residents felt that none of the armed actors offered them security. On the contrary, they were involuntarily immersed in escalating confrontations. An official report by the security forces gave a body count of 1,891 guerrillas killed in 2005; 2,184 in 2006; and 2,717 as of November 2007.[7]

A number of FARC commanders were killed after October 2007, including Gustavo Rueda, alias "Martín Caballero," who commanded the Thirty-seventh Front on the Caribbean coast; Tomás Medina, alias "el Negro Acacio," leader of the Sixteenth Front; Marco Aurelio Díaz of the Bloque Occidental; and alias J.J. in Valle del Cauca, among others. Three members of the FARC's top leadership fell in March 2008. Second-in-command Raul Reyes was killed in a joint operation by Colombian ground, air, and river forces in Ecuadorian territory. Commander Iván Ríos was assassinated by an underling and his right hand delivered to authorities for a bounty. FARC founder and maximum leader Manuel Marulanda died of natural causes.[8]

As a result of peace negotiations with AUC, 504 paramilitaries of the Bloque Central Bolívar under the command of Mario Jiménez, alias "Macaco," demobilized in Puerto Asís in March 2006. The paramilitary phenomenon, however, persists. A new group called the Rastrojos is one of the many that have appeared in various regions to fill the void left by the demobilized AUC (CODHES 2006, 1). According to the mayor of Valle del Guamués, the Rastrojos include former paramilitaries of the Southern Front of the Bloque Central Bolívar. They are described in the region as "paramilitaries who no longer wear uniforms but who walk the streets with handguns in their waistbands intimidating anyone who might turn them in."[9] This group and others like it "no longer have the territorial influence or capacity that their predecessors had, but their geographical range coincides with that of the old groups. In fact, mid-level commanders who are now working in the new groups take advantage of their close relations with the territories and the inhabitants [that they once controlled] to maximize their mobility," according to the National Reparation and Conciliation Commission (Comisión Nacional de Reparación y Conciliación 2007, 46). This is particularly significant in light of the Special Report of the Foundation for Security and Democracy, which states: "These are relatively disarticulated armies. They do not respond to a coherent command structure and their activities are limited to controlling the cultivation of drug crops, clandestine laboratories, and smuggling routes" (Fundación Seguridad y Democracia 2007, 21).

In May 2007, a special group of investigators from the judicial police uncovered the fifth and largest mass grave found in Putumayo that year in the town of La Hormiga (municipality Valle del Guamués). It contained the remains of 105 victims of the paramilitaries, bringing the total number of remains found in Putumayo since January 2007 to 211.[10] Twelve bodies were found in a grave in the town of La Dorada (municipality San Miguel), and more were found elsewhere in Valle del Guamués: twenty-one in the inspectorate of El Placer, twenty-six in the inspectorate of El Tigre, and forty-seven in the vereda of La Esmeralda. These bodies were among the nearly one thousand that had been uncovered between 2006 and 2008 throughout the country.[11] By October 15, 2010, the Justice and Peace Unit of the Attorney General's Office reported that the number had reached 3,524. Three hundred sixty-eight of these bodies had been exhumed in Putumayo, of which 51 had been identified.[12] The existence of these mass graves confirmed the 1998 reports of paramilitary killings by the mayors and residents of these municipalities.

Prosecutors reported that the mass graves were located thanks to information provided by demobilized AUC commanders, victims' families, and other residents. The population also helped to identify thirteen bodies positively and many more preliminarily. On the other hand, prosecutors reported that people in Putumayo continued to be more intimidated than those in other regions, and that due to their fear of new generations of paramilitaries, very few people came forward to provide testimony.[13] The social and economic conditions associated with the armed conflict and drug trafficking have evolved, but there has been no structural change. The underlying social dynamics and processes examined in this book that revolve around the growing of coca remain the same. If anything, policy formation is even more centralized and the central government continues to favor a more military and less social response to campesino activities. The repeated demands of campesinos dependent on small coca crops for their subsistence continue to be ignored.

Letter from Five Putumayo Mayors to the Minister of the Interior

Letter to Interior Minister Horacio Serpa

August 3, 1996

Señor Minister:

The mayors of the municipalities in conflict in the department of Putumayo met in this city [Puerto Asís] to analyze the social situation affecting the region. We emphasize the following points of view from this analysis:

1. The municipalities of Lower Putumayo find themselves at imminent risk of social emergency due principally to two factors resulting from the Civic Strike in the zone:

   a) Because the strike affects all economic sectors of the region, the civilian population is beginning to feel the stresses of economic inactivity, and added to the lack of clarity on the possibility of a visit from a high-level Government Negotiating Commission, this is affecting the mood of the population. Consequently the people are trying to find new pressure tactics in an attempt to get the Government to accelerate sending the Commission. For their part the Security Forces are repelling the attempts of the demonstrators, with regrettable numbers of dead and injured.

   b) The overcrowding in seven of the department's towns has begun to generate serious health problems. The lack of adequate hospital infrastructure, medicines, and medical personnel in the zone means a risk level that is too high if epidemics are to be controlled, and if the injuries from clashes between demonstrators and the Security Forces are to be treated with existing resources.

2. For the foregoing reasons, we ask the Central Government to:

   a) Treat the situation as a social problem, not one of war.

   b) Urgently send a high-level Negotiating Commission to the zone, to normalize the situation and avoid greater upheaval.

c) Do not criminalize the attempt that we mayors are making to help
find legal alternatives to bring the central government and the communities closer together. On the contrary, we ask that you to try to
coordinate with all the civilian authorities of the region to find a
peaceful solution to the problem.

Respectfully,

Alcibíades Enciso Galvis
Mayor of Puerto Asís

Luis Alfredo Urbano
Mayor of Orito

Miguel Ángel Rubio
Mayor of Puerto Leguízamo

Luis Alfonso Agudelo
Mayor of Puerto Caicedo

Felipe A. Guzman M.
Mayor of La Hormiga

Negotiating Teams

Composition of the government commission

Eduardo Díaz, National Director of the Solidarity Network and presidential representative. Díaz was head of the commission.

Jaime Navarro, advisor to Minister of the Interior Horacio Serpa. Navarro was granted decision-making authority.

Rafael Echeverry, Vice Minister of Agriculture

César García, PLANTE official

Gustavo Restrepo, INCORA official

Juan José Arango, Director of Development at the Ministry of Agriculture

Yolanda Pinto de Tapias, National Highway Institute

A representative from the local office of the National Highway Institute

Luis A. Tovar, Ministry of Education

Mauro Santamaría, Ministry of Health

Marcos Barreto García, Ministry of the Environment

Fernando Salgado, Health Ministry

Gustavo Adolfo Cabrera, President's office

Luis Edmundo Maya, Director of CORPOAMAZONÍA

Luis A. García, National Director of ICEL

Manuel Peña Suárez, ICEL Planning Director

María Carolina Samper, ECOPETROL journalist

Gelver González, ECOPETROL

Composition of the civic movement commission:

Luis Emiro Mosquera, head of the Civic Movement and team coordinator

Gilberto Sanchez, Civic Movement leader from Puerto Asís

Richard Avella, Civic Movement leader from Puerto Asís

Ramiro Grisales, Civic Movement leader and deputy in the departmental Assembly

Fabio Carvajal, President of the Association of Communal Action Committees of Puerto Guzmán

Julio Cesar Ortiz, Council Member and representative for Puerto Guzmán

Jaime Burbano, representative for Valle del Guamués

Ruby Tejada, representative for Valle del Guamués

Luis Alberto Arias, representative for San Miguel

Euler Guerrero, representative for Orito

Arquímedes Ceballo, Council Member from Orito

Maria Murcia, representative for Villa Garzón

Miguel Melo, representative for Puerto Leguizamo

Julian Vallejo, President of ASOJUNTAS and representative for Puerto Asís

Hugo Cuaran, representative for Puerto Caicedo

Martin Posada, President of the Association of Communal Action Committees of Puerto Caicedo

Edilberto Imbachí, leader of OZIP and representative for the indigenous communities

Daniel Mavisoy, representative for the indigenous communities

Agreements by Working Group

Working Group One: For the Consolidation of Alternative Development, Agricultural, and Agro-industrial Development Programs, and Rural Development Policy in Putumayo

The strengthening of finances and operations in the region (bodies attached to the Ministry of Agriculture and Rural Development, the PLANTE program, and programs of the Solidarity Network intended to generate employment)

Working Group Two: Electrification and Road Infrastructure

Electrification

Electrification contract with ICEL (Colombian Institute of Electric Energy, or Instituto Colombiano de Energía Eléctrica)

Electrification of localities within the municipality of Puerto Guzmán

Upgrading of substation at Puerto Guzmán

Design of transmission line to the inspectorate of José María, passing through El Bombón, Puerto Rosario, El Cedro, Las Perlas, La Esmeralda, and Puerto Pradera

Provision of diesel-powered generator for Puerto Guzmán

Agreement on studies for the connection of Arizona to the El Cedral substation

Construction of hydroelectric plant in the upper Caquetá basin

Commitment of the national government to pre-feasibility studies

Construction of hydroelectric plant on the Río Mocoa

Proposal to begin studies on the feasibility of distributing cooking gas for domestic use

The Colombian Electric Power Institute is committed to providing the inspectorates and veredas with generators and to increase investment in the municipality of Puerto Leguízamo

Road Infrastructure

Paving of Mocoa–Pitalito road

San Miguel–Villagarzón–Mocoa international bridge

Widening and maintenance of Pasto–Mocoa road INVIAS

Construction of Orito–Manopamba road (National Fund for Local Roads, or Caminos Vecinales)

Construction of Las Perlas–José María Mayoyoque road (Caminos Vecinales)

Construction of Santa Lucía–Buena Esperanza–Arizona road (Caminos Vecinales)

Construction of road from Puerto Vega to the international bridge

Construction of bridge over the Caquetá River in the Guayuyaco sector and completion of the Putumayo–Florencia road (Caminos Vecinales, INVIAS)

Construction of the Orito–Villagarzón road (Caminos Vecinales; CORPOAMAZONIA to conduct the environmental impact study and design the environmental management plan)

Construction of the Mocoa–San Francisco alternate route (INVIAS, Ministry of Environment)

Construction of the Bordines–El Tigre road

Design and construction of the Picudo–Puerto Ospina road (departmental government, Caminos Vecinales, CORPOAMAZONIA)

Paving of second lane on the Puerto Leguízamo–La Tagua road (Caminos Vecinales)

Financing of environmental management plans on the above roads (Caminos Vecinales)

Strengthening the pool of machinery and other resources for the construction and maintenance of roads through the establishment of machinery banks (Caminos Vecinales)

Protection of hydrographic basins (Amazon Fund, or Fondo Amazónico; Amazonian Fund for the Environment, or Fondo Ambiental de la Amazonia; Royalties Fund for the Environment, or Fondo Ambiental de Regalías)

Expansion, and modernization, and bringing on line of regional airports

Compliance with border regulations concerning fuel prices. Prices of
gasoline and its derivatives to match those in Bogotá (Ministry of Mines
and Energy)

River transportation (construction of docks and warehouses; dredging of
channels)

Working Group Three: Health, Basic Sanitation, and Social Security

Pre-agreements: the resources needed to execute the Comprehensive Emergency Plan will differ from those already legally appropriated

Indigenous Health

Formulation of an Indigenous Health Plan for the subsequent five years,
training workshops on Social Security Law 100, determination of
Compulsory Health Plans (Planes Obligatorios de Salud, POS) and Basic
Health Care Plan (Plan de Atención Básica, PAB) (Social Investment
Fund, Ministry of Health, Ministry of the Interior, Putumayo
Administrative Department of Health)

Execution of the Plan (Administrative Department of Health)

Subsidies to the Plan (Guaranteed Solidarity Plan, or Fondo de Solidaridad
y Garantía; Department of Putumayo)

Technical assistance (Ministry of Health, Social Investment Fund)

*Strengthening of the Network for the Prevention
and Response to Emergencies and Disasters*

Promotion of the plan for training, technical assistance, and education,
according to the Law on Firefighters

Support and training for Local Emergency Committees (National
Directorate for the Prevention and Response to Disasters, affiliates of
the National Emergency System)

Financing of local emergency committees (Office for the Prevention and
Response to Disasters, Administrative Department of Health, hospitals
and other response organizations)

Hospital Infrastructure

Supply of Level II hospitals in Puerto Asís and Mocoa (Ministry of Health,
Social Investment Fund)

Supply of hospitals in Orito and La Hormiga and the health center in La Dorada (Ministry of Health, Social Investment Fund)

Complementary resources for supply of hospitals (Putumayo departmental government)

Supply of Level I hospitals in Puerto Leguízamo, Puerto Caicedo, Villagarzón, and Puerto Guzmán and the health center in Puerto Ospina (Ministry of Health, Social Investment Fund)

Social Security Health Coverage

Technical advice on the provision of health care (Ministry of Health)

Hold workshops to design and implement regional programs of the Basic Health Care Plan

Commitment to enroll 68,678 people by the end of 1996, 100,000 in 1997, and 135,000 in 1998 in a plan subsidized through the Administrative Department of Health or the Guaranteed Solidarity Plan (or Fondo de Solidaridad y Garantía)

Amendments to Law 60

Present, define, analyze, and support pertinent criteria for the amendment of Law 60, allowing for increased resources to be channeled to subnational entities such as departments and municipalities (Ministries of Health, Education, Development, Treasury, and Planning)

Environmental: Water and Sanitation

Approval of financing for basic sanitation programs presented for 1996 (Ministry of Mines and Energy)

Construction of aqueducts, Planadas–Puerto Asís

Construction of aqueducts, Teteyé–Puerto Asís

Construction of aqueducts, Puerto Umbría–Villagarzón

Construction of aqueducts, Mayoyoque–Puerto Guzmán

Studies and design for the provision of potable water and the sanitary disposal of human waste, Puerto Limón–Mocoa (DRI, departmental and municipal governments)

Studies and design for the provision of potable water and the sanitary disposal of human waste, Yurayaco–Puerto Leguízamo (DRI, departmental and municipal governments)

Studies and design for sanitary sewerage, Puerto Leguízamo–Puerto Ospina (DRI, departmental and municipal governments)

Studies and design for sanitary sewerage, Mayoyoque–Puerto Guzmán (DRI, departmental and municipal governments)

Studies and design for sanitary sewerage, Puerto Rosario–Puerto Guzmán (DRI, departmental and municipal governments)

Studies and design for the provision of potable water and the sanitary disposal of human waste in indigenous communities, Condagua–Mocoa (DRI, departmental and municipal governments)

Studies and design for the provision of potable water and the sanitary disposal of human waste in indigenous communities, Cecilia Cocha–Puerto Leguízamo (DRI, departmental and municipal governments)

Working Group Four: Education, Recreation, Sports, and Culture

Technical and financial assistance for feasibility studies and the provision of resources for the construction of a university in Valle del Guamués, Orito, and San Miguel, and the outlay of resources for its subsequent staffing, supply, and the initiation of operations

Services will be provided in Putumayo as part of the Universalization Plan in the municipalities of Puerto Leguízamo, Puerto Asís, San Miguel, Valle del Guamués (La Hormiga), Orito, Puerto Caicedo, Puerto Guzmán, Villagarzón, and Mocoa

Institutional strengthening and supply of the Putumayo Technological Institute (Social Investment Fund)

A program of incentives to expand the availability of basic educational services

The payment of 20 teachers' salaries in each of the municipalities in conflict: Puerto Leguízamo, Puerto Asís, San Miguel, Valle del Guamués (La Hormiga), Orito, Puerto Caicedo, Puerto Guzmán, Villagarzón, and Mocoa (Ministry of Education, Coordinator of Municipal Education, municipal governments)

Youth and the Struggle Against Drug Addiction

Plans for the development of education and health services (Social Investment Fund)

Consultancy and training on addiction and on sexual education (Ministry of Education)

Seminars, workshops, and programs for health promotion, disease prevention, and a plan for basic health care (Basic Health Care Plan, Ministry of Health)

Development of programs to cover the basic needs of communities, including indigenous and black communities and communities of vulnerable groups (Social Investment Fund)

School maintenance and supply (Ministry of Education)

Establishment of co-financing projects for recipients of housing subsidies from the National Institute of Low-Income Housing and Urban Reform (INURBE, Social Investment Fund)

Ethno-education

Professionalization and technical assistance to 140 indigenous people affiliated with normal schools and universities (Social Investment Fund, Ministry of Education)

Curriculum development for the eleven ethnicities (Social Investment Fund, Ministry of Education)

Technical assistance and logistical support in the formulation of a plan for ethno-education (Social Investment Fund, Ministry of Education)

Development of workshops, formulation of projects to define the needs for educational services in the municipalities

Culture, Artistic, and Artisanal Production

Formulation and execution of projects for supply, training, and infrastructure

Technical assistance to the educational sector in carrying out its responsibilities in the areas of oversight, mentoring, and feedback (Social Investment Fund)

Working Group Five: Housing

Additional funds provided through the emergency plan for urban and rural housing programs in Puerto Leguízamo, Puerto Asís, Orito, Valle del Guamués, San Miguel, Puerto Caicedo, Puerto Guzmán, Villagarzón, and Mocoa

Urban Housing

Commitment to establish a regional office of INURBE (central government)

Priority for participants in the Comprehensive Development Plan

Rural Housing

For the rural sector 1997

For indigenous communities 1997

For the rural sector 1998

For indigenous communities 1998

Establish a housing department in the Agricultural Development Bank, or
    Caja Agraria (central government)

Working Group Six: Land-Use Planning

The formation of a working group made up of the central government, the
    departmental government, and the civic movement to analyze the land
    use question and formulate and execute a land-use proposal

It is decided to set the first meeting of this working group for September
    11, 1996, in Mocoa.

Allocate necessary resources for the formulation and execution of the
    Putumayo Land-Use Plan (central government)

Technical teams for the development of the Land-Use Plan to be made
    up of leaders, technical personnel, and professionals with ties to the
    development of the region and approved by the community

Working Group Seven: Human Rights

Colombian–Ecuadorian agreement for border security

Fact-finding for the agreement (Presidential Human Rights Office)

Victims of Violence

Financing for relocation of leaders for their security

Establishment of a hotline for strike leaders and participants needing to
    report on human rights issues

Verification

Verification of human rights abuses during the course of the movement (Strike Committee, Presidential Human Rights Office)

Case of Colombian residents of Montepa, Putumayo detained in Ecuador

Commitment to monitor the trial of six Colombians detained by the Ecuadorian government in Montepa, Putumayo

Guarantees Subsequent to Demobilization

No disciplinary or legal action will be taken against workers or public officials who did not report to work and they will not be economically penalized

Working Group Eight: Follow-Up and Social Control

Follow-Up

The members of the negotiating committee, both from the government and the Putumayo Strike Committee, agree to adhere to the points of the agreement and to make their work public.

Social Control

The members of the negotiating committee, both from the government and the Putumayo Strike Committee, commit themselves to call upon the community, NGOs, sectoral economic organizations, and civil society to monitor and evaluate compliance with the provisions of the agreement.

Public meetings will be called periodically in order to conduct these evaluations (departmental governor, mayors, Ministry of the Interior)

Composition of Base Group

Community Sector

Thirteen (later eleven) community leaders, one for each municipality

One representative of indigenous organizations

One Putumayan women's representative

One representative of the Afro-Colombian population

One merchant representative endorsed by the Chamber of Commerce

Three professional community advisors

(Note: Two of the four municipalities in the non-cocalero Upper Putumayo region subsequently withdrew from the base group. The Afro-Colombian and merchant representatives were never active in the group, and only one of the three professional advisors was ultimately hired.)

National Delegation

Head of *Plan Sur*

Solidarity Network

Plan for Alternative Development, PLANTE

Ministry of Agriculture

State agricultural bank (Caja Agraria)

Comprehensive Rural Development Fund (Fondo de Desarrollo Rural Integral, Fondo DRI)

Colombian Institute of Agrarian Reform (Instituto Colombiano de la Reforma Agraria, INCORA)

Regional Delegation

One representative of the Amazonian Regional Council of Economic and Social Planning (Consejo Regional de Planificación Económica y Social de la Amazonia, CORPES Amazonia)

One representative of CORPOAMAZONIA

Departmental Delegation

Thirteen mayors, one from each municipality

The governor or his representative

One representative from the Departmental Planning Secretariat

One representative from the Putumayo Administrative Department of Health

One representative from the Department of Agricultural Development and Promotion

One representative from Putumayo Education Secretariat

Notes

Introduction

1   The Colombian national territory is divided into thirty-two departments (*departamentos*). Although each department has an elected governor and departmental assembly, economic transfers from the central government make up the majority of each departmental budget, particularly in the less developed and peripheral departments, and most legislation and decision making takes place at the national level.

The southern region of the department of Cauca, known as the Baja Bota of Cauca, or the "Boot" of Cauca, is the largest municipality in Cauca at 4,479 square kilometers. Until 1996 it had only one municipal seat, Santa Rosa, located in the upper, mountainous part of the Bota. Due to rugged terrain, it takes up to twelve hours to get from there to the lower, Amazonian part of the Bota (the Baja or Lower Bota). Because of this isolation, the people there have often looked more to Caquetá or Putumayo than to their own department for administrative services like health and education.

The area of Colombia is 1,138,388 square kilometers, more than twice the size of France. Its Amazon region is 423,473 square kilometers, larger than the state of California. This area makes up 37 percent of Colombian territory but only 6 percent of the vast Amazon basin. The Colombian Amazon includes the departments of Caquetá, Putumayo, Guaviare, Amazonas, Vaupés, Guainía, and southwestern Meta (map 2). The department of Putumayo has an area of 24,885 square kilometers, a little larger than the state of New Hampshire.

2   Das (1995, 6) adds that "the terrain on which these events were located criss-crossed several institutions, moving across family, community, bureaucracy . . . state and multinational corporations."

3   Interview with Lucero, campesino and member of ANUC-Putumayo. La Hormiga, September 13, 2003.

4   For a more extensive comparison of the cocalero movement in the three departments, see M. Ramírez et al. 1998–99 ICAN-Colciencias study.

5   The municipality (*municipio*) is the most local unit of public administration. Similar in size to the county in the United States, it has an elected mayor (*alcalde*) and municipal council.

6   Each municipality has a town center, where the administrative offices of the mayor and the official entities are located, called the *casco urbano*. Valle del Guamués and San Miguel were the last two municipalities to be established in Putumayo, in 1985 and 1994. Unlike other municipalities, they each have a casco urbano that uses a traditional name (La Hormiga and La Dorada, respectively) different from that of the municipality itself.

7　The municipalities of Putumayo are mostly rural. Outside of the casco urbano, they have three administrative subdivisions: *corregimientos*, inspectorates (*inspecciones de policía*), and veredas. Corregimientos are geographically delimited but have no administrative autonomy. They are governed by the municipality in which they are located. The inspectorate is defined by the presence of a police inspector and his authority over the area. Veredas are rural areas within larger corregimientos. To give one example, the municipality of Puerto Asís is made up of 148 veredas organized into five corregimientos and seven inspectorates.

8　Since the relative values of the Colombian peso and the U.S. dollar are variable, all currency conversions in this book are made at the average exchange rate for the particular calendar year being referenced. Readers should keep in mind that the average annual value of the U.S. dollar in terms of Colombian pesos varied by as much as 283 percent between 1996 and 2008, but that these changes were not unidirectional. The value of both currencies rose and fell.

9　In 1993 the index of unsatisfied basic needs in Putumayo was 79 percent and roads so poor that people cannot get their perishable crops to market (DANE 1993).

10　Human Rights Watch (2000) amply documented close ties between nearly half of the Colombian army's eighteen brigades and paramilitary groups. Furthermore, the report specified that many paramilitaries who used dirty war tactics in their anti-guerrilla activities had come out of the ranks of the armed forces.

11　"No debe haber agresiones en la jornada," *Semana*, February 1, 2008, http://www.semana.com.

12　Unlike Bolivia and Peru, the government of Colombia has accepted and adopted the forced eradication and fumigation promoted through the United States's war on drugs.

13　Dryzek (1996, 482) differentiates two types of state exclusion: "Active exclusion implies a state that attacks and undermines the conditions for public association in civil society. Passive exclusion implies a state that simply leaves civil society alone." Dryzek (1996, 482) also points out that "a degree of exclusion in the pattern of state interest representation is desirable if civil society and so democracy itself are to flourish." In the Anglo-American world authoritarian liberalism is one means of exclusion by the state.

14　While the words "paternalist" and "paternalistic" in English have negative connotations of authoritarianism, of arrogantly treating citizens as children who are unable to make important decisions for themselves, a "paternalist state" (*estado paternalista*) in Spanish may have the positive connotation of a state that takes care of its citizens, just as a responsible parent protects, takes care of, and meets the needs of his offspring.

15　For a wide-ranging discussion of new social movements and their specificities in Latin America, see Escobar (1992a, 1992b), Escobar and Alvarez (1992), Alvarez, Dagnino, and Escobar (1998), and Foweraker (1995).

16　Interview with Ballesteros, board member of the National Agricultural Union

Federation (Federación Nacional Sindical Unitaria Agropecuaria, or Fensuagro). Bogotá, January 27, 1998.

17 I refer to "social capital" and "cultural capital" in the sense proposed by Pierre Bourdieu (Bourdieu and Waquant, 1992, 119).

18 Interview with Sánchez, Civic Movement leader, Puerto Asís, August 23, 1998.

19 The PNR had been established in 1982 "in response to the sharpening of social conflicts and the emergence of new manifestations of violence," and lasted until 1994. Its objective was "to create the minimum necessary social, economic, and infrastructural conditions for a higher integration of those population sectors that have traditionally been excluded from the country's economic, political, and social development process" (National Rehabilitation Plan 1994).

20 The Colombian Institute for the Promotion of Science and Technology (Instituto Colombiano para el Desarrollo de la Ciencia y la Tecnología, COLCIENCIAS) is a state body that funds scientific research.

Chapter One

1 This depiction of an empty territory echoes the colonialist strategies in Africa analyzed by Comaroff and Comaroff (1988), who demonstrated that portraying territories as desolate and lonely—empty of the kind of human markers that Europeans associate with culture—was a way to legitimize colonization.

2 Colombia's Agustín Codazzi Geographic Institute (Instituto Geográfico Agustín Codazzi, IGAC) and Colombian Agricultural Research Corporation (Corporación Colombiana de Investigaciones Agropecuarias, CORPOICA) reported that in 2001, 57.3 percent of landowners in Colombia held less than 3 hectares each, and that all of these small properties together formed just 1.7 percent of the land suitable for agriculture. Only 0.4 percent of landowners held more than 500 hectares each, but this group owned 61.2 percent of the land suitable for agriculture (IGAC-CORPOICA 2002).

3 Regional landowners (predominantly cattle ranchers), establish patron-client relationships with the campesinos working their lands. There is a strong expectation that campesinos will become affiliated with the traditional political party to which "their" landowner belongs. The clergy has also exercised local political influence in rural areas ever since the church established missions in the nineteenth century.

4 In the 1993 census, the Department de Caquetá reported a population of 311,464 inhabitants, 204,309 in Putumayo and 57,884 in Guaviare. By 1999, the population had increased dramatically to 410,368 in Caquetá, 323,549 in Putumayo, and 114,083 in Guaviare (DANE 2002).

5 In the 1993 census, 37,764 inhabitants were counted in the department of Amazonas, 18,235 in Vaupés, and 13,491 in Guainía. By 1999 the population was calculated as follows: 68,569 in Amazonas, 29,395 in Vaupés, and 35,964 in Guainía (DANE 2002).

6   Human Rights and Conflict Resolution Workgroup, Puerto Asís, February 1998.

7   Letter to President Samper, March 1998. This and the other letters cited in the book reside in the archive of the Government of Putomayo, Mocoa.

8   For an extensive analysis of the cultural complexities of the interactions between colonizers and the colonized during the rubber boom period in Putumayo, see Taussig's seminal text (1987).

9   Remarks by Ramiro Grisales, Civic Movement leader, during negotiations on the formulation of the crop substitution plan, Orito 1996; emphasis added.

10   Remarks by Grisales at forum, May 1997.

11   Statement to *AM PM News* in February 1998. A video copy of the segment is on file with the author.

12   Remarks from August 14, 1996 meeting of the First Working Group in Orito 1996.

13   Remarks of a Baja Bota community leader in a workshop at Yapurá, October 1998.

14   The conversion of campesino self-defense groups into mobile guerrilla units has been a recurrent phenomenon since 1946. As Pizarro Leongómez (1989, 7) argues: "In fact, Colombia has seen a recurring cycle of violence–amnesty–rehabilitation–violence since 1946. Roughly speaking, this cycle coincides with the different modalities of armed action inspired by the Communist Party, self-defense units–guerrillas–self-defense units–guerrillas."

15   This government, the only military government Colombia has had in the twentieth century, was fostered by the traditional Liberal and Conservative Party elites and deposed when they agreed to establish the National Front.

16   William Ramírez (1981, 204) explains: "FARC, despite their doctrine of mobility, offensive capability, and the widespread dispersion of their fronts; despite the revolutionary innovations they attribute to themselves in their public statements and despite their relationship with the Communist Party, are no more than the vanguard of a campesino colonization movement. In service to this movement, their fundamental project is resistance to the super-exploitation of the campesino by big capital and the establishment of a democratic agrarian reform regime."

17   In 1958, the two traditional political parties, the Conservatives and the Liberals, agreed to establish a National Front. Under the terms of this pact, the two parties would end *La Violencia*, alternate in power, and divide patronage offices between them. The agreement precluded the participation of any third party and lasted until 1974.

18   Operation Marquetalia was approved in Congress on May 27, 1964, and was signed by President Guillermo León Valencia, launching a military operation against the so-called independent republics of the Communists. The institutionalized monopoly of power held by the two traditional parties during the National Front period characterized the operation as a state military action representing the elite social sectors. The objective was to enter the area held by the Communist campesino self-defense groups and destroy them. The cold

war–era United States government promoted the operation. This aggression became the foundational myth of FARC.

19 In 1983 the EPL established the Aldemar Londoño Front, which operated in the oil-producing areas of Putumayo (Orito and Valle del Guamués) for eight years. The EPL ceased all military activities at the end of 1990, signed a truce with the government of César Gaviria in 1991, and demobilized. That same year, FARC occupied the areas of Orito and Valle del Guamués that had been abandoned by the EPL (*Comisión de Superación de la Violencia* 1992, 102).

20 This guerrilla movement was established in 1974 by members of a populist political party called National Popular Alliance (Alianza Nacional Popular, ANAPO).

21 See chapter 3 for an analysis of the Patriotic Union's genesis and its national and departmental electoral activities.

22 Alternative political movements in Putumayo and their persecution are discussed in greater depth in chapter 3.

23 Conversation with Laura, local pharmacist and nurse in Puerto Asís, 1998.

24 In Colombia, the Security Forces (Fuerza Pública) are defined by the Constitution to include both the military forces (Army, Navy, and Air Force) and the National Police. All police in Colombia are national; there are no local or departmental forces. While the police are defined as civilian, in many respects they resemble the military in terms of their uniforms, responsibilities, weapons, and system of ranks. However, military forces report to the Armed Forces General Command while the police report directly to the Ministry of National Defense. The national police has a number of subordinate bodies with special responsibilities, including an intelligence unit, anti-narcotics police, judicial police, *carabineros*, and others. Several of these bodies engage in counterinsurgency activities.

25 Interview with Imbachí, director of the Putumayo Regional Indigenous Organization (OZIP), Bogotá, July 14, 1999.

26 Ibid.; emphasis added.

27 For an in-depth anthropological analysis of the set of social relations which mediates the distribution of surplus value among different groups of actors in the chain of coca production in Putumayo, see Jansson 2008.

28 A number of military officers have been investigated, tried, and convicted for promoting paramilitaries and ignoring their illegal activities. In July 1997, paramilitaries killed seven campesinos and disappeared forty-one others in Mapiripán, Meta. The commander of the Seventh Military Brigade of Villavicencio was arrested two years later. He had known of the paramilitaries' plans for the massacre and had done nothing to prevent it. The prosecutor explained that he had been arrested "for having acted in such a way as to assure a result, that is, a massacre" ("Coronel mata general," *Semana*, no. 897, July 12, 1999; 38). The Twentieth Brigade, an Army intelligence unit, was dismantled in May 1998 when it was found to be involved in the murders of two human rights activists and threats to more than a dozen other union leaders and peace and human

rights activists ("B-20 investigada por muerte de activistas de DH," *El Especta-dor*, May 11, 1998; and "El desplome de la Brigada XX," *El Espectador*, May 21, 1998).

29 This was the case in Serranía de San Lucas, Bolivar; La Gabarra, Norte de Santander; and in Putumayo, all places to which coca cultivation had been displaced and where it was intensified as a result of aerial fumigation in Caquetá and Guaviare ("La guerra blanca," *Semana* no. 904, Aug. 30, 1999, 32–34).

30 Serrano, "Con la guerrilla o con las convivir?" *El Tiempo*, July 20, 1997.

31 FARC's attacks on security forces increased after 1996, notably on military bases and mobile counter-guerrilla units, demonstrating FARC's military power in contrast to the weakness of the army. That was the case of the attack to the military base of Las Delicias in Putumayo on August 31, 1996 ("Guerra en el fin del mundo," *Semana* no. 824, February 16, 1998; 30–32), to the military communications headquarters for southern Colombia at Patascoy military base in Nariño on December 20, 1997 ("La Caída," *Semana* no. 819, January 12, 1998; 18–23), and to the army's Twenty-fourth Mobile Brigade at El Billar, Caquetá, on March 24, 1998. This latter confrontation was called the army's greatest debacle (*Semana* no. 832, April 20, 1998, and "El desastre militar del río Caguán," *El Espectador*, March 7, 1998). As a result, FARC held 249 military and police prisoners ("Los olvidados," *Semana* no. 852, August 31, 1998; 26–31). In June 1997 the soldiers kidnapped at Las Delicias were released by the Southern Front of FARC in Cartagena del Chairá (Caquetá). However, the soldiers captured at Patascoy and El Billar are still prisoners of FARC. By mid-2008 those captured at Patascoy had been held for ten and a half years.

32 Amilkar Serrano, "Con la guerrilla o con las convivir?" *El Tiempo*, July 20, 1997.

33 Alfredo Molano, "Las Convivir," *El Espectador*, July 17, 1997.

34 "Golpes de pecho," *Semana* no. 828, February 16, 1998; 46–50.

35 "DAS y Convivir harán inteligencia conjunta," *El Tiempo*, November 11, 1997.

Chapter Two

1 Data available from United Nations Office on Drugs and Crime (UNODC) Illicit Crop Monitoring Programme (ICMP), current through 2008. For one such report, see http://www.unodc.org/documents/crop-monitoring/Andean_report _2008.pdf.

2 Diana Jean Schemo, "U.S. Seeks Sharp Increase in Funds to Fight Drugs in Colombia," *New York Times*, April 1, 1998.

3 The National Narcotics Council enacted two resolutions to authorize aerial spraying in indigenous territories: Resolution 0013 of June 27, 2003, and Resolution 28 of November 24, 2005. The first authorized aerial spraying in National Parks, where many indigenous people live, and the second one explicitly called for aerial spraying in specific *resguardos* in Guaviare, Sierra Nevada de Santa Marta, and Catatumbo-Barí (Norte de Santander).

4 The National Narcotics Council categorizes coca producers as large (more than

ten hectares), medium (from three to ten hectares), and small (less than three hectares).

5 As Thoumi (1995) documents, marijuana production decreased in Mexico at the end of the 1960s as a result of a successful eradication program there. Traffickers sought new sources to supply the United States market and marijuana began to be grown in Colombia, at first in the Sierra Nevada de Santa Marta, a northern mountain range. By the middle of the 1970s, business was booming and the plantations had spread to the eastern plains. In 1978, Colombian President Julio César Turbay initiated a manual and aerial eradication campaign using the chemical paraquat. Another factor in the waning of the marijuana bonanza was the success of a new variety being grown in the United States. Production levels recovered between 1982 and 1984, though. President Belisario Betancur began a second fumigation campaign in 1985 that reduced but did not eliminate marijuana cultivation, which in fact rebounded once again in 1986 and 1987. Not until 1989 did the area of planted marijuana shrink dramatically, and this was not necessarily the result of the various eradication campaigns, but rather of the relatively low profitability compared to the United States's crop.

6 "La Batalla del Glifosato," *Semana* no. 659 (December 20, 1994).

7 "Como arar en el mar," *Semana* no. 821 (January 26, 1998).

8 For an expanded analysis of the relation between the internal armed conflict in Colombia and the international war on drugs see Ricardo Vargas (1999 and 2004).

9 In March 1998, the *Washington Post* analyzed the 350 percent increase of U.S. assistance to the Colombian military and National Police from $28.5 million in 1995 to nearly $100 million in 1997, concluding: "The efforts to help the Colombian armed forces reflect changing U.S. attitudes about the gravity of the threat to the government posed by drug-financed rebels." Dana Priest, "U.S. May Boost Military Aid to Colombia's Anti-Drug Effort," *Washington Post*, March 28, 1998.

10 Both the anti-narcotics police and army counterinsurgency units operate in Putumayo.

11 Tod Robberson, "U.S. Policy in Colombia May Face Revision. Rebels' Gains, Drug Trade Ties Could Change Military Aid," *Dallas Morning News*, March 18, 1998.

12 Two FARC commanders were extradited to the United States on drug trafficking charges in 2005: Ricardo Ovidio Palmera, also known as Simón Trinidad, and Anayibe Rojas Valderrama, known as "Sonia."

13 President Virgilio Barco declared war against drug traffickers in August 1989, driving up the wholesale price of cocaine in the United States. At the same time, the price of Peruvian coca leaf and coca paste fell dramatically. The Colombian government's suppression of the trade destabilized some Colombian organizations that had been importing coca from Peru, resulting in an oversupply of coca leaf in that country accompanied by a relative decrease in demand in the

United States market (Uprimny 1994, 80). Moreover, Barco's anti-drug offensive "provoked, one year later, a forty percent increase in the wholesale price, while the price to the final consumer was unchanged. Instead the purity of the product deteriorated by fifty to sixty percent" (Uprimny 1994, 82).

14   "Capos de la mafia disfrutan de mansiones en plena selva," *La Nación*, April 6, 1997.

15   "Nuevas rutas para transportar coca," *La Nación*, April 11, 1996.

16   Conversation in Cuembí, Puerto Asís, with a campesino cocalero, March 1998.

17   Comments at a workshop conducted by the author in Orito to assess alternative development projects promoted by USAID under Plan Colombia, July 17, 2004.

18   "Of the 11,884 hectares of coca in Puerto Asís in 1996, 2,733 (23 percent) were in the hands of large growers with an average of eighteen hectares per farm; 4,159 (35 percent) were in the hands of medium producers with an average of seven hectares per farm; and the remaining 4,992 (42 percent) were in the hands of small growers with an average of 2.3 hectares per farm. In Valle del Guamués and San Miguel, it was found that of the 11,112 hectares in coca, 2,000 (18 percent) were in the hands of large growers with an average of sixteen hectares per farm; 3,334 (30 percent) were in the hands of medium producers with an average of 5.6 hectares per farm; and 5,778 (52 percent) were in the hands of small producers with an average of 2.6 hectares per farm" (Alomía et al. 1997, 51).

19   "If the campesino is responsible for three hectares of coca, he will have to dedicate an average of twenty full days per harvest cycle exclusively to fertilizing, controlling disease and plague, harvesting, and processing. If he produces sweet Peruvian coca this work cycle will repeat itself six or seven times per year and if it is the bitter variety, it will repeat itself nine times" (Sabogal 1998, 35).

20   Alomía et al. (1997, 104) notes that in Middle Putumayo, "Approximately sixty percent of the coca workforce is minors under the age of twenty-five. Coca producers and workers have little education; approximately 20 percent have finished elementary school, 10 percent have attended some or all of high school, and the remaining 70 percent have less than a fifth grade education."

21   For a detailed study of daily life of young raspachines in coca and poppy-growing areas, see Ferro et al. 1999.

22   Conversations in Puerto Asís with raspachines, March, 1998.

23   Conversation with a female coca worker in Vereda La Española, Lower Cuembí area, Puerto Asís, March 1998.

24   "About 6,808,800 *arrobas* of coca leaf are being processed annually in Puerto Asís, Valle del Guamués, and San Miguel in 5,000 small laboratories, which are also 5,000 small sources of contaminated water, since along with the macerated coca leaf they discard all the precursors that they use in their industrial process" (Alomía et al. 1997, 72).

25   "Small campesino producers ... make large investments per hectare in the cultivation and processing of coca ... If you consider the totality of the agricultural processes and the initial preparation of the same land each time around, you will see that they devote a lot of capital to it. In this way they incur expenses of

from 21.7 million pesos or US$10,850 to 68.3 million pesos or US$34,150 in a five-year period. . . . On average, the maintenance and processing of one hectare of coca costs the equivalent of one day of agricultural wages every day" (Sabogal 1998, 35).

26 Interview with Jairo, former traqueto, in Puerto Asís, April 28, 1998.

27 Ibid.

28 Ibid.

29 Ibid.

30 In 1998, for each kilo processed, a chemist earned 10,000 pesos, or US$7. A manager earned 4,000 pesos, or US$2.80. The oven tender and the recycler each earned 2,000 pesos, or US$1.40, and the rest of the employees earned 1,000 pesos, or US$0.70.

31 Interview with Jairo, former traqueto, in Puerto Asís, April 28, 1998.

32 Ibid.

33 Violent deaths include homicides, suicides, and accidents.

34 Remarks by a campesino from the Mandur vereda of Puerto Guzmán at the Forum on Peace and Social Harmony in Puerto Asís, 1997.

35 Conversation with a woman in Puerto Asís, 1998.

36 Ibid.

37 Interview with Agudelo, Puerto Asís, October 12, 1998; emphasis added.

38 Conversation with a woman in Puerto Asís, 1998.

39 Interview with Agudelo, Puerto Asís, October 12, 1998.

40 Conversation with Laura, Puerto Asís, 1998.

41 For a definition of place that combines objective components of locale and location with the subjective sense of place, see Agnew (1997, 28).

Chapter Three

1 Interview with Gonzalo Portilla, civic leader, Mocoa, 1998.

2 Ibid.

3 "Llueve Glifosato," *La Nación*, November 22, 1994.

4 The approval of areas to be fumigated would be coordinated among the Institute for Renewable Natural Resources and the Environment (Instituto de Desarrollo de los Recursos Naturales Renovables, INDERENA), the Colombian Institute of Agriculture (Instituto Colombiano Agropecuario, ICA) and Ministry of Health officials, giving all of these bodies input about the aerial application of herbicides, including risks, effectiveness, and social and environmental impact. The National Narcotics Directorate (Direccón Nacional de Estupefacientes, DNE) would engage an outside contractor to supervise the authorized fumigations on environmental, operational, and technical execution levels. Special management areas and natural reserves were not to be fumigated without a specific ruling by the Ministry of the Environment. To avoid spraying subsistence agriculture, only areas greater than two hectares would be subject to fumigation; smaller plots would be eradicated manually or mechanically.

5   "Controlarán uso del glifosato," *La Nación*, November 30, 1994.

6   "Fumigación no se suspenderá," *El Tiempo*, November 22, 1994.

7   The National Rehabilitation Plan was in effect from 1982 to 1994 during the presidencies of Belisario Betancur, Virgilio Barco, and César Gaviria. Its goal was to develop marginal regions, by providing incentives for participation in decision making. When President Ernesto Samper took office in 1994 the Plan was renamed the Solidarity Network and its focus largely changed from participatory programs to financial assistance. Forms of assistance included urban and rural employment and housing subsidies in cooperation with the National Affordable Housing and Urban Reform Institute (Insituto Nacional de Vivienda de Interés Social y Reforma Urbana, INURBE) and the Caja Agraria. In addition a program called REVIVIR was settled to provide 70,000 pesos monthly to needy seniors from each municipality, educational subsidies for poor children of single mothers, food subsidies and other assistance to community daycare facilities, and subsidies for rural childcare services (Solidarity Network 1998).

8   "Puerto Asis: La fumigación no podrá erradicar la injusticia," *Diario del Sur*, November 22, 1994; "Guerrilla culpable de paro en Putumayo," *El Tiempo*, January 3, 1995.

9   "Ataque campesino a la planta de Ecopetrol en Putumayo," *El Tiempo*, January 5, 1995.

10   "Colombia esta semana," *El Tiempo*, January 8, 1995. Army Special Forces were transferred from the military base at Tolemaida, located in Melgar, Tolima, in January, and carried out a violent raid on ECOPETROL's Churuyaco facility in the municipality of Orito. Juan Carlos Gómez, a six-year-old boy, died as a result of tear gas used by the soldiers to break up the demonstration. Several campesinos were injured in the same operation (*Justicia y Paz* 1995).

11   "Colombia esta semana," *El Tiempo*, January 8, 1995; and "El Putumayo continúa el debate por la fumigación," *El Tiempo*, January 11, 1995.

12   "By the end of 1986, the victims included a senator, a representative, a deputy, and twenty municipal councilors. Their first presidential candidate, Jaime Pardo Leal, was assassinated in October 1987. The killings continued and their second candidate, Bernardo Jaramillo Ossa, was killed in March 1990. This assassination brought the death toll to 1,044 in the 'dirty war' against this organization" (Gaitán 1992, 132).

13   The UP acknowledged and supported the spread of a Civic Movement in Colombia: "It is the most complex movement in the country . . . organized around economic and social demands, it has been growing so much that it has now been structured as a national movement [with] a coordinating body [Coordinadora Nacional de Movimientos Cívicos y Comunales]" (Harnecker 1989, 21). Given the presence of the UP in Putumayo during these years, it is possible that it influenced the mobilizations ideologically. Since it was not electorally strong in Putumayo, however, the degree of autonomy between the Civic Movement, and the Patriotic Union and Communist Party, is an open question.

14   Interview with Gonzalo Portilla, 1998.

15   Ibid.

16   Interview with Rubio, 1999.

17   "Luis Alfredo Urbano, nuevo alcalde," *La Nación*, July 3, 1996.

18   Interview with Diego Peñuela in Orito, April 26, 2001.

19   Interview with Gonzalo Portilla, 1998.

20   "Romería a la Machaca," *Cambio* no. 311, May 31, 1999.

21   "Los Alcaldes de la Guerrilla," *Semana* no. 785, May 19, 1997.

22   Interview with Rubio, 1999.

23   "Alcaldes deciden organizarse," *La Nación*, March 22, 1996.

24   Interview with Rubio, 1999.

25   Ibid.

26   Interview with Hugo Zambrano, a journalist and local historian in Mocoa, 1998.

27   "Plante: Alternativas de Vida," *Diario del Sur*, September 3, 1996.

28   Héctor Moreno Reyes, address to the Universidad de los Andes, April 1997.

29   "El Plante sí ha cumplido," *La Nación*, February 2, 1996.

30   "Lo del Plante . . . en veremos," *La Nación*, June 28, 1996.

31   Interview with Ruben Darío Pinzón, local PLANTE official in Puerto Asís, 1998.

32   ¿"Plante y pa dónde?" *La Nación*, April 4, 1996.

33   "Por qué no le ha cumplido al Putumayo," *La Nación*, January 25, 1996; and "Comunidad no muy conforme ante evaluación de la Comisión del Gobierno Central," *La Nación*, January 31, 1996.

34   "Denuncian oscuros intereses en paro de Putumayo," *El Tiempo*, January 5, 1996.

35   "Sustitución gradual y no erradicación,"*La Nación*, April 23, 1996.

36   Ibid.

Chapter Four

1   Each community action committee has a president and a number of other officers called "dignitaries" (*dignatarios*), all elected for three-year terms, as well as many "affiliates" (*afiliados*), in this case the vereda residents. The president and the board members are in charge of establishing relations, demanding services, and proposing projects to improve living conditions in their vereda.

2   For an interesting discussion of the contextuality of stigma and how "an attribute that stigmatizes one type of possessor can confirm the usualness of another, and therefore is neither creditable nor discreditable as a thing in itself," see Goffman (1963, 3).

3   In their discussion of the Mothers of the Plaza de Mayo in Argentina, Calderón et al. (1992, 20) point out that "social movements derive their power not so much from opposing the state as from the fact that the state has systematically opposed them."

4 "Se gesta otro paro en el Putumayo," *El Tiempo*, January 4, 1996.

5 "Alcaldes piden solución al problema del cemento y la gasolina," *La Nación*, October 12, 1996.

6 This type of restriction on materials that are used in cocaine processing but are also necessary for daily life has continued to be imposed. On September 10, 1996, Resolution 0004 restricted some additional products used in clandestine cocaine processing laboratories such as urea ammonium, diesel fuel, and kerosene. In May 1997, the Ombudsman of Putumayo (Defensor del Pueblo) asked the National Narcotics Council to annul this resolution, arguing that the department's infrastructure had been seriously affected, almost to the point of paralysis. Construction workers had unionized in response to the lack of work and were calling for modifications to the restrictions ("Piden nulidad para control de cemento y gasolina," *La Nación*, May 20, 1997). In October 1997, Resolution 0003 was enacted to modify Resolutions 0001 and 0004 of 1996, accounting for price inflation and raising the threshold quantities for restrictions on distribution of these chemicals and products. The sale of cement in the region was restricted again in August 1999. Authorization was required for the sale of more than half a sack. Only 600 kilos were permitted in wholesale transactions, and discontent continued. In 2002, Resolution 006 was passed in order to further restrict the sale of cement, gasoline, urea ammonium, diesel fuel, and kerosene in Putumayo, and resolutions were enacted in this same year and with the same goal in the departments of Caquetá, Guaviare, Amazonas, Vaupés, Arauca, Meta, Vichada, Nariño, and some municipalities in Norte de Santander. This reflected the migration of coca cultivation in response to massive aerial spraying in the departments of the western Amazon. Similar legislation was passed in 2003 in Huila and Casanare; in 2004 in Guainía, Santander and some municipalities of Cauca and Bolivar; in 2006 in other municipalities in Nariño, Córdoba, Antioquia, and Chocó.

7 "No a las zonas de Orden Público, Sí a la zona especial de Inversión Social," *La Nación*, June 10, 1996.

8 "Palabras del Presidente Ernesto Samper Pizano en la Presentación del Balance del Plan Córdoba y los resultados de la Operación Conquista," *La Nación*, July 10, 1996.

9 Ibid.

10 This point would be debated during the marches by movement leaders, because it was central to their analysis of the government's motivation in promoting the fumigation policy.

11 "El paro en el Guaviare es una bomba de tiempo," *El Tiempo*, July 17, 1996.

12 "Reinician Fumigación," *La Nación*, July 27, 1996.

13 "Crece Concentración, cinco mil campesinos en Santuario," *La Nación*, August 1, 1996.

14 "Caquetá se sumó al paro," *La Nación*, August 2, 1996.

15 "Lo que queda de lo social," *El Espectador*, August 2, 1996.

16 "Paro indefinido en 12 pueblos del Putumayo," *El Tiempo*, July 28, 1996.

17 "Bedoya Acusa al Gobierno," *El Espectador*, August 7, 1998.

18 *Noticiero AM/PM*, "Marchas Campesinas del Caquetá, Guaviare y Putumayo," New York: Colombia Media Project, July 7, 1996; emphasis added. This one-hour television broadcast, produced by the news show *Noticiera AM/PM*, compiled coverage of the cocalero protest marches in the departments of Guaviare, Caquetá, and Putumayo, including coverage of the army's brutal repression of the marches.

19 Ibid.

20 Ibid., emphasis added.

21 Ibid.

22 "Siete días de paro y no hay ningún acuerdo. Completo Abandono Estatal," *La Nación*, August 1, 1996.

23 *Noticiero AM/PM*, "Marchas Campesinas del Caquetá, Guaviare y Putumayo."

24 "Afirma el general Mario Galán: hay intereses de la narcoguerrilla," *La Nación*, August 2, 1996.

25 Mary Douglas has called attention to how "dirt is the by-product of a systematic ordering and classification of matter, insofar as ordering involves rejecting inappropriate elements" (1966, 35–40).

26 *Noticiero AM/PM*, "Marchas Campesinas del Caquetá, Guaviare y Putumayo," 1996.

27 Elver Monge, "Cocaleros mandan en Mocoa," *El Tiempo*, August 16, 1996.

28 "Una Crónica de lo Absurdo," *La Nación*, August 11, 1996.

29 *Noticiero AM/PM*, "Marchas Campesinas del Caquetá, Guaviare y Putumayo."

30 Conversation with school teacher in Mocoa, 1998.

31 Interview with Hugo Zambrano in Mocoa, 1998.

32 Interview with Octavio, campesino from the Baja Bota of Cauca, Piamonte, 1998.

33 For Lacan, *identification* implies "the transformation that takes place in the subject when he assumes an image—whose predestination to this phase—affect is sufficiently indicated by the use, in analytic theory, of the ancient term *imago*" (1977, 2).

34 S. Nugent (1993, xxi) maintains that campesino communities in Brazilian Amazonia "have not been granted full status as integrant social forms," and moreover, they are "defined in terms of what they are not (aboriginal, national) rather than in positive terms."

35 Letter to Ombudsman's Office, July 26, 1998. Emphasis added; grammar and spelling reflects the original.

36 First comment by Albeiro, JAC leader from the vereda La Consolata, Piamonte. The second comment is from Euraldo, JAC leader from the vereda El Porvernir, Piamonte, October 1998.

37 Interview with Jaime Navarro, advisor to the interior minister for the 1996 Putumayo negotiations, in Popayán, 1999.

38 Interview with Marino Rincón, director of the Mocoa Hospital and advisor to the Civic Movement during negotiations in Mocoa, 1999.

39 Legislation enacted by the United States Congress in 1986 requires the president to "certify" illegal drug-producing and transit countries depending on whether they were cooperating effectively with the United States's counternarcotics efforts or not. In this certification process, the administration must provide annual reports evaluating progress and defend its policies before Congress. Those countries that do not make the grade face stiff penalties—including withdrawal of U.S. aid (with the exception of counter-narcotics and humanitarian aid), American opposition to loans from multilateral development banks and possible trade sanctions. Colleta Youngers has also pointed out that the certification process "guarantees members of Congress an opportunity to present a tough position in the 'war on drugs' to win votes back home" and that "in the end, drug-war politics and domestic politics are inextricably intertwined" ("Drug Decertification: The Process has become an Annual Charade," *Washington Post*, March 27, 1999).

40 Interview with Edilberto Imbachí in Mocoa, 1999.

41 Interview with Marino Rincón, 1999.

42 Interview with Edilberto Imbachí, 1999.

43 Ibid.

44 Ibid.

45 Ibid., emphasis added.

46 Strike leader at the Civic Strike follow-up meeting, Puerto Caicedo, September 25, 1996.

47 "Guerrilla culpable de paro en Putumayo," *El Tiempo*, January 3, 1995.

48 Interview with Jamioy, Indigenous Inga woman, La Floresta, Piamonte, March 5, 1999.

49 Interview with Albeiro, campesino member of the Central Organizing Commission of Baja Bota of Cauca, and community action committee leader, La Consolata, Piamonte, February 25, 1998.

50 Testimony in Puerto Asís, 1999.

51 Interview with Narcilo Castillo, Negotiating Commission member for the Baja Bota Civic Strike, 1998.

52 Interview with Rincón, 1999.

53 Interview with Oliva Macías, Piamonte, 1999.

54 Interview with Jamioy in vereda La Floresta, Piamonte, 1999.

55 Ibid.

56 Ibid.

57 Ibid.

58 Interview with Albeiro, 1998.

59 Interview with Jamioy in vereda La Floresta, Piamonte, 1999.

60 Conversation with campesino, Puerto Asís, 1998.

61 Interview with Octavio, 1998.

62 "Las Marchas ya no son Pacíficas," *La Nación*, August 10 1996.

63 Interview with Eduardo Díaz, director of the Solidarity Network and presidential representative at the negotiations, Bogotá, June 5, 1999.

Chapter Five

1 In evaluating the accomplishments of the 1991 Constitution, Velásquez (1991, 65) emphasizes the role of citizen participation: "Participation is not only a desirable practice in the political behavior of Colombians. It is an *essential goal* of the state. This means that the state is obligated to promote and facilitate it in the distinct spheres of citizens' lives. This holds true not only for the central state, but for every level of political and territorial organization. . . . It has an obligation to foster the participation of the citizenry in the essential decisions that will affect their future."

2 Marshall (1965, 78–79) distinguishes the civil, social, and political elements of citizenship in his classic work *Class, Citizenship, and Social Development*: "The civil element is composed by the rights necessary for individual freedom— liberty of the person, freedom of speech, thought, and faith, the right to own property and conclude valid contracts, and the right to justice. . . . By the political element I mean the right to participate in the exercise of political power, as a member of a body invested with political authority or as an elector of the members of such body. . . . By the social element I mean the whole range from the right to a modicum of economic welfare and security to the right to share to the full in the social heritage and to live the life of a civilized being according to the standards prevailing in the society. The institutions most closely related with it are the educational system and the social services."

3 Dagnino (1998, 50–52) establishes for this "new citizenship" the following characteristics: "It includes the invention and creation of *new* rights, which emerge from specific struggles and their concrete practices." Second, "the new citizenship requires the constitution of active social subjects (political agents), defining what they consider to be their rights and struggling for their recognition. . . . In this sense it is a strategy of the noncitizens, of the excluded, to secure a citizenship 'from below.'" Third, "what is at stake in fact, is *the right to participate in the very definition of the system, to define what we want to be members of*, that is to say, the invention of a new society." Fourth, "The new citizenship is a *project for a new sociability*: a more egalitarian format for social relations," which implies the recognition of the other as a bearer of legitimate rights. Fifth, this new citizenship "is no longer confined within the limits of the relationship with the state or between the state and the individual but must be established within civil society itself . . . for society as a whole; this strategy requires learning to live on different terms with these emergent citizens, who refuse to remain in the places that were socially and culturally defined for them. This is the point in which the radicality of citizenship as a cultural politics seems quite clear."

4 Analyzing the objectives and achievements of the new social movements, Cohen and Arato (1994, 526) point out that they seek to influence the hegemonic political discourse and to an even greater extent the political institutions, by deploying both a politics of influence "aimed at altering the universe

of political discourse to accommodate new interpretations, new identities and new norms," and a politics of reform that seeks "the further democratization of political and economic institutions" (Cohen and Arato 1994, 526).

5   See Uprimny and Vargas Camacho (1989, 143) for an analysis of the government's crisis of hegemony during the decade of the eighties. They hypothesize that "the dirty war was a symptom of the weakness of the Colombian regime at the beginning of the eighties, the result of a double crisis of hegemony . . . for the traditional power bloc with respect to the subordinated classes due to the relative exhaustion of the traditional mechanisms of domination and a crisis of hegemony within the same power bloc due to the presence of drug entrepreneurialism, a powerful new fraction of the dominant class that had no channel for the social and political expression corresponding to its economic and military power."

6   "Crece Concentración, cinco mil campesinos en Santuario," and "Siete días de paro y no hay ningún acuerdo. Completo Abandono Estatal," *La Nación*, August 1, 1996. There is a JAC in each of the 148 veredas in the municipality of Puerto Asís.

7   "La Hormiga agitadora," *El Espectador*, July 30, 1996.

8   Letter from General Mario Galán, commander of the Army's Third Division, to the governor of Putumayo, Puerto Asís, July 29, 1996.

9   Letter from Putumayo police commander, entitled "An Assessment of the Civic Strike Situation," to the governor, Mocoa, July 28, 1996.

10 Ibid.

11 For a more detailed account of the confrontation, see Vásquez 1996.

12 "Sangrienta Jornada en Puerto Asís," *El Tiempo*, August 3, 1996.

13 "Amenaza a Ecopetrol," *El Espectador*, August 1, 1996; emphasis added.

14 "Por la coca, suspendido el diálogo," *El Tiempo*, August 8, 1996.

15 "Putumayo paralizado por 24,000 campesinos," *El Tiempo*, July 30, 1996.

16 "Sangrienta Jornada en Puerto Asís," *El Tiempo*, August 3, 1996.

17 "La cosa en el Putumayo se puso color de hormiga," *El Espectador*, August 3, 1996.

18 "Putumayo paralizado por 24,000 campesinos," *El Tiempo*, July 30, 1996.

19 "Hoy viaja a Orito una comisión del Gobierno," *El Tiempo*, August 3, 1996.

20 "Puerto Asís marcha sin rumbo fijo," *El Espectador*, August 2, 1996, 6A.

21 Mayor Alcibiades Enciso, recorded on videotape at the Puerto Asís Municipal Building by journalist Carlos Mauro Rosero, 1996.

22 Statements to *Noticiero AM-PM*, July 7, 1996.

23 "Calma chicha en territorios calientes," *El Espectador*, August 4, 1996.

24 Letter sent by General Mario Galan to the Mayor of Puerto Asís in August 2, 1996, cited in "Puerto Asís convertido en campo de batalla," *El Espectador*, August 3, 1996, 7A.

25 "Puerto Asís convertido en campo de batalla," *El Espectador*, August 3, 1996, 7A.

26 "Amenaza a Ecopetrol," *El Espectador*, August 1, 1996.

27 "Dialogan de nuevo," *El Tiempo*, August 10, 1996.

28 Civic Movement for the Comprehensive Development of Putumayo, "Reality and Alternatives to the Social Problem of Illegal Crops," 1996.

29 Ibid.

30 "Opción para conciliar en el Putumayo," *El Espectador*, August 2, 1996.

31 "El gobierno no va a negociar cultivos ilícitos," *El Espectador*, August 3, 1996.

32 Ibid.

33 Statement on *Noticiero AM-PM*, August 4, 1996.

34 "Gobierno no negociará las fumigaciones de cultivos," *El Espectador*, August 5, 1996.

35 Interview with Eduardo Díaz, Bogotá, June 5, 1999. See appendix 2 for a list of negotiating team members.

36 Interview with Ana Beiba Rincón, Puerto Asís, February 22, 1999.

37 "Comisión Nacional negociadora en Orito," *La Nación*, August 8, 1996.

38 Civic Movement for the Comprehensive Development of Putumayo's first draft proposal for an agreement, 1996, courtesy of Teófilo Vásquez, CINEP advisor to the Civic Movement.

39 Interview with Díaz, 1999.

40 Government of Colombia's first draft proposal for an agreement, Orito negotiations, 1996, Courtesy of Teófilo Vásquez.

41 Ibid.

42 Interview with Diaz, 1999.

43 Ibid.

44 Civic Movement's first draft proposal, 1996; emphasis added.

45 César García, PLANTE representative speaking at negotiating session, 1996; emphasis added.

46 Interview with Navarro, Popayán, July 28, 1999.

47 "Paños de agua tibia para el polvorín del Putumayo," *El Espectador*, August 6, 1996.

48 "No somos subversivos ni narcotraficantes, alcaldes," *El Tiempo*, August 6, 1996.

49 "La cosa en el Putumayo se puso color de hormiga," *El Espectador*, August 3, 1996.

50 "Puerto Asís sigue viviendo entre la bala y el miedo," *El Espectador*, August 4, 1996.

51 "Paños de agua tibia para el polvorín del Putumayo," *El Espectador*, August 6, 1996.

52 Quoted in Alfredo Molano, "Perro viejo late echado," *El Espectador*, August 15, 1996.

53 Interview with Palou, conducted by Elsy Castillo, Bogotá, September 15, 1998.

54 Remarks of Jaime Burbano, Movement representative, during the negotiations.

55 Government of Colombia's first draft proposal for an agreement, Orito negotiations, 1996.

56 Civic Movement's first draft proposal, 1996.

57   Ibid.
58   Statement of a community spokesperson during negotiations, Orito, 1996.
59   Contribution of an agricultural technician to the discussion on crop substitution, Orito negotiations, 1996.
60   "Respuesta social y no militar piden cocaleros," *El Tiempo*, August 7, 1996.
61   Statement of Euler Guerrero, community spokesperson during negotiations, Orito, 1996, emphasis added.
62   Interview with Díaz, 1999.
63   Comments during the negotiations, 1996.
64   Civic Movement's first draft proposal, 1996.
65   Interview with Marino Rincón, Mocoa, February 1, 1999.
66   Comments by César García at the Orito negotiations, 1996.
67   Ibid.
68   Comments by Echeverry during the Orito negotiations, 1996.
69   Campesino at the Orito negotiations, 1996.
70   Interview with Díaz, 1999.
71   "Dialogan de Nuevo," *El Tiempo*, August 10, 1996.
72   "Nueva Agenda en Putumayo," *El Espectador*, August 10, 1996.
73   Interview with Díaz, 1999.
74   Interview with Marino Rincón, 1999.
75   Remarks of Jaime Navarro at the negotiations.
76   Civic Movement for the Comprehensive Development of Putumayo's proposal for development plan, August 1996.
77   "La fumigación no tiene limitaciones," *El Tiempo*, August 13, 1996.
78   Interview with Díaz, 1999.
79   Negotiating Commission of the National Government and Negotiating Commission of the Civic Strike of the Department of Putumayo, "Comprehensive Emergency Development Plan for a Coca-free Putumayo Sustained in an Economy of Solidarity," Orito, August 19, 1996.
80   Remarks by Serafin Merino Rosero, Civic Movement leader at the negotiations, Orito, 1996.
81   Remarks of unidentified campesino spokesperson during negotiations recorded by Nancy Sanchez, DASALUD official, Orito, 1996.
82   Remarks of Heraldo Vallejo, agricultural technician at the Orito negotiations, 1996.
83   Interview with Ana Beiba Rincón, 1999.
84   "Confusión por atentado de Orito," *El Tiempo*, August 14, 1996.
85   "Confusión por atentado de Orito," *El Tiempo*, August 14, 1996.
86   Negotiating Commission, "Comprehensive Emergency Development Plan," 1996.
87   Ibid.
88   "Levantado el Paro: Campesinos a sus parcelas," *La Nación*, August 21, 1996.
89   Interview with Peña, Piamonte, March 1, 1999.

90 Conversation with JAC leader in Bogotá, May 1998.

91 "La fumigación no tiene limitaciones," *El Tiempo*, August 13, 1996.

92 Ibid.

93 Interview with Ospina, Bogotá, July 11, 1999.

94 Remarks by Palou at the plenary round table, "Peace and the Environment," at the Environmental National Congress, Guaduas, Cundinamarca, July 26, 1998, emphasis added.

95 Interview with Navarro, 1999.

96 Negotiating Commission, "Comprehensive Emergency Development Plan," 1996.

Chapter Six

1 See J. Scott (1998) for a discussion on "legibility as a central problem of state craft" where population registers are identified as a strategy for control of the population, in other words, a technique of governance.

2 "Tirofijo se destapa. Por primera vez el jefe de las Farc habla sobre el canje y el proceso de paz," *Semana* no. 872 (January 18, 1999), 22.

3 Interview with Navarro, Popayán, July 28, 1999.

4 Ibid.

5 Interview with Marino Rincón, Mocoa, February 1, 1999.

6 Interview with Arturo Ospina, Bogotá, July 11, 1999.

7 Interview with Diaz, Bogotá, June 5, 1999.

8 Interview with Navarro, 1999.

9 Interview with Diaz, 1999.

10 Interview with Ospina, 1999.

11 Interview with Navarro, 1999.

12 Interview with Rincón 1999, emphasis added.

13 Interview with Diaz, 1999.

14 Ibid.

15 Interview with Navarro, 1999.

16 Interview with Nestor Hernández Iglesias, mayor of Puerto Asís from 1998 to 2000, September 14, 1998.

17 Interview with Navarro, 1999.

18 Ibid.

19 "Fondos de cofinanciación, mano derecha de alcaldes," *La Nación*, September 16, 1997.

20 Ibid.

21 Interview with Hernández Iglesias, 1998.

22 In this same vein, Wendy Brown (1995, 170) in her analysis of the state from the perspective of gender theory, points out that "to be 'protected' by the same power whose violation one fears perpetuates the very modality of dependence and powerlessness."

23   Letter from Vereda Villanueva Ad Hoc Leadership Committee to the ombuds-
      man, Puerto Guzmán, July 26, 1998; emphasis added.
24   Interview with Luis Emiro Mosquera, Puerto Asís, August 27, 1998.

Chapter Seven

1   Gilberto Sánchez at a civic strike follow-up meeting in Puerto Caicedo, Septem-
     ber 25, 1996.
2   Negotiating Commission of the National Government and Negotiating Com-
     mission of the Civic Strike of the Department of Putumayo, "Comprehensive
     Emergency Development Plan for a Coca-free Putumayo Sustained in an Econ-
     omy of Solidarity," Orito, August 19, 1996. See appendix 4 for composition of the
     base group.
3   Proceedings of the meeting to monitor the Orito Agreement between the Nego-
     tiating Commission of the National Government and the Negotiating Commis-
     sion of the Civic Strike of the Department of Putumayo, Puerto Asís, October
     28, 1996.
4   Interview with Luis Fernando Correal, Bogotá, July 8, 1999. *Plan Sur* (the Plan
     for the South) was designed by the Samper administration after the signing of
     the 1996 Orito Agreement. It was intended to implement, assist, and evaluate
     the national government's compliance with the commitments that the agree-
     ment entailed. It also mediated between the president and the various other
     government bodies involved in the agreement, as well as between commu-
     nity leaders and these bodies. The Samper administration called Plan Sur "the
     hotline between the communities of Putumayo and the President" ("Plan Sur,
     línea directa con el presidente Samper," *La Nación*, May 14, 1997).
5   Comment by movement leader Richard Avella in Puerto Caicedo, 1996.
6   Remarks of Serafín Merino Rosero in Puerto Caicedo, 1996.
7   Proceedings of the founding meeting of the base group and the definition of its
     proposed activities. Puerto Asís, October 18, 1996.
8   Remarks of Gilberto Sánchez in Puerto Caicedo, 1996.
9   Proceedings of the Orito Agreement's first working group, August 14, 1996.
10   The UMATAS had been established in 1993 and had by then earned the good
     will of communities and local and municipal authorities. As an example, the
     regional office of PLANTE channeled their centrally-allocated funds for mu-
     nicipal institutional and infrastructural assistance through the UMATAS and
     allowed the UMATAS themselves to decide how best to invest and distribute
     them (interview with Orozco 1996).
        The campesinos knew that additional funds for technical assistance and re-
     sources were crucial to the success of substitute crop programs. They pointed
     to the case of a pilot program run by CORPOAMAZONIA to plant rubber as an
     example of how paying for technical assistance out of pocket could drain alter-
     native crop programs to the point of bankrupting them. CORPOAMAZONIA paid
     campesinos 1,000 pesos per rubber tree planted, but at the pace of planting

that they were able to maintain, they had to spend virtually all of this money on fees for an engineer to design an agricultural management plan. On the other hand, they lauded a decision of the regional office of PLANTE to strengthen the UMATAS by providing them with five technicians, three agricultural professionals, seven motorcycles, nine computers, and six high-powered motor boats for riverine municipalities such as Puerto Guzmán, Caicedo, and San Miguel ("Si venimos cumpliéndole al campesino," *La Nación*, May 25, 1996).

11 Proceedings of the Orito Agreement's first working group, 1996.

12 Remarks at Orito negotiations in the Proceedings of the Orito Agreement's first working group, August 14, 1996, emphasis added.

13 Comment by Richard Avella, 1996.

14 For a discussion of the importance of *capacidad de gestión* in Latin American social movements, see Foweraker (1995) and Foweraker and Craig (1990).

15 Interview with Correal, 1999.

16 Interview with Ignacio Muñoz, Mocoa, February 10, 1999.

17 Ibid.

18 Interview with Galarza, Mocoa, March 10, 1999.

19 Interview with Imbachí, Bogotá, July 14, 1999.

20 Interview with Ana Beiba Rincón, Puerto Asís, February 22, 1999.

21 Base Group proposal for continuation presented to the Commission for the Monitoring of the Orito Agreements, Mocoa, June 27, 1997.

22 Interview with Marino Rincón, Mocoa, February 1, 1999.

23 Interview with Navarro, Popayán, July 28, 1999.

24 Interview with Correal, 1999.

25 Interview with Díaz, Bogotá, June 5, 1999.

26 Interview with Ospina, Bogotá, July 11, 1999.

27 Official Report of the Second Commission, follow-up to the Orito Agreement, Puerto Asís, October 17, 1996, emphasis added.

28 Civic Movement, main presentation at the regional forum, "Peace and Human Rights," Puerto Asís, May 7, 1997, emphasis added.

29 Tilly (1996, 8) proposes that we "confine the definition of citizenship to a certain kind of tie: a continuing series of transactions between persons and agents of a given state in which each has enforceable rights and obligations by virtue of (1) the person's membership in an exclusive category, the native-born plus the naturalized and (2) the agent's relation to the state rather than any other authority the agent may enjoy."

30 For Hall and Held (1989, 176–77), "a contemporary 'politics of citizenship'" must take into account not only the role that social movements have played in expanding the claims to rights but also questions of membership. They call attention to the complex interplay of identity and identification in modern society and to the differentiated ways in which people now participate in social life. However, they point out that citizenship "has tended to absorb 'differences' into one common universal status—'the citizen.'" Therefore they recognize that, "there is now an irreconcilable tension between the thrust to equality

and universality entailed in the very idea of the 'citizen,' and the variety of particular and specific needs, of diverse sites and practices which constitute the modern political subject."

31   Comments by campesino leader at the Orito negotiations in the Proceedings of the Orito Agreement's first working group, August 14, 1996.

32   Young (1995, 207) argues that social movements "have offered an emancipatory meaning of difference to replace the old exclusionary meaning." She also argues that social equality, the goal of these movements, should be reconceptualized in order for group-specific rights and policies to stand together with the general civic and political rights of participation and inclusion of all in public life and in the democratic process. She points out that the recognition of group-specific rights may lead to a restigmatization of oppressed groups, justifying new exclusions, and she states that "group representation can help protect against such a consequence. If oppressed and disadvantaged groups can self-organize in public and have a specific voice to present their interpretation of the meaning of and reasons for group-differentiated policies, then such policies are more likely to work for than against them" (1995, 222).

33   Remarks of Emiro Mosquera, Puerto Caicedo, 1996.

34   As one of the results of the United States' "decertification" of Colombia as a partner in the war on drugs, President Samper was barred from travel to the United States.

35   Remarks of a campesino representative, at the the Orito negotiations in the Proceedings of the Orito Agreement's first working group, August 14, 1996.

36   The Amazon Alliance is a network of nearly one hundred indigenous organizations and allied NGOs. Founded in 1990 in Iquitos, Peru, the mission of the Amazon Alliance is to ensure that indigenous peoples have power in the processes that affect them and that their voices and perspectives are clearly heard around the world. The Coordinating Office of the Amazon Alliance works to ensure effective coordination between the Amazonian indigenous movement and other important actors in the region. The Amazon Alliance is a unique vehicle for addressing the urgent situation of environmental degradation and cultural annihilation in Amazonia. See http://www.amazonalliance.org.

37   Interview with Rodrigo Alfaro, sociologist and advisor to the Base Group, Bogotá, June 17, 1999.

38   This Departmental Committee was supported by Catholic clergy, the mayor of Puerto Asís, and the national NGO CINEP.

39   Proceedings of the meeting with the Inter-American Human Rights Commission, Puerto Asís, December 4, 1997.

40   Ibid.

41   Interview with Navarro, 1999.

42   "Guerra en el fin del mundo," *Semana* no. 824 (February 16): 30–32.

43   Ibid.

44   Civic Movement, main presentation, 1997, emphasis added.

45   Foweraker (1995, 77) has pointed out a similar strategy for survival in the case

of Latin American urban social movements which, by engaging with municipal politics, "have had some success in pressing the state to fulfill its legal and normative obligations of guaranteeing individual security, protecting the property of the poor from fraud and violence, and enforcing its own rules, regulations, and price controls."

46   The national press identified one of the leaders of the 1996 cocalero movement as an ex-guerrilla. With the headline "Cocalero Agreement signed by Guerrilla," an article in *El Tiempo* reported that "To judge by the accusations of criminal activity against him and by testimony in the possession of the Regional Prosecutor, at least one man accused of being the ex-leader of FARC's Forty-fifth Front and a current member of the Thirty-second Front in Putumayo was participating as a coordinator and was the second signatory to the agreement reached last Sunday." His political activities were investigated and he was "exposed" as having previously been an active member of the Communist Party and the Patriotic Union, the political party that emerged from the peace agreement reached with FARC in 1985 ("Guerrillero habría firmado Acuerdo Cocalero," *El Tiempo*, August 15, 1996). In February 1998 Amnesty International reported that civic movement leaders Luis Emiro Mosquera, Gilberto Sánchez, and Serafín Merino Rosero, as well as Father Harold López, had to leave Puerto Asís because of rumors that their names appeared on a list of 250 people being pursued by the paramilitaries (Amnesty International 1998; "37 sepelios en sólo dos semanas en Puerto Asís. 'El cementerio se quedó pequeño,'" *El Tiempo*, February 13, 1998). Alirio Romo Guevara, mayor of Puerto Asís from 1994 to 1997, was assassinated in Cali on January 30, 1998, just after leaving office. The paramilitaries publicly claimed responsibility for his killing.

47   A cocalero movement spokesperson was assassinated in San Vicente del Caguán, Caquetá, on January 5, 1997. From November 1996 until his death he had participated, with national government representatives, in the departmental commission monitoring compliance with the agreement signed in Caquetá on September 12, 1996 ("Matan a vocero de campesinos cocaleros," *El Tiempo*, January 10, 1997). On March 7, 1997, the secretary general of the Agricultural Union Federation (FENSUAGRO) was assassinated. He had been a Communist Party activist and had participated in the cocalero mobilization initiated on July 16, 1996, in Guaviare. At the time of his death he was participating in regional commissions to evaluate compliance with the agreements reached between the movement and the national government in Putumayo and Caquetá ("Asesinado un vocero de cocaleros," *El Tiempo*, March 6, 1997).

48   Campesino at the May 1997 Forum on Peace and Human Rights.

49   "Respuesta social y no militar piden cocaleros," *El Tiempo*, August 7, 1996.

50   This statement echoes Harvey (1998), who follows Foweraker (1990) in his analysis of the Zapatista social movement in Chiapas, Mexico, and maintains that what is innovative about Latin American popular and social movements is their struggle for effective citizenship through the demand that their rights and above all their dignity be respected, an essential prerequisite for democratic discourse.

51   Interview with Marino Rincón, 1999.

52   "Renuncian 318 candidatos de un total de 354 inscritos," *La Nación*, September 18, 1997.

53   "Las Farc amenazan jurados de votación," *La Nación*, October 1, 1997.

54   "En Putumayo, 14 poblaciones cercadas por las Farc," *La Nación*, October 3, 1997.

55   Speech by Luis Emiro Mosquera, September 27, 1997. Recorded on videotape by Putumayo journalist Carlos Mauro Rosero.

56   "Polémica sobre garantías electorales crea Alcalde de Puerto Asís," *La Nación*, October 25, 1997.

57   Conversation with municipal council member, Piamonte, March 31, 1999.

58   Interview with Díaz, 1999.

59   Ibid.

60   Interview with Nestor Hernández Iglesias, Puerto Asís, September 14, 1998.

61   Conversation with council member, Puerto Asís, 1998.

62   "Paras les quitaron el sueño a las Farc," *El Tiempo*, February 15, 1998.

63   "Confirman crímenes en el Putumayo. La situación se puso color de Hormiga," *El Espectador*, February 15, 1998.

64   This information was provided by a publication of CINEP and Justice and Peace, called *Noche y niebla: Panorama de derechos humanos y violencia política en Colombia* ("Night and Fog, An Overview of Human Rights and Political Violence in Colombia"). Issues numbered 1–10 present data covering the period from July 1996 to December 1998. The quantitative data was compiled within the scope of a research project financed by Colciencias and the Colombian Institute of Anthropology and History.

65   Interview with journalist, Mocoa, 1998.

66   La Batalla decisiva," *Semana* no. 962 (November 6, 2000), 54.

67   Conversation with Doña Laura, Puerto Asís, 1998.

68   Ibid.

69   "'Lo peor está por venir en el Putumayo.' Entrevista a Nestor Hernández Iglesias, alcalde de Puerto Asís," *El Espectador*, February 13, 1998.

70   "Putumayo, nuevo escenario de barbarie," *El Espectador*, February 12, 1998.

71   "'No hubo Masacre', dice el Ejército," *El Espectador*, February 13, 1998.

72   "Son muertes que preocupan," *El Tiempo*, February 15, 1998.

73   Mayor Iglesias's comment comes from the interview in *El Espectador*, February 13, 1998. The paramilitary group led by Gustavo Gómez, called Self-Defense Forces of the South (*Autodefensas del Sur*) was originally from Urabá. At the beginning of the 1990s it was affiliated with the paramilitaries of Gonzalo Rodríguez Gacha. They appeared in Putumayo in January 1998 (CINEP and Justicia y Paz, nos. 7 and 8, June 1998, 39).

74   "Las funerarias en temporada alta," *El Tiempo*, February 15, 1998.

75   "Estupor por Barbarie de 'Paras,'" *El Espectador*, January 11, 1999.

76   "Fin de semana violento en el sur del Putumayo," *El Espectador*, May 18, 1999.

77   "29 muertos dejan 'Paras' en el Putumayo," *El Tiempo*, November 9, 1999.

78   In this vein see Lechner (1992) for an analysis of how authoritarian states use

the power of fear to depoliticize the citizenry without recourse to open repression. Violence is attributed not to the dictatorship but to chaos, to the enemy that infiltrates and subverts the established order, and people cling to the dictatorship as the alternative to this danger and chaos.

79 "Denuncian más crímenes selectivo en el Puerto Asís," *El Tiempo*, September 6, 1999.

80 Conversation with Doña Laura, 1998.

81 Remarks of a Civic Movement leader at the takeover of the Ombudsman's office in Bogotá, May 28, 1998.

82 From a treetop, a man observing the massacre in El Tigre identified community members working as hooded informers with the paramilitary death squad.

83 Interview in *El Espectador*, February 13, 1998; emphasis added.

84 Letter from the Puerto Asís Municipal Council President, the Municipal Secretary of Administration, and the Office of the High Commissioner for Peace to the Interior Minister, November 14, 1997.

85 Interview with Germán Martínez, Putumayo human rights delegate, Puerto Asís, September 17, 1998.

86 Ibid.

87 "Marcha contra la incredulidad," *El Tiempo*, February 14, 1998.

88 Final Declaration, Forum for Peace, Puerto Asís, February 20–21, 1998.

89 Final speech at the demonstration in Bogotá, May 28, 1998.

90 Conversation with Putumayan at the occupation of the Ombudsman's Office, Bogotá, May 28, 1998.

91 Proceedings of meeting at Nariño Palace, June 4, 1998.

92 Interview with Oscar Gaviria, Putumayo Secretary of Departmental Planning, Mocoa, February 27, 1998.

93 Lechner (1993) discusses what he calls "a deficit of modernity" in Latin America. As economic structures evolve and the social order stagnates, new forms of exclusion emerge, and with them the linked demands for community and civility. The meaning that the word *community* acquires "refers, more than to an opposition to the military, to a demand for citizenship," or more precisely, to "a community of citizens," since what is upheld is the collective. This reflection is pertinent to the case at hand. The Putumayan movement was essentially aimed at developing and giving voice to such a community of citizens.

Chapter Eight

1 "El Plan Colombia: Una gran alianza con el mundo contra el delito internacional, por los derechos humanos, los derechos sociales y por la ecología," speech delivered in Santafé de Bogotá, October 22, 1998.

2 Colombia's Contraloría General de la República is similar to the U.S. Government Accountability Office.

3 In 2003, trainers from the United States began setting up a second counternarcotics brigade to operate in the country's remote eastern departments.

4 The appropriation allocated $68.5 million for alternative development, $37.5

million for aid to the internally displaced, $51.0 million for human rights, $13.0 million for judicial reform, $45 million for the rule of law, and $3 million for peace.

5   In 2002 Colombia ranked second in the world after Sudan in terms of the number of internally displaced people (IDPS). By February 2008, the government recognized 2,266,000 IDPS ("Desplazados siguen a la espera de sus derechos," *El Tiempo*, February 6, 2008). The Consultancy for Human Rights and Forced Displacement (Consultoría para los Derechos Humanos y el Desplazamiento, CODHES), an NGO monitoring internal displacement, reported more than 4 million people displaced between 1985 and 2007 (CODHES 2008). The government's estimate was much lower at 1.75 million, largely due to the fact that it started registering IDPS systematically only in 2000.

6   Interview with Alzate, Puerto Asís, April 23, 2001.

7   Interview with Cecilia Anaya, member of ANUC-Putumayo, Puerto Asís, April 18, 2001.

8   Interview with Sánchez, Puerto Asís, April 29, 2001.

9   "La Batalla decisiva," *Semana* no. 962, November 6, 2000, 56.

10 Interview with Sánchez, 2001.

11 Interview with Alzate, 2001.

12 "El Plan Putumayo," *Cambio* no. 381, October 9, 2000, 36.

13 "53 muertos," *Semana* no. 964, November 20, 2000: 24–36. By April 2003, CODHES reported a total of 39,397 people displaced by fumigation in Colombia, 15 percent of the total displaced population in the country. The highest level of displacement was reported in the Catatumbo area in the department of Norte de Santander (13,751 people), followed by the departments of Caquetá (10,956) and Putumayo (10,813). The National Solidarity Network registered 22,184 displaced persons in Putumayo and 20,086 who had left the department in 1997–2003. The armed conflict and fumigation were the principal causes of displacement in middle and lower Putumayo. A total of 9,979 applications by Colombians for refugee status were filed in Ecuador from January 2000 to January 2003, mostly as a result of displacement from Putumayo (Ecuadorean Ministry of Foreign Relations in Salgado 2004). The director of the Solidarity Network in Mocoa clarified that "although people displaced due to fumigation are not registered, in Putumayo we know that at least 50 percent of the displaced in 2002 were displaced because of aerial spraying" (interview with Eduardo Alomia, Mocoa, July 10, 2003). As the CODHES report makes clear, displacement continued and increased. During the first nine months of 2006 a total of 7,372 Colombians applied for refugee status in Ecuador.

14 Remarks by Grisales, Puerto Guzmán, April 26, 2001.

15 "Estados Unidos preocupado por suspensión de fumigaciones," *El Espectador*, June 4, 2001.

16 Ibid.

17 Interview with Pinzón, Local PLANTE official, Puerto Asís, September 21, 2001.

18 Statement by Orduz in the Plenary Session of August 14, 2001.

19 "UE concreta apoyo a paz de Colombia," *El Espectador*, May 1, 2001. In a September 2003 evaluation of Plan Colombia, the National Planning Department of Colombia reported that "by December 2002, US$5.61 billion had been committed, 75 percent of the total cost projected at the beginning of the Plan. Of this amount, $3.981 billion (71 percent) was provided by Colombia, and the remaining $1.628 billion (29 percent) derived from non-reimbursable assistance provided by the international community. Eighty-eight percent of this international assistance ($1.464 billion) came from the United States, and other countries contributed $128.6 million, or 2.3 percent of total commitments. Overall, only 44 percent of the nonreimbursable assistance offered by countries other than the United States resulted in firm commitments, owing in part to European disappointment at being excluded from discussions of the plan's design and fundamental disagreements over counter-drug strategy, as well as a lack of interest in a country outside Europe's "sphere of influence" (Armenta, Jelsma, and Vargas 2001).

20 "La otra diplomacia por la Paz," *El Espectador*, April 15, 2001.

21 A Verification Committee was constituted for this purpose, comprising representatives from the Defensoría del Pueblo (Ombudsman's Office), anti-narcotics police, central government, community, and a cooperating international NGO.

22 In answering this question, Holston and Caldeira (1998, 276) note in the case of Brazil that "neither civil rights, nor access to justice, nor due process of law has become a prominent concern for the principal forces of democratization in the new social movements, unions, or universities."

23 Foweraker (1995, 98) quotes Cohen and Arato (1992, 127), indicating how the notion of social rights implies benefits obtained in the role of "clients rather than citizens."

24 The Páez indigenous community in the Calderas reserve (*resguardo*) in Tierradentro was producing coca leaf products like herbal tea, a beverage common in Bolivia and Peru, and is promoting an informational campaign to promote the plant's medicinal properties. This exemplified the attempt to redefine coca and its cultivation. Not only are the Páez taking up and promoting the way that coca was used in other Andean countries, but by adopting and defining a collective identity as coca leaf producers, they rejected its criminalization. Residents of the resguardo petitioned the National Narcotics Council for the right to produce and market coca tea ("Coca de la buena," *Cambio* no. 432, October 1, 2001, 44).

  Bolivian coca producers are organized into unions with a strong tradition of struggle. Beginning in early 2000, they repeatedly blocked the main highways of the Yungas region to protest government plans to destroy coca crops. Although there were thirty thousand hectares of legal coca in Bolivia, the government estimated that in 2000 there were also five thousand illegal hectares of the crop, which then-President Hugo Banzer proposed to destroy within one year. The campesinos of the Chapare region demanded the right of each one of the thirty-nine thousand families living there to grow sixteen hundred square meters of coca. In September 2000, after another mobilization and another blockade of the Santa Cruz–Cochabamba highway, Bolivian cocaleros accepted a government proposal to invest US$80 million in alternative projects. Cocalero leader and later Bolivian president Evo Morales insisted, however, that "the Quechuas and Aymaras cannot lie to the people or to the international community. There will not be 'zero coca' as the government wishes" ("Coca o muerte. Evo Morales, líder de los campesinos bolivianos, advierte que erradicar la planta no acaba con el narcotráfico," *El País Digital Internacional*, November 5, 2000).

In October 2000 cocaleros in the Alto Huallaga of Peru blocked access to Tingo María and adjacent towns, demanding a realistic proposal for coca substitution and saying that fifteen years of alternative projects had failed to bring results. They demanded a serious evaluation of possibilities for alternative development based on soil analysis and other concrete factors ("Bloquean carreteras y exigen suspender erradicación de sembrados de coca," *La República* [Lima], November 1, 2000). Bolivian campesinos shared the Peruvians' disillusionment, saying that sixteen years of coca eradication programs had benefited no one other than small groups of campesinos who did not belong to the unions ("Hacia la clandestinidad de la coca. Los cultivadores bolivianos creen que la planta sobrevivirá a las prohibiciones y a las amenazas de la comunidad internacional," *El País Digital Internacional*, December 22, 2000).

25 State Department Fact Sheet on U.S. Policy towards the Andean Region, May 17, 2001: "U.S. support for counter-drug actions in the Andes is designed to reduce illicit coca production by 20 percent by the end of 2002 (base year 1999) and 40 percent by the end of 2007. This includes a 30 percent reduction in Colombian coca production and the elimination of illegal coca production in Bolivia by the end of 2002." The fact sheet indicated that coca production had been reduced by about 70 percent in Peru and Bolivia in the previous five years, but that there had been no reduction in overall coca supply due to expanded production in Colombia, adding that "to prevent traffickers from simply relocating elsewhere, we need to reinforce our counter-drug efforts in neighboring countries." For that reason, US$180 million in the Plan Colombia appropriation was designated for other countries in the region.

26 "Coca o muerte. Evo Morales, líder de los campesinos bolivianos, advierte que erradicar la planta no acaba con el narcotráfico," *El País Digital Internacional*, November 5, 2000.

27 Interview with Grisales, Mocoa, April 26, 2001.

Epilogue

1 "3,100 erradicadores vuelven al monte," *El Tiempo*, August 3, 2007.

2 "Marcha cocalera está forzada con fusil: Policía," *El Tiempo*, April 22, 2008.

3 Remark by a spokesperson for the Sibundoy Municipal Council, August 25, 2006.

4 Letter from the Putumayo Coalition of Campesino Organizations to President Alvaro Uribe Vélez, October 7, 2006.

5 Testimony of May 8, 2007, by a participant in the March 2007 mobilization.

6 "Crisis humanitaria denuncian campesinos del Putumayo y se declaran en movilización permanente," *El Tiempo*, March 28, 2007.

7 "En qué están las FARC?" *Cambio* no. 752, November 29, 2007.

8 "Cronología de los más recientes golpes a las FARC, que viven el peor momento de su historia," *El Tiempo*, May 26, 2008.

9 "La Madre," *Revista Semana*, May 12, 2007.

10 "Hallan restos de 105 personas en fosas comunes en el Putumayo," *Caracol Noticias*, May 2007.

11 "A 3.000 podría llegar el número de víctimas enterradas en fosas comunes en Putumayo," *El Tiempo*, May 5, 2007.

12 See http://www.fiscalia.gov.co/justiciapaz/EXH/imagenes/mapa-de-colombia .jpg.

13 Ibid. See also "A dos años de la Ley de Justicia y Paz, las víctimas corren con la peor suerte," *Revista Semana*, July 25, 2007.

References

Abrams, Philip. 1988. "Notes on the Difficulty of Studying the State." *Journal of Historical Sociology* 1, no. 1, 58–89.

Acción Social. 2006. *Colombia, otra vez record mundial en erradicación manual forzosa.* Bogotá. October 23. http://www.accionsocial.gov.co.

Agencia de Noticias Nueva Colombia (ANNCOL). 1998. "Los soldados del ejército sienten que esta guerra no es de ellos." Entrevista con el comandante guerillero Joaquín Gómez, jefe del Bloque Sur de las FARC-EP de Colombia, November 17, 1998.

Agnew, John. 1987. *Place and Politics: The Geographical Mediation of State and Society.* Boston: Allen and Unwin.

Alomía, Eduardo, et al. 1997. *Estudio de impacto socioambiental generado por el cultivo y proceso de la hoja de coca erytroxilon coca lam, en los municipios de Puerto Asís y el Valle del Guamués, Departamento del Putumayo.* Monografía para optar al título de Especialista en Ecología, Medio Ambiente y Desarrollo. Bogotá: Universidad Incca de Colombia.

Alvarez, Sonia. 1997. "Reweaving the Fabric of Collective Action." *Between Resistance and Revolution: Cultural Politics and Social Protest,* ed. Richard G. Fox and Orin Starn, 83–117. New Brunswick, N.J.: Rutgers University Press.

Alvarez, Sonia, Evelina Dagnino, and Arturo Escobar, eds. 1998. *Cultures of Politics and Politics of Cultures: Revisioning Latin American Social Movements.* Boulder, Colo.: Westview.

Amnesty International. 1998. "Colombia: Fear for Safety / Extrajudicial Excecution / Disappearance." Press release, February 17, http://www.amnesty.org.

Aranguren Molina, Mauricio. 2001. *Mi confesión: Carlos Castaño revela sus secretos.* Bogotá: Editorial Oveja Negra.

Archila, Mauricio, Alvaro Delgado, and Martha Cecilia García. 2002. *25 Años de Luchas Sociales en Colombia 1975–2002.* Bogotá: CINEP.

Arendt, Hannah. 1949. "The Rights of Man, What Are They?" *Modern Review* 3, no. 1, 124–37.

Aretxaga, Begoña. 1993. "Striking with Hunger: Cultural Meanings of Political Violence in Northern Ireland." *Violence Within: Cultural and Political Opposition in Divided Nations,* ed. Kay B. Warren, 219–53. Boulder, Colo.: Westview.

———. 2000. "A Fictional Reality: Paramilitary, Death Squads and the Construction of State Terror in Spain." *Death Squad: The Anthropology of State Terror,* ed. Jeffrey A. Sluka, 46–69. Philadelphia: University of Pennsylvania Press.

———. 2003. "Maddening States." *Annual Review of Anthropology* 32, 393–410.

Ariza, Eduardo, María Clemencia Ramírez, and Leonardo Vega. 1998. *Atlas cultural de la Amazonia Colombiana: La construcción del territorio en el siglo XX.* Bogotá: Ministerio de Cultura-Instituto Colombiano de Antropología, Corpes Orinoquia, Corpes Amazonia.

Armenta, Amira, Martin Jelsma, and Ricardo Vargas. 2001. "Europe and Plan Colombia: Chronicle of a Commitment with an Uncomfortable Plan," Debate Papers, no. 1. Amsterdam: Transnational Institute. http://www.tni.org.

Arrieta, Carlos Gustavo, Luis Javier Orjuela, Eduardo Sarmiento Palacio, and Juan Gabirel Tokatlian. 1990. *Narcotráfico en Colombia: Dimensiones políticas, económicas, jurídicas e internacionales.* Bogotá: Ediciones Uniandes y Tercer Mundo Editores.

Asociación Nacional de Usuarios Campesinos (ANUC). 1998. *Lineamientos sobre los Concejos Municipales de Desarrollo Rural.* Décimo Congreso Nacional Campesino. Bogotá: Escuela Nacional de Formación Campesina.

Asociación Nacional de Usuarios Campesinos (ANUC) Putumayo. 2001. Seminario Taller Seguimiento y Monitoreo Plan Colombia, Santiago, August 11–12.

Bauman, Zygmunt. 1990. "Modernity and Ambivalence." *Global Culture: Nationalism, Globalization and Modernity,* ed. Mike Featherstone, 143–70. London: Sage.

Bejarano, Ana María. 1992. "Democracia y sociedad civil: una introducción teórica." *Análisis Político,* no.15, 68–85. Bogotá: Instituto de Estudios Políticos y Relaciones Internacionales.

———. 1995. "Para repensar las relaciones estado, sociedad civil y regimen político: Una nueva mirada conceptual." *Controversia,* no. 167, 9–32. Bogotá: CINEP.

———. 1998. "Tensiones y dilemas de la representación política." *Controversia,* no. 172, 11–28. Bogotá: CINEP.

Bonamusa, Margarita. 1997. "Qué es la sociedad civil?: Una mirada a Colombia." *Sociedad civil, control social y democracia participativa,* ed. Juan Fernando Londoño, 65–88. Bogotá: Fescol.

Borneman, John. 1992. *Belonging in the Two Berlins.* New York: Cambridge University Press.

Bourdieu, Pierre. 1994. *Language and Symbolic Power.* Cambridge: Harvard University Press.

Bourdieu, Pierre, and Loïc J. D. Wacquant. 1992. *An Invitation to Reflexive Sociology.* Chicago: University of Chicago Press.

Brown, Wendy. 1995. *States of Injury: Power and Freedom in Late Modernity.* Princeton, N.J.: Princeton University Press.

Calderón, Fernando, Alejandro Piscitelli, and José Luis Reyna. 1992. "Social Movements, Actors, Theories, Expectations," *The Making of Social Movements in Latin America: Identity, Strategy, and Democracy,* ed. Arturo Escobar and Sonia E. Alvarez, 19–36. Boulder, Colo.: Westview.

Cardoso, Ruth Correa Leite. 1992. "Popular Movements in the Context of the Consolidation of Democracy in Brazil." *The Making of Social Movements in Latin America: Identity, Strategy, and Democracy,* ed. Arturo Escobar and Sonia E. Alvarez, 291–302. Boulder, Colo.: Westview.

Center for International Policy (CIP). 2000. "The Colombia Aid Package by the Numbers." Washington, July 5. http://www.ciponline.org.

Centro de Investigaciones y Educación Popular (CINEP) and Comisión Intercongregacional de Justicia y Paz. 1996–1998. *Noche y niebla: Panorama de derechos humanos y violencia política en Colombia*, nos. 1–10. Bogotá: CINEP.

Chernick, Marc, and Michael Jimenez. 1990. "Popular Liberalism and Radical Democracy: The Development of the Colombian Left, 1974–1990." Conference paper 43. Columbia University–New York University, Consortium for Latin American Studies.

Comisión Andina de Juristas (CAJ). 1993. *Putumayo*. Serie Informes Regionales de Derechos Humanos. Bogotá: Códice Editorial.

Consultoría para los Derechos Humanos y el Desplazamiento (CODHES). 2003. "Destierro y Repoblamiento." *CODHES Informa*. Bulletin 44, Bogotá. April 28. http://www.codhes.org.

———. 2006. "Paro Armado Putumayo." Informes. March 3. http://www.codhes.org.

———. 2008. "Ahora por los desplazados." *CODHES Informa*. Bogotá. February 5. http://www.codhes.org.

Cohen, Jean. 1995. "Interpreting the Notion of Civil Society." *Toward a Global Civil Society*, ed. Michael Walzer, 35–40. Providence, R.I.: Berghahn.

Cohen, Jean, and Andrew Arato. 1994. *Civil Society and Political Theory*. Cambridge: MIT Press.

Comaroff, Jean, and John Comaroff. 1988. "Through the Looking Glass: Colonial Encounters of the First Kind." *Journal of Historical Sociology* 1, no. 1, 6–32.

Comisión de Superación de la Violencia. 1992. *Pacificar la paz: Lo que no se ha negociado en los acuerdos de paz*. Bogotá: IEPRI, CINEP, CAJ, y CECOIN.

Comisión Intercongregacional de Justicia y Paz. 1995. *Boletin Justicia y Paz*. Information Bulletin on Human Rights Violations in Colombia. Bogotá: CINEP.

Comisión Nacional de Reparación y Reconciliación. 2007. "Disidentes, rearmados y emergentes: ¿Bandas criminales o tercera generación paramilitar?" Informe 1 del Área de Desmovilización, Desarme y Reintegración (DDR). Bogotá.

Consejo Nacional de Estupefacientes (CNE). 1997. *Política antidrogas en Colombia*. Sudirección Estratégica e Investigaciones. Bogotá.

Consejo Nacional de Política Social y Económica (CONPES) *Document 2734 of October 12, 1994*. Departamento Naciónal de Planeación, Bogotá. http://www. dnp .gov.co.

Constitucion Política de Colombia. 1991. Bogotá: Editorial Panamericana.

Contraloría General de la República. 2001. *Plan Colombia: Primer informe de evaluación*. August, Bogotá.

Coronil, Fernando. 1997. *The Magical State: Nature, Money and Modernity in Venezuela*. Chicago: University of Chicago Press.

Coronil, Fernando, and Julie Skurski. 1991. "Dismembering and Remembering the Nation: The Semantics of Political Violence in Venezuela." *Comparative Studies in Society and History* 33, no. 2, 288–337.

Corporación Colombiana de Proyectos Sociales (CORPOS). 1991. *Putumayo, historia de su poblamiento y situación actual*. Plan Nacional de Rehabilitación. Bogotá.

Corporación Nuevo Arco Iris. 2007. "Paramilitares y politicos." *Arcanos*, Año 10, no. 13, 4–32.

Corrigan, Philip Richard D., and Derek Sayer. 1985. *The Great Arch: English State Formation as Cultural Revolution*. Oxford: Basil Blackwell.

Corsetti, Giancarlo, Massimo Tommasoli, and Maura Viezzoli. 1987. *Migrantes y colonos de la Sierra en la Selva Tropical Colombiana*. Rome: Bulzoni Editore.

Crandall, Rusell. 2002. *Driven by Drugs: U.S. Policy toward Colombia*. Boulder, Colo.: Lynne Rienner.

Dagnino, Evelina. 1998. "The Cultural Politics of Citizenship, Democracy and the State." *Cultures of Politics and Politics of Cultures: Revisioning Latin American Social Movements*, eds. Sonia Alvarez, Evelina Dagnino, and Arturo Escobar, 33–63. Boulder, Colo.: Westview.

Das, Veena. 1995. *Critical Events: An Anthropological Perspective in Contemporary India*. New York: Oxford University Press.

Das, Veena, and Deborah Poole, eds. 2004. *Anthropology in the Margins of the State*. Santa Fe, N.M.: School of American Research.

Davis, Diane. 1989. Review of *Power and Popular Protest: Latin American Social Movements*, ed. Susan Eckstein, *Journal of Interamerican Studies and World Affairs*, 31, no. 4, 225–34.

Departamento Nacional de Planeación (DNP). 2003. *Balance del Plan Colombia*. Bogotá: September 17.

De Rementería, Iban. 1989. "La sustitución de cultivos como perspectiva." *Coca, cocaína y narcotráfico: Laberinto de los Andes*, ed. Diego García-Sayán, 361–88. Lima, Perú: Comisión Andina de Juristas.

———. 1996. "La decertificación de Colombia y la certificación de Perú." *Análisis Político*, no. 27, 58–61.

De Roux, Carlos Vicente. 1989. "El bien jurídico protegido." *Coca, cocaína y narcotráfico: Laberinto de los Andes*, ed. Diego García-Sayán, 319–26. Lima, Perú: Comisión Andina de Juristas.

Decree 356 of February 11 of 1994. Presidency, Bogotá.

Defensoría del Pueblo. 2001. *Las fumigaciones y los derechos humanos*. Amicus curiae. Bogotá.

Del Olmo, Rosa. 1989. "Leyes paralelas." *Coca, cocaína y narcotráfico: Laberinto de los Andes*, ed. Diego García-Sayán, 277–305. Lima, Perú: Comisión Andina de Juristas.

Departamento Administrativo Nacional de Estadística (DANE). 1993. *Necesidades Básicas Insatisfechas (NBI)*. http://www.dane.gov.co.

———. 2002. *Proyecciones de población*. Bogotá. http://www.dane.gov.co.

Dirección Nacional de Estupefacientes (DNE). 2001. *La Lucha de Colombia contra las drogas ilícitas. Acciones y Resultados*. Bogotá: DNE-Plan Nacional de Lucha contra las Drogas, Observatorio de Drogas de Colombia (ODC). http://www.odc.dne.gov.co.

Douglas, Mary. 1966. *Purity and Danger*. London: Penguin Books.

Dryzek, John S. 1996. "Political Inclusion and the Dynamics of Democratization." *American Political Science Review* 90, no. 1, 475–87.

Echandía, Camilo. 1998. "Evolución reciente del conflicto armado en Colombia: La guerrilla." *Las violencias: Inclusión creciente*, ed. Jaime Arocha, Ferando Cubides, and Myriam Jimeno, 35–65. Bogotá: Facultad de Ciencias Humanas, Universidad Nacional.

Equipo de Alternativa. 1997. "Convivir, embuchado de largo alcance." *Alternativa*, no. 8, 9–19.

Escobar Arturo. 1992a. "Culture, Practice and Politics: Anthropology and the Study of Social Movements." *Critique of Anthropology* 12, no. 4, 395–432.

———. 1992b. "Culture, Economics and Politics in Latin American Social Movements: Theory and Research." *The Making of Social Movements in Latin America*, ed. Arturo Escobar and Sonia Alvarez, 62–85. Boulder, Colo.: Westview.

Escobar, Arturo, and Sonia Alvarez, eds. 1992. *The Making of Social Movements in Latin America. Identity, Strategy and Democracy*. Boulder, Colo.: Westview.

Fajardo, Darío. 1998. Preface to *Atlas cultural de la Amazonia Colombiana: La construcción del territorio en el siglo XX*, Eduardo Ariza, María Clemencia Ramírez, and Leonardo Vega, 13-15. Bogotá: Ministerio de Cultura-Instituto Colombiano de Antropología, Corpes Orinoquia, Corpes Amazonia.

Fals Borda, Orlando. 1990. "El papel político de los movimientos sociales." *Revista Foro*, no. 11, 64–74.

FARC. 1998a. "El Poder Local" *Revista Resistencia* 17.

———. 1998b. "Las FARC llaman a la abstención electoral en el 34º Aniversario de su fundación (comunicado íntegro)."

———. 1998c. "Las FARC-EP: 30 años de lucha por la Paz, Democracia y Soberanía." http://www.analitica.com/bitblio/farc/30.asp.

Feierman, Steven. 1990. *Peasant Intellectuals: Anthropology and History in Tanzania*. Madison: University of Wisconsin Press.

Feldman, Alan. 1991. *Formations of Violence: The Narrative of the Body and Political Terror in Northern Ireland*. Chicago: University of Chicago Press.

Ferguson, James. 2001. "Global Disconnect: Abjection and the Aftermath of Modernism." *The Anthropology of Globalization*, ed. Jonathan Xavier Inda and Renalto Rosaldo, 136–53. Oxford: Blackwell.

Ferro, Juan Guillermo, et al. 1999. *Jóvenes, coca y amapola: Un estudio sobre las transformaciones socioculturales en zonas de cultivos ilícitos*. Bogotá: Pontificia Universidad Javeriana, Facultad de Estudios Ambientales y Rurales.

Foucault, Michel. 1971. *The Archaeology of Knowledge*. New York: Harper and Row.

———. 1973. *The Order of Things*. New York: Vintage.

———. 1979. *Discipline and Punish: The Birth of a Prison*. New York: Random House.

———. 1991. "Governmentality." *The Foucault Effect: Studies in Governmentality*, ed. Graham Burchell, Colin Gordon and Peter Miller, 87–104. Chicago: University of Chicago Press.

———. 1994. "Two Lectures." *Culture/Power/History: A Reader in Contemporary Social Theory*, ed. Nicholas B. Dirks, Geoff Eley, and Sherry B. Ortner, 200–221. Princeton, N.J.: Princeton University Press.

Foweraker, Joe. 1990. "Popular Movements and Political Change in Mexico." *Popular Movements and Political Change in Mexico*, ed. Joe Foweraker and Ann L. Craig, 3–20. Boulder, Colo.: Lynne Rienner.

———. 1995. *Theorizing Social Movements*. London: Pluto.

Foweraker, Joe, and Ann L. Craig. 1990, ed. *Popular Movements and Political Change in Mexico*. Boulder, Colo.: Lynne Rienner.

Fox, Richard. 1985. *Lions of the Punjab: Culture in the Making*. Berkeley: University of California Press.

Fundación Seguridad y Democracia. 2007. "Pacto por la verdad: Colombia y la experiencia internacional. El rearme paramilitar," Bulletin 16. Bogotá: Fundación Seguridad y Democracia.

Gaitán, Pilar. 1988. "Primera elección popular de alcaldes: Expectativas y frustraciones." *Análisis Político*, no. 4, 63–83.

Gaitán, Pilar, and Carlos Moreno Ospina. 1992. *Poder local: Realidad y utopía de la descentralización en Colombia*. Bogotá: Instituto de Estudios Políticos de la Universiad Nacional y Tercer Mundo Editores.

Gaviria, Oscar, Claudia Bonilla, and Rocío Arenas. 1997. *Economía de la coca*. Mocoa. Unpublished document.

Gianni, Matteo. 1997. "Multiculturalism and Political Integration; The Need for a Differentiated Citizenship?" *Rethinking Nationalism and Ethnicity*, ed., Hans-Rudolf Wicker, 127–42. Oxford: Berg.

Giraldo Javier and Santiago Camargo.1978. "Paros y movimientos cívicos en Colombia." *Controversia* 128. Bogotá: CINEP.

Goffman, Erving. 1963. *Stigma: Notes on the Management of Spoiled Identities*. New York: Simon and Schuster.

González, Fernán, Ingrid Bolívar, and Teófilo Vázquez. 2002. *Violencia política en Colombia: De la nación fragmentada a la formación de estado*. Bogotá: CINEP.

González, José Jairo. 1992. *El estigma de las Repúblicas Independientes, 1955–1965*. Bogotá: CINEP.

Government of Putumayo. 1998. *Plan piloto territorial de convivencia 1998–2000*. Mocoa: Gobernación del Putumayo.

Gramsci, Antonio. [1944] 1992. *Prison Notebooks*. Vol. 1. Ed. Joseph A. Buttigieg, trans. Joseph A. Buttigieg and Antonio Callari. New York: Columbia University Press.

Gupta, Akhil. 1995. "Blurred Boundaries: The Discourse of Corruption, the Culture of Politics and the Imagined State." *American Ethnologist* 22, no. 2, 375–97.

Gupta, Akhil, and James Ferguson. 1997. "Culture, Power, Place: Ethnography at the End of an Era." *Culture, Power, Place: Explorations in Critical Anthropology*, ed. Gupta and Ferguson, 1–29. Durham: Duke University Press.

Guzmán Campos, German, et al. 1980. *La violencia en Colombia*. 9th edn. Bogotá: Carlos Valencia Editores.

Hall, Stuart, and David Held. 1989. "Citizens and Citizenship." *New Times: The Changing Face of Politics in the 1990s*, ed. Stuart Hall and Martin Jaques, 173–88. London: Verso.

Hann, Chris. 1996. "Introduction: Political Society and Civil Anthropology." *Civil*

Society: Challenging Western Models, ed. Chris Hann and Elizabeth Dunn, 1–26. New York: Routledge.

Hansen, Thomas Blom, and Finn Stepputat, eds. 2001. Introduction to *States of Imagination: Ethnographic Explorations of the Postcolonial State*, ed. Thomas Blom Hansen and Finn Stepputat, 1–38. Durham: Duke University Press.

Harnecker, Marta. 1989. *Entrevista con la nueva izquierda. Bernardo Jaramillo (Unión Patriótica)/Nelson Berrío (A Luchar)*. México City: Centro de Documentación y Ediciones Latinoamericanas.

Harvey, Neil. 1998. *The Chiapas Rebellion: The Struggle for Land and Democracy*. Durham: Duke University Press.

Herbst, Susan. 1994. *Politics at the Margin: Historical Studies of Public Expression outside the Mainstream*. Cambridge: Cambridge University Press.

Herzfeld, Michael. 1985. *The Poetics of Manhood: Contest and Identity in a Cretan Mountain Village*. Princeton, N.J.: Princeton University Press.

———. 1992. *The Social Production of Indifference*. Chicago: University of Chicago Press.

Holston, James, and Arjun Appadurai. 1996. "Cities and Citizenship." *Public Culture* 8, no. 2, 187–204.

Holston, James, and Teresa Caldeira. 1998. "Democracy, Law and Violence: Disjunctions of Brazilian Citizenship." *Fault Lines of Democracy in Post-Transition Latin America*, ed. Felipe Agüero and Jeffrey Stark, 263–95. Miami: North-South Center Press.

Huertas, María Antonieta, Carlos F. Pressacco, and Jesus Puente. 2000. "Colombia." *Descentralización, municipios y participación ciudadana: Chile, Colombia y Guatemala*, ed. Carlos F. Pressacco, Consuelo Ahumada, and María Antonieta Huerta, 355–72. Bogotá: Editorial Ceja, Universidad Javeriana.

Human Rights Watch. 2000. "The Ties That Bind: Colombia and Military-Paramilitary Links." *World Report*, 12, no.1 (B).

ILSA, CINEP, and Revista Colombia Informa. 1995. "Nuevas Movilizaciones Campesinas." *Actualidad Colombiana*, no. 169, 1–2.

Instituto Geográfico Agustín Codazzi (IGAC) and Corporación Colombiana de Investigaciones Agropecuarias (CORPOICA). 2002. "Cobertura y Uso Actual de las Tierras de Colombia" *Zonificación de los conflictos de uso de tierras en Colombia*. Bogotá: IGAC-CORPOICA. http://www.siac.gov.co.

Jansson, Oscar. 2008. *The Cursed Leaf: An Anthropology of the Political Economy of Cocaine Production in Southern Colombia*. Uppsala: Uppsala Universitet.

Jelin, Elizabeth. 1987. *Ciudadanía e identidad: Las mujeres en los movimientos sociales Latinoamericanos*. Geneva: UNIRSD.

Jelin, Elizabeth, and Eric Hershberg, eds. 1996. *Constructing Democracy: Human Rights, Citizenship and Society in Latin America*. Boulder, Colo.: Westview.

Joseph, Gilbert, and Daniel Nugent, eds. 1994. *Everyday Forms of State Formation*. Durham: Duke University Press.

Keane, John. 1998. *Civil Society: Old Images, New Visions*. Stanford, Calif.: Stanford University Press.

Kearney, Michael. 1996. *Reconceptualizing the Peasantry: Anthropology in Global Perspective*. Boulder, Colo.: Westview.

Kirk, Robin. 2003. *More Terrible Than Death: Massacres, Drugs, and America's War in Colombia*. New York: PublicAffairs.

Lacan, Jacques. 1977. *Écrits: A Selection*. Trans. Alan Sheridan. New York: Norton.

Laclau, Ernesto. 1985. "New Social Movements and the Plurality of the Social." *New Social Movements and the State in Latin America*, ed. David Slater, 27–42. Amsterdam: CEDLA.

———, ed. 1994. *The Making of Political Identities*. London: Verso.

Laclau, Ernesto, and Chantal Mouffe. 1985. *Hegemony and Socialist Strategy: Towards a Radical Democratic Politics*. London: Verso.

La Hormiga Accords. "Acuerdo entre el gobierno nacional y la Comisión Negociadora del Movimiento Cívico." January 11, 1995. La Hormiga, Putumayo. Unpublished document.

Laraña, Enrique, Hank Johnston, and Joseph R. Gusfield, eds. 1994. *New Social Movements: From Ideology to Identity*. Philadelphia: Temple University Press.

Leach, Edmund. 1972. "Anthropological Aspects of Language: Animal Categories and Verbal Abuse" *Mythology*, ed. Pierre Maranda, 39–67. London: Penguin.

Lechner, Norbert. 1992. "Some People Die of Fear: Fear as a Political Problem." *Fear at the Edge: State Terror and Resistance in Latin America*, ed. Juan E. Corradi, Patricia Weiss, Fagen, and Manuel Antonio Garretón, 13–35. Berkeley: University of California Press.

———. 1993. "Modernización y modernidad: La búsqueda de ciudadanía." *Modernización económica, democracia política y democracia social*, ed. Centro de Estudios Sociológicos, 63–75. México City: El Colegio de México.

———. 1996. "La problemática invocación de la sociedad civil." *Revista Foro*, no. 28, 24–33.

Lefebvre, Henri. 1991. *The Production of Space*. Trans. Donald Nicholson-Smith. Cambridge, Mass.: Blackwell.

Mallon, Florencia. 1995. *Peasant and Nation: The Making of Postcolonial Mexico and Peru*. Berkeley: University of California Press.

Marshall, Thomas H. 1965. *Class, Citizenship and Social Development*. Garden City, N.Y.: Anchor Books.

Marulanda Vélez, Manuel. 1994. "Texto completo del discurso pronunciado por el Comandante en Jefe de las FARC-EP, Manuel Marulanda Vélez en el 30º aniversario de las FARC," Speech delivered on May 27. http://www.analitica.com/Bitblio/marulanda/30.asp.

Medina, Gallego, Carlos Téllez, and Mireya Téllez. 1994. *La violencia parainstitucional, paramilitar y parapolicial en Colombia*. Bogotá: Rodriguez Quito Editores.

Melucci, Alberto. 1988. "Getting Involved: Identity and Mobilization in Social Movements." *International Social Movements Research* 1, 329–48.

Ministry of the Interior. Database of Communal Action Committees, April 1996. Bogotá.

Mitchell, Timothy. 1991. "The Limits of the State: Beyond Statist Approaches and Their Critics." *American Political Science Review* 85, no. 1, 77–95.

———. 1999. "Society, Economy and the State Effect." *State/Culture: State Formation after the Cultural Turn*, ed. George Steinmetz, 76–97. Ithaca: Cornell University Press.

Molano, Alfredo. 1988. "Violencia y colonización." *Revista Foro*, no. 6, 25–37.

Moliner, Maria. 1998. *Diccionario de uso del Español*. 2nd edn. Madrid: Editorial Gredos.

Moore, Sally. 1987. "Explaining the Present: Theoretical Dilemmas in Processual Ethnography." *American Ethnologist* 14, no. 4, 727–36.

Moran, Emilio. 1988. "Social Reproduction in Agricultural Frontiers." *Production and Autonomy: Anthropological Studies and Critiques of Development*, ed. John W. Bennett and John R. Bowen, 199–212. New York: University Press of America.

Moreno Reyes, Hector. "Plan de Acción del Plante 1995–1998." Address at the *Universidad de los Andes*, April 1997.

Nielsen, Terry. 1995. "Reconceptualizing Civil Society for Now: Some Somewhat Gramscian Turnings." *Toward a Global Civil Society*, ed. Michael Walzer, 41–67. Providence, R.I.: Berghahn.

Nugent, David. 1994. "Building the State, Making the Nation: The Bases and Limits of State Centralization in Modern Peru." *American Anthropologist* 96, no. 2, 333–69.

Nugent, Stephen. 1993. *Amazonian Caboclo Society: An Essay on Invisibility and Peasant Economy*. Oxford: Berg.

Observatorio para la Paz. 2000. "Plan Colombia: Juego de máscaras." *Cultivos ilícitos, narcotráfico y agenda de paz*, ed. Darío Posso, 165–76. Bogotá: Mandato Ciudadano por la Paz, la Vida y la Libertad.

Padilla, Nelson Freddy. 1996. "Estamos en la dolorosa." *Cambio* 16, no. 164, 18–20.

Peñaranda, Ricardo. 1996. "Los movimientos sociales: un año intenso." *Síntesis 96. Anuario Social, Político y Económico de Colombia*, 25–32. Bogotá: IEPRI, Fundación Social y Tercer Mundo Editores.

Pile, Steve. 1997. "Introduction: Opposition, Political Identities and Spaces of Resistance." *Geographies of Resistance*, ed. Steve Pile and Michael Keith, 1–32. New York: Routledge.

Pizarro Leongómez, Eduardo. 1989. "Los orígenes del movimiento armado comunista en Colombia (1949–1966)." *Análisis Político*, no. 7, 7–31.

———. 1992. *Las FARC. De la autodefensa a la combinación de todas las formas de lucha: 1949–1966*. Bogotá: Tercer Mundo Editores e Instituto de Estudios Políticos y Relaciones Internacionales de la Universidad Nacional de Colombia.

———. 1996. *Insurgencia sin revolución: La guerrilla en Colombia en una perspectiva comparada*. Bogotá: IEPRI y Tercer Mundo Editores.

Plan Nacional de Desarrollo Alternativo (PLANTE). 2001. *Fondos municipales de desarrollo alternativo y acuerdos de erradicación temprana*. Bogotá.

Plan Nacional de Rehabilitación (PNR). 1994. *Memoirs*. Bogotá: PNUD.

Presidencia de la República. 2000. *Plan Colombia: Plan para la paz, la prosperidad y el fortalecimiento del estado.* Bogotá.

Presidencia de la República and Ministerio de Defensa Nacional. 2003. *Política de defensa y de seguridad democrática.* Bogotá.

Ramírez, Constanza. 1998. "Conflicto agrario y medio ambiente." *Revista Foro* no. 35, 5–28.

Ramírez, María Clemencia. 2001. *Entre el estado y la guerrilla: Identidad y ciudadanía en el movimiento de los campesinos cocaleros en el Putumayo.* Bogotá: Instituto Colombiano de Antropología e Historia-Colciencias.

Ramírez, María Clemencia, Henry Salgado, Elsy Castillo, and Luz Piedad Caicedo. 1998–99. "Los Colonos en la Region Amazonica de Colombia: Violencia, Coca, Descentralizacion del Estado y Reconstitucion de Identidades." Proyecto de Investigación ICAN-Colciencias. Bogotá: Unpublished document.

Ramírez, Luis. 1998. "Del Campo a la Alcaldía: un campesino que sin quererlo llegó a ser el Alcalde de Orito." *Así es: Orito, un pueblo que lucha para conseguir sus ideas.* Mocoa: Industria Gráfica.

Ramírez, Roberto. 1991. *Aquel rincón del Cauca: Rincón del olvido.* Proyecto Historias Locales, PNR. Florencia: Universidad de la Amazonia, Instituto Amazónico de Investigaciones.

———. 1998. "Conflictos sociales en el Putumayo." *Conflictos regionales: Amazonia y Orinoquia,* ed. José Jairo González, 71–130. Bogotá: IEPRI-FESCOL.

Ramírez, William. 1981. "La guerrilla rural en Colombia: Una vía para la colonización armada?" *Estudios Rurales Latinoamericanos* 4, no. 2, 199–209.

Restrepo, Darío I. 1995. "La participación social como construcción del interés público entre el estado y la sociedad." *Revista Nómadas* no. 3, 52–59.

Revelo, Diva, comp. 1998. *Epidemiologia de la mortalidad en el Putumayo: Estadísticas según sistema de registro civil y estadísticas vitales.* Mocoa, Putumayo: DASALUD.

———. 2001. *Efectos de la fumigación: Valle del Guamués y San Miguel Putumayo.* Mocoa, Putumayo: DASALUD.

———. 2002. *Mortalidad por homicidios en el Putmayo entre 1991 y 2002.* Mocoa, Putumayo: DASALUD.

Ríos, José Noé. 1997. *Cómo negociar a partir de la importancia del otro.* Bogotá: Editorial Planeta.

Roseberry, William. 1994. "Hegemony and the Language of Contention." *Everyday Forms of State Formation: Revolution and the Negotiation of Rule in Modern Mexico,* ed. Joseph Gilbert and Daniel Nugent, 367–77. Durham: Duke University Press.

Routledge, Paul. 1993. *Terrains of Resistance: Non-violent Social Movements and the Contestation of Place in India.* Westport, Conn.: Praeger Publishers.

Sabogal, Melquisedec. 1998. *El negocio del cultivo de coca a escala de producción campesina.* Bogotá: PLANTE.

Salgado, Henry. 1995. *La coca y su impacto socio-económico y político en el campesinado del Putumayo Colombiano.* Tesis de Maestría, Facultad Latinoamericana de Ciencias Sociales, Ecuador.

————. 2004. "El Plan Colombia, una política de (In)seguridad humana para las poblaciones de Putumayo." *Desplazamiento forzado: Dinámicas de guerra, exclusión y desarraigo*, ed. Martha Nubia Bello, 253–76. Bogotá: UNHCR-ACNUR, Universidad Nacional de Colombia.

Salazar, Alonso. 2001. *La Parábola de Pablo: Auge y caída de un gran capo del narcotráfico*. Bogotá: Editorial Planeta.

Sanabria, Harry. 1993. *The Coca Boom and Rural Change in Bolivia*. Ann Arbor: University of Michigan Press.

Sanchez, Nancy. 1998. *Coca y región*. Mocoa, Putumayo: Escuela Superior de Administración Pública, Especialización en Gestión y Planificación del Desarrollo Urbano y Regional.

Sánchez, Nancy, and Diva Revelo, comps. 1996. *Mortalidad violenta en el Putumayo*. Mocoa, Putumayo: DASALUD.

Sayer, Derek. 1994. "Everyday Forms of State Formation: Some Dissident Remarks on 'Hegemony.'" *Everyday Forms of State Formation: Revolution and the Negotiation of Rule in Modern Mexico*, ed. Gilbert M. Joseph and Daniel Nugent, 367–77. Durham: Duke University Press.

Scott, Alan. 1991. *Ideology and Social Movements*. London: Allen & Unwin.

Scott, James. 1998. *Seeing Like a State: How Certain Schemes to Improve the Human Condition Failed*. New Haven, Conn.: Yale University Press.

Sibley, David. 1995. *Geographies of Exclusion*. New York: Routledge.

Silva, María Cecilia. 1991a. "La Coca y la Situación del Colono." *Raigambre* 2, no. 3, 41–47.

————. 1991b. "Eramos Esclavos." *Raigambre* 2, no. 3, 39–40.

Slater, David. 1998. "Rethinking the Spatialities of Social Movements: Questions of (B)orders, Culture, and Politics in Global Times." *Cultures of Politics and Politics of Cultures: Revisioning Latin American Social Movements*, ed. Sonia Alvarez, Evelina Dagnino, and Arturo Escobar, 380–96. Boulder, Colo.: Westview.

Solidarity Network. 1998. *1994–1998, Memoirs*. Bogotá: Antares Editores.

Solidarity Network and Interamerican Institute of Agricultural Cooperation (IICA). 1998. "Activities report July-September 1998." Mocoa, Putumayo.

Solomon, Keith R., Arturo Anodón, Antonio Luiz Cerdeira, Jon Marshall, and Luz-Helena Sanin. 2005. "Environmental and Human Health Assessment of the Aerial Spray Program for Coca and Poppy control in Colombia." Report presented to the Organization of American States–Interamerican Drug Abuse Control Commission (OAS-CICAD). Washington D.C, March 31.

Taussig, Michael. 1987. *Shamanism, Colonialism and the Wild Man: A Study in Terror and Healing*. Chicago: University of Chicago Press.

————. 1992. "Maleficium: State Fetishism." *The Nervous System*, 111–99. New York: Routledge.

————. 1997. *The Magic of the State*. New York: Routledge.

Taylor, Charles. 1995. "The Politics of Recognition." *Campus Wars. Multiculturalism and the Politics of Difference*, eds. John Arthur and Amy Shapiro, 249–63. Boulder, Colo.: Westview.

Thoumi, Francisco E. 1995. *Political Economy and Illegal Drugs in Colombia*. Boulder, Colo.: Lynne Riener.

Tilly, Charles. 1996. "Citizenship, Identity and Social History." *Citizenship, Identity and Social History*, ed. Charles Tilly, 1–17. Cambridge: Cambridge University Press.

Tovar, Hermes. 1993. "La coca y las economías exportadoras en América Latina: El paradigma Colombiano." *Análisis Político* no. 18, 5–31.

Trouillot, Michel-Ralph. 2001. "The Anthropology of the State in the Age of Globalization: Close Encounters of the Deceptive Kind." *Current Anthropology* 42, no. 1, 125–38.

Tsing, Anne Lowenhaupt. 1993. *In the Realm of the Diamond Queen: Marginality in an Out-of-the-Way Place*. Princeton, N.J.: Princeton University Press.

———. 1994. "From the Margins." *Cultural Anthropology* 9, no. 3, 279–97.

United Nations Office on Drugs and Crime (UNODC) and Governments of Bolivia, Colombia, Ecuador, and Peru. 2007. *Coca Cultivation in the Andean Region*. http://www.unodc.org.

United Nations Office on Drugs and Crime (UNODC) and Government of Colombia. 2002. *Colombia: Annual Coca Cultivation Survey*. March. http://www.unodc.org.

———. 2003. *Colombia: Coca Survey for December 2002 and Semi-Annual Estimate for July 2003*. http://www.unodc.org.

———. 2004. *Colombia: Coca Cultivation Survey*. June. http://www.unodc.org.

———. 2006. *Colombia: Coca Cultivation Survey*. June. http://www.unodc.org.

———. 2007. *Colombia: Coca Cultivation Survey*. June. http://www.unodc.org.

———. 2008. *Colombia: Coca Cultivation Survey*. June. http://www.unodc.org.

———. 2009. *Colombia: Coca Cultivation Survey*. June. http://www.unodc.org.

———. 2010. *Colombia: Coca Cultivation Survey*. June. http://www.unodc.org.

Uprimny, Rodrigo. 1994. "Narcotráfico, régimen político, violencias y derechos humanos en Colombia." *Drogas, poder y región en Colombia*, vol. 1, comp. Ricardo Vargas, 59–146. Bogotá: CINEP.

Uprimny, Rodrigo, and Alfredo Vargas Camacho. 1989. "La palabra y la sangre: violencia, ilegalidad y guerra sucia en Colombia." *La irrupción del paraestado*, comp. Germán Palacio, 105–65. Bogotá: Ilsa-Cerec.

Uribe López, Mauricio. 2005. "¿Es posible un acuerdo humanitario?" *Actualidad Colombiana*, no. 412, 4–18.

U.S. Department of Justice. 2006. *National Drug Threat Assessment 2007*. Washington: National Drug Intelligence Center. October.

U.S. General Accounting Office. 2002. *Drug Control: Efforts to Develop Alternatives to Cultivation of Illicit Crops in Colombia Have Made Little Progress and Face Serious Obstacles*. GAO/01–26, February.

Varela, Andrea. 1998. "Por qué se pierde la guerra en el Caguán." *Cambio* 16, no. 249, 20–22.

Vargas, Ricardo. 1996. "Colombia y el Area Andina: los vacíos de la guerra." *Controversia* no. 169, 53–72. Bogotá: CINEP.

————. 1999. *Drogas, máscaras y juegos: Narcotráfico y conflicto armado en Colombia*. Bogotá: Tercer Mundo Editores y TINI-Acción Andina.

————. 2004. "State, Esprit Mafioso and Armed Conflict in Colombia." *Politics in the Andes: Identity, Conflict, Reform*, ed. Jo-Marie Burt and Philip Mauceri, 107–25, Pittsburgh: University of Pittsburgh Press.

Vásquez, Teófilo. 1996. "Violaciones a los Derechos Humanos durante el paro campesino en el departamento del Putumayo." *Noche y Niebla* no. 1, 112–21. Bogotá: CINEP.

Velásquez, Fabio E. 1991. "Una democracia participativa para Colombia." *Revista Foro* no. 16, 60–72.

Villamarín, Luis Alberto. 1996. *El Cartel de las Farc*. Bogotá: Ediciones El Faraón.

Walsh, John M. 2007. *Connecting the Dots: ONDCP's Reluctant Update on Cocaine Price and Purity*. Report by the Drug Policy Program of the Washington Office on Latin America, April 23.

Walzer, Michael. 1991. "Constitutional Rights and the Shape of Civil Society." *The Constitution of the People: Reflections on Citizens and Civil Society*, ed. Robert E. Calvert, 113–26. Lawrence: University Press of Kansas.

————. 1995. "The Civil Society Argument." *Theorizing Citizenship*, ed. Ronald Beiner, 153–74. Albany: State University of New York Press.

Whitten, Norman. 1985. *Sicuanga Runa: The Other Side of Development in Amazonian Ecuador*. Urbana: University of Illinois Press.

Young, Iris Marion. 1990. *Justice and the Politics of Difference*. Princeton, N.J.: Princeton University Press.

————. 1995. "Social Movements and the Politics of Difference." *Campus Wars: Multiculturalism and the Politics of Difference*, ed. John Arthur and Amy Shapiro, 199–223. Boulder, Colo.: Westview.

Newspapers and Periodicals

Cambio
Caracol Noticias
Diario del Sur
El Espectador
La Nación
La Prensa (Bolivia)
La Razón (Bolivia)
La República (Lima)
Revista Semana
Semana.com
El Tiempo

Index

Page references in italics indicate illustrations or captions

256n15; Operation Marquetalia and, 42. *See also* National Front

Constitution (1968 reform), 95–96

Constitution (1991): on freedom of movement, 139; on *intendencias*, 96; on participatory democracy mandated by, 96, 134, 166, 267n1; on petitions to the government, 139; on protection to vulnerable/marginalized groups, 231; respect for, 194–95; territorial entities created by, 179–80

Consultancy for Human Rights and Forced Displacement (CODHES), 278n5, 278n13

Contraloría General de la República, 215, 277n2

Convivirs, 51–53

Coronil, Fernando, 167

CORPES (Regional Councils for Economic and Social Planning), 96

CORPOAMAZONIA, 189–90, 217, 272n10

CORPOICA (Colombian Agricultural Research Corporation), 255n2

Corporación Nuevo Arco Iris, 51

Correal, Luis Alberto, 192–93

corregimientos, 254n7. *See also specific corregimientos*

corruption, 101–2, 107

Cuban revolution (1959), 40

Curillo (Baja Bota), 30

currency conversion, 254n8

Dagnino, Evelina, 134–35, 267n3

DAINCO (Administrative Department for *Intendencias* and *Comisarías*), 96

Dallas Morning News, 63–64

Das, Veena, 3, 253n3

DASALUD (Putumayo Health Department), 80

Decree 5367 (1994), 179

Defensoría Del Pueblo, 231

de Francisco, Gonzalo, 221, 224–25

Delgado, Holdan, 140

democracy. *See* citizenship rights/democracy

Departmental Development Plan, 190–91

Departmental Human Rights Committee, 196–97, 274n38

Diario del Sur (Pasto), 93

Díaz, Eduardo, 132–33, 147, 153–57, 175–76, 178–79, 186, 193, 203

Diaz, Marco Aurelio, 237

Díaz Plata, Orlando, 120, 140

dictatorships, fear used by, 276n78

difference, emancipatory vs. exclusionary meaning of, 274n32

dirt, 265n25

DNE (National Narcotics Directorate), 261n4

dollar, value of, 254n8

Douglas, Mary, 119, 265n25

drug traffickers: arrival in Putumayo, 21–22, 43–50, 79; autodefensas financed by, 47; Barco's war against, 259n13; coca grown by, 60; cocaine laboratories funded by, 73; debt-for-work system of, 50; drug dependence created among workers by, 44; FARC and, 21, 45; government suppression of, 43; guerrillas and, 61, 63; mansions built by, 65; traquetos working for, 72–73; U.S. State Department on, 231–32; workers as virtual slaves of, 44. *See also* Cali drug cartel; Medellín drug cartel

Dryzek, John S., 9, 254n13

Echandía Sánchez, Oscar de Jesús, 47

Echeverry, Rafael, 155

ECOPETROL (Empresa Colombiana de Petróleos), 84, 90, 93–95, 142–43, 262n10

Ecuador, refugees in, 278n13

education: of harvest workers, 69–70; of municipal officials, 100–101; working group on, 185–86, 247–48

El Azul (Putumayo), 43–45, 47–48

electrification, 243

ELN (National Liberation Army), 64

Maria Clemencia Ramírez is a senior research associate and former director (2005–7) of the Colombian Institute of Anthropology and History in Bogotá, and author of *Entre el estado y la guerilla: Identidad y ciudadania en el movimiento de los campesinos cocaleros del Putumayo* (2001). She is coauthor, with Eduardo Ariza and Leonardo Vega, of *Atlas cultural de la Amazonia Colombiana: La construccion del territorio en el siglo XX* (1998) and author of *Frontera fluida entre Andes, Piedemonte y Selva: El caso del Valle de Sibundoy, Siglos XVI–XVII* (1996).

Library of Congress Cataloging-in-Publication Data
Ramírez, María Clemencia.
[Entre el estado y la guerrilla. English]
Between the guerrillas and the state : the cocalero movement, citizenship, and identity in the Colombian Amazon / María Clemencia Ramírez ; translated by Andy Klatt.
p. cm.
Includes bibliographical references and index.
English translation, revised from first Spanish ed.: Entre el estado y la guerrilla (Bogotá : Instituto Colombiano de Antropología e Historia, Colciencias, 2001).
ISBN 978-0-8223-5000-2 (cloth : alk. paper)—ISBN 978-0-8223-5015-6 (pbk. : alk. paper)
1. Cocaine industry—Political aspects—Colombia—Putumayo (Dept.)
2. Coca—Political aspects—Colombia—Putumayo (Dept.) 3. Paramilitary forces—Colombia—Putumayo (Dept.) 4. Guerrillas—Colombia—Putumayo (Dept.) 5. State-sponsored terrorism—Colombia—Putumayo (Dept.) 6. Drug control—Political aspects—Colombia. I. Title.
HD9019.C63R36513 2011
986.106'35—dc22
2011015674